SPORT AND THE SPIRIT OF PLAY IN CONTEMPORARY AMERICAN FICTION

CHRISTIAN K. MESSENGER

Sport and the Spirit of Play in Contemporary American Fiction

Columbia University Press
New York

Columbia University Press
New York   Oxford
Copyright © 1990 Columbia University Press
All rights reserved

Library of Congress Cataloging-in-Publication Data

Messenger, Christian K., 1943–
    Sport and the spirit of play in contemporary American fiction/
    Christian K. Messenger.
        p.   cm.
Includes bibliographical references.
ISBN 0-231-07094-2 (alk. paper)
1. Sports stories, American—History and criticism.
2. American fiction—20th century—History and criticism.
3. Play in literature.
I. Title.
PS374.S76M44   1990
813'.0109355—dc20   89-29640
                                  CIP

Casebound editions of Columbia University Press books are Smyth-sewn
and printed on permanent and durable acid-free paper

∞

Printed in the United States of America

c 10 9 8 7 6 5 4 3 2 1

For Janet, Carrie, Lucas—and Ellen

Contents

Preface   xiii
Introduction   1

   The Play Spirit   3
   A Structural Semantics for Sports Fiction   10
      Mapping the Arena   12
      Describing and Animating the Quadrants   16

Part I
Individual Sports Heroism: Male Physical
Self-Definition   27

1. The Decline of the Ritual Sports Hero   29

   Dickey and Concealment   36
   McGuane and Exposure   42

"Feeding the Ape": Mailer and the Bad Death of Ernest
  Hemingway   46

2. Mailer: The Body as Arena   51

   Father and Son Days: Ritual Sport and Sacrifice in *Why
     Are We in Vietnam?*   55
   Mapping Mailer's Arena   60
   Killer Brothers for the Team   65

3. Mailer: Boxing and the Art of His Narrative   69

   The Enormous Present   71
   The Bad Death of Benny Paret   75
   The Carnage of *An American Dream*   78
   Passivity and Working the Corners: Mailer and Ali   85

4. Fictions of Boxing   95

   Ring-Masters   95
   Youth and Age   97
   Predator and Prey   105
   The Great White Hope   113

Part II
*Individual Sports Heroism: Responses of the
Play Spirit*   123

5. Play, Sacrifice, Performance: Kesey and Coover   125

   The Dynamics of Ritual and Play: Kesey's *One Flew Over
     the Cuckoo's Nest*   126
   Ritual and Play: The Good Death of McMurphy   129
   Ritual Sport and Play: *Sometimes A Great Notion*   135
   Ritual Performance: *The Public Burning*   145
   Conclusion   150

6. Women in Sports Narrative: The Strategies of Mimicry   154

   The Strategy of Mimicry   155
   Cat on a Hot Tin Roof: Maggie Re-Gendered   161

The Hotel New Hampshire: Tough Girls at Play   163
Personal Best: Nurture and Competition   168
Water Dancer: The Multiples of Touch   175
Conclusion   185

7. The Decline of the School Sports Hero   192

The Last Amateurs   194
The Sacrifice of the Natural   200
   A Separate Peace   201
   The Huge Season   204
Conclusion   208

8. Anti-Heroism: The Witness at the Center   210

Heroes and Witnesses: A Brief Literary History   212
Fleeing the School as Arena: The Witness "On the Road"   217
The Field of Vision: Witnessing and Reader Response   221
A Fan's Notes   224
Goodbye, Columbus: Suburban Games   229
   Brenda Patimkin: School Sports Heroine   232
   Ron Patimkin and Neil Klugman: School Sports Hero
      and Witness   236
The Sportswriter: Epiphanies without Cause   239
Conclusion   244

Part III
Collective Sports Heroism: Fictions of Team Sport   249

9. Fictions of Football: Between the Lines   251

The Team Sports Hero: A Man for Our Season   252
Between the Lines   254
Field Structure and Symbolism   258
Football as Education: The School Sports Story   262
Football and the Configuration of the Body   267
The Texas Connection   271
   Dan Jenkins and Texas Triumphant   275
   Dallas, 11/22/63: "Why Are We Playing?"   280

The Professional Plot   282
    Peter Gent: The Professional and Pain   286
    The Franchise: The Professional and "Control" 290

10. Fictions of Football: "Why We Are Playing"   294

    Gloomy Gus: Football Aestheticized   295
    Joiner: Football Historicized   298
    End Zone: Football, Nuclear War, Language   302
        The Collision of Differences   305
    Conclusion   313

11. Fictions of Baseball: Baseball and Passages   315

    Creating the Field/Book   319
    Coming Home: Fathers and Sons   322
    Baseball and Education   328
        Harris: The Education of Henry Wiggen   331
    Baseball and Myth   334
        Malamud: The Passion of Roy Hobbs   336
        Coover: The Diamond Alive in the Sun   341

12. Fictions of Baseball: Baseball Historicized   346

    Contextualizing the Passages   346
    Benign Myth and Demonic Reality: Roth's *The Great
    American Novel*   353
    Coover: Baseball and Metahistory   357
    Exile and Exclusion: Blacks and Baseball History 362
    Neugeboren and Charyn: Counterhistories   366
    Expansion Draft: Baseball Fiction 1980-88   371

13. Fictions of Basketball   387

    Basketball's Arena: The Playground   389
    Basketball and the Black Experience   395
    "I Have My Game": The Pursuit of Upward Space 403
    Upward Space: Updike's *Rabbit* Trilogy   407
    Conclusion   417

Conclusion 419
Notes 429
Bibliography 443
    Primary Works Cited 443
    Secondary Works Cited 453
Index 459

Preface

THIS VOLUME is the concluding half of my inquiry that began with *Sport and the Spirit of Play in American Fiction: Hawthorne to Faulkner* (1981). I have kept references to Book 1 to a minimum here. Although I do not carry forward the tripartite division of subject from my previous book—the Ritual Sports Hero, the School Sports Hero, the Popular Sports Hero—I have provided a summary of my conceptions of these three different fictional sports heroes at the outset of chapters 1, 7, and 9, respectively. These conceptions still have resonance as residual namings and appear throughout the book even as I write of their decline or transformation.

Readers of Book 1 will here find a familiar game with slightly altered rules. That earlier game was of necessity a different con-

test. My first book on sport and American fiction drew heavily
on the cultural history of American sport and leisure as well as on
a century of American popular literature. Because of its time span
and diverse materials, the book was somewhat encyclopedic,
combining chapters on dime novels, boys' school sport stories,
and sportswriting with "major author" chapters. *Sport and the
Spirit of Play in Contemporary American Fiction* is more fundamentally a literary study that looks at a synchronic cut of the fiction
for its evidence and gauges the full coming-of-age of the American sports fiction subject since World War II.

Contemporary authors sense that play and sport exist in a more
problematic relation than play theorists and literary critics might
allow. First, authors must confront the relation of sport to play
and freedom. There is a general strife between play as un-
grounded potential and sport as grounded context, with play as
freedom and sport as discipline. In considerable degree, sport is
counter to play, a brief for actual, physical competition, material-
ity, potential victory and loss, public acclaim, commodification:
all the powerful facets of a social and cultural world that would
channel play and present rewards in return for the loss of the
player's freedom. On the other hand, authors see potential growth
through sport that play can only gesture toward: fellowship,
harmony, cooperation, social growth—all point beyond the differing, deferring, metaphor-making power of play. Sports, then,
models roles while play veers us away from fixed roles. Sport is
the religion of the positivists in investing selves in development
and the setting of goals. Play suspects such overtures and counters
them in subversion. Extrapolating from remarks on play theory,
I have sketched out a structural semantics for the study of sport
and play in contemporary American fiction and these subjects
comprise the introduction.

I am concerned here with major developments such as the turn
from modernist to postmodernist representation in American fiction, the roles of women in the play and language of sports
fiction, and the establishment of theories of play as vital underpinning to much current literary theorizing. Certain authors, such as
John Barth, Kurt Vonnegut, Thomas Pynchon, and Ishmael Reed,
may be noticeable for their absence in the discussions. The criteria

for omission are quite simply that while they are deft fictional players, the rhythms and structures of American individual and team sport have not engaged their imaginations to any appreciable degree. While all writers of sports fiction are welcome here, only authorial players whose characters compete in some recognizable arena receive their admission ticket. Nonfiction about sport and play is not considered, for the most part, except as it influences the use of ritual by writers such as Norman Mailer. Films and drama about sport are examined when relevant to various strands of sports narrative.

I want to cite all those involved in the nascent study of sports literature, both in the Sport Literature Association in the United States and in the Deutsche Vereinigung für Sportwissenschaft in West Germany, for their scholarship, good talk, and mutual encouragement. Such activity has meant a great deal to all of us in the research into fictional sport and play in the past several years. A 1984–85 Institute for the Humanities Fellowship at the University of Illinois at Chicago was of enormous value in allowing me to complete a first draft of this long manuscript. Portions of this text appeared in altered form in *Coroebus Triumphs, Arete* (now *Aethlon: the Journal of Sports Literature*), and *Modern Fiction Studies*. I am grateful for their permission to reprint. My colleagues in English at UIC—Jonathan Arac (now at Columbia University), Judith Kegan Gardiner, Clark Hulse, John Huntington, Ned Lukacher, David Spurr, Virginia Wexman, Linda Williams (now at University of California, Irvine)—have been my continuing source of education. They have challenged me to think and write more clearly and I am better for having such scholars as friends. Special debts are owed to Michael Oriard and Terry Smith, as well as to Jennifer Crewe and David Bain at Columbia University Press. My family, despite occasional exhortations that I should write the Great American Sports Novel and make our fortune, has, as always, supported me with understanding and love.

SPORT AND THE SPIRIT OF PLAY
IN CONTEMPORARY
AMERICAN FICTION

Introduction

There was a man in my class at Princeton who never went to football games. He spent his Saturday afternoons delving for minutiae about Greek athletics and the somewhat fixed battles between Christians and the wild beasts under the Antonines. Lately—several years out of college—he has discovered football players and is making etchings of them in the manner of the late George Bellows. But he was once unresponsive to the very spectacle at his door, and I suspect the originality of his judgments on what is beautiful, what is remarkable and what is fun.

F. Scott Fitzgerald, *"The Bowl" (1927)*

FITZGERALD'S STORY is about a Yale football player learning to love his sport. The story by extension is a treatise on coming to understand what is "beautiful," "remarkable," and "fun" in our lives and learning to care about it for itself as something intrinsically valuable. Sixty years later, Americans are squarely in Fitzgerald's corner, almost slavishly attentive "to the very spectacle at [their] door." America has long since "discovered" football players as subjects and objects to be transformed by aesthetics. The same holds true for many other sports and their competitors. Sportsworld *is* the American environment: we need look no further for the pattern of our lives, the rhythms, victories, and defeats. We know now that the spectacle is not just "at our door," but in our daily round and expressive of life beyond that specta-

I

cle. Our conception of sport in America is recognized as a record of our cultural preferences and the contradictions of our social arrangements.

The shift that Fitzgerald describes is one that leads from historical study to popular cultural appreciation, the creation of art out of the close at hand. Certainly the legacy of sport in American fiction is that of authors such as Ring Lardner and Fitzgerald who proved that modern American society may be imaginatively conceived and explained through its games and players. Contemporary American authors write in their wake, both in subject matter and mode of narration. During the past four decades, American authors have repeatedly turned to sport more than to any other popular cultural activity. These authors range from the major figures of our literary climate—Norman Mailer, Ken Kesey, Philip Roth, Bernard Malamud, John Updike, Don DeLillo, and Robert Coover—to authors such as Peter Gent and Dan Jenkins who arise from the sports culture itself.

As in the work of Fitzgerald, Ernest Hemingway, and William Faulkner, the best use of sport in contemporary American fiction confronts the question of play as an individual human necessity, a drive toward a complex freedom for the individual beyond teams, codified rules, organized competition, and defined arenas. The free exercise of the imagination in and through language is ultimately the category that links play and sport most closely to aesthetics. *Sport and the Spirit of Play in Contemporary American Fiction* is a book about the range of fictional transformation of American sport and play after the subsiding wake of the classic modernists—the contemporary response.

The relations of sport and play are keys to understanding the problem of freedom as a master trope in contemporary criticism, an issue repeatedly raised by Frank Lentricchia in *After the New Criticism* (1980). A goal in my book is the identification of a continuing social drama of sport in society that actualizes the issues of freedom (play) and constraint (rules, competition). This identification of such a contradiction within the fiction of sport and play is raised to a discussion of how the contradictions might function in the criticism of the sport and play subject.

The Play Spirit

FROM KANT and Schiller in the eighteenth century down through Nietzsche and Heidegger, to Gadamer, Marcuse, Derrida, and Jameson in our time, concepts of play have been central and vital to the articulation of the individual subject's freedom as well as to that subject's ability to perceive beauty and to create it in language. Play has provided us with images, symbolic activity, joyful "purposeless" production, a safe harbor, a boundary space, a disguise, a vertigo, an existential errand, a structure, a freedom, a choice. Play is a powerful hermeneutic device in contemporary Western metaphysics and in musings on the death of that metaphysics. It is provocative when positioned betweeen terms such as the sensual and the ethical, rite and myth, content and form, and the material and the spiritual where it then seeks to bring out the essence of each polarity while always reserving the power to dance away from capture by one pole or another. As an expressly subject-centered phenomenon in many of its guises, play remains the free individual's last best card in the deck, the one that may keep him or her alive in time and space by creating temporary structures of time and space that the individual can stand and learn from in the larger game.

Sport itself is that larger game in so much contemporary American fiction, an object-centered phenomenon. As a sharply defined, rule-bound structure of time and space, sport accepts play's freedom and limits it for specific ends. The subject player submits to the sport where he is both player and play-thing in the larger game, a competitor and a pawn. Sport utilizes the exhilaration of the player while it presents a challenge to the player to retain a freedom within constraint. A ceaseless infusion of play drives sport but, at the same time, sport challenges the player's freedom, the very freedom of play.

Play theory has become an accepted mode of inquiry in this century but often has been depicted in more functional or humanist models: behavioral psychology (Piaget), history (Huizinga), theology (Eliade), sociology (Goffman); other contemporary sociologists walk the borders of play and sport while defining them (Loy, Luschen, Sutton-Smith, to name a few). The thought of Schiller and Nietzsche gave to Marxist and formalist critics on the one hand and to post-structuralist and phenomenological critics on the other, new modes of "playing between" and "playing beyond," a fresh rhetoric of rebellion and astonishment, of vision and of free space. Play became the mode in which to speak of the largest of contradictions. In sports fiction, the play mode confronts the sportsworld of determined roles, rules, collective domination, and external reward. Within the powerful rhetoric of play, sport as social subject competes to be an equal partner.

What Schiller took from Kant's *Critique of Aesthetic Judgment* (1790) was the concept of freedom that inhered in the beautiful derived from aesthetic experience. Yet Schiller in "Letters on the Aesthetic Education of Man" (1795) went much further by emphasizing the realm of the aesthetic as the reflection of human essence, which is fundamentally moral within itself. Thus from the outset of play theorizing, Schiller's privileging of the aesthetic was to leave himself and his program vulnerable to charges of idealism and subjective conceptualizing, pushing play toward art and marginal utility, toward the "not-serious." Visions of autonomous imaginations and unquestioned primacy of the beautiful have dogged aesthetic play theory ever since Schiller's formulation at the dawn of German romanticism. Such visions are primary reasons why aesthetic play appears so far from the social world of sport and why American sport sociologists and sports fiction critics have little interest in Schiller's legacy. Yet this legacy is crucial in determining the art of sports fiction.

Through play, the sensuous might receive an object while the formal impulse might produce an object (Schiller 51). The object of the play instinct is "living form" in both the realms of matter and of form. That living form Schiller designated as "beauty" (53–54). The impulse of form to mastery must be "played" back through the sensuous impulse to a semblance of intuitive individual freedom from rationality. According to Schiller, the mediation of play in aesthetics looks like this:

Stofftrieb ⟷	Spieltrieb ⟷	Formtrieb
"Sense Drive"	"Play Drive"	"Form Drive"
Sensuousness	Aesthetics	Reason
Matter	Beauty as Objective	Ethics
Content	Freedom as Goal	Spirit

Play becomes the place where matter and form are satisfied together. "Reality," then, cannot be positioned outside play, or counted "more serious" than play, because the play drive itself must finally determine the constitution of the entity, its positioning lodged between major oppositions in human personality.

If Schiller's play is potentially revolutionary, it is also nostalgic, evoking at one and the same time the return to an original plenitude before the dissociative split into sense versus reason or matter versus spirit and the impossibility of such a return.[1] Play reconstitutes the broken unity of the sensual and the moral in what Schiller would have called a "state of nature." Such nostalgia for the completeness of content and form is real and powerful, as it works on any writer's synthesizing imagination or on any artist or thinker's quest for truth.[2] This concept of a broken pattern and play's tentative or provisional healing of it occurs again and again in play theory. We are seen to play (depending on the ideological bent of the play theorist) to approximate a prior unity or to stave off the intolerable present. In *Ecce Homo*, Nietzsche writes, "I do not know any other way of associating with great tasks than with *play*" (258; italics Nietzsche's), which will hurl him beyond categories into the most extreme of individualities. Nietzsche's "play beyond" is not in time or in a utopian future but in thought itself, where the intellectual hero may be free from antitheses.

Heidegger is the great figure between Nietzsche and Derrida, realigning thinking on being in his literal astonishment at existence and our subjective relation to Being. He would find what is recaptureable and full when an object is fully itself in the gaze of a subject who is truly in-the-world. Heidegger's vision has the highest conception of *mimesis*, both the most all-encompassing and the simplest. Heidegger believed that "the play of Being is a playing *with* human being" (Hyland 85), a serious play, for "this floundering in commonness is part of the high and dangerous game and gamble in which, by the nature of language, we are the stakes" (Heidegger, *What Is Called Thinking?* 119).

Heidegger in "Language" (1959) expresses the terms that Derrida will make central in his essay "Differance" (1968). Heidegger writes of "world" and "things" "penetrating" each other only as they "traverse a middle" where "they are at one" ("Language" 202). "The intimacy of world and thing" comes to pass when "in the between of world and thing, in their *inter*, division prevails: a *dif-ference*" (202). What Heidegger prepares for Derrida is a continuity of mediation, an elusive "between" in difference that allows definition of the material and the sensible (earth, thing) and the knowable, the cultural (world).[3] Yet with Heidegger, we are also in the presence of the philosopher who would define a very inclusive frame for world play. He identifies a "play of the same" where play mediates between time and space ("The Nature of Language" 106; Thiher 59–62). His repeated emphases on tools and equipment, his metaphors of the "clearing" and of sudden instrumental illumination, of a "standing within" for the subject, all suggest an intimate understanding for the physical knower and a knowledge of and by the body's relation to earth and world. To "come to the between of the dif-ference" is to come to the work of art, but also to the work-place, to the arena, to the lighted pathway, to the space of a full earth. Here is where sport "worlds" in all its guises. Here the sportsman in nature or in the set-apart arena knows himself most intimately.

The two most prominent post-Heideggerian philosophers in terms of contemporary play theory are Gadamer and Derrida. Gadamer's *Truth and Method* (1955, trans. 1975) suggested that in the realm of the aesthetic, it is not the playful activity of the player-subject that is primary, but *play:* "the structure of play absorbs the player into itself and thus takes from him the burden of the initiative" (94). Gadamer's view absorbs all freedom into the world "as played." Gadamer consistently attacks the notion of the play-ful subject. He posits instead a world play in which the game itself would be a firm totality and would have primacy over the players involved in it (95–96). Art itself is absorbed into this game structure and cannot be privileged over and against reality, for "beauty and art give to reality only a fleeting and transfiguring radiance" (74); freedom is only in aesthetics, not in reality. Following Heidegger, Gadamer believes nothing less than that "in the representation of play, what *is* emerges" (*Truth and Method* 101; italics mine).[4] Such a conception is far more encompassing than Huizinga's more rigid distinctions between play and the serious in *Homo Ludens:* between play as powerfully determining the origins of art and social institutions but as completely absent in the present. The primacy of the game almost stipulates the sports subject as world where sport is a cultural and social unit that plays out all relations of subjects and objects.

Derrida made language the subject of his play conceptions as well as the object making them up. Two seminal essays, "Structure, Sign, and Play in the Discourse of the Human Sciences" (1966) and "Differance" (1968) provided a bold conceptual advance in play theory. "Differance" is the more fundamental of the essays in which Derrida wishes to describe what the irreducible differing, deferring, and substituting mechanism within language is that allows us to speak of differences at all and that fundamentally frees us to make sense of any concepts within language. Such positioning of differance between sense and reason, between speech and writing, recalls Schiller's positioning of play. Schiller's domain was, of course, an idealist aesthetics, but, structurally, Derrida's differance is play in the same semantic mode: play as the force that is more than real, yet is not in itself captureable in language; play as that which dictates meaning and yet cannot be located. The power of differance lies in making up what we call "power." This remarkable and challenging essay of play-as-differance concludes with a quest for the single and the unitary without losing its alternative and insurgent voice.

Derrida's definition of play as the "disruption of presence" in "Structure, Sign, and Play" is a definition waiting for his radical concept of differance in the article by that name. The criticism in "Structure, Sign, and Play" of the "ethic of nostalgia for origins," the longing for a "purity of presence," is not glossed with the majesty of a Heideggerian reading. Instead Derrida presents us with a fundamental double reading of play, one with major consequences in the assigning of this or that play impulse to authors, characters, and conceptions in the fiction of sport and play:

> Turned towards the lost or impossible presence of the absent origin, this structuralist thematic of broken immediacy is therefore the saddened, *negative,* nostalgic, guilty, Rousseauistic side of the thinking of play whose other side would be the Nietzschean *affirmation,* that is the joyous affirmation of the play of the world and of the innocence of becoming, the affirmation of a world of signs without fault, without truth, and without origin which is offered to an active interpretation. (292)

Such choices are continual when Derrida invokes play. They are his inscription of nothing less than philosophy's spanning the oppo-

7

sition between Nature and Freedom or Necessity and Freedom, as Heidegger described it in his *Schelling's Treatise on the Essence of Human Freedom* (57–59). In a study of sport and the play spirit, such "spanning" of oppositions is crucial in the analysis of disparate sports narratives and figures. The play toward origins is evident in the studies of the sporting "natural," the heroic romantic individual, or the competitor who pushes toward the ultimate test in nature or against his own body, who without any irony wants to move to the limit of the real or the sacred. On the other hand, the play of the sporting hero beyond categories is existential and individualizing, often dark and dionysian. The play beyond categories revels in paradoxes and the freedom of its own thesis-making. Here is the verbal play of the rebelling confessional hero, the mimesis of the female player, the athlete who plays *with* his sport, and the play of the athlete who sees a future not bound by the performance principle or competitive imperative and who plays toward that future. All authors in the fiction of sport and play are consciously or unconsciously thinking about play in their own choices of subject and representation and in the figuration of the drama within which their players and athletes move.

The political-social thrust of play's hermeneutic dictates the ways in which it may be conceived as a radical tool for the articulation of cultural dissatisfaction with the dominant ideology. Such dissatisfaction provides a major dramatic tension in the contemporary fiction of sport and play. Schiller's program reveals social and political implications, as Marcuse and Jameson have been well aware. Schiller wrote, "I hope that I shall succeed in convincing you that this matter of art is less foreign to the needs than to the tastes of our age; nay, that to arrive at a solution even in the political problem, the road of aesthetics must be pursued, because it is through beauty that we arrive at freedom" (Schiller 7). Even though Marxist critics would question that beauty is the path to freedom, they nonetheless are challenged by the yoking of concepts and see them as a way to combat reification.[5]

Jameson's controversial and highly useful ploy of transcoding from one semantic universe to another has as one of its bases his admiration for Schiller's vision of the freedom growing out of play.[6] Jameson is quick to point to Schiller's political influences, how Schiller's program is deeply affected by the chaos of the French Revolution, how it is a bourgeois aesthetic of idealistic order. Yet for all that, Jameson takes from Schiller the liberating energy of play in what Jameson calls freedom's "privileged instrument of a political hermeneutic" (*Marxism and Form* 84).[7]

Clearly, then, Jameson's program casts the two "interpretations of interpretation" (Derrida, "Differance" 292) in familiar opposing modes, from the two interpretations of play at the conclusion of Derrida's "Structure, Sign and Play" all the way back to Schiller's initial opposition of content and form. Jameson is vitally interested in freedom as what he calls "an interpretive device," and its application in contemporary Marxist theory. Jameson derives new paired oppositions out of the terms of which freedom may operate and conceives of other, more materially dictated contradictions in the social world—public and private, work and leisure, sociology and psychology, politics and poetics—all summed up in the largest contradiction, "society and the monad." Here is where freedom will operate as the third drive between matter and form: "Such a drive is the *Spieltrieb,* the impulse to play, which underlies artistic activity in general" (89).

Schelling's treatise *On Human Freedom* (1809) was German idealism's highest attempt to delineate the various kinds of freedom: freedom as that which needs no foundation; freedom "from"; freedom "for"; freedom as "standing within one's own essential law"; freedom as the capability of good and evil; and, lastly, freedom as complete indeterminacy (Heidegger, *Schelling's Treatise* 84), indecisive in itself, but, as Heidegger has written, "rather that which in its turn can only be understood and overcome in terms of freedom" (102). Jameson wants expressly to appropriate this concept of negative freedom as a revolutionary tool. Freedom may be negatively defined as coming to consciousness in a very personal definition for the individual: "Freedom (n.) – 'What I don't have,' the realization of a bondage to content or form that must be redressed." Freedom is a drive to play ourselves out of the intolerable present toward the utopian future. Yet the present is where the game always must be: we are in it nor can we be out of it, as Gadamer would tell us.[8] In Jameson's case, play in the guise of freedom becomes the actively determining agent of the mediation of history, which is itself the agonistic ground of all play.

What finally comes forth in contemporary play theory derived from Schiller and continuing through Gadamer, Derrida, and Jameson is a group of fundamental questions that play helps to answer: How to retain a kinetic, fluid center of human thought and feeling that is supplely capable of extending to the boundaries of physical and moral experience without being included in or excluded from matter or form? How to resist premature unification and fight both sublimation and spiritualization? How to cancel domination by seizing the very process of conceptualization? Play is that figure of figures for the athlete, the novelist, the philosopher, the critic.

A Structural Semantics for Sports Fiction

PLAY IS a fundamental mechanism for heroes and heroines of sports fiction and indeed for all people but, more immediately and powerfully, for people designated already as players, competitors in a determined space in game time. The operations they undertake in the arena are public rituals of mediation *between* content and form. They are expressions of their spirit in physical glory and perfection while representing the deep sense-reason production of language as well as aesthetics.

All the play modes—"playing back to," "playing beyond," and "playing between"—are represented in sport, and, by extension, in sports fiction. Thus, while sport is often counter to play in its rules and disciplines, it nonetheless functions structurally as the supplement to play of social reality, as the physical activity that plays off the differences. We "play back to" a sense of our physical well-being in a natural drive to mastery and expression. Such a drive is toward our most intimate or "original" knowledge of our physical selves. Physical sport momentarily "frees us from" the domination of mind and reason. We "play beyond" such control in sport, outside the oppositions of our daily lives, which include our work roles and sexual roles. We defer these oppositions in sport as surely as we mime them in substitution of rules, space, time, and degree of difficulty. Finally, in sport, we mime our deeper life patterns of voyage and return, of youth and age; we play life and death "between" the starting pistol and the final gun, "between" the lines, "within" the rules. The "play between" in sport is a deeply felt mimetic response both to mortality and to the tyranny of conceptual oppositions, portraying, as Coover writes in *The Universal Baseball Association,* "old rituals of resistance and rot" (Coover 165).

We need a structural model in which play and sport may co-exist in a full field of relations where play may be seen as the basis for sport but also as its implied opposite and critic in many ways. I would like to propose a structural field description of sports fiction, one that might prove useful in charting a significantly large number of texts from many areas of sports fiction. If we carry forward Schiller's mediation of the play impulse of Stofftrieb–Spieltrieb–Formtrieb, we possess the fundamental model for the individual subject as he or she plays between content and form in the realm of aesthetics. However, this opposition is not sufficient to account for the true complexity of the hero's relation to late capitalist society in which the individual sports figures are caught in the mechanism of a network of productive and consumptive relations that alter their material status and often their psychic balance.

Jameson believes that Stofftrieb, defined as "sense drive" or "content," has "ceased to exist" as such in the twentieth century and "has given place to commodities which are intellectual forms, or the forms of intellectualized satisfactions" (*Marxism and Form* 96). Jameson simply stops referring to Spieltrieb or "Play Drive" in the discussion, which suggests the deformity that he sees content and form to have undergone. No balance remains between them in a market economy. I would like to retain the "Play Drive" in a manner to be described shortly, but I want first to suggest an alternate mediation that Jameson's severe criticism of the content-form distortion provokes. That mediation would be a "Commodity Drive" of which Schiller at the dawn of Western industrial capitalism could not have conceived. The Commodity Drive would be fundamentally identified with reification: with consumption as objective and production as goal. I would present a more idealistic retention of content and form as states that in their purity are still desired by individual subjects who nonetheless become caught in Commodity Drive between the body and the spirit. If Play Drive and Commodity Drive are related to one another, we have

Play Drive ⟷	Commodity Drive
Aesthetics	Reification
Beauty as Objective	Consumption as Objective
Freedom as Goal	Production as Goal

Commodity Drive would in fact be involved in the play of production itself. The primary difference would be that while Schiller determined Play Drive as the privileged balance-wheel between sense and reason that enhanced them both through a positive neutralization, Commodity Drive draws on the life and potential from matter and form. Commodity Drive neutralizes the oppositions to destroy them as entities. A problem immediately becomes apparent. How can Play Drive and Commodity Drive *both* be present at the same time in any discussion of content and form? Second, how can these various impulses be made into paradigms that may be inhabited by individual subjects in the fiction of sport and play?

Mapping the Arena

TO GAIN a wide perspective on the coding of sport in fictional texts, I propose a structural dynamic that is jerry-built in the best American tradition. I want to bend Schiller's mediation of play between content and form into a semiotic square of binary opposites, retrieve it for dialectical criticism, and then center on a few well-known fictional texts for examples.

The semiotics of A. J. Greimas appear most helpful in an initial formulation of a semantics for sports fiction. In his essay, "The Interaction of Semiotic Constraints," Greimas posits what has come to be known as the "semiotic square," a four-term homology designed in quadrants to elicit "semes" of meaning. Greimas' construct begins with a figure of four terms that defines the "conditions of existence for semiotic objects" and is labeled the "elementary structure of signification." An initial term S generates its contrary (S_1: S_2) and then the negation of the two terms ($\overline{S}_2$ and $\overline{S}_1$) produce the bottom of the square (Greimas and Rastier, "The Interaction of Semiotic Constraints" 86). Greimas' mechanism functions by a series of contraries, contradictories, and implications and provides "a visual

representation of the logical articulation of any semantic category" (Greimas and Courtes, *Semiotics and Language* 308). If we attempt to portray the relations between the Sense Drive (Stofftrieb) and the Form Drive (Formtrieb) and their alternate mediations of Play Drive (Spieltrieb) and Commodity Drive, can we devise a semiotic square in which all the impulses may be grasped in a single dynamic?

If we posit Sense Drive (S_1) as the logical contrary of Commodity Drive (S^2) and Form Drive ($\overline{S}_1$) as its relation of contradiction, then Play Drive ($\overline{S}_2$) becomes the direct contradictory of Commodity Drive and the logical contrary to Form Drive. The semiotic square would look like this:

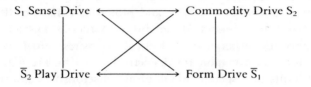

S_1 Sense Drive ⟷ Commodity Drive S_2

$\overline{S}_2$ Play Drive ⟷ Form Drive $\overline{S}_1$

If we nominalize the drives into object relations, the square may look like this:

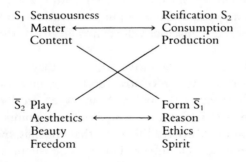

S_1 Sensuousness   Reification S_2
Matter ⟷ Consumption
Content   Production

$\overline{S}_2$ Play   Form $\overline{S}_1$
Aesthetics ⟷ Reason
Beauty   Ethics
Freedom   Spirit

Content and form are in contradiction; they may be reached only by the mediations of Play Drive and Commodity Drive; they can never meet in any economy. Such a representation allows us to propose a cycling in which matter is both played and reified, depending upon the emphasis of the text. The supple possibility occurs that play can be either a *paradigm* denoting freedom, separateness, unproductiveness, and uncertainty or that play may be in a *syntagmatic* relation to content and form and only elucidated as play by what enhances or keeps the two contradictory terms apart.

Greimas has been consistently concerned with his system's implications for literary study, stating that what is revealed is the author's journey "punctuated with compelling choices," that "leads through a series of exclusions and options, manifesting personal and social phobias and euphorias to the constitution of an original and unique work" ("The Interaction of Semiotic Constraints" 86). Greimas' mechanism is intricately calibrated as far as the level of the individual sentence. While most critics have doubted the validity of any lexical set of categories to fully explain an imaginative work, they have cited the organizational tool that Greimas provides for the reduction of an inventory of characters, scenes, and plot to a constructed series of contraries and their generated negations.[9] Greimas' system is one of binary opposites rather than dialectical opposites, but Jameson sees the procedure as retrievable for dialectical criticism. He states that "it maps the limits of a specific ideological consciousness and marks the conceptual points beyond which that consciousness cannot go, and between which it is condemned to oscillate" (*The Political Unconscious* 47). What I suggest is that the relations of play to content and form and the relations of play and sport within a social network of forms can be mapped by developing a structure that describes a specific ideological consciousness common to authors of sports fiction.

We need, then, a way to move from the diagram of drives and object relations to a diagram of structural congruity, one dictated by a different code, that of individual characterological roles and passages. These roles represent the most significant points in the lives of sports heroes and comprise a life cycle that touches sports heroes at every stage of their development. Transposing the previous semiotic squares into one that actively maps the fiction about sport and play, yields

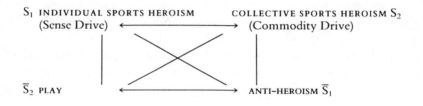

S_1 INDIVIDUAL SPORTS HEROISM   COLLECTIVE SPORTS HEROISM S_2
(Sense Drive)   (Commodity Drive)

$\overline{S_2}$ PLAY   ANTI-HEROISM $\overline{S_1}$

Such a grid placed over disparate authors and texts maps out the field of sports fiction and gives us conceptual points among which individual authors must range, wherever they may choose to concentrate any given cluster of characters and themes.

In essence, the sports hero begins in free Play, delighting in the freedom and self-mastery of his body. In a liberal rhetoric, sport is the province of the "free" individual where he may test self through and against limit, rule, record, and physical barriers. Play informs the generating skill of the sports hero, one converted into Individual Sports Heroism as he wins some notable victory. Individual Sports Heroism is a coming-of-age, the first encounter in competition. Individual heroes with a great skill are most often appropriated in American sport by the larger society which in sports fiction is collectively represented by the team in a *sports heroism in and for the collective*. How the individual hero utilizes his great skill within strict patterns of achievement and reward creates the tension between the individual and the collective. The sports heroism in and for the collective (hereafter called Collective Sports Heroism) is not simply an objective the Individual Sports Hero strives for but is an active societal role and concrete model that challenges him through its needs as an entity. He is most surely "in the game" and is both player and played.

The sports hero's crisis is dramatized in an Anti-Heroism in which he is cast out of the team world by the collective against his will or voluntarily in an act of self-knowledge and/or martyrdom. Here the sports hero realizes the form of his being and learns his spirit. Anti-Heroism as a conceptual point leads either back to an ironic relation to Collective Sports Heroism or returns the hero to the freedom of Play from which he began. Play is the individual's free point where he or she may reign provisionally with dominion over all signifiers but with no ultimate relation to the collective. Here the individual resists capture by either the sensuous or the rational, by the physical victories of the Individual Sports Hero or by the personal crises of the Anti-Hero. The traversal of the above relations and the currents that are generated map out the form of the individual's free potential (Play), heroic encounter and sensuous production (Individual Sports Heroism), initiation into the group and commodification (Collective Sports Heroism), disaffection, rational insight, and potential sacrifice (Anti-Heroism), and return to Play.[10]

I do not wish to call the two versions of the semiotic square—that of the drives/object relations and that of the versions of heroism— absolutely congruent in meaning. Yet I believe there is a significant correspondence between the series of binary oppositions created from the impulses and drives proposed by Schiller and amended by Jameson and the series of oppositions proposed as controlling sports fiction. Individual Sports Heroism does have a specific correspondence with Sense Drive, for it is material and content-centered. It inheres in the exercise of the athletic body, its pushing to physical limits, as well as its quantified accomplishment: runs, points, touchdowns, and knockouts. Individual Sports Heroism is also a relational competition in which the athlete physically engages something or someone, an opponent, nature, the record book, the clock, the tape. Collective Sports Heroism does find the hero in crisis as a commodity for the team, compelled to reproduce his heroism over and over again as he is "consumed." Anti-Heroism may be simple victimization but more often it involves an ethical judgment on the collective's means and goals, a rational decision to detach self from the team to salve the spirit. Thus Anti-Heroism is Form Drive's logical end state. Play functions similarly in both versions of the semiotic square. As a drive, it is active and generative of momentary control as it "plays between." As a fixed category, Play remains the paradigm where the hero may perform momentary acts of conversion of matter and form at a point of recuperation. Play is also a revolutionary starting place for further reference to Individual Sports Heroism and to Anti-Heroism.[11]

Describing and Animating the Quadrants

ALL THE critical texts on sport and fiction state that sport recapitulates the problems of the individual in society. How can we deal with that major representation and include the generating power of play as well?[12] With this question in mind, the resolving of the initial opposition of individual heroism to collective heroism is an impossible synthesis to achieve and, of course, the subject of great debate and representation throughout the history of American life and literature. The individual hero in American sport is a richly physical and material standout. He enters freely into the constraints of competition to test himself to the physical limit (Hyland 68). The individual sports hero moves swiftly through all barriers to recognition in society and becomes a striking success, one not bound by class or race.

The heroic achievement of the individual sports hero is then absorbed by the power of institutions in the larger society. As one of our strongest and most pervasive cultural experiences, team sport is a model of our American socialization into competitive groups for external reward. In our simplest sports fiction narratives, assimilation to the team after initial misgivings and strife is the most common tale: reconciliation with the collective without the denial of the individual's identity. Very seldom is such reconciliation achieved in complex fiction about sport. However, the exception that proves the positive interaction between the individual and the collective might be a novel such as Mark Harris' *Bang the Drum Slowly* (1953) in which the initial suspicion of the team and its adversary relationship to Henry Wiggen and the dying Bruce Pearson is overcome. The players support and learn from one another and, not incidentally, win the pennant (the economic carrot, the victory for the team).

However, *Bang the Drum Slowly* is decidedly in the minority. In the great majority of team sports fiction, the team is owned and operated by a pack of low capitalist wolves; the coaches and managers are "characters" or have no character. The individual sports hero falls into a crisis against the authority of the collective, his great skill consumed eagerly, his integrity threatened by his inability to get along or to go along. Bernard Malamud's *The Natural* (1952) documents Roy Hobbs' disaffection as he treads a minefield of sportswriters, evil owners, and temptresses in a world that devours heroes. *Bang the Drum Slowly* and *The Natural* are matched in their benign and malignant views of the collective by two football novels, Dan Jenkins' *Semi-Tough* (1972) and Peter Gent's *North Dallas Forty* (1973).

Caught in a mode contradictory to play, the individual sports hero desires a way out of inauthentic experience in a renunciation of the bad collective. The fall into anti-heroism is the decline of the hero into crisis in an individual rebellion that is either forced or voluntary. The pressure comes from being benched, scapegoated, cut by a surgeon or a general manager, or cast out as a "loser" or "quitter."

The individual sports hero is now isolated again as an anti-hero. The glare is solely on him, not for his achievements but for the lack of them now that he contradicts all that he has been in the public eye. There is an ironic centering on him as a problem where he once was the solution. Such a crisis may lead simply to a truism that "Big Sport" is a dirty business. Sports novels of anti-heroism, most often those of football and boxing, have a strong emphasis on physical suffering and economic manipulation, the biological and environmental underpinnings of American literary naturalism, and they endlessly traverse the collective sports heroism/anti-heroism quadrant with no real resolution beyond pain and defeat. Yet anti-heroism may also lead to a wiser, more wary, and renewed relation to collective sports heroism as the individual hero returns to his sport. Or, the sporting anti-hero is seen at a point of existential revolt where his experience in the collective may be a turning to self-knowledge and ethical choices. Finally, play allows the sports hero to return to a limited freedom and to pursue his vision, either of renunciation, revolt, or a renewed drive for individual sports heroism.[13]

The Greimas semiotic square *itself* models the play of differences in sport. The square displays a constant movement between oppositions in which the individual subject is determining what is "me" and "not me": what belongs to the self and what belongs to the team. The sports hero or player often desires the "play back to," the desire merely to feel his or her body as a smooth-running whole or to "get back to" the elements of sport before it was taken over in his or her life by patriarchs, coaches, fans, leagues, and schedules. Players wish to "play back to" the origins of their physical delight. Just as often, they wish to "play beyond" limits, get beyond self and the body's limitations to do what has never before been achieved. Most often, the semiotic square will remind us that we "play between," not in absolutes or terminal crises but in complex and shifting relations between our individual and collective selves, between our allegiances and our rebellions. Such modeling further reveals that we are "in the game," in a Gadamerian sense, fully participating in the play of the world. We find ourselves in the play and sport of sports fiction.

I want to take three novels — *The Natural, Rabbit, Run* (1960), *One Flew Over the Cuckoo's Nest* (1962) — through some paces in terms of the semiotic square and focus on play's power to mediate between matter and form. I begin with *The Natural* (see chapter 11) both in its novelistic and recent cinematic (1984) presentations. In the novel, Bernard Malamud's Roy Hobbs keeps cycling through the binary oppositions; in the film, he makes two complete circuits. He begins in play in the film, in the nostalgic pose of a farm boy having a catch with his father: the father-son relation is the one most stressed in baseball narrative as a whole. Hobbs then moves to his first act of individual sports heroism in film and novel as he vanquishes the Whammer on three pitched balls at the carnival, but he is immediately seduced and violated by the Dark Lady, Harriet Bird, avatar of the collective sports heroism's violent and wounding attention. She is the resentful witness to heroism. Hobbs is sent spiraling down into anti-heroism, into a literal "wandering in the wilderness" before he returns at age thirty-four, a disciplined quester instead of a bright youth. When manager Pop Fisher finally consents to let Hobbs bat in a game, he tells him "to knock the cover off of it" (63), which he does, *literally,* the ball unravelling as outfielders can find little to retrieve. Lightning flashes, thunder roars, rain pelts down as the Knights and their wasteland team managed by Pop, "the Fisher King," are regenerated. Hobbs has arrived as an individual hero through Malamud's play with literalizing the manager's command.

Here, the author's play is a point of coincidence that highlights both the hero's sport and the novelist's resources. To "knock the cover off the ball" is to perform an amazing physical feat that converts matter (the ball) into form (magical disappearance, extraordinary occurrence, "deconstruction"). Like all play, the scene re-works a mimetic moment into an activity outside ordinary life, yet one that begins in the known activity. As play, Hobbs' feat is free, separate, uncertain (no one has seen anything like it), unproductive (anti-productive), and fictive (a fantasy).[14]

Play is the clear mediation that lifts Hobbs out of anti-heroism and into individual sports heroism once more. But Hobbs is not done cycling through the oppositions. Now as individual hero he falls into the collective's hands once again as he duels the team's satanic owner, an evil sportswriter, and another temptress, Memo Paris. He descends into another anti-heroism, the victim of desire and the collective's resentment. Yet the film by dint of one burst of *Star Wars* effects—a pennant-winning home run setting off a galactic ballpark light show—redeems Hobbs in director Barry Levinson's "play." The home run triggers the explosion of matter that signifies Hobbs' physical and spiritual triumph. We last see Hobbs in Iris Lemon's field throwing the ball to their son; we are back at the tale's origins, having made two complete trips around the diamond/square.

The film completely alters Malamud's ending, which stops short of redemption with Hobbs mired in a negative anti-heroism, having sold out and struck out, answering that most agonizing of baseball cries, "Say it ain't true, Roy"—"I'm afraid it is, kid." This is an appropriately bleak ending for a Camelot tale of Arthurian knights. However, for the film version to invent a sixteen-year-old son for Roy Hobbs and Iris Lemon, to invent a perforated stomach lining from the earlier shooting as the reason for his retirement from baseball, is to link the two complete heroic cycles and take the action away from Hobbs' will. It is a fine piece of Hollywood packaging entirely consistent with fictional baseball narrative which stresses, as does the sport itself, journeying, "coming home," recurrence, and origins. Levinson and Robert Redford get closer to the appeal of baseball's satisfying rhythms than Malamud.

To play with and through the injunction "to knock the cover off the ball" is to use language immediately and playfully as an example of freedom for the character and author. Yet much of sport and play is "flow" experience, essentially physical and nonverbal, and thus difficult to retrieve in narrative. An example of this play's mediating power, one in which language can be converted in and through action, occurs in John Updike's *Rabbit, Run* (see chapter 13) in which Rabbit Angstrom hits a "perfect" golf shot. The scene finds Rabbit in a golf match with the Reverend Eccles who, in this contemporary version of a parish visit, wants to find out why Rabbit has left his pregnant wife and young son to live with another woman. Rabbit is a natural athlete and former high school basketball star who is imbued with a delicate touch and sensuous control. Yet he is wallowing in an anti-heroism, hounded by the collective's moral displeasure at his flight from society. He feels clumsy; the golf clubs will not respond to his touch, but finally,

> Very simply he brings the clubhead around his shoulder into it. The sound has a hollowness, a singleness he hasn't heard before.

His arms force his head up and his ball is hung way out, lunarly pale against the beautiful black blue of storm clouds, his grandfather's color, stretched dense across the east. It recedes along a line straight as a ruler-edge. Stricken; sphere, star, speck. It hesitates, and Rabbit thinks it will die, but he's fooled, for the ball makes this hesitation the ground of a final leap: with a kind of visible sob takes a last bite of space before vanishing in falling. "That's *it!*" he cries and, turning to Eccles with a smile of aggrandizement, repeats, "That's it." (133–34)

The moment of sports excellence liberates Rabbit from Eccles' reasons and forms. Nature had fled Rabbit's control. Now in the realm of plenitude, in response to society, he converts club and ball to a transcendence, an orgasmic fullness, both a re-conversion of matter to form (stricken; sphere, star, speck) and a re-integration into fullness and weight. Rabbit's triumphant phrase, "That's it!", truly signifies "That's me!"; "that's my physical skill and the only peace I know in space." Rabbit has regained control of the sensuous and, by extension, his control over the women in his life.[15]

Rabbit demonstrates momentary dominance of "touch," the grace of the male sports natural, but it is important to see it as a liberation from anti-heroism and a direct rebuttal to the collective. For an instant, the aestheticizing impulse has given the golf club, the ball, the moment, and Rabbit's material predicament a freedom, a liberation of sensuousness through Updike's artistic form, which creates Rabbit's adeptness.[16] Nothing is resolved on the golf course in *Rabbit, Run*. Play does not resolve. Play mediates by playing oppositions, here in the momentary perception of perfection and transcendence that refers to Rabbit's individual heroism in sport and that controls his status as male sexual outlaw, as anti-hero.

A third example of play's power would be in the final scenes of Ken Kesey's *One Flew Over the Cuckoo's Nest* (see chapter 5) when Chief Bromden kills the lobotomized body of Randall Patrick McMurphy and escapes from the mental ward. The Chief's physical act is a freeing of McMurphy's spirit, a conversion of matter to form. He does so even as the ward's inmates could deny the living "dead" body was McMurphy's, for they had been taught the power of play *by* McMurphy, the confidence man and illusionist. The smothering of McMurphy, the master-player, is an ethically complete act that will free McMurphy and the Chief. The act is a ritual sacrifice but begins in play. The act is free, separate, and fictive in the sense that the Chief has constructed a fiction that it is not Mc-Murphy's body at all, even as the men on the ward had been taught by McMurphy to see a World Series forbidden to them by Nurse Ratched on a dead, gray television screen; they had been taught to convert recalcitrant matter in play. Likewise, the Chief's final action is to hurl the Combine's huge control panel through a plate-glass window. The material object soars into the moonlit night, its "absence" providing the Chief's path to freedom. This moment, too, has been prepared for by McMurphy's playful wagering at the novel's outset as to whether the panel could be lifted. By passing through the realm of play, the degraded body of McMurphy has been reconverted through the Chief's individual heroism; the Chief has passed through psychic and physical barriers to freedom as well.

Malamud, Updike, and Kesey have all used play to mediate between the pressures of matter and form. They satisfy our yearning to speak of matter and form together without being placed in bondage to sense or reason. All three heroic actions have taken place against the terms posed by the collective that would control thought and lives.

To test the usefulness of the diagram's oppositions and the potential mediations, I want to speculate as to the position of a variety of sports fiction categories and anticipate how I will enlarge on them in the succeeding chapters. In novels of individual sports heroism where males violently seek self-definition, sports narratives of man-in-nature (chapter 1), of the body as arena (chapter 2), or of fighters in the deterministic boxing arena (chapters 3–4) work strongly in the individual sports heroism and collective sports heroism quadrants with ritual as collective act being underscored, whereas play is comparatively absent as an option for characters. Ritual freezes and rigidifies into rule-dominated behavior in the face of a world where nothing is left free or uncertain and the body is violated. Such a sporting world was intimately known to Hemingway whose inheritors include Mailer, James Dickey, and Thomas McGuane.

In more playful responses to plights of individual sports heroism, authors veer sharply away from capture or imprisonment in some driven, determined culture of the male body. The threats of sacrificial crisis and of the pressure of performance demand both the play of characters and of authors in novels such as Kesey's *Cuckoo's Nest* and Coover's *The Public Burning* (1977) (chapter 5). A study of the inscription of women in play and sports fictional narrative (chapter 6) centers on the women's struggle for representation through a male dominant language. Women athletes are represented as individual sports hero-ines since their bodies are always intensely visualized and coveted. The embodied state of physical perfection is for women what cannot be overcome, but a politicized mimesis may allow them in sport to at least temporarily neutralize the power relations and gain some control within the male sports culture. Such awareness is still more a potential development in sports fiction but is evident in the unique work of Jenifer Levin's *Water Dancer* (1982) and *Snow* (1983) and in Robert Towne's film *Personal Best* (1982).

The "last" school sports heroes, with all the attendant ironies of their position (chapter 7), traverse the play-individual sports heroism-collective sports heroism quadrants. The school sports hero's major defeat and frustration is in his inability to convert matter to form, to convert individual heroism into any lasting victory for the spirit; he cannot play the sensual into the ethical. The physical perfection in individual sports heroism cannot locate the self-knowledge of anti-heroism as in John Knowles' *A Separate Peace* (1960) and Wright Morris' *The Huge Season* (1954). Novels that deal with the fan or the witnessing confessions of the anti-hero (chapter 8) traverse the quadrants of play-anti heroism-collective sports heroism in comic renunciation where protagonists refuse to play for any "team." The missing term here is individual sports heroism. The witness will not or cannot be a hero. He remains mired in form, in rational or irrational abstention from heroics where he cannot "produce" for himself or for the team. He cannot play the ethical into the sensual but instead controls the language of "see-ing." Such heroes are both self-deprecating and defiant in texts such as Frederick Exley's *A Fan's Notes* (1968) and Philip Roth's *Goodbye, Columbus* (1959).

The three major team sports—football (chapters 9–10), baseball (chapters 11–12), and basketball (chapter 13)—have definite fictional patterns and are most fully about the collective paradigm of sport, about individual sports heroes being immersed in the game, both personally and in a structural sense. Football narratives most often chart the deterministic fall through collective sports heroism to an anti-heroism. The hero is a martyr-victim, ritual has turned to spectacle, and play is denied. Chapter 9 describes this beleaguered team sports hero while chapter 10, "Why We Are Playing," chronicles the few football novels that raise the physical inquiry to a metaphysical one. Baseball narratives keep cycling, as oberved in *The Natural*. The endless returning "home" moves through all quadrants in passage. It is no mistake, then, that baseball fiction has been the most supple and imaginative of all sports fiction, allowing authors the greatest range of imaginative inter-play (chapter 11). Authors may create counter-histories of whole leagues (indeed, universes) that textualize historical contradictions and allow for individual spiritual journeys (chapter 12). Basketball fiction (chapter 13) is always concerned with transcendence and upward space—and it is often simply spacy, comfortable in the play–anti-heroism negations where each player dances to his or her own moves.

No novel or group of novels exists solely in one quadrant or another of the semiotic square. All partake of the system's dynamics. The semiotic square may not only identify the locus of tensions of specific analyzed scenes but also may enhance the grouping of similar or disparate sports fiction texts. Finally, however, the semiotic square is a starting point for categorization, a way to map the sports fiction universe. It is not a substitute for intelligent reading and interpretation. The adaptation of the Greimas square is meant to enhance the precision and compass of these operations.

I want to conclude this introduction (in the spirit of Yogi Berra, the noted critic of closure: "It ain't over till it's over") with an initial estimate of my own structure that will be returned to throughout this study. The play and sport variation of a semiotic square proposed here is expressly subject-centered and displays a model that suggests that the pattern of contemporary American sports fiction is best described through the passages of its individual heroes. However, I do believe that collective sports heroism, that team sport and public realm of the social and economic world, is by far the most dominant point in the structure, as is the commodity drive which that collective sports heroism represents. The individual sports hero's tensions and achievements within the sports collective is the obsessive subject of the authors of American sports fiction, no matter what ideology of the hero and of society the authors espouse. My critical operation is that of playing the trump card of play at every promising opportunity, championing freedom through play in the liberal sense while not forgetting the larger political struggles in which play may be enlisted to fight. When we "freely" make rules and disciplines in sport, we are miming a whole set of determinisms to which we then "freely" submit.

In the best of our sports fiction, play presides over the transformation of matter into grace and spirit, and spirit into matter and content—which is, after all, why we care about sport and play at all in the articulation of our earth-bound, mortal bodies against space and time and against less lyrical but more obdurate barriers such as reification. We value authors who dramatize these struggles in all their complexity. They deserve our complex response in turn.

PART I

Individual Sports Heroism: Male Physical Self-Definition

I.

The Decline of the Ritual Sports Hero

THE MALE body itself is the place to begin an analysis of individual sports heroism. Authors see the male body under threat where it seeks mastery over nature, self, an animal, or another person in a natural arena. Ritual sport has traditionally provided codification and structure to male physical experience in sustaining ceremony. However, in contemporary American fiction, the figure of the Ritual Sports Hero is in real decline. He is a hero in new deployments, often as a player where suspension of ritual's sacrificial threat is the goal. Or he joins the collective in a team sport where his primary physical definition is distilled into wins, losses, and submersion in a larger structure. Sports heroes who are defined more by play and team sport comprise the large majority of subjects under discussion in the book (chapters 5–13).

Here we begin with the Ritual Sports Hero as the male body under acute stress in a narrative as old as American fiction itself.

The Ritual Sports Hero in American fiction had been a well-tested figure from Cooper's Natty Bumppo down through Hemingway's classic bullfighters and fishermen to Faulkner's Ike McCaslin. The Ritual Sports Hero had always been a solitary figure coming to learn what he was capable of in a primal arena. Although most often portrayed as an isolate, it was just that quality that enabled him to comment on the ills of the larger collective society. He had been a natural aristocrat, the stance presupposing an abstention from murderous conduct in the name of an integrated sportsmanship. Before the contemporary era, the figure always had a purity of conception, a breadth of vision, and an innocence that made him both vulnerable and heroic.

The Ritual Sports Hero's goal is to become "same," "like," "at one with." He wishes to be unified with a fixed center that will hold. The Ritual Sports Hero definitely seeks to move *beyond* play, in states inimical to free play that would cancel play in a transcendent moment or in the violence of a sacrificial moment. If ritual does indeed begin in play, which threatens the stability of all signifiers, ritual re-constitutes play in rigid forms. The Ritual Sports Hero freezes at a pole of matter or spirit where he may either experience competitive mastery of the physical world and gain the resultant blood knowledge or "become the woods," become nature in a spiritual witnessing. The Ritual Sports Hero desires space to be "like himself"; indeed, in the case of Mailer, the hero desires to *be* that space.

The Ritual Sports Hero touches all the sports heroisms—*individual, collective, anti-heroism.* As an *individual sports hero,* he seeks mastery in technique that would allow him to be, in Hemingway's phrase from "Big Two-Hearted River," "in the good place," as a co-equal in the physical world. As a *collective sports hero,* he is an initiate desiring mentors through which he can gain in society's passages as a man. He can be merged into the collective body. Finally, as an *anti-hero,* he divests self of competition and technique, privileged to be allowed to be "at one" with the natural world, as in Ike McCaslin's sublime identification with the wilderness in "The Bear," Part I (1942). Far from the freedom of *play,* the Ritual Sports Hero desires a constraint, a limit, and a discipline in the processes of ritual and/or in the rules and competition of sport.

What the ritual experience yields in contemporary fiction are a frustrating isolation for the individual sports hero and ineffective community in the collective, the husk of effective ritual action. The private rites are anxious and concealing; the public rites are incomplete and often humiliating. Such rites are in great contrast to the rites in earlier American sporting fiction. Hemingway attempted control of the ritual sports tale by tightening its perception and banishing the authority of all mentors and public ceremony. How much, finally, do "Big Two-Hearted River" (1925) and *The Old Man and the Sea* (1952) resemble each other, three decades apart? The youthful Nick Adams and the aged Santiago both perform surely in a world without people, as if all inhabited arenas are already canceled in contamination. "There were plenty of days coming when he could fish the swamp," thinks Nick Adams in the last lines of "Big Two-Hearted River," and this metaphor describes well Hemingway's wariness toward what waits, unritualized and out-of-control.

Hemingway fought all his career to gain control over such terror, most notably through sporting heroism and heroic witnessing, which was elevated into a rite as well.[1] Denying other games-masters or father-authorities, he became "papa" so very young, the mentor-father himself, the aesthetician and sportsman with his meticulous disquisitions on technique and courage that merge into a more abstracted sense of form. The Hemingway story most similar to the contemporary ritual sports tale is "The Battler" (1925), the actual narrative of "fishing the swamp," where Ad Francis and Bugs reside and educate Nick Adams. Apart together, the grotesque faceless boxer and his coy, crooning companion level all Nick's questions and distinctions.

Nick's initiation is into the possibility of limitless incestuous, racial, and economic distortions in the individual and collective life of Ad Francis, the game competitor whose boast is "they all bust their hands on me." Nick can't "read" Ad Francis' featureless face and Ad's language oscillates violently as well. Nick is turned back toward civilization, having seen not clearly but too well the disorder of the unsanctified, set-apart arena. Yet Ad and Bugs are strictly defined *by* that civilization from which they and Nick have fled. The boxer and his keeper, as well as the young initiate, are at home neither in civilization nor in nature. The distortion and layers of evil and the deteriorating human relations mark the wilderness and portrayal of primal arenas in contemporary ritual sports fiction. Hemingway's ploy was to place correctly the boxer, the arena-bound avatar of the individual sports hero, back into the natural world, a setting in which he glares forth in all his distortion, "like" no one and "at one" with nowhere. For Nick Adams, the question is how to keep from becoming "like" Ad Francis, a faceless, defeated sports figure, a male whose physical self-definition is violent and skewed.

Chapter 1 looks at two novels of male anxiety in the despoiled natural environment, Dickey's *Deliverance* (1970) and McGuane's *The Sporting Club* (1969), and ends in speculation about Mailer's intense identification with Hemingway as ritualist. The ritual sports narrative records the fragmenting encounters of would-be individual heroes with their physical natures and with opposing forces in a menacing natural world. The environment does not yield exalted witnessing and is not majestic as much as viscerally threatening. One reason the natural world is so terrifying is that *we* are in it or want to "be" it. Such yearning for absolute merger is continually frustrated as our apprehension of nature's limitlessness produces a sacrificial or sublime response in conflict with our ego-dominant desires for mastery. The sacrificial or sublime response is encoded in ritual; the desire for mastery is encoded in competitive sport. Instead of Ike McCaslin or Santiago becoming re-integrated with creation at whatever cost by Faulkner and Hemingway, we have brutal messages: the homosexual rape and anonymous murders for survival in *Deliverance;* a tragi-comic class war and ritual insanity in *The Sporting Club;* the Alaskan God-beast in *Why Are We in Vietnam?* (1968) telling D.J. and Tex to "go forth and kill" in Vietnam (see chapter 2).

Thus the Ritual Sports Hero may be expressed in a violent literary naturalism as well as in a more philosophical and historical fiction that runs him squarely through the collective's radical altering of nature. To lift the individual sports hero out of society and its down-drag had never been the aim of Cooper, Hemingway, or Faulkner. Instead, they used the individual sports hero as an anachronism, a prior heroic vision to oppose trends of collective modern society: the rapacity of a growing Templeton in *The Pioneers* (1823), a hero-worshipping Madrid (and Brett Ashley) bent on seducing Pedro Romero in *The Sun Also Rises* (1926), the Edmonds line of McCaslins and its continuing violence toward women and the earth in *Go Down, Moses* (1942). The narrative of the Ritual Sports Hero had always been an archaic narrative thrust into a dominant present reality.

The Ritual Sports Hero as an ideal American natural man had never, even in his strongest configurations, been an adept individual hero without contradictions. Hemingway drew the figure as always subject to real physical danger. Pedro Romero's great victory in *The Sun Also Rises* is climaxed when he is carried out of the bullring by the crowd. The scene is emblematic of Christ entering Jerusalem's gates in Easter Week and describes a dangerous straddled position that leaves him sexually vulnerable to the crowd; he is theirs for their purposes. Other moments in Hemingway suggest the collective society as both predatory and unmindful of the Ritual Sports Hero. *The Old Man and the Sea* concludes with tourists gazing stupidly at the skeleton of Santiago's great marlin, "now just garbage waiting to go out with the tide"; they look right past the evidence of the agon to discuss the shark's "handsome, beautifully formed tails" in a defective aesthetic response. In *To Have and Have Not* (1937), Harry Morgan, the working-class ritualist, is countered by Mr. Johnson's view of sport fishing: "If it hurts, why do it?"—while Frederick Harrison, a Washington, D.C. predator, wonders, "If you can't eat 'em, where's the sport?"

Faulkner, too, showed that a ritualist was subjected to the dominant collective contradictions. Ike McCaslin's series of negations and renunciations move him into an anti-heroic witnessing, a spiritual absorption into nature that is complete. However, the larger crimes of Yoknapatawpha society against women and blacks rage on. The saint-martyr of Hemingway and Faulkner in ritual sport was never a soaring, noncontradictory figure of mastery. That hero functioned with surety in a sexless natural world beyond seductions and blandishments, either in the world of the Gulf Stream where individual sports heroism could be practiced unencumbered by Santiago, or in the woods without compass, map, or gun, where Ike McCaslin has become spatially "same" and has abolished all difference with his environment. Ike has reached an almost pure sublime relation to objects of nature, the representation of which, according to Kant, *"determines the mind to regard the elevation of nature beyond our reach as equivalent to a presentation of ideas"* (Kant 119; italics Kant's). But back of all that majesty remained an unyielding world of sexual confusion, spectacle, and materialism in society that resisted the Ritual Sports Heroes, in effect, drove them out to perform for themselves in individual sports heroism and witness for themselves in antiheroism.

The relations of ritual, play, and sport must be clarified to speak of a specific category such as ritual sport. In general, ritual implies a formal set of procedures in performance that possess validity that is justification for the action itself (Fox 53). The performance of ritual affects the participants and provides a heightened dimension to existence. The associations within this formalism may or may not be associated with an active dimension of religion.

Play may be enlisted in the service of ritual or it may be opposed to it. Ritual often takes the freedom and uncertainty of play for its own purposes and regulates play as do games and sports. In ritual, play is not free potential but rather "miming in the service of" in symbolic motions that have a narrative of their own. Rituals are then ceremonial and demonstrate a social situation (Fox 53), whereas play is more personal and is revelatory on that basis alone.

When ritual is opposed to sport, the major difference is that the semiotic form of ritual is mimetic (Duthie 93) while that of sport is agonistic. Ritual is representation; sport is competition. Alternatively, competitive sport in a social and collective context is also a ritual of representation. Within performance, sports competition is painful, physically exhausting, and full of encounter and risk. Yet at a transcendent level, all our agreed-upon motions of sport are ritualized responses to spatial "otherness," to temporality, and to mortality. Sports always have a ritual dimension waiting to be invoked. Ritual does not necessarily have a competitive dimension. Ritual can do *without* an active encountering and may be represented as slow, sure, ceremonial, sacrifical, and solemn.

The Ritual Sports Hero has always pushed toward the limits of his skill in sport or of his knowledge through performance in the rite. He had known that natural environment and felt most whole there. The natural world or the arena was his good place where all contradiction ceased, where, as Mailer believes, the boxer is more alive than anywhere else, where as Faulkner knew in "The Bear," Part 1, that "the wilderness coalesced." In the contemporary ritual tale, the wilderness is often *within* the individual, a bankruptcy of motives and goals that dictates a pushing of the individual male body into the natural arena. The Ritual Sports Hero feels that, rather than play in recoil from reification, the salvation is to become more physical or sensuous in direct relation to the natural world or to become more spiritual. Play is not an option because it is capricious, free, and out-of-control. The Ritual Sports Hero desires a bonding that only the rites may perform or a primary competition that sport may satisfy. He seeks to mime a stance of "this I know" that coheres, is fixed in ceremony, and enhances reality. As rest point and dynamic, play and its freedom are resisted and suppressed.

When men in contemporary American sports fiction go into the natural world, they have varying physical impulses. They may be compelled in attraction-repulsion to want to "be" nature or "be in it," to assume its power and signify "like" or "same" with nature, space, time, and mortal process. This is the drive to ritual. Alternately, characters in sport want to test themselves to the physical limit in nature to defeat nature, to kill it, to master it. This is the drive to competitive sport. The sport in ritual sport is in the service of a ritual response. The sporting drive to external and internal reward, to recognition, to heroism, is in ritual subordinate to the need to come into some sort of correct relation to existence. The conflicting poles of human and thus individual physical response in ritual sport move from desire for dissolution into the sacred to utter ego-mastery in the kill: to become "it" or to obliterate "it."

Dickey and Concealment

RITUAL SPORTS Heroes from the chaos of the collective's competition do not divest themselves of their conflicts; rather those conflicts survive and multiply. The nominal Ritual Sports Hero's experience in nature is that of a frustrating search for a proper rite, one that ends in a sacrifical crisis and in an even more pronounced competition. Mailer in *Why Are We in Vietnam?* portrays the dramatic difficulties that potential Ritual Sports Heroes experience as they attempt to be "at one with" nature, to possess its great animal or spirit. In Mailer's tale, the violence is projected onto a sacrificial "other," an entire substitute culture. Three other models are instructive for the erratic course of the sacrifice in contemporary sports fiction: Dickey's *Deliverance,* McGuane's *The Sporting Club,* with Kesey's *One Flew Over the Cuckoo's Nest* and Coover's *The Public Burning* as contrasts to be discussed in chapter 5.

René Girard in *Violence and the Sacred* (1977) has articulated a complete system of ritual sacrifice whereby society identifies certain classes of victims. He firmly believes that it is not a matter of averting violence as much as seeing to it that violence is contained and not a part of a vengeance cycle. The quest by society is for the correct sacrificial victim, a stand-in for the surrogate victim who cannot be sacrificed without communal rage and disruption. In the case of the sacrifical victim, there is always a crucial link with community missing so that the victim can be exposed to violence without reprisal: "The function of ritual is to 'purify' violence; that is, to 'trick' violence into spending itself on victims whose death will provoke no 'reprisals' " (Girard 36). The Ritual Sports Hero may be a priest or sacrificial victim. However, tension understandably surrounds the question of who will be dismembered and who will administer the rite. The identity of priest and victim is in doubt and characters fight to gain the priesthood and to deny their own sacrifical status.

Hemingway's insistence on the bullfight and Santiago's disquisition on the correct death of the great marlin are prime examples of properly purified ritual violence that sustains culture and yields insight. Faulkner had a more complex vision of ritual. Old Ben in *Go Down, Moses* is a true sacrificial victim, but Ike McCaslin sacrifices *himself* into the sacred. Faulkner's contradictions about the values of ritual dominate the novels of Dickey and McGuane. Dickey's suburban men take to a wild Georgia river for a weekend of white water canoeing and "wilderness experience" but conclude with at least three murders and concealed horror. McGuane constructs a bitter class war at a venerable Michigan private sporting club where all distinctions fall apart and destructive combat escalates. Each novel is obsessed with testing and competition. Dickey portrays a survival anxiety akin to that expressed in vintage literary naturalism: Is *Deliverance's* narrator, soft city man Ed Gentry, capable of becoming as hard and sure of himself as the situation demands? Can he become a predator and still retain ties to the world he has left? For McGuane, there is Vernor Stanton, a malevolent gamester whose energy turns competition and play malignant while he compels others to play in his frame, calling into question the efficacy of play itself.

Stanton's more straightforward counterpart in *Deliverance* is Ed Gentry's Ritual Sports Hero, Lewis Medlock, a wilderness adept and survival fanatic who articulates the charge to Ed after he (Lewis) has been cruelly injured in a canoeing accident and murder has overtaken the group: "It's you. It's got to be you" (129) and "We've killed a man. So has he. Whoever gets out depends on who kills who. It's just that simple" (131). Dickey has reduced the struggle to the human body, and Lewis' ability to be predator is what will be prized. "Preparedness" for tests is what Lewis preaches, a disaster mentality based on fear of nuclear war but more a proto-fascist desire for will and strength to be the ultimate determinants. Lewis' constant erection of barriers against the potential apocalyptic destruction in actuality is a longing to feel its great weight, a privatizing desire for a time when "a few men are going to take to the hills and start over" (40).

Lewis wants no rituals, with their delicate symbolic promise of repetition and renewal. Instead he says at the outset of the canoe trip, "The kind of life I'm talking about depends on its being the last chance. The very last of all" (42). Far from sustaining civilization through rite, Lewis wants to begin antedating civilization. He had developed mystiques about several demanding sports—fly-casting, archery, weight-lifting, spelunking, canoeing—but none of them really show his links to the land itself, but to survival. He is rock hard in response to softness. His goal, unlike Rusty Jethroe's in *Why*

Are We in Vietnam?, is to strip down to himself, smash the machines, and insert *his* body, what in other contexts might herald a vicious fascist preening toward authority. Ed states his wonder: "I had never seen such a male body in my life" (90).

This glorification of the strong body is a staple of ritual sports fiction. McGuane's Quinn in *The Sporting Club* is the narrator-witness to Stanton's menace, of Stanton's Hemingwayesque bulk and power: "His muscular frame was covered only by the pleated linen shorts he wore and sweat ran down his chest. In his right hand hung a duelling pistol" (14). Similarly, though in a positive vein, McMurphy in *Cuckoo's Nest* is revealed in all his phallic power to Chief Bromden, his narrator, as they shake hands: "The fingers were thick and strong closing over mine, and my hand commenced to feel peculiar and went to swelling up out there on my stick of an arm, like he was transmitting his own blood into it. It rang with blood and power" (24). Dickey has Ed Gentry see Lewis as degenerating society's last defense, "I would have liked nothing better than to touch that big relaxed forearm. . . . I would have followed him anywhere" (111).[2]

The impossibility of converting the body's power into something spiritual or ritually correct is a truth that underscores the various defeats in Dickey and McGuane. Buggery is the nightmare priming *Deliverance*—the body violated. As Bobby is buggered by the grotesque backwoodsman, Ed Gentry watches helplessly and conjures up Lewis' potent leg "with the veins bulging out of the divided muscles of his thigh, his leg underwater wavering small-ankled and massive as a centaur's" (97). But this leg is gored open by the river, burst like a sore as Lewis' power, so close to the surface of his skin, is almost over-ripe. The truth of Ed's impotence is that he can only watch Bobby's degradation. Dickey conveniently displaces the humiliation onto one "other" (the first backwoodsman) while giving Lewis the strength to kill the *other* "other." The scene is shocking but it happens to others and by others. The death of the rapist by Lewis's arrow dictates a cycle of vengeance in which no one will be safe.[3]

Thus the other side of the glorification of the body in ritual texts is the great anxiety about its violation: the grisly arrow murders in *Deliverance* as well as Ed's counterpoint terror when his shirt is zipped down to the belt "as though tearing me open" (98); the humiliating and painful duels with dummy bullets that Stanton puts Quinn and Earl Olive through in *The Sporting Club;* and Mc-Murphy's lobotomy in *Cuckoo's Nest.* All the concerns of ritual sport are here: the search for ritual; the sexual competition and insecurity; the inability to construct meaningful rites; the "bad deaths" of victims; the inevitable inability to get past the world the men have left.

Personal moments of ritual mastery in *Deliverance* are not viable. Even the "transfiguring power of full draw" (163) in archery with its erect imagery is an immediate prelude to Ed's murder of an unknown victim on the surmise of a prior crime in *Deliverance,* as well as the subsequent tracking of the victim over a gore-clotted trail to make sure that he is dead. Ed can "not tell which was [his] blood and which was [mine]" and becomes an animal himself on all fours as he crawls in through a tangle of bush to track his victim. When he finds the body, "it bunched at the foot of a dead tree. It could have been a bush or a stone, but I knew when I first saw it that it was neither. . . . I walked over to it, and it was a man lying face-down, holding on to one of the roots of the dead tree. He had long thin dirty fingers, and his back was soaking with blood" (169). Here is no transfiguring death but a murder, furtive and private with the victim not elevated to any sacrificial status but slowly, painfully raised from an "it" to a "he." Ed has his moment of sacrificial impulse and atavistically imagines cutting off head, genitals, and/or cannibalizing the body. He imagines his dominion over life and death. He could sight down on and kill Bobby on the river and he imagines the corpse urging him to test his new power. " 'Do it,' the dead man said. 'Do it; he's right there' " (171), a voice such as Mailer's Alaskan god-beast of death mandating "fulfill my will" in *Why Are We in Vietnam?.* The kill leads not to a cessation of violence but to a desire to test the momentary omnipotence of violence.

Each death on the river leads not to ceremony but to anxious concealment. The query of the individual hunter, "Am I man enough to kill and be Predator?" is replaced by the more familiar line of collective man, "Can I cover it up?" Dickey thus recreates the passage of the individual male subject from the physical anxiety to the acculturated one. After the burial of Lewis' first victim, the suburban men manage the funeral rite: "We shoveled and scrambled the dirt back in, working wildly. I kept throwing the stuff in his face, to get it covered up quick. But it was easy, in double handfuls. He disappeared slowly, into the general sloppiness and uselessness of the woods" (117). Lewis, in effect, gives Ed the sanction to kill the buggers who have brought the sexual terror. Ed does so in revenge to complete the cover-up and to seal the experience per agreement; in effect, to close the whole (holes), both anus and story, and stop the tale's violation.

The inability to ritualize hangs over *Deliverance* like a pall and best shows the decline of the contemporary Ritual Sports Hero. Ultimately, getting out alive and "innocent" is the highest goal of the suburban men and at odds with their initiation. The "good kill" and the "proper burial," the tracking of the wounded animal in courage: these large motions of the rite are impossible. McGuane, too, uses the occasion and setting of ritual sport but guts its strongest statements literally and figuratively. In *Deliverance,* the strongest image is of rising water, a man-made placid lake destroying the primitive natural setting of gorge and river, the water that *conceals*. Sequestering as a first condition of ritual instruction in the private liminal rite is extended to controlling symbol of all *Deliverance*'s messages with this difference: what is buried in *Deliverance* cannot be acted upon, is impacted barbarism, and is left at the level of nightmare. In *The Sporting Club,* a man-made lake of privilege and exclusion is blown up and drains back into the river exposing the tangled, ugly bottom, the bankruptcy of the Centennial Club's lofty sporting ideal. These opposing motions of liminal ritual—concealment and exposure—set the terms of the two novels in the voided and powerless mapping of topography.[4]

Dickey would further muddle the lessons of the nightmare weekend and cancel the class antagonisms that he creates and then leaves unresolved. His redneck victims, lurching, degenerate, stage-mockery vicious, are, as Jameson has commented, spectres of the 1930s in some deflected, unacceptable scapegoating ("The Great American Hunter" 185). They not only look like Walker Evans characters caught (literally) with their pants down in decidedly anti-populist, anti-sainthood, they are the unritualized, unromantic descendants of Faulkner's Frenchman's Bend cast in *The Hamlet*—yeomen and Snopeses alike without their humor, sense of play, or individuation.

The sacrificed backwoodsmen are completely expendable "others" in every sense. Economically marginal, their communal life is so alien from the suburban men that in Girard's terms, "a crucial social link with the community is missing" (Girard 13). The only community that matters in *Deliverance* is the Atlanta world that the men have left. Even the victims' homosexuality makes them marginal for their potency will not foster community.

Dickey has allowed the gap between victim and community to grow too wide (Girard 39); Dickey has naturalized all the symbols of oppression. All similarity between murderer and victim is suppressed. No gravity of gesture nor lasting consequence can occur when concealment dominates; no ritual may take place that might signify "like" or "same." Of the three murders, two are of unknown victims, and one, that of Drew on the river, is problematic. There is no way to "sanction" the killings in response to sexual terror. The hesitancy of the characters' actions is contrasted to their stark survival presence. Finally, the burial of the river arena itself under placid dammed water mirrors the concealing of Ed, Lewis, and Bobby. As the river has claimed its victims, so have the developers (whom Lewis and Ed symbolically represent) claimed the river. It is "as if" nothing has really happened there. The "general sloppiness and uselessness of the woods" may be extended to *Deliverance's* despair about ritual and its mimesis.

"Concealment" in *Deliverance* finally extends to the fiction itself, which does not open to a dialogue between forces in the wilderness, between the suburban men and the rural men. There is no "double-voicedness" in Bakhtinian terms (Bakhtin 324–31), no fully experienced confrontations, but instead, the tightly controlled and anxious consciousness of Ed Gentry about the male body under threat. Ed Gentry's voice replaces the similarly monologic voice of Lewis Medlock. In Lewis, Dickey presents an authoritative, oracular voice in utter seriousness. Lewis is an almost mythical insertion. His language is impregnable since no alternative world-view can break into his consciousness. Lewis will be ready to begin again as a solitary ritualist upon the disappearance of the society that the novel as a genre thrives on. The world will have become "himself." A nightmare unity would be achieved.

McGuane and Exposure

MCGUANE'S TECHNIQUE in *The Sporting Club* is to expose the underlying relationship not only of individuals but also of the Centennial Club to society. McGuane's exposure is politicized and dialogized realistic fiction. He desires to de-construct the monolith of the Centennial Club into its ugly origins. He torments different social classes into a forced dialogue, opening the narrative to fiction itself, to the dismay of the participants.

McGuane attempts to criticize both aristocrats and yeomen, to level class distinctions through saturnalia that leads to degradation and despoliation. He is especially effective with the incongruous and flashy natural scene. His imagery is always harsh and elegantly grotesque. For example, the obligatory ritual sports scene, the tracking of a wounded animal, which Mailer and Dickey effect, is, in McGuane, the pursuit of a Harley-Davidson motorcycle: "The spoor of the Harley was clearly down the face of the hill; feather-shaped blades of earth turned up, smashed twigs and ferns down to a broad skid mark in soft ground and a place where the rear wheel had dug in half a foot and the exhaust had scorched and withered the foliage behind" (126). Instead of a deer, bear, or bugger in blood extremis, "the twilight glinting of the huge motorcycle was visible through the vegetation and there was the smell of leaking gasoline harsh and unnatural in the decay of the lowland, the smell of which was as sweet as yeast" (127). On the motorcycle are a fat naked girl and a boy assaulting her from behind as she guns the engine on his command and thrust: "*Now razz the pipes! . . . Now first gear! . . . Now pop the clutch!*" (128).

McGuane transforms sylvan sex into a machine rape, all climaxing at the end of a "hunt" for the beast (motorcycle). The sensory deflection of sights and smells, so important to the hunter, the delicate animal tracks changed to skid marks, and the murderous sacrificial scene altered to anal rape with complicity and engine accompaniment blur all messages into de-familiarized sensation. McGuane's tactic is to recode the natural hunter's world through capitalist and technological impersonality and barbarism. His characters who hunt each other are more dangerous than any animal or natural phenomenon. His narrative consistently turns all sex and potential murder into violent humiliation. It is as if Nathanael West had claimed possession of the Big Two-Hearted River.

McGuane also creates a brutal gamester and huntsman in Vernor Stanton, whose rituals are exposures in a humbling and leveling with no higher reference. Stanton is a mentor like Lewis Medlock. Whereas Lewis veers away from society to construct a myth of himself, Stanton's goal as the mad authority-father figure is to drag everyone in society into the pitiless light of their true social and political relationships. Stanton is a rich man's son, Harvard graduate, and cruel dilettante-artist without a canvas. His playfulness is combined with physical menace.[5] Stanton incarnates the massive resentment of an insolent aristocrat who exposes both his impotence and the collapse of the social structure. Stanton wants to bring the club down, and his ire is directed against the bad form of all classes. The very existence of the Club as a decaying, compromised structure exposes a rotted base: the Detroit businessmen who now own the Club, their ancestors who wrested the land from farmers in the 1870s, the Chippewa Indian labor that built the lodge, the current farmers who poach the land, the yeomen who oppose the club members.

Stanton is a perfect example of an Abject Hero (Bernstein 299). His play is transformative but never toward an aesthetic completeness. Rather he represents the *negation* of difference as he equilibrates all social positions, characters, and forces. He is the fool turned destroyer who wishes to extend the individual player's dominance to include institutions that he refuses to respect. Through Stanton's destruction of matter and form, McGuane hints at the potential madness of a willed dialogization. Stanton is the player-god of *The Sporting Club* who, without a belief any longer in nature or in the individual, would force ritual action in all its individual sports hero, collective sports hero, and anti-hero paradigms. The player unmoors ritual as he/she overturns constraint and limit. Without being placed in the service of art or rebellion, play merely dismantles. Stanton as malevolent fool underscores the need for play to be at the behest of *some* production.

None of Stanton's games will signify. They make other people angry and foolish much as those crafted by Guy Grand in Terry Southern's *The Magic Christian* (1960). McGuane's philosophy is comically nihilistic. Stanton exclaims, "We could make it so insane for these bastards" (163) after the Club members revert to joining primitive hunting parties as they stalk Earl Olive's plebeian revelers and mockers. This is Stanton's goal, the spreading of madness; he "liked it when the tension was up . . . it was for these moments he lived" (177). This sentiment, passed from Hemingway to Mailer and to writers such as Dickey and McGuane, produces a real ugliness when the tension seems capable of generating only destruction. The chaos of *ilinx* in McGuane is not toward some goal of expanding consciousness in a mimetic scene (as with Kesey and his Merry Pranksters) but in angry bewilderment with ritual sport and the social order.

This bewilderment extends to the question of proprietorship of the Centennial lands: to whom do they truly belong? Stanton has the insouciance of a medieval lord and a lordly contempt as he calls all the shots. Yet the actual title of "manager" of the Centennial properties passes in the text from Jack Olson to Earl Olive, from the "good" yeoman to the "bad" yeoman, from a Natty Bumppo figure to a Michigan Snopes. McGuane writes, "Olson was a serious sportsman, with rigid and admirable ideas of sporting demeanor," and "Olson's study of problems natural to the taking of trout and bringing grouse to the gun had made him so knowing a woodsman that many of the members whose forebears had formed the association resented him" (60). This character, already marginal to Cooper's Templeton in *The Pioneers,* survives as an archaic figure in the text, carrying a trace of Natty Bumppo's rather spectral authority. Olson is the only man at Centennial who has even an adequate relation to the natural world; the Club members "wanted to kill as he killed without the hard-earned ritual that made it sane" (62). "Olson had his unique alchemy and fished for sport. He kept only the fish he needed" (65), an echo of Natty's "Use. Don't waste!" in *The Pioneers.*

In contrast, Olson's successor, Earl Olive, is a criminal and cohort of a sort of Michigan Hell's Angels group of misfits. He is a "purveyor" of "live bait" which he becomes to "hook" the rage-filled Club members when Stanton successfully deflects their violence toward Olive, his "play-thing." Olson, who truly affects nothing, is part of McGuane's knowledge of the tradition of Ritual Sports Heroism but he is a mythical minor character to be disposed of quickly. Only three pages past Olson's "unique alchemy" comes McGuane's statement, "Short of the pieties of woodland life to which the club subscribed so heartily, nothing pleased them more than internecine strife" (68). McGuane's dexterity and coyness expose the Club's facile appropriations of "hard-earned ritual" to "woodland pieties." Unfortunately, McGuane himself appears as the arch-appropriator, having purposely fragmented the ritual tale into a comedy of manners in the woods. Although the Club members and their antagonists are murderous, there is never a hint of real sacrificial crisis. *The Sporting Club*'s action never coheres to this point.

"Exposure" in *The Sporting Club* begins with Earl Olive's dynamiting of the lake and finally dictates a leveling of all characters into "play-things" with no advantage over one another and no arbiter but Stanton. Stanton concludes by erratically firing a machine gun from a hole where the Club's century-old time capsule had been exhumed (it had contained a pornographic group photograph "exposure" of the founders and their women). Stanton has exposed the prophecy and has become the future. As he is led away into his final madness, the Club's lands are offered for developers, even as the Cuhulawassee River has become a track for speedboats in *Deliverance,* even as Major DeSpain wanted to sell the bottom lands for a "hunt club" in "The Bear." Detroit, Atlanta, Memphis, and in *Why Are We in Vietnam?,* Dallas finally dictate the collapse of the wilderness into lots, lakes, and "vacation" land. The collective has control there, having converted the ritual arena into settings and landscapes. Quinn last sees Stanton as an aging, shrunken madman, "heroic and at one with his illusions" (218), who "no longer had his pistols, but he had plywood cutouts that were much the same; and they paced off, turned and said 'Bang, bang!' at each other soberly. Then someone invisible upstairs announced Stanton's bedtime" (220).

It is clear that Natty Bumppo is not the only iconographic figure McGuane draws on but, more centrally, Hemingway himself in his last days, more of a hospital patient than a sportsman.[6] At the conclusion of *The Sporting Club,* the "patient" is all that is left of the ritual sportsman and "bedtime" is announced for the child at play. Stanton had tried to contort ritual by ironic intellect and then had attempted to destroy it by public spectacle forged through his play. An aging, satanic Nick Adams has returned to the Michigan woods to construct a theatre of the sporting absurd.

The civilized man cannnot be injected back into nature and find any peace. Dickey and McGuane show a yearning for the sublime through nature's superior power but ritual concealment and exposure only gesture in weakness toward the possibility. We bring ourselves to the natural arena and that seems to be enough to defeat us. As Kant first pointed out, our intuition of magnitude, of power in nature, is finally quite independent of nature (Kant 92). We introduce sublimity into wildness. Its ground is in ourselves as is our subversion of sublimity itself. Dickey and McGuane show the collapse of the "strong man" into physical and psychological impotence, respectively. Ritual sport becomes a narrative wherein the satisfactions of performance, of participation, of form itself in ritual procedure, are set against the survival imperatives of competitive sport for struggle, domination, and victory. The natural arena in Dickey, and McGuane, is often the male physical body itself in its drive for oneness with something "other," or for the ego-dominant defeat of that "other."

"Feeding the Ape": Mailer and the Bad Death of Ernest Hemingway

ONE OF the greatest crises in the representation of ritual sport has been the Hemingway early senility and suicide, a crisis that culminates in a failure of belief in the fictional strengths thus posited in the Ritual Sports Hero. Twenty-five years later, Kesey remembered feeling that he had been left "holding this bag of dead Hemingway bones" ("Blows to the Spirit" 268). The legacy of Hemingway is everywhere in contemporary American sports fiction and nowhere more so than in the ritual sport story. No American author had told us more about our competitive nature, about the strict adherence to rule-bound categories of experience, and about the balance between heroism and spectating. Yet this balance was extraordinarily tense and fragile. Mailer began *Of A Fire on the Moon* (1970) by meditating on Hemingway's 1961 suicide "with thoughts of Hemingway's brain now scattered in every atmosphere—what a curse to put upon his followers": "Hemingway had constituted the walls of the fort: Hemingway had given the power to believe you could still shout down the corridor of the hospital, live next to the breath of the beast, accept your portion of dread each day. Now the greatest living romantic was dead. Dread was loose. The giant had not paid his dues, and something awful was in the air. Technology would fill the pause" (*Of A Fire on the Moon* 9–10).[7]

Mailer views Hemingway's death as that of a primitive ritualist but without ritual. A powerful shaman has died under dreadful circumstances and so what are the consequences for the tribe? Mailer's martial image of Hemingway and the "walls of the fort" is very apt because Hemingway's defenses had been intricate and formidable, his heroes and witnesses obsessively constructing rule-dominated ritual experience to control an implacable determinism and a menacing, anarchic free-play. By Mailer's own accounts, the deaths of Hemingway and Marilyn Monroe by suicide in 1961 and 1962 left him pondering that terminal course and loathing the demons thus suggested. In the opening paragraph of *Moon,* Mailer allows that "Hemingway's suicide left him wedded to horror. It is possible in the eight years since, he never had a day which was completely free of thoughts of death" (9). Mailer had by 1969 worked through a period that had tested his will and had driven him to the edge of his own sanity. Hemingway is imagined working through the ritual with shotgun to mouth, testing his trigger finger, to "come close to death without dying" (*The Presidential Papers of Norman Mailer* 104–5). In the early 1960s, Mailer evolves the same ritual testing, one designed to keep him alive by probing that wound.

Mailer initially imagined Hemingway and his pressures in "The Metaphysics of the Belly," written in June-July 1962 and published and re-published in *The Presidential Papers* (1963) and in *Cannibals and Christians* (1966). The fable of Hemingway's self-destructive tendencies is refuted by Mailer, who rather believes that Hemingway died taming his "dirty ape," what Mailer calls "a better word than id or anti-social impulse" (*Cannibals and Christians* 270). "Hemingway was on the one hand a man of magnificent senses. There was a quick lithe animal in him. He was also shackled to a stunted ape, a cripple, a particularly wild dirty little dwarf within himself who wanted only to kill Hemingway. Life as a compromise was impossible" (271).[8] Hemingway was forced out into close contact with death "to propitiate" the dwarf who, in order to live, *had* to live close to death or "they were doomed to dull and deaden one another" (a sin for Mailer in one's relationships with all other people as well as with the dirty ape). Logically and devastatingly, the death ultimately demanded by the ape was Hemingway's. Thus came the repeated "raids" (a familiar Mailer noun) on death through violence to let Hemingway's "psyche out of the dungeon"; "He could work" (271) and thereby achieve some equilibrium and write his way through the trauma Hemingway's compulsive testing was thus defined by Mailer as both a survival imperative and a creative necessity.[9]

Hemingway's need to encounter, to feed his "stunted cripple ape" is a grotesquely binding mode of existence toward repeated small rituals and one that ends in personal disaster. A possible alternative for Mailer would be the good sex linked to creativity, an act productive of the soul's liberation from madness and violence. Stephen Rojack's union with Cherry Melanie in *An American Dream* (1964) hints at this synthesis but also carries with it the suggestion of how Mailer absorbs Hemingway into his own sexual drama. With Cherry, Rojack can drop the enormous competitive weight of attack-defense that had begun in *An American Dream* with his murder of his wife, Deborah. He first reveals to the reader the depths of the battle sex had always been for him: "I did not go on [to tell Cherry] that when I was in bed with a woman, I rarely felt as if I were making life, but rather as if I were a pirate sharpening up a raid on life" (*An American Dream* 115). However, Cherry was "exquisite": "I was alive in some deep water below sex, some tunnel of the dream where effort was divorced from price" (121). Rojack concludes, "For the first time in my life without passing through fire or straining the stones of my will, I came up from my body rather than down from my mind, I could not stop, some shield broke in me, bliss and the honey she had given me I could only give back" (122). Mailer here has reached a most singular point for him, a beautiful description of orgasm as sustaining and untainted by competition. In creativity, we create love itself, generated from the body without defense. Mailer is here close to the "natural," the sexual athlete flowing in performance without the pride of attack or plan on the blunt edge of keen training. "Giving back" is the re-curring generous wonder, not the raid or defense.

The question arises as to why and how Mailer was finally able to write of such an effectively generative sexual act between Rojack and Cherry.[10] Certainly part of the reason for the success of Rojack's sexual liaison with Cherry is that Mailer elevated her to mythic Marilyn Monroe-like status as a radiant blonde who could be anything from mob tart to innocent little girl. Monroe as popular culture heroine fits into the pop mythography of *An American Dream,* while her suicide ranks with Hemingway's in bringing on Mailer's dread. She is thus a fitting partner for Rojack who immerses himself in all [-] American nightmares.

Yet Cherry's ultimate power, the reason she can make Rojack find the good sex at last, is because she is not just Monroe but Hemingway as well. Mailer's conceptualization and language point to the fact in many instances. Mailer had spoken of Hemingway's "quick lithe animal," of his "magnificent senses"; Cherry's singing has a "lithe riding beat" (93) and in sex she is "exquisitely sensitive" (121), and thus Rojack "had never moved so well" (121). Beyond this similar phrasing is Mailer's athletic tribute: Rojack believes Cherry to have "simple honest muscle in her heart" (105). Describing her kiss, "It was exactly as if I'd been sparring with a bigger man and got hit with a full right hand. . . . It was not the nicest kiss I ever had, but it was certainly the most powerful" (105). Thus Rojack is sparring with a "bigger man" and a real fighter. Cherry also articulates Mailer's beliefs about Hemingway tempting death by continually gesturing toward death's darkness (114); she feels a "crazy killer right inside" (163), her particular dwarf-ape. The ape is personified in black singer Shago Martin (see chapter 3) who tells Rojack, " 'It's never over with her and me' " (177). Thus Cherry is inhabited by Hemingway's killer and can philosophize about it with Rojack who understands her dread immediately.

"We were equals" (120) in sex, believes Rojack, and the depth of Mailer's belief in himself as Hemingway's true successor/equal is given credence here. Even Cherry's other side, "masks of greed and cruelty" and a "vulgar egomania" (123) resemble Mailer indictments of Hemingway. Yet Rojack is most clear that Cherry must be loved and saved. If he could accomplish that ("let me love that girl, and become a father, and try to be a good man, and do some decent work," 153) the obsession with sex and murder could be broken and he would have achieved what Mailer saw Hemingway duelling the ape to achieve: the space in which to create the book (child). Rojack protects the "lithe animal"—Cherry/Marilyn/Hemingway. If he could save Cherry, he could save his creativity from the Devil. To divorce creativity from murder (Rojack's murder of wife Deborah) and buggery (Rojack's assault of Ruta, Deborah's maid, and of Shago Martin), Mailer needed to see an ultimately private realm of sexual intercourse and creativity that lies over and against the fallen public world of *An American Dream* where his desperate rituals take place (see diagram, chapter 3, p. 81). The birth imagery of sex with Cherry (labor, contractions, water) would yield the novel that is *An American Dream*. Mailer could save his creative space by transmuting Hemingway into the feminine and posing a non-combative union with him. Here is a sleight-of-hand that prepares Mailer for his more extreme sexual metamorphoses in *Ancient Evenings*.

To get to the point of the "good sex," Mailer has defused the buggery nightmare with males by aligning Cherry with creativity, ascribing Hemingway's traits to her—in boxing, philosophy, suicidal dread—and saving her from Shago's evil. Not the least of Mailer's ego-conceptions is his positing a psychosis for Hemingway and then repeatedly showing his own characters inhabiting it. For one, totally disarming moment, though, Rojack is at peace after orgasm with Cherry, suffused with knowledge and simplicity absolutely singular in Mailer's work. It has taken only the combined sensual power of Cherry, Marilyn Monroe, and Hemingway. Rojack rests at Cherry's breast but that rest is tentative in the extreme. The ape claims Cherry and Shago by novel's end and Mailer remains in thrall to the metaphor. Another way in which Mailer was able to reify his dread and shape a brief for himself and his vision of the ape is through the voice of D.J. in *Why Are We in Vietnam?*. D.J. taunts the reader, speculating, "Am I the ideational heat of a real crazy-ass broken-legged Harlem Spade?" (59); is he "some fucked-up little bedridden spade," "a figment of a spade gone ape in the mind from outrageous frustrates wasting him and so now living in an imaginary white brain?" (60). With this identification, Mailer has given another identity of the driving power source of the language in *Why Are We in Vietnam?*: it is Hemingway's "stunted cripple ape, the wild dirty little dwarf" (*Cannibals and Christians* 271). The voice of D.J., the hipster's nervous shriek of creation and de-creation is pure id speech. D.J. activates the "daily portion of dread." D.J.'s savage discourse is the activated voice of the "stunted cripple ape," murderous and in control. Hemingway's "bad death" had not been exorcised by the time of Mailer's writing *Why Are We in Vietnam?* in 1967.

2.

Mailer: The Body as Arena

A language and a style are data prior to all problematics of language, they are the natural product of Time and of the person as a biological entity.

Roland Barthes, *Writing Degree Zero*

OF ALL major writers in contemporary America, Norman Mailer is the most challenging to position in relation to sport and play. He does not believe in school sport romantics as did Fitzgerald. He possesses no sense of wonder at play's strong currents as did Faulkner and has none of the self-reflexive world-projecting impulses of his fabulist contemporaries such as Barth and Coover who present fiction as a doubly playful exercise. Finally, the rich traditions of American team sport have never engaged his imagination on a symbolic level as is the case with Malamud, Roth, Updike, and DeLillo.

While Mailer ignored or discarded all the forms and conventions that he might have chosen to work with, it is nonetheless certain that in a diverse body of work over four decades he has told us more about the meaning of aggressive male competition and the physical roots of its compulsion than any other current American writer. His language in relation to sport has been more primally powerful, more relentlessly inquisitive. He has not always transformed this language of competition into story or novel but has used the language to explain his form which is intensely ritualized.

Jameson best expressed Mailer's commitment to "some more primary form of the *agon* or ontological combat" that points not to merely "unresolved aggressive impulses" (a favorite psychoanalytic shorthand for critics dismissing what they believe to be Mailer's privatizing tendencies) but rather to "some hypostasis of *competition* itself as a social and historical mode of being. It is as though within the competitive society Mailer had chosen not to repudiate the dominant value but to adopt it with the fanatical exaggeration of the newly-converted, to live it to its ultimate existential limits" ("The Great American Hunter" 193). Thus Mailer has chosen to live and create in the very maw of *collective sports heroism,* a move that determines the current between his physical responses and his extreme philosophical choices, between his attempt to master experience through *individual sports heroism* on the one hand and his role beyond society as an outlaw in *anti-heroism* on the other.

Mailer's instincts are those of a warrior-athlete. He is always advancing in battle or defending his territory in a terminal contest. He does not want to describe the athlete in the arena as much as he wants to be in the arena itself or, to take it one step further, his strongest desire has been to *become* the arena with his body as the warring ground. In the most radical act of the individual sports hero, Mailer will become the space for battle or identification. To "get back to" such a unity for Mailer is to become that ritualized warrior. He is writing of the "sexual athlete" or the "athletic sensualist" as a heroically engaged individual who enacts, as he has said, form as a war (*Cannibals and Christians* 270). Competition *itself* has become the repeated ritual for Mailer. The form of his recording narrative is for him the form of his sexuality. He has had a continual horror of all experience and reaction that has not been self-contained: indeed, the inner cry of his first adept killer-hunter, Sam Croft in *The Naked and the Dead* (1948), has been Mailer's as well: "I HATE EVERYTHING WHICH IS NOT IN MYSELF" (*The Naked and the Dead* 130).[1] The sensible would *be* the intelligible. No mediation is attempted or desired.

On one level, this is the agonized cry of "the natural," that lonely, gifted, isolated figure of so much American sports fiction —Malamud's Roy Hobbs, Updike's Rabbit Angstrom, Knowles' Phineas in *A Separate Peace*—but Mailer drives the vision to pathology in an overdetermination of the individual hero. Mailer is a "natural" in the sense that nothing beyond his sensibility may truly impinge on his consciousness without its conversion to his personal physical form in a truly fundamental ritual act. Mailer's role in the collective world is always imagined as physical crisis and then converted to spiritual crisis symbolic of associations beyond the mundane world. The male body as the seat of wounded sexuality and displaced male aggression triggers the resultant enormous competitiveness. His "hero"-self only ventures forth protected by the most formidable psychic armature that has been fastened in place by prodigious syntheses of contraries and fashioned by intricate small motions of grace as well as by grand and overbearing utterances. These are Mailer's ritual preparations for the most intense competition.

After *The Deer Park* (1955), Mailer was developing a style not adequate so much to fiction itself but adequate to render his agon in private and public life, a competition not matched in American letters since Hemingway's from 1925 to 1940. Sex *is* male physical experience for Mailer and all meditation on sport by him comes from that central fact and dominates its usage. He sees no substitute positioning of the body in symbolic sporting rites on genteel playing fields. His meditations on sport are enlisted in the search for a form to counteract the dread of death and de-creation; and since it is imperative that Mailer continue his search and combat the dread, the encounters and tests of his physical body with other bodies are of the greatest importance.

In the "Higher Laws" chapter of *Walden,* Thoreau wrote of fishing as a suitable endeavor for the embryo sportsman who upon becoming adept might then metamorphose into the naturalist who would seeks the "hook of hooks" and become a "fisher

53

of men." In Mailer's case, there are more left hooks and right hooks than fish hooks, but the search for spiritual value is very similar. As in the most enduring American narratives, there is a soul to be salvaged by intellectual and visionary endeavor; a transcendent relationship to experience must be established. Yet just as surely, that relationship must be forged through the body and, for Mailer, this often takes the form of the most competitive sport.

Clearly for Mailer, the search began in a quest for the mysteries of the orgasm based on the intimate turns and shifts of the male organ, the sensitive, violent, mercurial fulcrum of the aggressive male world. Like any good athlete, Mailer's search for "condition" and "tone" is a prerequisite for any victory. If Mailer can make it all seamless—the search for physical validity, the competitive advantage it attains, the aesthetic form it fosters—he can fashion, while keeping the search within "himself," a coherence among individual sports heroism, its currency in the collective sports heroism, and its conversion to form from which knowledge may grow. Such a coherence is fundamental in exposing the ritual arena that Mailer feels himself to be.

Its first organ of perception is what Mailer in "The Time of Her Time" (1958) with no irony or self-consciousness called "my third eye, the athlete's inner eye which probed its vision into all the corners, happy and distressed of my body whole" (446). This is Whitmanian coding for the phallus as privileged organ of sensibility and Mailer is no less an incantatory chanter of male authority. In Mailer, the body indeed becomes the body politic.[2] For him, aggressive sport and its ritualized form suggest ways to control the death instinct, regulate anxiety about male homosexual violation, trace out the courage that may be in us, define much of the aesthetic sense that may be vouchsafed to us. In his fierce singularity, Mailer gestures with contempt toward a larger competitive culture that has driven American men to the corporation and Mailer himself back to the desperate primary scenes of maleness. As Jameson suggests, being a male "becomes the privileged place of [Mailer's] self-dramatization" where he labors "to overcome the tensions of his unhappy consciousness and to be reunited with the social order itself ("The Great White Hunter"

187). Within this self-dramatization, Mailer is able to suggest the intensely physical root of all male competition and to construct a powerful obsessive argument for male sexual fear at the center of competition and in the ritual sport story in general.

Father and Son Days: Ritual Sport and Sacrifice in *Why Are We in Vietnam?*

THE SURVIVAL of the individual sports hero is a subject that Mailer meets squarely in *Why Are We in Vietnam?*. By examining how Mailer integrates personal obsession with individual and collective sports conventions in *Why*, we may find the congruent passage between *his* arena, and the larger mapping of intense ritual sport and its subversion/conversion in the collective arena in recent sport and its fictions. Mailer had been fascinated with the power relationships in American society long before he had evolved a personal philosophy with eclectic psychological positions in the late 1950s. *The Naked and the Dead* introduced Sam Croft, a Texas son of great determination, who in retrospect is Mailer's prototype of the young D.J. Jethroe and Tex Hyde in *Why*. In *The Naked and the Dead*, General Cummings and Lieutenant Hearn play out their own Oedipal battles of anxious authority and reluctant submission. In *Why*, Rusty Jethroe is an amalgam of the two figures with a bit of Sam Croft as well. He is a new breed of corporate manager, a big, disillusioned white male, yet a Texas son of instinctive competitiveness. The Croft possessiveness, an anal fury, heralds the Mailer heroes of the 1960s and D.J. Jethroe gives it the most manic articulation.

Yet *Why* is not an excremental shrieking; it is the most thorough contemporary account of the American sportsworld's confrontation with the natural environment and the locus of Mailer's ritual deployment of the private and public grids of his nightmare. *Why* is the ritual sports narrative in which the central figures compete to keep from being sacrifices. *Why* provides a relocation of Mailer's discourse in the material world where social practices of the collective reveal their compulsive and competitive root. In *Why*, there is a disturbed *national* body which may be linked to Mailer's sense of the individual body's disturbance. The sensual and murderous contradictions are given their individual and collective consequences. Humiliations and fears have their coordinates in the sports behavior which is intensely individualized.

D.J. Jethroe is in liminal encounters where humbling and leveling are coded in power relationships that dictate humiliation rather than elevation, psychological crises where initiation is in suppression and defeat. His mentor is his father, Rusty. What passes for a primal sporting scene in *Why* and highlights the Oedipal battle between Rusty and D.J. is a father-son football contest "on the back lawn of the Dallas ass mansion" (40). Rusty, "a competitive prick, you know, he played for TCU, third All-American AP, 1936, 1937, like back in there! look it up!" (40) wanted to demonstrate to D.J. how he (D.J.) could not run around him but D.J. did so repeatedly "cause D.J. at thirteen had a presumptive hip dip halfback's butt about as big as Scarlett O'Hara's waist and he could use it like a double pin universal swivel and Rusty had acquired a considerable amount of dead ass sticking his brave plunger up all blindly into the cunt-refined wickedness of Hallelujah's [Hallie Lou Jethroe, his wife and D.J.'s mother] sophisticated rumps and vaginal radar rays masers and lasers" (40–41). Mailer has Rusty so furious at D. J.'s conquering of him, "running Third Team All America TCU tackle Rusty Death-row's middle-aged dead ass into the Dallas lawn fertilizer"(41) that when D.J. makes the "fatal misestimate" and feels sorry for Rusty, his father bites him "in the ass, right through his pants, that's how insane he was with frustration" (41). Rusty then proceeds to throw a bleeding D.J. all over the lawn for ten minutes before ending with a speech on how D.J. must be a fierce competitor, whereupon D.J. "limped broke-ass to the gardener's shed, picked up a pick-axe handle, and bopped his daddy over the dead center of the head, blood still running down from that bite" (43).

Here is a familiar Mailer configuration where sex is deflected from Hallie Lou Jethroe, the wife and mother, toward a ritual murder of the son in lieu of the mother/woman Rusty can't truly possess. Its signature is the bite on the ass, the gesture of male frustration that defeats the son in humiliation, compensating for Rusty's emasculation. The curve of the deflection is from Sexual Intercourse to Murder to Buggery (the bite) with D.J.'s retaliation in defense of his own hole, the proper Oedipal denouement: the "form" is a record of their "war." The scene prefigures the final Alaskan scene between D.J. and Tex Hyde where D.J. is feminized psychically in Tex's desiring imagination. The prior scene shows father and son murderously blocked in apprehensive combat that allows for no weakness. Their battle is cleverly constructed by Mailer through the nominal frame of father-and-son sports tutelage, a hallowed sportsworld referent that is, of course, a conventionalized, unthreatening Oedipal passing of potency from mentor to acolyte, a feature of the ritual sports story through Santiago and his boy companion as well as through Sam Fathers and young Ike McCaslin. Rusty has no surety as mentor in a private liminal rite, for he is still as insecure as any adolescent and terribly eager to prove himself. D.J. is the son as initiate and distorted sexual object and threat to Rusty. Together, their private Dallas drama constitutes D.J.'s real baptism in competition not by a Sam Fathers, but by his father. Cast in character roles from *The Naked and the Dead,* Rusty Jethroe is a Hearn pretending to be a Cummings but closer to a Croft whose rage courses through Rusty. Now father and son are ready to go on patrol together in Alaska with no remaining innocence.

Rusty's fears are genuine and Mailer articulates them in sports frames. Rusty's sexual anxieties center on his performance and "the time is soon coming, thinks Rusty, when fornication will be professional athletics, and everybody will watch the national eliminations on T.V. Will boys like D.J. and Tex be in the finals with a couple of Playboy bunnies or black ass honeys? well, shit-and-sure, fifty thousand major league fuckers will be cleaving and cutting to get in the big time . . . in happy magnification by Color Vision RCA" (114). Here is the clearest of Mailer's examples in which individual physical experience will be regulated and re-cast by the collective as sports competition and spectacle. Mailer gives Rusty a seventeen point proof that is a telling catalogue of the white corporation male's insecurities. Rusty's fears are many: of women, minorities, his own son, the rest of the world, the decline of American products, the "dues" Communism will demand, of the primacy of "fucking" and its demand for performance, of Jews, karate, motorcycles, and LSD. In his rendition of the great "decline and fall," he also mentions that "the white men are no longer champions in boxing" and that "the great white athlete is being superseded by the great black athlete" (115–16). In summary, "He, Rusty, is fucked unless he gets that bear, for if he don't white men are fucked more and they can take no more. Rusty's secret is that he sees himself as one of the pillars of the firmament, yeah, man—he reads the world's doom in his own fuckup" (116). Rusty's discourse is a concise amalgam of WASP tensions and insecurities, all intertwined sexually, racially, and nationally into massive resentment and coming to focus on the bear hunt in Alaska as a test of surviving will and blessing. Rusty's needs are messianic. He sees himself in Protestant incarnation, the WASP moving in history, as Mailer expressly textualizes the historical moment through Rusty's ideology. He must kill the bear to relieve the sexual night-mare of a world breaking loose, a world where even athletics are no longer under his control but where competition is all he knows. Rusty's need is to make everything *himself.* His competition, his victory or defeat will reveal society's future.

The safari to the Brooks Range where Rusty, D.J., Tex, and Rusty's corporate minions all find out who they are is the clearest contemporary fictional portrait we possess of the invasion of tech-nology and commodities and their mental conditioning into a here-tofore reserved (if only in nostalgia) area of practice,[3] the wilderness and how to live in relation to it. Mailer renews the ritual sports story's search for lasting value in sustaining ceremony. And, like Cooper, Hemingway, and Faulkner, he finds slaughter and misap-propriation, the default of the dominant culture as it probes its own wounds in the wilderness for symbolic victories and trophies and rapes what it will never understand. What Ritual Sports Heroism informed by a code has come to is explained by Rusty in the field: "Maybe a professional hunter takes pride in dropping an animal by picking him off in a vital spot—but I like the feeling that if I miss a vital area I still can count on the big impact knocking them down, killing them by the total impact, shock! it's like aerial bombardment in the last Big War" (88). And in the new Big War in Vietnam, as Mailer knows. Rusty advises a real working-over, a total destruction of all opponents. The other side of victory at any cost is the gutted and vacant emphasis on sport's "good form," which lingers as a trace in the Texas hunters only in the selection of the right gun and ammunition, the commodified objects as symbols of power and probity. To know what brand of equipment to take into the woods has replaced knowing what it might mean to be there. Thus about "M.A. [Medium Ass-Hole] Bill," Rusty's lieutenant: "He's not interested in where the bullet goes, he just wants to stuff it full of the right sort of smokeless" (91–92), a succinct deflation through commodified language in blood sport.

Mailer repeatedly shows the lunacy of the Alaskan hunt, the outsized weapons that blast huge holes, the helicopters hopping hilltops to run down goats and caribou for the "sportsmen." The carcasses are so torn and blasted that the real work of art is getting the mess into trophy condition to be shipped back to Dallas. The hunting scenes are grotesquely fascinating but Mailer never loses sight of where the real competition lies: within the corporation in its contracts and hierarchies of fear. Rusty must get exactly the right bear for his corporate standing. There is hell to pay when poor M.A. Pete shoots "Rusty's bear" and then "Pete began to think of moving to Kansas City. That corporation land is mother, father, children, wife, hot weekend fuck, and romantic sorrow all in one" (125). Thus the Alaska safari to escape technological Dallas merely reinforces its patterns: alienation and the resultant response for domination.

During the week of their departure for Alaska, "the real hoedown . . . was between Fiberglas and Tendonex to see who was going to get the contract to put a plastic Univar valve and plug into the collapsible built-in space suit chemical toilet in the Gemini" (48), and Rusty is now disappointed that his boss had to cancel out on the trip for that would have been his competition. The real "sport" is the Univar contract. Its product is to control shit's flow with the astronauts dependent on it. Rusty, in D.J.'s favorite theory, is a surrogate for America's "mysterious hidden mastermind . . . who's got a plastic asshole installed in his brain" (37). The dogged and hysterical fixation on shit throughout *Why* underscores Mailer's disgust at the commodities, mindsets, and goals of Rusty and the corporation men, but more to the point, it is a deft fragmenting and imprinting of the negation of buggery into the language of every material scene and description. Such negation is the imprint of D.J.'s renunciation of the individual and collective modes of sports heroism. His will be the outlaw's voice of anti-heroism.

The competitive world in *Why* is fouled utterly and only D.J.'s playful energy sustains the reader. D.J.'s language is the differing and deferring mechanism that allows him to "play between." His monologue allows him to veer away from his physical obsessions as well as from his spiritual crisis to construct provisionally a play-space not dominated by Rusty or Dallas or Alaska's immensity. Yet even D.J. gets bogged down "in the brackish backwaters of a sluggish narrative" (95), desiring a way to break out into open country away from all the technical gun terms and the oneupsmanship of Rusty and his minions: "We have been hung up in numbers, details, and all sorts of overspecific technical data as if it were scum, slime, pollen slick . . . all meandering down a dead ass [Rusty's signature] stream" (95). Here Mailer writes that it is easier to describe all the materials from "the high technological nexus" rather than deal with the "riptide impact and collision marginated halfway between civilization and a nature culture-primitive constellation" (95). Such a collision is a space that can only be mediated by language play. D.J. finds psychic relief in word-play, punning, obscenity, high hipsterdom, verbal riffs, and fantasy, before confronting his deeds and future. The question becomes how to get "the purification ceremony straight" (187), how "it's terrifying to be free of mixed shit" (197). This is Mailer's narrative problem; he identifies the plight of the contemporary individual sports hero as well, one familiar from Dickey and McGuane.

Mapping Mailer's Arena

BEFORE D.J. and Tex can make their doomed attempt at purification and freedom, Rusty and D.J., father and son, look for something beyond the mechanized battles, the slaughter, and the gored-ass trophies. Rusty is terribly frustrated because the grizzly has not been sighted, so he and D.J. take off on their own. For awhile they are at relative peace. Rusty really does know woods lore and tells D.J. stories about his childhood as the liminal mentor-initiate frame is once more tentatively advanced. Yet as soon as they see bear tracks, the competitive tension grips them in awful detail through a return to a primal scene. D.J. remembers having been beaten at age five for walking in on his mother and father in bed and now expresses clear murderous rage toward Rusty: "his life is hip to the hole of his center" (144); he wonders if a "little pretty seed of backed-up murder passed from valve asshole Rusty's heart to the seat of D.J.'s brain" (145) at that time.

Sexual intercourse and murder are fused for D.J. here. He recalls his mother saving him ("little man saved by cunt"), "memory of father near to murdering the son" (145). Now they confront one another in the Brooks Range with weapons and with scores to settle and achieve in the form of ritual and the war of competition. Mailer deflects the current from father and son as they turn "to contemplate the beast" (147). When the grizzly comes roaring like a locomotive, they get in bad shots and must search for a wounded bear. In a Hemingwayesque revelation of form, Rusty first regrets not bringing another gun; neither father nor son dares to suggest going back to camp. They descend in great fear through a bloody trail down a steep slope where a "bad kill" must await them. The bear has been violated, not dispatched, and this adds to their anxiety. Rusty wants to end it right away but D.J. is moved to take blood knowledge of the bear's eyes and fancies he sees intelligence of enormous battles yet to be fought: "Baby, you haven't begun" (156), he imagines the bear telling him. As the bear is about to die peacefully, Rusty sends in a last overload of murder and D.J. disgustedly watches Rusty claim the bear as his own: "Whew. Final end of love of one son for one father" (157). The knowledge imparted by the mentor to the initiate is over-kill and possession at all costs. Competition overrides all attempt at proper form in the rite.

The 900–pound bear is Rusty's guaranteed contract trophy and the hunt is over for him. But he has murdered more than the bear in the rite; any current between father and son is gone. D.J. must still seek the heart of the Brooks Range with Tex but the sportsworld segment of the journey has concluded. With the Alaskan hunt that remains unsanctified and unritualized, Mailer has provided a map to his own essential conflict. Yet he has written it within the culture's competitive obsessions. Re-instituting the semiotic square mapping sport and play fiction, we have

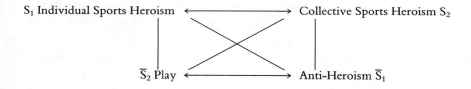

In the introduction, the theory was advanced that the traversal of these relations mapped sportsworld's conceptual universe and provided a grid that expressed their contradictions and contraries. In *Why*, the square is operative on the public level as well as on Mailer's psychic level. Mailer comes to his truth that American men are deflected away from expressions of mutual love toward the only activity they can undertake together—that of the kill—which has its corporate body where Rusty reigns as executive-predator, half-mad with sexual fears and frustrations of his own. At the level of *Why*'s action, D.J. and Rusty's personal obsessions and the public attempt at ritual sport may be seen as congruent and passing into one another. Thus we have

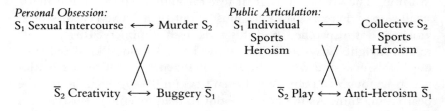

Personal Obsession:
S_1 Sexual Intercourse $\longleftrightarrow$ Murder S_2

$\bar{S}_2$ Creativity $\longleftrightarrow$ Buggery $\bar{S}_1$

Public Articulation:
S_1 Individual $\longleftrightarrow$ Collective S_2
Sports   Sports
Heroism   Heroism

$\bar{S}_2$ Play $\longleftrightarrow$ Anti-Heroism $\bar{S}_1$

The bottom terms for the squares are generated from the negations of the initial oppositions and in Mailer's case show the potentially generative, physically natural acting with the physically canceling anti-generative. The negation of Sexual Intercourse is the not-creative ($\bar{S}_1$), a neutral term that most often in Mailer is represented by Buggery, his terminal state of male defeat and horror; the anti-womb in females, the violated hole for his males, the "Devil's storehouse," as he has called the anus. The negation ($\bar{S}_2$) of the contrary is the difficult term to articulate. It is literally the not-murder, the not-not sexual. This tentative state suggests the pure possibility for the term. To reiterate, Jameson calls this ($\bar{S}_2$) construct "the primary work which the semiotic mechanism is called upon to establish," observing that the "absent fourth term comes to the center of the stage" (*The Prison House of Language* 167). The fulcrum of all Mailer's blood knowledge must be described as Creativity (in the sense of the creation of new "circuits") and the creation of children, as well as of violence (Murder) and degradation (Buggery).

Rusty and D.J. do unresolved battle on the line of intent between

Sexual Intercourse and Murder. The death of the animals is always a bloody slaughter with innards ripped apart by over-powerful bullets. The angels of this death are M.A. Bill and M.A. Pete: ass-holes as hunters, maiming carcasses while they humiliate themselves. Tex and D.J. meet in the wired brilliance of Alaskan night poised between Buggery and the fear of the knowledge it might provide, of the metamorphoses possible. Finally, the current between Sexual Intercourse and Creativity is potentially canceled in *Why* as the de-creative beast is in control of the concluding action. The call is to go forth and kill, to deflect all sensuality into Murder. D.J. craves that dark moment when—Hot dam!—the id will be in control. Mailer's vision of anti-heroic knowledge is only possible when the boys turn from Buggery toward an even greater power in the momentary exalted witnessing in the Alaskan night where they are touched by something huge that they respect, where they touch hands in a sublime equilibrium with no competition and may equally possess the field of wonder. Yet the motion of their relationship will not stop there and they return to murderous competition.

In Mailer, there are opposites that are enormous and that work to break his characters and threaten the very sanity of his writings. "An artist is usually such an incredible balance of opposites and incompatibles that the wonder is he can even remain alive," Mailer wrote about Hemingway (*Cannibals and Christians* 271), and surely we can include Mailer as well in this statement. In Mailer's universe, there is always a war between life and death, the impulses wavering counter to his vision, subject to philosophical realignment. Yet we can chart the largest generating term as Sexual Intercourse. Its direct contrary for Mailer would appear as Murder, the de-creative, the killing of life as Sexual Intercourse may bring it into being. Sexual Intercourse —Murder is an initial impossible circuit for Mailer, one he traverses again and again searching for a synthesis of its complex term.

This attempt at synthesis itself may be interpreted as a tormenting of concepts into confrontation. Roland Barthes in *S/Z* (1970, trans. 1974) has called attention to the great violence necessary to breach the barrier of meaning that an antithesis would erect. Barthes states that the function of the antithesis (of which the Greimasian "contrary" is the right hand term) is to "consecrate (and domesticate) by a name, by a metalinguistic object, the division between opposites and the very irreducibility of this division" (*S/Z* 26–27). Thus the attempt to reduce the paradox brings forth Barthes' most disruptive imagery: "paroxysm of trangression," "paradigmatic conflagration," and, most revealingly, "a headlong flight of two bodies brought together in so unseemly a manner" (65). As usual, Barthes is most incendiary when discussing the violence of a concept whereas Mailer drives any violence toward conceptualization, that of opposites and their clash.

Barthes knows that "the body is the site of the trangression effected by the narrative" (*S/Z* 28). Mailer has in *Why* provided a bridge from his conception of the body to its cultural representation through the ritual hunt and its styles, its aggressions, its codified example of the excesses of the corporate world that yields a Rusty and his lieutenants. Rusty must perform an individually heroic action in taking that grizzly bear or he is "fucked more." The bear becomes an object that he must murder to regain himself as well as his status on the corporate team. Rusty must score a victory in both the sexual and competitive sense. Thus the complex term Sexual Intercourse–Murder may also be rendered through the ritual sports narrative in *Why* as *individual sports heroism-collective sports heroism*. Rusty not only kills the bear for the corporation. He kills his relationship with D.J. as well. There is an individual effacement amounting to the killing of his own best impulses regarding D.J., whom he relegates to a status below that of the bear he must have.

Rusty's desperate drive for the kill in sportsworld's system of rewards — the heroic hunter seeking his guaranteed trophy — recapitulates his frustration on the lawn with D.J., the bite that moves D.J. to thoughts of murder. The complex term Sexual Intercourse-Murder always hovers over Mailer's individual heroes, ready to wrest the text from the comedy of technological hunters and their blasted kills back to the primacy of the original Oedipal conflict. The complex term represents the psychic pressure that the hunt was supposed to ritualize and control. However, Mailer returns D.J. and Tex to the "knife of the divide" (219) where they are sequestered in liminal relation, poised in sexual tension on their way to a murderous resolution. The inadequate ritualizing of their conflicts in the hunt cannot hold the center for long in its essential falsity and the boys work their way back to another codification of the real world. It is one not controlled by sacrificial animal victims but by surrogate victims. Heroic Texas soldier boys hunt Vietnamese in the "team" enterprise of the collective American commitment in Vietnam.

Killer Brothers for the Team

BEFORE THEY conclude on this pact, D.J. and Tex concentrate on clearing their systems of what Mailer repeatedly calls "mixed shit," the entire load of commodified attitudes, assumptions, competitions, and material that is their baggage on the hunt. They attempt a Brooks Range trek that would bring them into an exalted state of witnessing, a spiritual response to the amoral power and beauty around them. This pursuit has generations of American Adams in ritual sport as an ancestral chorus, and the immediate lines of descent from Hemingway in "Big Two-Hearted River" and *The Old Man and the Sea* and Faulkner in "The Old People" and "The Bear" are obvious. However, for Mailer, as for Dickey, McGuane, and the post-World War II generation of authors approaching the American wilderness tradition, the continuing truth is that there is no unmediated, sanctified "good place" that does not exist in severe circumscription and ironic relation to both the material world and to unconscious drives.

D.J. and Tex go beyond the hunt to see if they can cleanse their relationship to the natural world and to each other. Their attempt is to make some imaginative relation to something sublime outside themselves that does not resonate with a sexual or murderous threat. This ritual purification's analogue in play-representation would be the "play back to" in quest for the plenitude of origin. The remaining terms of Mailer's oppositional psyche come into view, where Buggery is equated with anti-heroism, with form itself. The boys vacillate between a physical battle of humiliation, the most negative of victimizing anti-heroisms, and the self-knowledge of heroic merging with the natural world, a positive anti-heroism that will leave an imprint on them forever. Here they attempt to wrest momentary control of time and space beyond the competition in ritual ceremony.

Yet D.J. and Tex end in sexual deflection. They turn away from each other toward ritual sacrifice. The bad kills, the depredations of

M.A. Bill and M.A. Pete, are concluded in the cultural expression of Buggery: male bondage to a collective idea, a giving up of self to a cruel and destructive war machine, where they will have a job to do like Rusty in the corporation. From unsuccessfully stalking the animals without proper ritual, D.J. and Tex move back toward stalking each other, then finally veer away to kill the sacrificial alien from another culture. Murder becomes sanctioned as collective sports heroism. D.J. and Tex can't "know" each other in any sense of the term. They give up their individual status in the Brooks Range to be "killer brothers, owned by something, prince of darkness, lord of light" (219).

D.J. and Tex are never "at one" with the wilderness scene. The wilderness never "coalesces" for them, even as they leave behind weapons and compass in an Ike McCaslin-like gesture. They simply do not belong there; a wolf is "knocked on his psychic ass" (194) by the murderous thoughts of the boys. The survival images still predominate, though Mailer does create beautiful sensory images, shifting prose rhythms to more stately and formal description while never abandoning D.J.'s racy idiom. The tension is well-expressed by D.J.: "Man, it's terrifying to be free of mixed shit. And they got the unfucked heaven of seeing twelve Dall ram on an outcropping of snow two miles away across two ridges" (197). The "unfucked heaven of seeing" is witnessing in the pristine spectatorial sense and uncorrupted by sexual obsession. The imagination is referred by aesthetic judgment to record the scene before it. The Kantian sublime is a momentary option for Mailer and D.J.

However, D.J. is never far from his essential wariness that "Mother Nature" with all its "unfucked" beauty is "as big and dangerous as a beautiful castrating cunt when she's on the edge between murder and love" (197). Thus does Mailer cancel the sublimity by reversion to the largest conceptual contraries of the sensual in his writing. The analogy proves there is no neutral encounter with the sacred beyond libidinous terrain as Mailer refuses to void his arena of human drives. For Mailer, the hard-won truth about an adversary is that unless you want to "fuck" it, kill it, or humiliate it, there is no way to come into a relationship with nature in the root physical sense, for it will resist you, even as your individual ego-consciousness resists its vastness. The most visceral competition has become the only primary ritual. The fantasy that one can yield to nature and be at peace will not work for Mailer. Any male yearning for surrender must carry its feminization and potential for violation. No relation to the sublime may be allowed because the limitless, the powerful, is *always* the enemy. The generating but castrating power of nature "on the edge between murder and love" is and must be possessed. The Word ultimately uttered to D.J. and Tex is "Fulfill my will, go forth and kill"—God as de-creative beast. The command sends D.J. toward sanctioned murder.

There is no redemption possible in the God-beast's final command to D.J. and Tex in the Brooks Range night. "Fulfill my will, go forth and kill" is surely the clearest call from the de-creative voice within the boys. The beast is stripped of hipster accents but not of the essential message: male sexual desire deflected toward murder and better murder than buggery. D.J. and Tex reach a fearful stalemate together in the Arctic. Mailer's obsessive tale of male–male encounter is doubly blocked; D.J. and Tex are "never to be near as lovers again, but killer brothers" (219), too fearful of each other. D.J. and Tex are spooked into silence, Tex scared that D.J. in sex would turn into a murderous version of D.J.'s mother, Hallie, while D.J. fears that if he tried to "steal the iron from Texas' ass," he would be resisted to the death. Sexual disorientation and murder lies at the core of each dream of possession, the male become female, the male resisting assault as male: "They hung there each of them on the knife of the divide in all conflict of lust to own the other yet in fear of being killed by the other" (219). Here was the dialectic that activated Mailer's male nightmares. It remains the deepest blood representation of the physical tensions in his individual sports heroes. But here in *Why* there is no sport that can ritualistically deflect competition and aggression toward the channels of form. Beyond the balked expression of male love can only be the "will to kill," to cancel the stalemate. D.J. and Tex move forward into Vietnam in great relief because there they can kill for the collective.

What Mailer creates is the naked representation of the American male physical experience, stripped of any compensatory ritual. Back of all that mimesis, buried under the codification of rules, of boxing, bullfighting, hunting, of team sport, is the male sexual encounter on the chaste, menacing "knife of the divide," a phallic wall of danger that separates the two lovers. It is the barrier respecting the antithesis in Mailer's violent conceptualization. Faulkner's majestic "I saw it. I saw *him*" occurs in "The Old People" when Ike McCaslin approaches the sacred in a majestic moment of witnessing, in a renunciation of competition to gain the center in an anti-heroism. Mailer re-casts this perception for he stresses the obsessive American male fear of violation. The consequent drive to confront death is the *it,* while the "him" becomes the male other, the homoerotic opponent.

Mailer has materially relocated his obsessions in *Why* within social practices—the corporate competition, the ritual hunt, the war it encodes—that expose the personal-public fusion and define the primary configurations of ritual sport: *the sanctioned killing to obliterate sexual terror with another male, the killer-brother, for the team.* Mailer has momentarily exposed the conceptual limit of the ritual sport narrative. The sanctioned killing to obliterate sexual terror is the individual's isolated experience as he searches for a suitable "other" to eliminate. To ally with the killer-brother is to carry the killing into the collective experience where the individual can feel "at one" with self, with sexual double/adversary, and with nature. We hypothesize that in whatever deflected, mutated, or managed form, all variations of ritual sport narrative partake of this structure for their deepest generation in the individual and collective spheres.[4]

3.

Mailer: Boxing and the Art of His Narrative

So I do not care to approach the public as a lover, nor could I succeed for that matter. I seem to have turned into a slightly punch-drunk and ugly club fighter who can fight clean and fight dirty, but likes to fight.

Mailer, *Advertisements for Myself (1959)*

T HE BOXING narrative is American ritual sports fiction's elemental physical encounter, an intimate visceral war that cannot be told without the body's damage. As such, it has intrigued American authors for decades with its violent premises and potential for social thematics. The contemporary generation boasts Mailer as the last vital inheritor who restored the primacy of the physical drama while most of his peers privileged the economic and social codes in boxing. The young novelist of *The Naked and the Dead* who knew his Hemingway and Farrell was wedded to the existential essayist of the late 1950s who discovered boxing. His instincts for survival dramatics were as sharp as Jack London's, his rage for victory as keen as Hemingway's. The boxing narrative has been shaped and presented by generations of American writers steeped in the shifting emphases of American literary naturalism. Briefly, there have been three different eras of American naturalistic fiction: the first in c. 1900 was marked by a biologically determined naturalism whose avatars included Jack London, followed by a more environmentally determined naturalism of the 1920s and 1930s utilized by Hemingway, Steinbeck, Farrell, and Algren, and an ideologically determined naturalism of the 1940s and 1950s, strongly influenced by totalitarianism, the Cold War, and the McCarthyite period.

All of these naturalistic strains are evident, either singly or in combination, in the boxing narrative. They move out from the crisis of the threatened and damaged physical self to the contingent and precarious life in the economic and social sphere of the collective, to the wounding of the spirit. The emphases in the strains roughly correspond to those of the *individual sports hero* (the physical self), the *collective sports hero* (the boxer in a controlled sports setting) and the *anti-hero* (the boxer as victim, as martyr). The absent or anxious term for the boxer is *play,* as with the Ritual Sports Hero in nature and in society. The boxer is never in freedom, even potentially. He is bound to performance and ownership with nowhere to hide, with no appeal to teammates. He is matter to be consumed.

Mailer raised the physical to metaphysical speculation. Mailer wrote in 1975, "One of the reasons I've never written about great prizefighters in a novel is that the experience they have in the ring is, I think, considerably different from what we believe it is. More intense, more mystical, more 'spooky' if you will, than anything we see on the outside" ("Existential Aesthetics" 83). In 1974, he quotes Muhammad Ali as saying, "Nobody is ready to know what I'm up to. People in America just find it hard to take a fighter seriously. They don't know that I'm using boxing for the sake of getting over certain points you couldn't get over without it." (*The Fight* 79). These twin impulses, to veer away from boxing in his fiction and yet to mine it in his own style and messages, have combined to make Mailer's boxing narrative a labyrinthine one, often circuitous and analogous but nonetheless extremely important for his work.

Richard Poirier acknowledged in 1972 that Mailer's subject of buggery or the fear of the zones of waste in *Why Are We in Vietnam?* was a horror of de-creation as opposed to gestation. Poirier extended his insight to find Mailer sensing heterosexual sexual activity as an emblem for cultural creativity and writing (Poirier 150–53). Robert Solotaroff stated that Mailer's career is an attempt "to ground the intuitive in the factual, the mystical in the phenomenal, the psychic in the biological, and the apocalyptic in the historical." Solotaroff was the first of Mailer's critics to show in detail how his idea complexes never truly change: "they simply turn up late [sic] in a different context, in combination with other ideas" (Solotaroff 90, 94). Or, we might say, as combinations of lefts and rights from many angles of attack.

Thus acknowledging the strong anal pattern of Mailer's writing, his battle to see creativity and destruction in strict physical responses, and his retentive capacity to synthesize and integrate the consecutive stages of his thought, we can begin to see how maleness and competition form the marrow of his language and how boxing gives him keys to male mysteries of being. Boxing is one more arena in which grace and dread collide, where the form born of style responding to necessity defines the character of the individual sports hero. This chapter traces Mailer's formation of a boxing aesthetic and concludes with Mailer's problematics of predation and play in *The Fight* (1974).

The Enormous Present

MAILER'S FIRST three novels—*The Naked and the Dead, Barbary Shore* (1951), *The Deer Park* (1955)—are all enervating precisely to the degree that characters weaken physically at crucial moments of resolution where they are dominated or exposed. The crises point to their emotional and moral weaknesses as well. For all of Mailer's later identities (factual and fictional) as a wild, vanguard philosopher of the orgasm and murder, his first three novels are decorous and naturalistic at the same time, redolent of a sexual drive that is never allowed primacy over the meditations on politics and the social order. The left-wing radical liberal had not yet given way to the existential philosopher.

His seminal essay, "The White Negro" (1958), is the most direct statment of the hipster's pursuit of the essential violent and sexual release into new knowledge. To "take a step toward making it, toward creating," he must "find his courage at the moment of violence, or equally make it in the act of love . . ." ("The White Negro" 315). The commitments throughout the essay are to "movement,", "motion," and the present. The body must be thoroughly alive to all its circuits of chance and risk: "In motion a man has a chance, his body is warm, his instincts are quick, and when the crisis comes, whether of love or violence, he can make it, he can win . . ." (314–15). "Making it" is always fused with "creating" and "winning" for Mailer after "The White Negro." "Making it" thus denotes "making love" and "making art" but also the victory in competition. Mimesis and agon both feed his creativity at every moment.

"The White Negro" announces Mailer's metamorphosis into a special sort of sexual athlete who possesses the "burning consciousness of the present," true for the existentialist, psychopath, saint, bullfighter, and lover (307). The recurring phrasing throughout the essay articulates the power of inhabiting the present to the fullest possible extent: "the enormous present" (306), "the electric present" (308), and "the theatre of the present" (311). This is the arena for action that sport privileges to such a great degree. In an overdetermined world of past and future, of inhibitions and goals, athletes possess time and space perhaps more vividly than any other performers. They shape time to game time, performing action in the arena for the duration of competition. Mailer's hero would thrust to the center and inhabit it in time of his own ritual creation, a heightened realm where action reveals being.

The 1958 story "The Time of Her Time," is a meditation on the form of orgasmic competition between well-matched sexual athletes; it begins the series of boxing images and commentary that will dominate Mailer's writings on sport and determine what he would use sport to accomplish in his work. The central battle in "Time" between Sergius O'Shaughnessy and Denise Gondelman is for possession of that "enormous present," her orgasmic time and his time of blood knowledge of her. His separate encounters with Denise are, in reality, definitive bouts, each with its own shape and rhythm. When she falls away from him during sex, "using [him] as the dildoe of a private gallop," Sergius is furious: "My rage came back, and my rhythm no longer depended upon her drive, but found its own life, and we made love like two club fighters in an open exchange, neither giving ground, rhythm to rhythm, even to even, hypnotic" ("The Time of Her Time" 438).

Mailer had become enamored of club fighters in the mid-1950s and wrote, "They were tough men. One reason a club fighter is a club fighter, after all is because of his ability to take punishment and give a high durable level of performance" ("Ten Thousand Words a Minute" 225). "Punishment" in "performance" coalesces in time as Mailer finds in boxing his recurring image for the Sergius-Denise battle. Sergius refuses to be used by her as a phallus but moves antagonistically against her rhythm. Potentially in creative motion, their sexual rhythms are denied by Sergius who, as adversary in his own rhythm, slaps back until she is once again following him but he then steals her now receptive body: "Her body sweetened into some feminine embrace of my determination driving its way into her, well, I was gone it was too late" (439). The first round is over and he has gone beyond her, denying her an orgasm, and remaining in control and intact. In effect, the bell has sounded, denying her offensive. The only true pride has been in maintaining advantage.

Mailer's sexual athlete always hovers on the edge of a mutual experience but "timing" is wrong: "I gave her all the Time I had in me" (440), but most often the search for the creative ends in mutual exclusion in their battle. Sergius after sex, after "we had been belaboring each other in the nightmare of the last round," "lay collapsed beside her, alone in my athlete's absorption upon the whisperings of damage in the unlit complexities of my inner body" (441). To fail in establishing any creative communion is to lapse back into the phallic narcissist's post-battle inventory of his own injuries. He can only vanquish an opponent in the agon.

On their third night, he "gave her the first kiss of the evening" (445) as Mailer makes it sound like the opening punch, but she "clipped the rhythm" and he is congested, blocked in "my third eye, that athlete's inner eye"; Sergius is all too ready to take her. She delays and makes his desire foolish. After taunting him that she has just come from another lover, Sergius relates, "I wasn't with her a half-minute before I was over, gone, and off" (447). Sergius has lost the round, made to feel "like a pinched little boy," for "she it was who proved stronger than me, she the he to my silly she" (447). Believing himself feminized in defeat, he resolves to win, not to allow her the victory. The bad timing and its sadness is that in the absolute of competition, nothing is allowed creation. Sergius defeats *her* when he brings her through to her orgasmic "victory" against her will, which had sought never to allow him to succeed. The ironies of sexual possession multiply. For Mailer, possession is privileged as the only form of sexuality, the absolutely necessary materialism in the "enormous present."

Sergius finally vows to "beat new Time out of her if beat her I must" (448–49). With "cold calculation" and "driving mechanical beat," "I threw her a fuck the equivalent of a fifteen round fight":

> I wearied her, I brought her back, I drove my fingers into her shoulders and my knees into her hips. I went, and I went, and I went, I bore her high and thumped her hard, I sprinted, I paced, I lay low, eyes all closed under sexual water, like a submarine listening for the distant sound of her ship's motors, hoping to steal up close and trick her rhythms away. (449)

This intimate attack and thrust with its grudging circuitous motive culminates when Sergius enters her ass, "the seat of all stubbornness," and finally back to "love's first hole" again and as she comes to orgasm, he is exhausted physically and psychically. His victory is paramount as all currency is to be converted into advantage. In the ambiguous ending of "Time," Sergius and Denise confront each other, and in her lost wholeness, she accuses, " 'You do nothing but run away from the homosexual that is you' " (451). This accusation, spoken or implied, is a challenge to Mailer's heroes for a decade after "Time." Boxing, which provides him with the imagery to describe the male agon in orgasm in "Time," will be complicated further by its relation to the quality of one's death as Mailer beats back the charge against his sexual nature while including it in his metaphysics. He never buries the homosexual accusation but, by writing his own and continual "Letter to his Wound," gets his "timing" down like the most diligent of club fighters or literary craftsmen.

The Bad Death of Benny Paret

AFTER HIS daring and brutally explicit charting of the competition of the orgasm in "The Time of Her Time," Mailer was never again to be in such heartless and clinical control of the prose of love-making, such a cool tactician in that particular arena. Sergius incorporates Denise's final assault in his hipster's knowledge. They have both performed heroically as opponents. By 1961, Mailer had committed the knife-wielding attack on his second wife that has made him infamous, the stabbing dredged up any time any social or literary critic needs ammunition for a psychoanalytic theory to explain him. However, it *is* an important event because it signifies a shift from Sergius' physical sensitivity and control to a dread of the power of sex and a certainty that it may be intimately related to murder. Finally, boxing, too, presented its darkest tragedy when Emile Griffith knocked out and killed welterweight champion Benny Paret in the Madison Square Garden ring on March 24, 1962. Mailer witnessed the fight which he then used as the core for "Ten Thousand Words a Minute," perhaps his most revealing statement on death, published in *Esquire* (February 1963) and reprinted in *The Presidential Papers* (1964). Thus in the space of a few years, murder and the bad deaths of Hemingway and Benny Paret came to dominate his thought in relation to the homosexual accusation. The deaths were to be cycled through the athlete's search for sexual satisfaction and ultimate physical knowledge. The sexual intercourse–murder opposition so obvious in Mailer's later work such as *An American Dream* and *Why Are We in Vietnam?* begins here.

"Ten Thousand Words a Minute" is nominally about the first Floyd Patterson-Sonny Liston Heavyweight Championship fight on September 26, 1962. While it is Mailer's first meditation on reporting as a literary form and has much to say about the ambience of boxing and its relation to Sportsworld, its fulcrum is a condensed and striking account of the Griffith–Paret fight that contains Mailer's eloquent, if iconoclastic defense of boxing as a human activity.

What makes the Griffith-Paret pages so revealing is that Mailer picks up the homosexual accusation of Denise to Sergius in "Time" and makes it the direct cause for mayhem and murder in the ring, suggesting the latent force of the charge for Mailer and his confrontation with it. At the weigh-in for their fight, "Paret had insulted Griffith irrevocably, touching him on the buttocks, while making a few more remarks about his manhood" (225). The air for the fight is thus electric and malevolent and Mailer prepares the ring: "The accusation of homosexuality arouses a major passion in many men; they spend their lives resisting it with a biological force" (243). A homosexual man (which Mailer implies Griffith to be) who does not practice homosexuality is "entitled to the dignity of his choice. He is entitled to the fact that he chose not to become homosexual and is paying presumably his price" (243). Griffith's rage from the outset is enormous; Mailer describes both fighters as proud veterans, as were Denise and Sergius. Paret was a club fighter who could take and had taken a great deal of punishment. Finally,

> in the twelfth, Griffith caught him. Paret got trapped in a corner. Trying to duck away, his left arm and his head became tangled on the wrong side of the top rope. Griffith was in like a cat ready to rip the life out of a huge boxed rat. He hit him eighteen right hands in a row, an act which took perhaps three or four seconds, Griffith making a pent-up whimpering sound all the while he attacked, the right hand whipping like a piston rod which has broken through the crank-case, or like a baseball bat demolishing a pumpkin. (244)

"And Paret? Paret died on his feet. As he took those eighteen punches something happened to everyone who was in psychic range of the event. Some part of his death reached out to us. One felt it hover in the air" (244–45). The attack born of compensatory rage with sexual roots has yielded a bad kill. Paret dies, Griffith having killed the woman in himself, with Paret a ritual sacrifice to Griffith's manhood.

There is no more shocking description of boxing death than Mailer's Griffith-Paret account. Yet Mailer defends the sport immediately upon conclusion of the death scene by calling boxing an "older religion, a more primitive one, a religion of blood, a murderous and sensitive religion" (245). This faith "scores the lungs of men like D.H. Lawrence" and "burns the brain of men like Ernest Hemingway" (245). His choice of authors and their physical weak points is

consistent with his views of the psychic nature of disease: thus Lawrence's tuberculosis and Hemingway's early senility are metaphysical
and ritualistic in nature, and begin in what they have too deeply seen,
felt, and sought to deny. Mailer imagines Lawrence in *The Prisoner
of Sex* (1971) as boldly using his gift: "the soul of a beautiful, impe-
rious, and passionate woman. . . . What a nightmare to balance that
soul!" (110). Lawrence "had become a man by an act of will . . . he
had lifted himself out of his natural destiny which was probably to
have the sexual life of a woman, had diverted the vitality of his brain
down into some indispensable minimum of phallic force" (111). Like
Emile Griffith, he "chose" and "paid his price." Like Hemingway,
so "lithe" and "sensitive," he "chose" to feed his particular ape to
stay alive. For Mailer, being a male is not a biological fact but a
willed course of action in the face of the counterweight of the feminine.

Thus the two authors Mailer most identified with (along with
Henry Miller) know the "murder" and "sensitivity" for "it is the
view of life which looks upon death as a condition which is more
alive than life or unspeakably more deadening" ("Ten Thousand
Words A Minute" 245). The fascination with this extreme testing
toward the void; the barbarous truths to be won; the potential wisdom gained at great cost: all rhetorically coalesce in the boxer's act
here dramatized as physical defense of heterosexuality in pursuit of a
Promethean theft of the secrets of mortality without falling victim.
This defense and quest both lie at the heart of Rojack's journey in *An
American Dream* and crystallize here around the Griffith-Paret fight
itself, an extension of the Denise-Sergius bout of "Time." Mailer as
Lawrence/Hemingway (the delicate male remaining sexually intact,
the killer stalking his own death).

"Form is the record of a war," asserted Mailer in *Cannibals and
Christians*; "form is the detailed record of an engagement—war reveals the balance of forces, discloses the style of the forces" (370–
71). Forms are multifarious and infinite in "Ten Thousand Words a
Minute," with as many boxing styles as there are fighters and ways
to characterize and possess the truth about individual style. Mailer
lists no fewer than fourteen types of boxers in "Ten Thousand
Words a Minute" (247) and by their "form" we shall know them.
He sees boxing at its best as a fundamentally human activity: "It

showed a part of what man was like, it belonged to his ability to create art and artful movement on the edge of death or pain or danger or attack, and it had much to say about the subtleties of human style" (247). Boxing is the art of creating yourself in courage in response to attack, a vivid, personal, individual style, a form that each fight, each confrontation would take—the record, in short, of a war. Mailer's description on the "edge of death or pain or danger or attack" limns Denise-Sergius as much as Griffith-Paret or Hemingway and his dwarf-ape.

Mailer shades the heterosexual-homosexual encounters back and forth in his work in a complex dialectic of offense and defense, protection of organs and pursuit of demonic knowledge, creation of form and the abhorrence of waste which Mailer comes to see person-ified in buggery. The bad deaths of Hemingway and Paret, the author's death in offense/defense of creativity and the boxer's foul unritualized death in defense of masculinity move Mailer to duel these unacceptable conclusions at the same time he defends his own creativity and masculinity. He fought a two-front war for the rest of the 1960s, his most productive decade, with the time of creation, of art, of orgasm arrayed against the attack on his own body. To retaliate, he had totemically to raid the Devil's storehouse himself and this raid became the dominant engagement of *An American Dream*.

The Carnage of *An American Dream*

IN "TEN THOUSAND Words a Minute," Mailer casts Floyd Pat-terson and Sonny Liston as the nominal hero and villain in what turns out to be a farcical fight, after which Mailer must turn to the primacy of Griffith-Paret. But before the farce, Patterson, the choice "to every protagonist who tried to remain unique in a world whose waters washed apathy and compromise into the pores" (241), is contrasted to Liston, "the hero of every man who would war with destiny for so long as he had his gimmick . . . the fixer, the bitch, the faggot, the switchblade, the gun, the corporation executive. Anyone who was fixed on power" (242). Stephen Rojack in *An American Dream* is an anointed Patterson but he continually encoun-ters visions of a satanic Liston. He is also a Griffith needing to shatter his Paret to relieve the dread. Mailer manipulates much of the dramatic register of "Ten Thousand Words a Minute" to good effect in *Dream,* and much of the most violent of *Dream's* imagery can be traced in genesis to the boxing metaphors of "The Time of Her Time" and "Ten Thousand Words a Minute."

Murder for Rojack is explicitly sexual. Liston, the hugely formidable foe, the nightmare of power, is matched by Rojack's wife, Deborah, who is savagely linked to the underside of American greed and demonic possession. "Liston was near to beautiful," wrote Mailer at his training camp: "You did not feel you were looking at someone attractive, you felt you were looking at a creation" (234). Deborah Coughlin Mangaravidi Kelly is the most potent castrating female Mailer ever created, a Liston to Rojack's Patterson. Deborah "was a handsome woman . . . she was big. She had a huge mass of black hair and striking green eyes sufficiently arrogant and upon occasion sufficiently amused to belong to a queen" (*An American Dream* 25). Deborah had a voice that was "a masterwork of treachery" (25), as Mailer had described Liston's voice ("Ten Thousand Words a Minute" 235).

Rojack is enraged when Deborah "reached with both hands, tried to find my root and mangle me" (35). In describing Rojack's murder of Deborah in sexual fury, Mailer reinvokes the sexual and boxing images from "The Time of Her Time" and "Ten Thousand Words a Minute":

> My hand came up and clipped her mean and openhanded across the face which brought a cry from her and broke the piston of her hard speed into something softer, wetter, more sly, more warm, I felt as if her belly were opening finally to receive me. ("The Time of Her Time" 438–39)

> Griffith making a pent-up whimpering sound all the while he attacked, the right hand whipping like a piston rod which has broken through the crankcase, or like a baseball bat demolishing a pumpkin. ("Ten Thousand Words a Minute" 244)

> My mind exploded in a fireworks of rockets, stars, and hurtling embers, the arm about her neck leaped against the whisper I could

still feel murmuring in her throat and *crack* I choked her harder, and *crack* I choked her again, and *crack* I gave her payment—never halt now—and *crack* the wire tore in her throat, and I was through the door, hatred passing from me in wave after wave, illness as well, rot and pestilence, nausea, a bleak string of salts. (*An American Dream* 36)

Mailer had described Sergius and Denise's orgasmic encounters as boxing matches, while the actual Griffith-Paret bout had its origins in Griffith's compensatory fury in being called a homosexual. Rojack's murder of Deborah is as far as Mailer can go in describing a rancid orgasm. Once Rojack is through the door, the death of the opponent is terrifying. The remainder of the novel portrays Rojack running to possess the secrets of the murder he now knows to be in him. He is primed for ever more barbarous ritual behavior.

Rojack's sexual assault on Deborah's maid Ruta is the foul coda to the decreative murder of Deborah. Murder and then sodomy in succession prepare him for his demonic future. Mailer once more returns to his ur-scene—Paret murdered by Griffith—for the language to describe Rojack assaulting Ruta. As already quoted, "Griffith was in like a cat ready to rip the life out of a huge boxed rat. He hit him eighteen right hands in a row, an act which took perhaps three or four seconds" ("Ten Thousand Words a Minute 244). As Rojack looks to take Ruta, "the knowledge of a city rat, came out from her into me and deadened the head of my heat. I could go for a while now. And go I did. . . . I barreled in on a stroke" (*An American Dream* 47). The buggery is begun and Griffith/Rojack has satisfied his double fantasy by murdering Deborah/Paret and then buggering Ruta/Paret, both feeding the ape and "stealing" secrets of the forbidden. Griffith as "a cat ready to rip the life out" is reincarnated in Rojack: "Like some cat caught on two wires I was leaping back and forth . . . bringing spoils and secrets up to the Lord from the red mills, bearing messages of defeat back from that sad womb" (48). Intercourse and buggery are balanced on the opposites. Mailer is raiding the Devil's storehouse of evil here in the relentless physicalizing of his "raid" images in "On Waste."

Rojack has four encounters or "bouts" in *An American Dream,* all interlocked, none definitive, each revelatory. They define the shape of Rojack's arena and have direct reference to Mailer's personal conceptual arena, the body he knows his protagonist to inhabit. Jameson speaks of "semes" in the Greimas semiotic square or units of meaning that can be articulated by the joining of quadrants: "The place of characters and of a character system is opened up only at the point at which the mind seeks further release from its ideological closure by projecting combinations of these various semes." "To concretely imagine the life forms, or the characterological types" (*The Political Unconscious* 254) is in *Dream* to chart Rojack's different sexual bouts and to indicate how conjunctions into semes are fully embodied:

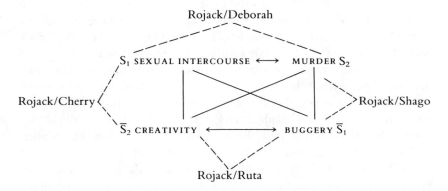

To begin clockwise on the right-hand side is to join Murder with Buggery and feel the destructive power of the rage generated there. The Griffith-Paret and Rojack-Shago bouts are those that affirm and then fundamentally deny the male sexual current, leading to Paret's death and to Shago's beating. The negative union on the bottom of the square is the current between Creativity (charged by Sexual Intercourse) and Buggery, the alternate choices of Sergius and Rojack with Denise and Ruta, respectively. The imagery is always of a march, a line of intent with Rojack between the opposites of womb and anus, a literal trap between zones of creation and waste, "a raid on the Devil and a trip back to the Lord" (*An American Dream* 48).[1] The traversal is the re-cast march between Sexual Intercourse and Murder. It is its darker, furtive twin, functioning as re-creation of the war, the "form" of attack and retreat made visceral and physically immediate.

To forge a style adequate to these sexual and homicidal nightmares, Mailer worked the boxing material over and over again in *Dream*. Rojack as World War II artilleryman hears the grenades explode "*blast, blast,* like a boxer's tattoo, one-two, and I was exploded in the butt from a piece of my own shrapnel, whacked with a delicious pain clean as a mistress' sharp teeth going 'Yummy' in your rump" (11). As if the cluster boxing/sexuality/murderous violence is not clear enough, Rojack's next horrific vision is of a German youth with a fat healthy "overspoiled young beauty of a face" whose rectum he imagines "tuned and entertained from adolescence on" (11). This walking ass-hole is obliterated, his face destroyed by Rojack who shoots him through the nose, the seat of shit's dread. In all of Mailer's work, the crescendo of atrocities is nowhere as concentrated as in the first fifty pages of *Dream*. The beast is really loose and all variants of male-female bouts have been realized.

Less intense boxing encounters surround the central acts of murder and rape. Rojack boxes at a party: "I was sliding my moves off the look in his eye and the shift of his fists . . . the kill was sweet and up in me" (22). Later, Rojack has a psychic battle with middleweight, now mobster "Romeo" Romalozzo, who even *looks* like Mailer: "He had curly black hair which he wore long and thick on the sides. . . . His eyes were dark and flat in expression, flat as Chinese eyes. He had put on weight. He would have looked like a young prosperous executive in Miami real estate if it had not been for the thick pads of cartilage on the sides of his temples which gave him a look of still wearing his headgear" (101). Indeed, Rojack banters that he'd play "Romeo" in a movie and promptly takes Romeo's girl, Cherry Melanie.

Rojack's "war" with singer Shago Martin carries Griffith-Paret into another rematch where Denise's accusation in "Time" (" 'You do nothing but run away from the homosexual that is you' "), receives a further answer. Shago brings a dangerous sensual athlete's style to his form. Athleticism dominates; Rojack hears in his voice the bounce of "a hard rubber ball off a stone floor" (172) by a squash champion. "So Shago Martin's beat was always harder, faster, or a hesitation slower than the reflex of your ear, but you were glowing when he was done, the ear felt good, you had been dominated by a champion" (172). So Shago's beat, like the sharp combinations of a boxer, finds its mark since neither of them can ever quite be parried.

Mailer's hero is left female after orgasm—glowing, dominated—the ear a vaginal substitute played by the "champion." Shago Martin is another familiar compound ghost of Mailer's re-creation. "I had decided long ago that Shago was the most talented singer in America" (170), says Rojack, and Mailer gives to Shago the persona of a vintage hipster conjured from "The White Negro" and his accounts of Liston-Patterson and Griffith-Paret.

Shago brings a dangerous sensual athlete's style to his form, but the other side of Shago's athleticism is in his experimentation in dissonances. Mailer catches two distinct accents in Shago's work, those of Miles Davis and other innovative jazz musicians as well as those of the young Cassius Clay:[2] "No average nightclub audience could follow him. He was harsh. Some of his most experimental work sounded at first like a clash of hysterias. It was only later that one discovered his power of choice—he was like a mind racing between separate madnesses, like a car picking its route through the collision of other cars" (172). This "clash of hysterias" will be animated linguistically through D.J. Jethroe's narration in *Why Are We in Vietnam*. Here Mailer introduces the character; the form that is the record of that war will follow. At the time Mailer was writing *An American Dream*, the American sports world was first noting and falling under the spell of Cassius Clay whose manic verbal performance before the first Liston fight had drawn almost as much attention as his boxing ability.

Shago Martin has many roles and many tongues. He menaces Rojack who, as Cherry's new lover, must retain his manhood against Shago, her ex-boy friend now cast as sexual challenger. As Shago taunts him with insults, Rojack moves toward Shago's knife, sensing "my reflexes were never a match for his. What I felt instead was an emptiness in his mood which I could enter" (175). This boxer's psychic opening parries Shago's accents which "flew in and out of his speech like flying peacocks and bats" (176). Finally, Shago gives the last challenge and pushes Rojack in the chest, exclaiming "Up your ass, Mother Fuck," and then "he turned around. . . . The pressure back of my neck let go of itself and I was a brain full of blood, the light went red, it was red. I took him from behind, my arms around his waist, hefted him in the air, and slammed him to the floor so hard his legs went" (181). Rojack has taken the devil from behind; Shago literalizes this when he cries " 'Let me go; I'll kill you, bugger.' " However, it is not so much buggery as a crushing of the anus that obsesses Rojack, much as Deborah had attempted a "mangling" of Rojack's "root." For Rojack, it is a compulsive annihilation of the hole as possibility in an orgasmic rhythm of obliteration: "I lifted him up and stomped him down I don't know how many times, ten times, fifteen, it could have been twenty . . . I kept beating the base of his spine on the floor" (181).

Mailer's grid overlaid on the Rojack-Shago fight was, of course, Griffith-Paret: "In the middle of the eighth round, after a clubbing punch had turned his back to Griffith, Paret walked three disgusted steps away showing his hindquarters" ("Ten Thousand Words a Minute" 244). Paret's action is the counterpart to Shago's turning his back on Rojack. Griffith's "eighteen right hands in a row" in the twelfth round that send Paret into a coma are the blows that generate Rojack's "ten . . . fifteen . . . twenty" "stomps" of Shago's spine. Furthermore, the motivation for Rojack's fury is similar to that of Griffith, to wit, the violent rejoinder to the repeated homosexual slur. "Say I'm anally oriented? O.K. Say I'm anally oriented. I'll say I'm Cassius Clay. Fuck you," said Mailer in a January 1968 *Playboy* interview. And by literally becoming Griffith/Clay/Rojack against Paret/Liston/Shago, he can dominate that charge, master the attack on the body through the body's language, and go on a relentless offensive to both destroy the hole and protect it at the same time. The violent physical act, "honorable" in the sense of choosing not to become homosexual, as in Mailer's perception of Griffith, is the closing of the hole, the denial of the male bugger. When Shago exclaims, "You just killed the little woman in me," the fact is that Rojack has ritualistically murdered the feminine in himself, has crushed Shago's assertion, has by a murderous tormented masculinity reclaimed his sexual identity in competition.

Each time Rojack learns about his nature, it is through a brutal bout of physical intimacy. For Mailer, to create "form," one must absorb the poisons of what one most fears. Some true cannibalizing of essence and being is a prerequisite for Mailer's ritualists from Sergius through Rojack and D.J. Jethroe. No barbarism without knowledge, Mailer might say, but equally, no knowledge without barbarism. Such are Mailer's maxims derived from working with boxing's images in his larger metaphysics.

Passivity and Working the Corners: Mailer and Ali

MAILER CAME late to boxing as an enthusiasm but its effect on his writing was immediate, just as the bullfight altered Hemingway's sense of courage and aesthetics in 1924–25 when he was working on *In Our Time* and *The Sun Also Rises*. Although he was interested in the fight world's characters and national icons such as the Great White Hope, Mailer cared most about what boxing meant to the fighter's intimate knowledge of his own body: "A man turns to boxing because he discovers it is the best experience of his life. If he is a good fighter, his life in the center of the ring is more intense than it can be anywhere else, his mind is more exceptional than at any other time, his body has become a live part of his brain" ("Ten Thousand Words A Minute" 255).

In effect, such a state is what Rojack strives to attain in *An American Dream*. However, through the manic intensity of *Why Are We in Vietnam?* and the spectatorial mode of Mailer's political reporting books and *Of a Fire on the Moon,* body and brain had been sundered for Mailer, first in decreative hysteria about waste, then in shrewd metaphysics. Mailer's consuming interest in Muhammad Ali resurrected his boxing imagery and enabled him to posit new forms. Mailer finally cast Ali as magician, the same trope he would use to characterize the vast resources of Menenhetet I in *Ancient Evenings* (1983), a book Mailer was beginning even as he completed *The Fight* (1975). Ali is surely a prototype for Meni, his "body" united with his "brain" to stave off mortality through wondrous art.

Mailer first met Cassius Clay in the summer of 1963 when Clay's Louisville syndicate sent him to Las Vegas before the second Patterson-Liston fight to generate support and publicity for a battle with Liston. Clay taunted Liston in a casino and by his own account was truly frightened when Liston pulled a gun (loaded with blanks) and chased him through the crowd (Ali 113). Before the first Clay-Liston fight in Miami in February 1964, Clay appeared at the weigh-in in what seemed to Maileras a "pain of terror or . . . a mania of courage" ("King of the Hill" 13), rolling his eyes and taunting the menacing Liston. There his verbal legend had began. This repeated act in later years with its marvels of nicknames, poems, and fight predictions established Clay/Ali as a national verbal resource.

Mailer entertained some doubts about Ali's manhood and courage for several years, but he quickly sensed the force of Ali's rhetoric. On March 8, 1971, Mailer covered the first Ali–Joe Frazier fight for *Life* and came to a final firm admiration for Ali. He cast the two fighters in his familiar Griffith-Paret, Patterson-Liston split with Ali as the endangered, softer, almost feminine fighter and Frazier as the powerful menacing force. "Every pedantic liberal soul who had once loved Patterson now paid homage to Ali" for "he was the mightiest victim of injustice in America . . . he was also the mightiest narcissist in the land" ("King of the Hill" 28). Mailer had begun to identify with Ali who had been exiled to anti-heroism and cast off the American team. His description of the Ali-Frazier fight contained the images of the Griffith-Paret sexual subtext: "The first fifteen seconds of a fight can be the fight. It is equivalent to the first kiss in a love affair" (29); in later rounds Mailer builds a post-orgasmic dream of competition that reads very much like Cherry Melanie and Rojack in intercourse in *An American Dream*: "[They] moved like somnambulists slowly working and rubbing one another, almost embracing, next to locked in the slow moves of lovers after the act until, reaching into the stores of energy reaching them from cells never before so used, one man or the other would work up a contractive spasm of skills and throw punches at the other in the straining slow-motion hypnosis of a deepening act" (31). Mailer repeatedly describes Ali as almost chastely effeminate and he regrets that Ali had not had a "real" second fight with Liston that would have baptised him as slugger, "more of a man crude to crude than Liston" (33). This inadequate knowledge of Ali's true disposition, the concept of the polarized possibilities, is familiar Mailer country. The terrain includes a sense of the aesthetic qualities of the hero—"exquisite" is Mailer's descriptive adjective for Cherry Melanie and Hemingway—as well as acute male insecurity. The Ali-Frazier fight would tell Mailer (and Ali) who Ali really was in terms of courage and sexuality and would be determined as well by his art.

The fight moves through the eleventh and twelfth rounds, "the longest round of the twelfth [Ali] working another bottom of Hell, holding off Frazier who came on and on, sobbing, wild, a wild hermit of a beast" (34). Mailer is back in the sexual swamps of the battle between Denise and Sergius in "The Time of Her Time." Not since that fifteen-round brawl had the strategy of a literal fight so engaged his senses in print. In the fifteenth round, Frazier, "his courage ready to spit into the eye of any devil black or white who would steal the work of his life" (35), resembles Tex Hyde in *Why Are We in Vietnam?* when D.J. wanted to "get in and steal the iron from Texas' ass" but Tex "was ready to fight him to death" (219).[3] Ali is on his feet at the end; defeated, he "had shown America what we all hoped was secretly true. He was a man . . . he could stand" (35). Mailer's admiration is voiced in Shago Martin's exact phrase to Cherry Melanie about Rojack in *An American Dream* when Rojack will not be intimidated. Shago says, "I be damn . . . you got yourself a stud who can stand" (173). Ali, then, is a potential Griffith who has come through not to a bad kill in frenzy but through a courageous battle that did no violence to his delicate aesthetic but reinforced it with endurance. His masculinity is a volatile mix of elements but it "stands." He can inhabit the masculine-feminine contraries without disintegration, achieving through the Frazier fight what D.H. Lawrence achieved through his sexual encounters in Mailer's conceptualization in *The Prisoner of Sex*. In the Ali–George Foreman fight in Zaire, Ali would truly come to utilize this dual nature and not battle it into submission.

Muhammad Ali became the one Mailer male character rich enough in possibilities to overcome the dominant fears of physical violation and obsessive mortal testing. In *The Fight,* Mailer identifies Ali in a number of familiar guises—narcissist, visionary, artist, philosopher, canny adept—but in his own role, Mailer has moved from the center of the stage to give full measure to the spacious realm of Ali's personality. It is not that Ali blinds Mailer's ego with his own, perhaps an impossibility. It is that Mailer may write comfortably through Ali and resolve, if only momentarily, his own masculine-feminine tensions.

The Ali-Foreman bout in Zaire on October 30, 1974 was an event impossibly rich for the imagination. Having been summarily stripped of his title in 1968 for draft evasion and more generally for anti-war remarks, the self-proclaimed champion of the Third World came to Africa to wrest his title back from the final pretender, an American black who had waved the American flag in the ring upon winning the Olympic Heavyweight Championship in Munich in 1972. Furthermore, Foreman had a tremendous record as a brutal puncher and knock-out artist. Once more, Ali would take his delicate balance of art and strength into battle against a dominant force.

Mailer believes "a Heavyweight Champion must live in a world where proportions are gone. He is conceivably the most frightening armed killer alive" (46). Here is the Mailer fear of "Ten Thousand Words a Minute" and *An American Dream* where the hero inhabited his murderous potential, where he tilted with precisely this lack of proportion and violent impulse to become Predator. Yet Ali redresses all of this for he "inspired love (and relatively little respect for his force). . . . Whereas Foreman offered full menace. In any nightmare of carnage he would go on and on" (46), a Griffith battering Paret or a Rojack strangling Deborah. The terms were thus set. How could Ali face destruction without a full complement of the killer's repertoire? How could his art and intelligence infuse a courage beyond the physical that might include the physical? How could he remake the "form of a war" into an aesthetic triumph and still survive? Or, to use the terms of Mailer's anxiety, if Ali were not a murderer, what could he bring to creativity?

By 1974, Mailer had come to a vision of himself as a sort of elder statesman of witnessing. Instead of Mailer as actor pushing his way onto the stage of history, he ceded heroic rights to Ali. However, the Ali of 1974 surely resembles Norman Mailer. In chapter 6 of *The Fight,* "Our Black Kissinger," Mailer gives Ali several points of identification with himself: "Never did a fighter seem to have so much respect for the magical power of the written word" (75); Ali had been deprived for years of ego, of strength, status, libido—his N'Golo or vital force. He had indeed been buggered by the collective morality of sportsworld into an outcast. Now Mailer muses on Ali entering history, "becoming that most unique phenomenon, a twentieth century prophet" (78), the role that Mailer in *Advertisements for Myself* had desired for himself: "I am imprisoned with a perception which will settle for nothing less than making a revolution in the consciousness of our time" (*Advertisements* 15). In the early 1960s, Mailer was driven to become the boxer, the killer, the sexual athlete. Now he can invest these figures and identify with their heroic virtue and vice. When Ali says he is "using boxing for the sake of getting over certain points," our dislocation as readers is complete, for it is Mailer who had used boxing again and again, had in fact used Ali and the whole championship fight tradition to "get over certain points" since "The Time of Her Time." When Ali concludes, Mailer simply adds, "I know what you're saying," as well he should, for ever since "The White Negro," he had been writing Ali's text, had been inscribing his own ambitions and obsessions onto and through a succession of black and white fighters in factual and fictional bouts. Ali can join the lover's triad with Hemingway and Cherry Melanie in *An American Dream,* the latter told by Rojack in the highest of compliments, "Sometimes I think in the same way" (186).

Ali in 1974 also has a historical specificity for Mailer. In 1974 Ali is attempting to regain his title after a shattering exile, feeling himself full of power and wisdom, much as Mailer felt poised to stage his own comeback in the late 1950s after his earlier "championship" of *The Naked and the Dead.* Also, they are (Mailer in 1958, Ali in 1974) artists, seers, sexually suggestive, and undefined. When Mailer tells Ali, "You better win this fight because if you don't, you are going to be a professor who gives lectures, that's all" (*The Fight* 80), he speaks an instinctive truth. The Ali who might fall to Foreman in the test of his life would be reverting to the status of a Rojack at the beginning of *An American Dream,* unformed, murderously blocked, full of theory, the ape unappeased; or he would become a 180-year-old Meni I in *Ancient Evenings,* at the desperate end of his physical magic, full of experience and defeat.

When Mailer exclaims, "what limitless curiosity could Ali generate" (80), it is no wonder, because the narcissistic fascination for Mailer reincarnating his own historical, visionary, serial selves is all very clear. Mailer has found a way to characterize himself by rounding Ali into a portrait of his own growth. Mailer resides in Ali's field of force which he relentlessly makes his own. Ali has become for Mailer what Santiago was for Hemingway in *The Old Man and the Sea,* what Meni I will be in *Ancient Evenings,* a classic veteran with technique, vision, and a skill in performance.[4] The art of one's sport becomes the art of one's life only in the performance of one's writing.[5] But when Hemingway wrote *The Old Man and the Sea* at the same age that Mailer wrote *The Fight* (c. age fifty), he aged Santiago to the point of senility while Mailer envisions Ali as the regenerative thirty-five-year-old Mailer of 1958, poised with Mailer's large knowledge and contradictions and ready for the battle of his life.

Mailer exposes some corner of this intimation when he analogically imagines Ali "through the two thousand nights of sleeping without his title after it had been taken from him without ever losing a contest—a frustration for a fighter doubtless equal in impact to writing *A Farewell To Arms* and then not being able to publish it" (175).[6] Mailer may also be encoding his own "title" as America's champion novelist, for in 1974, that title had increasingly eluded him. It had been seven years since *Why Are We in Vietnam?* and Ali returns to claim his crown as stand-in for the "Great White Hope" Mailer has always felt himself to be, enmeshing his readers in his own dramatization of his decades-long struggle to write "Great American Novels." Mailer may express his own hopes when he writes of Ali's "biblical seven years of trial through which he had come with the crucial part of his honor, his talent, and his desire for greatness still intact and light came off him at this instant" (175).

Honor. Talent. Desire for greatness. Mailer's defense of his body in anti-homoerotic competition, his creative ability, and his egomaniacal ambitions are incarnated in the light that is Ali. What sort of art does this apotheosis of Mailerian heroism perform? In the beautifully rendered chapters 13–14, "Right Hand Leads" and "The Man in the Rigging," we see Ali unfold his radical plan of attack/defense against Foreman. In Ali's blueprint for battle, Mailer finds a resolution of contraries that unite masculine-feminine and active-passive. In round two, "Ali introduced his grand theme. He lay back on the ropes. . .and from that position he would work for the rest of the fight" (185). Mailer exclaims, "What is genius but balance on the edge of the impossible?" (185), as he has taken us once more to "the knife of the divide."

Ali's great ploy moves Mailer to construct boxing emblems that resonate: "Before fatigue brings boxers to the boiler rooms of the damned, they live at a height of consciousness and with a sense of detail they encounter nowhere else. In no other place is their intelligence so full, nor their sense of time able to contain so much of itself as in the long internal effort of the ring" (188). The "long effort," "intelligence," "sense of detail," and "height of consciousness" are all terms that call up the writer's art and struggle as well. When Hemingway defensively and coyly described his own work and ranked that of other writers through boxing and baseball language, the result was an oddly silly profundity. However, Mailer provides organic metaphors with the aggressive sport he truly admired. Mailer aestheticizes boxing as labor that engages both body and brain. For once, the sense of play as mediation between matter and spirit describes Ali's creativity, as play finally is allowed possibility in the boxing narrative. The shift to the observing of Ali as a creative fighter, to lauding Ali's brain and heart, signifies Mailer's shift in 1974 from perception of the boxer as killer and protector of sexual identity to that of author and artist: Ali is "exquisite" on the "edge" and Mailer gives no surer compliment.

In the Ali–Foreman fight, we are in the realm of aesthetics and play. Ali is a philosopher-magician, playing the masculine and feminine, rather than a homoerotic compensating through murder as was Emile Griffith against Benny Paret. Although Mailer had spoken of man's "ability to create art and artful movement on the edge of death or pain" through boxing in "Ten Thousand Words a Minute," the reality of it had been a violent death in the Griffith-Paret fight as well as orgasmic competitiveness in "The Time of Her Time" and murderous impulses of destruction and violation in *An American Dream* and *Why Are We in Vietnam?*. It took Mailer over a decade to match his ideal of boxing's power to the ideal fighter (Ali) and fight (Ali-Foreman). Having satisfactorily established Ali's manhood in the first Ali-Frazier bout, Mailer could then go on to explore Ali's wisdom and art in *The Fight*.

For Mailer, Ali in the Foreman fight "is turning the pockets of the boxing world inside out. He is demonstrating that what for other fighters is a weakness can be for him a strength" (191). In society's most celebrated ritual of manhood and aggression—a Heavyweight Championship fight—Ali will play with potential destruction. Mailer announces Ali's freedom and his own from customary strategies and form. Ali will lay back on the ropes by offering himself as Prey. By allowing himself to be pummeled in the dialectic, he will absorb the murderous force of Foreman's blows. The "pockets" he turns inside out are precisely those of the Predator-Prey opposition. Poirier's intimation that Mailer associates the creative act with the feminine is given full credence in Mailer's appropriation of Ali's syle in boxing. After Foreman's early ejaculation and the gestation period of Foreman's growing exhaustion, Ali will bring to life his attack, one that would not be possible without Foreman's spent essence. Thus Ali creates, drawing off the power of the opponent and using it to forge victory.

The war of the decade 1958–67, or from "The White Negro" to *Why Are We in Vietnam?*, had been one of Mailer as heroic battler in ever more extreme modes of attack and defense. In boxing Mailer found a way to describe his mid-career in aggressive and aesthetic form. Now Ali gives him the clue to describe his role of witness, of heroic posture "in the corners" where he had placed himself since *The Armies of the Night* (1968). The concept of "working the corners" allows him to integrate Ali's passivity into a coherent male aesthetic even as the appropriation of Ali allows Mailer to "work the corners" in an honorable, tactical plan of attack.

Boxing began for Mailer as a way to animate the orgasmic war of "The Time of Her Time"; it ends as a more circuitous way to possess the considerably more complex sexual contraries in *The Fight*. The resolution of Ali's sexuality, his ability to mine his own sexual contraries and achieve creativity, is a sign that the Sexual Intercourse-Murder circuit was no longer where Mailer's imagination was to be torn apart in opposition. The sexual nature of Ali was not portrayed as embattled and murderous but as a cornerstone of his art that would stave off murder and defeat. To be "on the ropes" is to possess the dialectic of active-passive but it was possession of the center of the ring that made Mailer a great writer. He has not replaced the masculine rage and fear that enabled him to reach the pitch of the early-to-mid-1960's. Mailer tested himself, competed to the limit, and then, having walked all around the parapet in *An American Dream*, and having journeyed to the lair of the beast-god in *Why Are We in Vietnam?*, he retreated to the wisdom of senior magician status in *Ancient Evenings*, where Meni I fired the contraries to greatest use in reincarnation. However, that "senior status" has already been eclipsed by the return to visceral warfare in the person of Tim Madden, the veteran hero of *Tough Guys Don't Dance* (1984), who states, "I had gotten so evil in my last few street fights that they always had to pull me off. Something of my father's blood has passed on to me, and I seemed to have bought his code. 'Tough guys don't dance'" (*Tough Guys Don't Dance* 112). The Mailer charmed by the play of Ali in 1974 has since been recaptured imaginatively by the relation of murder to creativity in the sagas of Gary Gilmore in *The Executioner's Song* (1979) and Jack Henry Abbott. "Dancing" in whatever metaphorical guise is anathema to him as it stands for play itself.

With the exception of Hemingway and bullfighting, no American author has internalized a sport with such consequences for his form as Mailer had done with boxing. The ring as arena and the posed oppositions are his immanent spatial homes, both literally and figuratively. For decades he has moved within their ropes and strictures in brilliance. In the narrative in which Mailer's body becomes arena, males aggressively attempt to murder death itself and, until *Ancient Evening*'s justifications, refuse to yield to decreative sex with other males. Mailer's offensive tactic has been to feed the ape, to forge space and time for creativity. His defense has been the protection of his own female identity, the anus. Mailer's complex rendering of masculine aggression is thus the most extreme analysis of the compulsive root of the *agon*. Mailer's sense of boxing's power is strong but his sense of murder's thrall and sex's mystery are the profound states in which boxing as performance is enlisted. Boxing may be a bridge back to a mysterious death from which we came. Alternately, boxing may be where men can negotiate physical circuits together without female sexual parody. It's thus "honorable."

A curious and striking defect in Mailer's work is his complete failure to understand any sense of comedy in the body's dissolution. The body's usage in fiction may be liberating, grotesque, vulnerable, and democratic in the sense that bodies are what we all share in whatever conception of power relationships in society. Unlike a Rabelais or a Sterne, or, in American Literature, a Hawthorne or Faulkner, Mailer sees only struggle and domination in the body's figuration in literature, never satisfaction or ironic resignation. Ultimately, he takes no ironic stance toward the body's placement in history as necessity but rages at the terms without laughter or joy. Croft's cry, "I HATE EVERYTHING WHICH IS NOT IN MY-SELF," in *The Naked and the Dead* finally suggests by extension that Mailer may loathe only what is in other selves, in other bodies that cannot be made "like" with his own, or "same" through victory in competition and/or in physical humiliation. Once "like" or "same," Mailer may bring his work to birth in the labor of literary creation.

Here is the instinctive movement of the individual sports hero driven to pathology, both competitive and literary. Boxing, the sport which offers the bleakest of personal alternatives to its warriors, that denies play in its fundamental structures for survival, is thus most useful to him as a writer.

4.

Fictions of Boxing

Knew I'd never get t'be twenty-one anyhow.

Lefty Bicek in Nelson Algren, Never Come Morning

MAILER'S METAPHYSICS are the most challenging use of boxing in narrative for the reader. Yet Mailer's own admission that he has not fictionalized boxers in a novel leaves us with the canon of boxing fiction to which we now turn. What are its recurring subjects and conceptualizations and how do they relate to Mailer's work? How have Mailer's contemporaries shaped the boxing narrative in fiction?

Ring-Masters

BOXING IS the public spectacle in individual American sport and provides the subject for the most durable of the naturalistic sports stories in our literature. Boxing is the one major American individual sporting event, the one most produced and consumed. The arena is set for the fighters who are the quarry as well as the hunters, in constant metamorphosis. The arena is the sporting equivalent of the public square where all political and cultural associations may be writ large.

The majority of boxing narratives have been didactic and/or ideologically motivated. The boxing narrative has not been one of dispersing collective man into nature, nor the bourgeois anxiety tale, but rather the crisis of male courage and definition, as in most individual sport narrative. Boxing tales have been left-wing myths of some strong symbolic victory or of an equally devastating defeat and have been sharply critical of an economic system that takes brutal advantage. The collective draws every ounce of strength and courage from a fighter before leaving him as victim.

The boxing narrative is always stark, often simplistic, and vulnerable to a cluster of sentimentalisms. An anatomy of the oppositions in the boxing narrative from Jack London through Sylvester Stallone's *Rocky* films yields the largest of physical oppositions with many cultural controls. Boxing opposes Life to Death in a decision of power and finality. The boxing narrative supports the antithesis through the opposition of Youth to Age, often depicted through a more primitive physiology of the boxer as Predator stalking his Prey. Overarching these oppositions for more than seventy-five years has been the loose utopian configuration of the "Great White Hope," a figure which in its impossible synthesis would contain and arrest these deep oppositions. Thus we have, reinstituting a variant of the Greimas square:

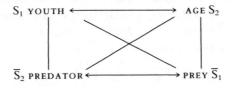

The "predator" has replaced the "player" who has no true place in the boxing narrative since freedom is never a possibility there. Play is a luxury for the boxer in elemental combat, except in Mailer's vision of Muhammad Ali in *The Fight*. The "Great White Hope" is the transhistorical synthesis attempting to defeat age and mortality. The "Great White Hope" stipulates that a boxing champion will be a young but immortal white male, immune to victimization and capable of becoming the beast in combat when necessary.

Youth and Age

YOUTH IS always in juxtaposition to its demise in the boxing tale. It is an unstable, endangered element. Youth is the most explicitly sexual of the boxing tropes and most often contains a radical sexual disorientation. A sexual delicacy surrounds the "youth": he fights it off but it is never far from the center of his being.

We begin with Jack London in each description of the boxing oppositions, because he initially shaped the boxing tale and anticipated most of its excesses. Joe Fleming in London's *The Game* (1905), the first boxing novel, is a young lightweight winning the bout of his life, only to slip on the canvas and give his opponent a chance for a strong knockout punch.[1] Joe reels backward, fractures his skull, and dies. An unmediated "destiny" claims the young boxer. London's choice of fight narrator is Joe's wide-eyed fiancée, Genevieve. Sexually disguised as a male "sport" to gain entrance to the males-only arena, she watches the fight through a peep-hole. Her description of Joe's body sounds as if a 'silly' Paret were describing a Griffith. Bad enough that she thinks of Joe clothed as "girl-cheeked, blue-eyed, curly-headed," but when he strips to his trunks, her virginal eyes see "his skin was as fair as a woman's, far more satiny, no rudimentary hair-growth marred its white lustre" (113). None of this is a good portent for Joe's survival. His abrupt death seals Genevieve's failure to comprehend the rules of the atavistic game that "had played [her] false" (172).

That Youth is overmatched, that his sexuality is blurred, are twin characteristics of structuring in the boxing tale. Hemingway's "The Battler" is a more ominous narrative of Youth and its powerful set of physical cancellations, as suggestive and dark as *The Game* was declarative and open, but similarly built on Youth's vulnerability and sexual indeterminancy. After boxer Ad Francis has been knocked senseless by Bugs—his "keeper"—"his blonde hair was down over his forehead. His mutilated face looked childish in repose" (78). Bugs' confused recounting of Ad Francis and Ad's sister in love; the menace of his relation to Ad; the succession and identification of fathers, brothers, sisters, and lovers: all leave protagonist Nick Adams with a vision of Ad as double, a "mutilated" boy as Nick will feel himself to be after the war.

Further extensions of Youth's fragility and sexual instability occur in Clifford Odets' Joe Bonaparte in *Golden Boy* (1936) and in Nelson Algren's Bruno "Lefty" Bicek in *Never Come Morning* (1942). Boxing becomes a way for Joe Bonaparte to punish everyone, including himself. With each fight he becomes coarser and more belligerent, as Odets contrasts this part of Joe with his father's ambition that he be a violinist in the boxing narrative's most celebrated and ridiculous "choice." Yet Joe himself is sexually suspect within the boxing profession, almost overmatched by his tough girlfriend, Lorna, who appears chameleon-like, both more aggressive than Joe and also as traditional heroine. Joe and Lorna are as unbelievable as were London's Joe and Genevieve. With Ad Francis, the two Joes share the boyishness that leads to death and mutilation; they are males of a deficient masculinity.

Never Come Morning is Algren's chronicle of the decline of seventeen-year-old Lefty Bicek, an intelligent, oddly courageous, always furious young Chicago delinquent who remains morally obtuse and unmindful of other people's pain. He commits his great sin when he allows his girl Steffi to be raped by members of his gang; she then becomes a prostitute. Lefty works as a bouncer and enforcer in the brothel where every night he is forced to confront her eyes. Algren carries the promise of the boxing frame through all sections of the novel as Lefty's continual hope for success; the boxing arena is also a spatial metaphor for violence and entrapment. What Lefty fails to understand is that by placing himself as a fighter in the hands of small-time gamblers, he has ceded all chance of his escape into a free life. Algren suggests that Lefty is not so much a creature shaped by economic realities as he is a boy caught in a social community dominated by Old World suspicion, brutality, and greed, which do not yield to American assimilation but become exacerbated by its pressure.

A copy of *Kayo: World's Foremost Boxing Magazine* "was all he had

on him when Adamovitch had collared him racing out of the alley"
(Algren 88) to bring him in for police questioning about the murder
of an old man. By extension, boxing itself was the only identity
Lefty possessed; in his mind, it was the one sure thing in his future.
Lefty's war of wits with the arresting detectives goes on for weeks as
the officers hold him in jail while they try and break his story. They
give him a stamp for a letter to write to his mother; he uses it to
write the question column of *Kayo,* asking for advice on how to gain
weight. *Kayo* is his imagined life line to the world. As the detectives
get closer to the truth of his crime, Lefty dreams of championship
fights. When he is released for lack of evidence, his isolation has
hardened his ambition and deadened his love and guilt. All he wishes
to do is follow his dream of boxing fame.

In his one big fight, Lefty wins the audience over with a hard-
earned victory full of low blows and illegal tactics. This victory
produces his only real elation in the novel, and he exults, "I'll butt
with anybody" (281), a crude articulation of the warped pride of Jack
Brennan in Hemingway's "Fifty Grand." At this moment of triumph,
the dogged detective Tenczara appears with the evidence that will
probably sentence Lefty to death. Lefty then concludes with the
fitting Tough Guy epitaph for boxing Youth: "Knew I'd never get
t'be twenty-one anyhow" (284). "Destiny" has appeared as in London's *The Game.* Now the fate is not biologically but environmentally determined. Youth will not grow to maturity. Rape is the
sexual distortion that really unites Lefty as Predator with Steffi as his
Prey, his first and, in effect, only victim who leads him to his self-
victimization. The world itself is Lefty's prison, which in its varied
settings of jail and boxing ring show the arena to be all there is.
Unlike Mailer, Algren did not have the radical art to posit the body
as arena itself, but the ceaseless positioning of Lefty's body in an
arena was the most inclusive boxing spatialization in sports fiction.

Sitting in jail, Lefty "was in his corner reading an article on Leo
Lonski's great fight with Loughran in 1927" (107) and "when the
murmur was past Bruno Bicek returned to his corner and fingered
the world's foremost boxing magazine" (131). The police already
have him between the ropes; their interrogations of him are the bouts
themselves. In the line-up, Lefty stands in full light, "the glare from
above like light on a long-caged animal's hide" (152). He dreams at

night in the cell block that the tier of cells is a ring: "He stood up in the darkened ring and listened for the sound of men from the darkened rows. No one. Nothing. No one at all" (157). At night at Mama Tomek's "house," the "world was a curtained brothel" (208). The family men who buy Steffi are "locked in for life" in their lust and hypocrisy: "not one would be paroled" (217). Lefty confuses Steffi's rape with his own knockdown in his climactic fight, the count of "nine" heard through his daze as Steffi's horrific "next" rasped out after several of her attackers had had their way. The very last line of the novel is simply "And the Bell" (284), the long rounds of resentment and attack, remorse and submission contained within the temporal boxing image. Youth is an innocence early lost for Algren. The purely naturalistic end to *The Game* is paralleled by the socially conditioned naturalistic conclusion to *Never Come Morning* and underscores the difference between the first and second generations of American literary naturalism.

The only recent contender for the boxing Youth tale would be Pete Hamill's *Flesh and Blood* (1977), which strives for the grit of the Lower East Side and Brooklyn and much of Mailer's sexual tension but falls short as both a naturalistic novel and as psychological realism. In Irish Bobby Fallon, we have a Joe Fleming, a self-described "choirboy," with "goddam yellow hair and blue eyes" (Hamill 7), but a "killer" who has the fighting instinct. The instinct surfaces after a stretch in prison where he must save himself from being a "white fuck." Such Maileresque activity is not the worst of Fallon's problems. He is deeply in sexual love with his mother and, in the fantasy-mode of a contemporary thriller, the Fallons (*mère* and *père*) wind up in Las Vegas where Bobby loses to a Sonny Liston–type for the heavyweight title. The syndicate controlling Fallon's opponent, Walker Lewis, is headed by Fallon's long-lost rakish father, who reclaims mother from son in an outlandish Oedipal ending. Hamill has painted by the numbers laid out from London through Mailer. but without nuance.

No passage into experience is possible for Youth in boxing. He does not survive into veteran status. Likewise, in the Age tale of boxing, there is no way back to Youth for the experienced fighter: who is not angry or passionately aggressive, but rather is reliable, tactical, a good craftsman. He is after money, not sexual definition.

No pathology sullies him; no rape, incest, or femininity confuses his selfhood. Instead, he very badly needs a payday from the collective. The Age tale is that of an economic coding of death's thrall and how to act professionally in the face of it. Again, London defined the tale in "A Piece of Steak" (*Saturday Evening Post,* November 20, 1909) in which the youthful Sandel dominates the veteran Tom King. When Sandel leads with his chin, King rushes in to take him down quickly because he knows his crippled knuckles and tired legs will not bear up under an extended assault. Yet his body gives way before he can knock Sandel out and he is flattened. London's "The Mexican" (1911) tells the story of Felipe Rivera, a youth who acts like a veteran, a stoical young Mexican revolutionary who journeys north of the border to fight "gringos" and wins $5,000 to buy rifles for his comrades: "Every face in the audience, as far as he could see to the high dollar seats was transformed into a rifle" (27).

As a Joe Fleming character turns up in "The Battler," transformed by Hemingway into an Ad Francis, so Tom King was to become Jack Brennan in "Fifty Grand," exemplifying a different vision of ring savvy and courage. Brennan loses his bout as well, but King's craftsmanship becomes Brennan's voluntary defeat on a foul when the mob double-crosses him. Thus a strong theme growing out of the age trope in boxing was the veteran in performance who did what he had to do to survive. However, if Youth was too fragile in sexuality and general experience to survive, so Age was diminished physically, if not spiritually.

In the contemporary era, Age has been presented as the collective wisdom of the fight game in W.C. Heinz's *The Professional* (1958), a realistic anatomy of boxing professionals and their roles. *The Professional* features a competent white middleweight fighter, Eddie Brown, who even has a manager named Doc! Assorted trainers, opponents, and hangers-on are "colorful." Heinz's novel has the look and smell of a musty gym while its form is the sports page feature story (the novel is narrated by a sportswriter). *The Professional* is perhaps the most informative novel about boxing and the fight game but lacks any real fictional agenda, thematically or ideologically, in relation to its boxing veterans as subjects. Instead, the boxers are more emblematic of boxing's theories and strategies. Eddie Brown loses his big fight when he ceases to be a cautious craftsman. He tries for a knockout punch and, when off balance, is knocked down and sent reeling toward defeat. What London in *The Game* ascribed to fate (Joe Fleming's "slip"), Heinz assigns to faulty technique. Indeed, technique is Age's best weapon and the manager, Doc Carroll, is the novel's true veteran voice. *The Professional* is about process and Doc Carroll is the artisan who shapes and molds his fighters to his requirements after decades in the fight game. *The Professional* gives boxing its most "Aged" feel in sports fiction.

Leonard Gardner's *Fat City* (1969) treated Youth and Age in boxing simultaneously, encoding a version of the truism that the way up and the way down in sport are the same. Boxers Ernie Munger and Billy Tully are chronicled at ages twenty and thirty, respectively, along with their forty-year-old trainer-manager, Ruben Luna. The characters are caught in Steinbeck country, here the central California town of Stockton in the Salinas Valley. Gardner's quiet realism has the undertone of naturalistic despair as the men—small-timers all—envision boxing not just as a way out of economic misery but as a clearer vision of themselves where they will at last take control of some part of their lives. The ring is safer than the chaos outside the ring, as Gardner reverses the imprisonment images of Algren.

What Gardner's characters share is a fear of and fascination with women that amounts to a general mystification. Mailer wrote that "sexual prowess is more revered than any athletic ability but a good straight right. It is precisely because women are strange and difficult, and not at all easy, that they are respected enormously as trophies" ("Married to Marilyn" 12). Far from the swagger of Mailer's lines, the diminished Ernie Munger and Billy Tully fight to attain a similar sense of themselves as capable of merely coexisting with their women. Yet they recoil from such intimacy at the same time. Tully's shining self-image is of himself after his early victories with his lovely young wife. Now she is gone and Tully is with Oma, a woman "near Tully's age, with thin pencil lines where her eyebrows had been and a broken nose much like his own" (11); her scar tissue makes her his double. Ernie is in panic when his wife-to-be says, "I want to be good for you. . . . I want to cook for you" (85). This domestic vision is frightening and claustrophobic to him as he kisses "the lax waiting mouth with exquisite unhappiness" (85). Ruben can't bear to look at his sloppy, overweight wife whom he has ceased to really acknowledge. Ruben privileges boxing as cleaner and simpler than his despair over domesticity, family, and home. Gardner sees men apart in boxing finding some momentary sense of self, but this has little relation to any current that can be transformed to their emotional relationships. Tully's yearning for women is immense but pathetic. His loss of Oma immobilizes him. The methodical Ruben, as always, proposes boxing's siren song, telling Tully, "If you'd get up and come down to the gym you'd work this out of your system. Anybody'd think about women laying in bed all day" (165).

Fat City concludes with Ernie winning a bout in Salt Lake City, but then Gardner adds a last scene on the highway back to California. There, in the dead of night, a hitchiking Ernie is picked up by two young women who "spar" with him verbally and then fling him out into the desert night, an encounter reminiscent of Nick Adams confronting Ad and Bugs in "The Battler." Here Gardner contrasts the victorious boxer with the sexually indeterminate female pair who box with each other through him. First, Ernie is diminished when the bigger woman tells him, "I saw you were just a boy so we stopped" (181); other men on the road are "tough guys," they might have been "rolled." The women are amazed Ernie is old enough to have a wife and baby. Their successive unmanning of Ernie climaxes when the women have a nasty argument about sex and power roles and demand that he, the symbolic cause of their lover's quarrel, leave the car. Just as Tully has concluded with a victory in the ring, but has lost Oma to her former lover, Ernie ends with a victory but is similarly powerless. This cycle of victory and defeat is unending suggests Gardner, echoing Algren in *Never Come Morning*. Even if Ernie could reach age thirty or forty, he would find a battered Billy Tully or Ruben Luna waiting in the mirror. Gardner fuses Youth and Age in boxing in a single vision: isolation from life's struggle outside the ring compounded by fear of women and emotional sharing. Finally, Gardner sees no biological clock in boxing. For him, fighters always have been, are, and will be "back in the gym" to take the known and safer blows.

Another vision of boxing that merged Youth and Age tales was that of James Jones in *From Here to Eternity* (1951) in which Robert E. Lee Prewitt is young but a bitter veteran in experience. A miner's son from Harlan County, Kentucky, Prewitt is a Depression child

whose scars from county road gangs, city lock-ups, and various fist
fights are described by Jones as his "history." When it would be time
to bury him, no one would be able to read the "memories that had
been written down on the book of his body" (Jones 675). Yet Prewitt's real story is in his stubborn individualist's spirit as Jones has
made him a throwback to past self-reliant Ritual Sports Heroes who
waged a continuing battle against the collective American society.

While boxing plays a pivotal role in Prewitt's life, it is precisely
what he *denies*. Jones goes against the grain with boxing. He suggests
how Prewitt will only fight aggressively with life really on the line;
the echo of Natty Bumppo's "Use. Don't waste," from *The Pioneers*
is in Prewitt's abstention from fighting after he blinds an opponent
in practice. The pre-World War II army in Hawaii appears organized
as one vast intramural program where athletics define the prowess of
each company. Prewitt initially is promoted to corporal and then
sergeant because of his boxing. After the blinding incident, enormous pressure is brought on Prewitt to fight in the company's bouts;
he has, after all, been "recruited" for that purpose. When he refuses
to compete, the company persecutes him as their Prey while he
retains an integrity in refusing Predator status.

The best example of Jones' use of boxing occurs in chapter 34
where Prewitt fights two bouts on the night of the company's scheduled matches. Neither of his matches is on the card. First, he mauls
Bloom, the company's middleweight, outside the mess hall after an
argument. After the matches (during which he spends his time drinking with the company's leading "jockstrap," Chief Choate, "the Jim
Thorpe of the Pacific") he decks Sgt. Galovitch who had drunkenly
come after him with a knife. Whereas Bloom wins his scheduled
bout in a one-round knockout and is promoted to corporal, Prewitt
wins his one-punch match against Galovitch and is sent to the stock-
ade. There Prewitt experiences the sadistic treatment of prisoners by
Sgt. Fatso Judson, a true Predator, whom Prewitt later kills in a knife
fight. Corporal Bloom, who has no more love for boxing than
Prewitt, feels increasingly isolated as a Jew in the army. When boxing brings him no closer to being accepted and he is beaten by
Prewitt, Bloom commits suicide. As Prewitt concludes, he and Bloom
had fought "for the amusement of all concerned, except themselves,"
which was "easier than trying to find the real enemy to fight . . .
since you did not know what it was to look for it" (499).

Prewitt never has a scheduled fight. From the tragedy in practice against Dixie Wells until he kills Fatso Judson, Prewitt is steadfast to himself and really cares only about "the Profession" in the sense of his love for soldiering and his "call" which is that of bugling. Prewitt was "good enough to play the Armistice Day Taps at Arlington" (18) and bugling was "the only code, the only language by which he could speak and be heard by other men" (95). Prewitt is an artist and Jones makes his music more plausible than Odets did in *Golden Boy*. Prewitt is mournful, apart, always, in effect, playing "Taps" for the common soldier, for the individual's struggle, for the army's melancholy, lonely sense of being the only community of men. What boxing represents for Gardner's characters in *Fat City*, the army represents for Jones' soldiers in *From Here to Eternity*. All is best rendered through Prewitt's song, "Re-Enlistment Blues." Prewitt thinks before he dies, "It was not true that all men killed the things they loved. What was true was that all things killed the men who loved them" (789).

Prewitt is a sacrificial youth in the novel's final scenes when he is shot on a golf course by his own side as he tries to return to his regiment after the attack on Pearl Harbor. Prewitt is dead at twenty-two but had the tune right in his head. He practices an economy of effort and pronounces the army's sports competition deficient and trivial in the best tradition of a Ritual Sports Hero's censure of the collective. Jones has created in his anti-hero an anti-boxer as well, the only solitary player among fictional boxing heroes. Prewitt won't be a Predator and will choose his arena, that is, until the larger forces of history and his army come forward to claim him.

Predator and Prey

THE MORE primitive Predator-Prey antithesis is a variant of the Youth-Age antithesis and is more of a dramatic statement than a biological-temporal statement of theme. So many heroic fighters metamorphose into the beast in combat, becoming killers at the ultimate moment. This mode of Predator is usually a momentary mask of fury but for some fighters it is a character classification that is direct and simplistic. Such aggression has its roots in the 1890s truism that all young athletes could become killers if necessary, a staple of the first generation of American literary naturalist writers, specifically London and Frank Norris in a legacy from Social Darwinism.

London introduced the prototype for the boxing Predator in John Ponta, Joe Fleming's opponent in *The Game:* "the beast with a streak for a forehead, with beady eyes under lowering and bushy brows. . . . He was heavy-jawed, bullnecked. . . . Here were coarseness and brutishness—a thing savage, primordial, ferocious" (*The Game* 117–18). Ponta attacks swiftly and violently, a hurtling force rather than a man. Lardner's "Champion" (1915) introduced Midge Kelly, a doggedly witless young thug of a contender whose combativeness extends to his knocking his crippled brother out of a wheel chair and flooring his own mother, telling her, "You're lucky I didn't land good" (241). Midge Kelly is relentless in his aggression as Lardner created a cartoon of a comic monster to prove his point that sportswriters would cover for the "champion."

Thus the Predator could either be the nightmare opponent (Ponta) or the dark side of a victor (Kelly). Beyond the naturalistic caricature and the comic caricature was a gallery of angry young men, especially in 1930s narrative, such as Algren's Lefty Bicek and Curly in Steinbeck's *Of Mice and Men* (1937), an ugly, roistering brawler. Odets' Joe Bonaparte wants to "go outside his weight and beat up the whole damn world." Most 1930s aggressive males are in a rage to "bust" someone. James Farrell's Studs Lonigan in *Young Lonigan* (1932) lives in a world of violent competition. His arenas are simply different outposts of Chicago neighborhood turf: schoolyards, parks, pool halls. Fights erupt at cards or billiards, about girls or religion. Studs and his pals are never more than a personal insult away from mayhem. In 1931, Studs is barely twenty-seven but feels old and weak as Farrell brings him to an early death. He is even cuffed around by his younger brother Martin, a more vengeful young punk than Studs himself had been. Studs' physical menace and militance were all that had propelled him; in later years, the deterioration of his body becomes his greatest sorrow.

In the contemporary era, there are fewer stark contrasts and caricatures. A more sophisticated "Predator anxiety" predominates: Can the individual fighter summon the state of Predator, and what are the consequences? Lefty Bicek in *Never Come Morning* is doomed when he becomes Predator by using up Steffi and beginning his guilty path toward murder. Ernie Munger and Billy Tully in *Fat City* fall far short of Predator status. Prewitt in *From Here to Eternity* refuses the pull to be Predator, yet blinds Dixie Wells and murders Fatso Judson.

Mailer's characters are the most complex when seized by "Predator anxiety." For Mailer, becoming Predator is far more than a survival imperative. It is the preliminary activity leading to the creative by which he could master death by a murder or by a raid of violation on the living essence of another being. A Predator's instinct always feeds Mailer's sense of creativity although he knows its irrational horrors. Rojack's murder of Deborah in *An American Dream* bids him to descend onto a frightening line of intent that claims Shago Martin and Cherry Melanie but leads Rojack to wish for a return to the rational. The "Predator anxiety" pushes D.J. and Tex off to the war in *Why Are We in Vietnam* after they are blocked in sexual possession of each other. They will displace their aggression onto ritual victims.

Mailer worked with the boxing oppositions in obsessive fashion. He canceled the Youth-Age opposition as premature and largely irrelevant, since he came to believe so strongly in reincarnation in artful attack-defense, a replenishment of the body's stores. His originality in appropriating boxing is in the linkage of predation to creativity in his own aesthetics, a cruel intimation that displaces play and its freedoms and makes Prey a living resource for the writer-creator. What Mailer has instead of play is predation in the consumption of others' force, of other forces. Mailer remains outside the play sphere, except in one dialectical excursion: how play helps Ali to be Predator against Foreman.

The state of Predator is achieved at great cost with murderous consequences. Robert Lowry's novel, *The Violent Wedding* (1953), works with the elements that Mailer would combine in *An American Dream*. Paris "Baby" James, a black middleweight fighter, has an intense affair with Laine Brendan, a falsely sophisticated, ingenuous white painter from Greenwich Village. Laine sees Paris in the ring as courage and beauty: "I saw that a person can only be beautiful and brave and right when he's involved in life, when he's keeping death away from him" (93). These leaden abstractions are far from Mailer's drama. Laine attends a fight and, like Genevieve in London's *The Game,* feels Paris' "alien nature" but has (a bad sign) an "urgent need to lose herself in his beauty and violence" (109). Lowry obliges. Paris kills in the ring and then rapes Laine after equating the two victims: "Her there on the round white string rug. And Jorgensen there on the square white canvas" (164); presumably, as an artist, she has taught him symmetry. The artist and female made him do it, Lowry suggests. This vision is unrealized in a novel that doesn't know what it thinks about violence, prejudice, men, or women, but is determined *to* think, to rationalize the Predator into something explicable. After Laine commits suicide, Paris wins the middleweight title and suffers some remorse but Laine's painting of him will see him through his guilt. Lowry has committed the real Predator's act on everyone involved. Laine Brendan is the perfect ritual victim, perhaps a central role for women in ritual sports fiction, as demonstrated by Mailer's Denise Gondelman, Deborah Kelly Rojack, and Cherry Melanie (and Shago Martin and Benny Paret as cross-gender compensatory victims).

Another female victim in the boxing narrative is teenage Enid Stevick in Joyce Carol Oates' *You Must Remember This* (1987), the Prey of her uncle, middleweight boxer Felix "the Cat" Stevick, with whom she has had an obsessive love relationship since she was fifteen. The prolific Oates has consistently represented inarticulate desirers of both sexes in clashes of helpless and violent duration. Oates has always been a throwback to American generations of biological and economic naturalistic writers. Her turn to boxing for thematics and physical imagery is thus not surprising. Felix Stevick in the ring is described by ten-year-old Enid ("her uncle's body exposed when he took off the white robe, so much of it covered in dark hair like an animal") in a female description of predator that dates back as far as London's Genevieve looking at Joe Fleming and John Ponta in *The Game.* In this case, however, Enid, no innocent spectator, can already "taste the trickle of blood," as she falls asleep imagining "a man in a white silk robe trimmed in gold his face crosshatched with blood whom she didn't know and who didn't know her" (Oates 35).

As Enid and Felix again and again come helplessly together, Oates frames their battle within the ring: "He didn't love her but there was this connection between them now, this bond. A blood bond as if between two men who'd fought each other to a draw. Or say one of them beat the other decisively but the losing fighter fought a courageous fight and pushed himself beyond his limit—the winner was forever in his debt" (166). Enid attempts suicide while keeping their awful secret from the Stevick family. Felix in retirement mixes with a minor sporting crowd and becomes interested in Jo Jo Pearl, a young lightweight boxer whom he helps train. Jo Jo is killed in the ring by a crafty veteran (the familiar Youth versus Age tale) and Felix is mutely devastated. Enid subsequently requires an abortion and Oates equates her suffering and blood with Jo Jo's death. Felix has blindly pushed them both into terrible punishment.

Each of the novel's three major parts climaxes with an imagined boxing image of violent resolution. At the end of part one, Felix intimidates Enid into silence about their relationship with "a ringing slap on the side of her face with the back of his hand . . . she hadn't seen it coming" (132). Jo Jo's death ends part two with Felix powerless to help. Finally, in part three, a drunken Felix is severely beaten in the men's room of a bar where he is caught by Jo Jo's father and another man. LeRoy Pearl strikes "any way he could" with a crutch and the heel of his boot. He sobs, "I know you! I know you! Stevick! Fucker! Bastard! Letting my boy die! Now it's your turn!" (410). All Felix's roles are reprised: illegitimate son, seducer, "murderer." In Oates' work, everyone gets his turn at punishment. Language always fails her characters as physical desire becomes reified into a terrible object-power. Existing in the uneven match are subjects such as Felix ("he was all feeling, emotion, desire . . . rarely did he respond to anything she said at such times, very likely he didn't hear" [182]) whose victim is Enid ("She heard herself cry out helplessly, crazily —the delirious words *I love you I love love love you* or no words at all, only frightened sounds like those of a small child being beaten" [182]). Yet she, too, desires the obliteration of this darkness: "Felix's weight on her was profound as the very weight of the world, she wanted it never to be lifted" (182). Oates never gives Felix and Enid a way out of the yearning, numb aggression that alternately proclaims itself as love and hatred. Her boxers stay within the ropes.

Most often in the contemporary fictional boxing narrative, fighters metamorphose into Predators when necessary. However, in the era of the anti-hero and the victim, the fighter as Prey has been more prevalent in the boxing tale's favorite theme of victimization. Ultimately, it must be the dialectical play between Predator and Prey that defines them as the poles of an unceasing opposition. Yet the brief for Prey, so ideologically weighted as social or cultural victimization, gains an intense physical coding as well. Physical destruction has often stood for moral destruction. London's "The Madness of John Harned" (1915) features an American boxer in Mexico who sharply criticizes the bullfight as nothing more than a slaughter. He is taunted by afficionados and winds up a mad bull himself, slaughtering spectators with a bayonet before he is shot to death and sacrificed.

Hemingway's Ad Francis in "The Battler" has already been discussed as a damaged youth. The ex-Bonus Marchers, the Key West veterans in Hemingway's *To Have and Have Not* (1937), are blasted and weak, a group of Ad Francis characters who take pride in their ability to absorb blows. A rejoinder to Hemingway's cruel portrayal of Jewish boxer Robert Cohn in *The Sun Also Rises* was Noah Ackerman in Irwin Shaw's *The Young Lions* (1948). The 135–pound Ackerman responds to anti-Semitic persecution by offering to take on, one-by-one, the soldiers who stole ten dollars from him. Ten men, none under 180 pounds, sign their names: "We took it, Jew Boy. We're waiting for you" (283). Ackerman absorbs nine horrendous maulings, then triumphantly destroys the tenth man, but when all his opponents wordlessly walk away, he deserts the army. He writes a letter saying he will not serve with men who won't respect him as a human being, although he still loves his country.

Such martyrdom most often defines Prey in the boxing narrative: a victim of some specific cultural oppression. The physical abuse directly relates to a spiritual abuse. An economic re-coding of Prey occurred in Rod Serling's teleplay, *Requiem for a Heavyweight* (1957), a landmark *Playhouse 90* production in which the cruelly scarred Mountain McClintock, at the very end of a dead-game career, faces the long night of no boxing and is warred over by managers and trainers who want to pick over the bones that remain. *Requiem* had no further ideological message beyond economic exploitation and human waste. More circuitous in intent was Budd Schulberg's *The Harder They Fall* (1947) and his story "Waterfront" which he adapted into the film script for Elia Kazan's *On the Waterfront* (1954). Schulberg's conception of Prey appears to have been shaped by his relationship to the American Communist Party and his appearance as a friendly witness before the House Un-American Activities Committee (HUAC) in 1951.[2] On the face of it, *The Harder They Fall* is the classic sentimental boxing exposé. It features Toro Molina, the pathetic "Man Mountain of the Andes," a giant, untalented Argentine heavyweight who is a cross between Luis Firpo and Primo Carnera. Molina is used up and discarded by the mob with no money or prospects, except for continual abuse by small-time managers when they pick him up as preliminary bout fodder. The novel is narrated by cynical press agent Eddie Lewis (literary kin to Jack Burden in Robert Penn Warren's *All the King's Men* [1946]) who sees all the injustice but sells out as a flack to the gangsters. The familiar fight mob is portrayed: the greedy second-rate managers, the mobster's sensuous wife, the blinded or punchy ex-fighters, even a whore with a heart of gold.

Molina's sacrificial outrage is undeniably one Schulberg target, although the "sell-out" tale of Eddie Lewis appears to be more of the Hollywood writer's parable than that of a boxer's degradation. Lewis apologizes for the abuses in boxing; he's "just a writer," what can he do but go along with the Molina juggernaut? However, he concludes in self-judgment that he was "the worst of them all. . . . The only one who knew right from wrong and kept his goddam mouth shut" (243). In other words, why didn't Eddie inform on the mob? He ends in disgust, admitting he had "enough brains to see it and not enough guts to stand up for it." Schulberg overturns this climax four years later as a witness against his previous "mob" in Hollywood, but clearly Lewis' speech is the seed of Schulberg's quandary exposed in narrative. In *On the Waterfront*, Schulberg and director Elia Kazan could vindicate themselves by making the boxer, Terry Malloy, the informer and battered Prey after his heroic testimony about the waterfront bosses. Marlon Brando's brilliant portrayal lifts Terry Malloy from the ranks of a Toro Molina into those of the informer-hero (Navasky 209–10). Johnny Friendly and his waterfront goons are the Communist party. Terry "coulda been a contenda" but his career was "state"-controlled. His brother Charlie wouldn't let him be part of a real market economy. Backed by an Academy Award for *On the Waterfront* and sentiment in favor of testifying, it is not surprising that in the film version of *The Harder They Fall* (1956), Schulberg has Eddie Lewis (Humphrey Bogart in his last role) begin to write his exposé of the fight game at the film's conclusion. No more indecision by witness Schulberg.[3]

Further Hollywood coding of Prey appeared in the films of Robert Rossen, including *Body and Soul* (1947) and *The Hustler* (1962). *Body and Soul,* with John Garfield as pugnacious middleweight Charley Davis, depicts the usual boxing evils of early success, mobsters, and loose women with money as the major villain. Davis rallies to defeat his challenger in a championship fight, even though he has agreed with the mob to throw the fight and bets $60,000 on his opponent. In a ringing climax, he eludes Prey status and walks away a victor with his long-suffering artist girlfriend, leaving the gangsters speechless.

Such a pat individual victory is made more complex in Rossen's *The Hustler* an adaptation of Walter Tevis' 1959 novel. While the sport in question is pool rather than boxing, the outline of Tevis' novel are familiar. A young sports hero of great ambition and potential is finally taken in by the mob and bent to their purposes, losing all of his humanity and freedom in the process. In Tevis' novel, Fast Eddie Felsen feels he must deny the loving part of himself that cares for his star-crossed girl friend, Sara. To win, he must be stronger than her vulnerability (there are echoes of Algren and Lowry in Tevis). Eddie beats Minnesota Fats utterly in a day-long match and joins the gamblers. Whereas Tevis simply had Eddie and Sara fail to connect, Rossen and Sidney Carrol's screenplay makes Sara a suicide after Eddie's neglect. Now that he has suffered and divested himself of personal feeling, his ambition can take him to new heights in his sport.

The difference between *Body and Soul* and *The Hustler* may be explained by Rossen's professional odyssey when pressured by HUAC. Originally named one of the "unfriendly 19" by HUAC in 1947, Rossen was not prosecuted and was reinstated by Warner Brothers when he wrote a letter stating he was no longer a Communist party member. In the second round of HUAC hearings in 1951, Rossen once more was subpoenaed, again renounced the party, but would not name names. Columbia broke his contract and he did not work for two years. On May 7, 1953, he voluntarily appeared as a friendly witness and verified fifty-seven names from HUAC lists (Casty 19, 28–32).

Reportedly, Rossen with a workaholic's mania, was terrified that he would not be allowed to direct in films again (Navasky 303–4). His self-condemnation because of his compromise with HUAC may be evident in his version of Fast Eddie's crisis: to be a champion, he must be inhuman and sell out those he cares about. Only then can he beat Fats, and Eddie Felsen's bitter monologue as he runs rack after rack of balls is perhaps the best cinematic sports discourse on competition and what men will do to achieve greatness. Like Schulberg and Kazan in *On the Waterfront*, Rossen appears to be giving personal testimony about the meaning of appearing as Predator-Prey. While Schulberg rang all the heroic changes as his defense, Rossen's harsh commentary through Fast Eddie was a dramatic confession. *The Hustler* split work and love radically to dictate what one must do: to avoid being Prey, be Predator. Mailer's intuition of what was needed to forge creative space is given not only the Hollywood "treatment" but is evident in Hollywood's treatment of Rossen and his response. Thus did Schulberg and Rossen create within the form of an ideologically determined literary naturalism where Predator-Prey appeared as the most expressive form.

The Great White Hope

WRITERS HAVE played the boxing oppositions of Youth-Age and Predator-Prey like a tune from Jack London to the present. Like the ring itself, and perhaps modeling its cloister, writers have had little choice but to stay within the ropes of the oppositions. Yet continuing as a refrain through all eras in this century has been the Great White Hope, the boxing narrative's overarching cultural myth. This figure has not been subject to the primary oppositions of Youth-Age or Predator-Prey. He is ageless and beyond vulnerability. He marches out of nature or from the surety of being a "natural" to confront corrupt civilization with his shining example. He will not be victimized and can kill when necessary. When this figure has appeared in fiction, he has been transcendent; in the culture itself, the figure has been presented as a "hope," a not-yet where all racial insecurities and economic contradictions would be solved.

Perhaps the first artistic expression of the Great White Hope was not in fiction at all but in the portraits of the American realist painter Thomas Eakins (1844–1916). Eakins battled the conservative art establishment for decades as he emphasized the fundamental, natural lines of the body. He strove for a spare, dignified realism that would affirm human individualism and achievement. Eakins strained after the same realism as did the best American fiction of the 1890s; he looked for an art that would be literal, descriptive, vital, and masculine (Matthieson 604–10). In 1898, Eakins completed "Taking the Count," the first in his series of boxing paintings, followed by "Salutat" (1898) and "Between Rounds" (1899). All the paintings suggest the dignity of the combatants, the heroism of the opponents, the spaciousness of the ring, and the fans in the mezzanine beyond. In "Salutat," the victorious fighter heads for his dressing room, acknowledging the fans' applause by raising his arm in a rippling display of muscle. The fighter himself is bathed in a soft light. Eakins' boxing prints contain no ironic presentation or criticism of the sport. His fighters are classically drawn in respect for the pain and violent beauty of the fighter's role.[4] Eakins was the first American artist to elevate the boxer from the milieu of violence, brutality, and illegal brawling that boxing had been associated with in the public eye since the Civil War. He portrayed the boxer as a figure closer to that widely accepted American sporting hero of the 1890s, the college sporting gentleman, who, of course, had always had the capacity to become the aggressor on command.

One of London's early newspaper accounts of a major fight, the 1901 match between heavyweight champion Jim Jeffries and Gus Ruhlin, suggested his indebtedness to an Eakins print such as "Taking the Count": London wrote of "the house in darkness and the ring a white blaze of light"; "in the blinding glare, the two battling elemental males, and all around the sea of faces stretching away and fading into the darkness." The picturesque quality of London's report, its dependence on perspective and angle, are artistic analogues shown to best advantage in *The Game*. London added to these new conventions of boxing's representation by his analysis of the July 4, 1910, Jack Johnson–Jim Jeffries heavyweight championship fight in

Reno Nevada. The bout was one of the pivotal sporting events for the American psyche. The thirtyseven–year-old Jeffries, an undefeated heavyweight champion, came out of a six-year retirement to face Johnson, the reigning black champion who had flattened "White Hopes" on three continents. Although London refused to acknowledge the years of suffering that might lie behind Johnson's perennial mocking smile, he gave him his due as a great fighting machine and seldom descended to racial stereotyping. London filed twelve days of copy on the fight for the New York *Herald* and produced the most detailed description of a sporting event in American journalism up to that time. When Jeffries was destroyed by Johnson in fifteen rounds, London's lead summed up the shock for white America and did not even mention Jeffries: "The greatest battle of the century was a monologue delivered to twenty thousand spectators by a smiling negro who was never in doubt and who was never serious for more than a moment at a time" ("The Battle of the Century" 140–41).

London's boxing fiction could do for the Great White Hope what Jeffries could not do. London's pre-fight Jeffries had been a rock-hewn superman matted with thick, dark hair, full of primitive vigor, a Predator eager to feast on whatever he found. In his 1913 novella, *The Abysmal Brute,* London rehabilitated Jeffries as Youth, a young blond super-hero, Pat Glendon, who doesn't have to deal with a Jack Johnson but with easier opponents (to London) of greed and organized gambling.[5] Pat Glendon is bred in rustic California isolation by his father, supposedly a fabled fighter from the pre–John L. Sullivan days. The old man has a Natty Bumppo-like abhorrence of civilization and a love of purity and fair play. Young Pat is Deerslayer or Pathfinder, a splendid vessel, the man-in-nature primed to be the "natural" in sports competition. When he reaches civilization, Pat acquires a strong wife who is rich and an intellectual (their honeymoon is spent tenting in the redwood forests, presumably the only true equivalents to Pat's sexual equipment). Pat becomes a heavyweight contender and learns of the fight mob's dishonesty. In a fiery speech from the center of the ring before his biggest bout, he denounces the whole corrupt sport. When the heavyweight champion, infuriated by Pat's insults, rushes into the ring in dress suit, Pat knocks him out with one punch and then destroys his scheduled opponent. The faithful crowd, set right by Glendon, their champion, then destroys the automobile of the gambler–fight promoter. A heavyweight frontier hero has marched out of the California mountains to expose the corrupt civilized sport in London's fantasy.[6]

London veered away from confronting the Jack Johnson figure in fiction and converted the veteran plodder Jeffries into an invincible blond youth. The reality of Johnson remained unchallenged, even when he was dethroned in a suspect bout in sweltering Havana on April 5, 1915, by uninspired, awkward Jess Willard. Jack Dempsey's tremendous popularity in the 1920s was not without its taint of black Irish scowling, a hobo's past, and a brutal style, while Gene Tunney, perhaps the only live version of the Eakins hero, was actually too strange for the fickle boxing public which then mourned the loss of Dempsey, the brawler. The Great White Hope as some half-civilized, half-savage reincarnation of young Natty or Frank Merriwell appeared unattainable in American life or fiction.

Hemingway's early boxing heroes were all damaged victors or victims — Ad Francis, Jack Brennan, Ole Andreson, Robert Cohn. Yet Pedro Romero, Cohn's opponent in one major unscheduled bout in *The Sun Also Rises,* was Hemingway's Great White Hope. As Jake Barnes thinks after watching Romero in a bullfight, "This was a real one. There had not been a real one for a long time" (164). Romero is almost a Spanish natural resource as described by Hemingway, a champion of purity and grace who wins by courage and technique and who is the crowd's darling. Romero is a blend of dignity, artistry, and the killer instinct. He refuses to stay down when battered by the lovesick Cohn and thereby gains in stature. He has the powers of Youth, knows how to be Predator, is a hero to the people, and resolves contradictions.

Hemingway went outside of boxing and American culture to find his Great White Hope. Meanwhile, the American boxing public has devised its own curious compensatory rearrangement of the figure since the 1920s. The next shift for the Great White Hope was a rebirth in a black fighter, Joe Louis, who upheld the American standard in 1938 against Max Schmeling, Nazi Germany's "Black Uhlan," although Schmeling was personally blameless. Prewitt was potentially this figure in *From Here to Eternity,* but Jones had higher claims on Prewitt than he believed boxing might articulate. Mailer certainly expressed the figure of the Great White Hope when he cast

Floyd Patterson as the force of the Lord against Sonny Liston, the Devil's agent in "Ten Thousand Words a Minute." Mailer then commented that Liston's victory had rearranged American "psychic seismographs."

The continuing need to place opposing boxers in the positions of Great White Hope and antagonist has at this point as much to do with moral and political gesturing as with racial identification. Thus Muhammad Ali became the Great White Hope at long last, appropriating a strong liberal patriotic message about the Vietnam War while destroying brute force in Joe Frazier and George Foreman. Ali completed the realignment by not only containing Jack Johnson's prowess but also the mocking sense of Johnson's rhetoric which was finally recognized as the fighter's offensive and defensive weapon. Having performed a psychic conferral of Great White Hope status onto black fighters for decades, the American public shed such contortions in the mid-1970s and conferred the title on a totally fictional creation, Rocky Balboa.

While there was a decided shift in Great White Hope authority to black fighters such as Louis, Patterson, and Ali, Howard Sackler's spectacle-drama, *The Great White Hope* (1968), in effect picks up the subject raw, where London had left it over a half century before. Sackler's Jack Jefferson is the focus in a portrait of an America so driven by fundamental race hatred that no reconciliation is even remotely possible. The fight promoter, Cap'n Dan, explains America's plight: "But Heavyweight Champion of the World, well it feels like the world's got a shadow across it. Everything's . . . kind of darker and different, like it's shrinking" (57). In response, Sackler makes Jefferson/Johnson a hard, experienced black man who expects nothing from his title. Jefferson is spokesman for no position but rather deals practically in turns with the array of forces against him. In effect, the heavyweight championship becomes his albatross, as much a "Black Man's Burden" to him as to the white American society that loathes him.

Sackler's final images finally crystallize the Great White Hope in powerful iconography which is Sackler's strength as a dramatist. Tired, bitter, and broke, Jack Jefferson is goaded into a title defense after the suicide of Eleanor Backman, his white lover who follows in the tradition of fighters' women as ritual sacrifices in Lowry and

Rossen. Jefferson's opponent is the latest White Hope, a fighter known only as "The Kid." Sackler makes him a grotesque as Jefferson realizes: "Sho a funny size fo a kid, ain he? Soun like somethin gone wrong wid his glans" (215). "The Kid" is in the fictional tradition of Toro Molina and Mountain McClintock, themselves fictional copies of the 6'7" Jess Willard and pituitary Primo Carnera. "The Kid" is, by the end of the fight, a huge, blind, bloody, flailing boy, who outlasts an ill-trained Jefferson rather than defeats him. In the play's last image, the surging crowd bursts through the stadium gates, pushing Jefferson aside: "The Kid rides on their shoulders: immobile in his white robe, with one gloved hand extended, the golden belt draped around his neck and a towel over his head—his smashed and reddened face is barely visible—HE resembles the life-like wooden saints in Catholic processions. Joyfully his bearers parade him before the audience, and with a final cheer fling their straw hats into the air" (264). Sackler's final stage directions expertly realize the artificiality of the Great White Hope conception. "The Kid" is a sacred relic held aloft to the crowd. His actual humanity is still unimaginable, his pulped face unrecognizable. "The Kid" is on a frieze exactly taken from an Eakins painting such as "Salutat" while his featureless gore is reminiscent of the boxing paintings of George Bellows. Sackler unites the visual images of America's two most prominent painters of boxing scenes as Great White Hope and Predator-Prey. This final image in the play literally absorbs Jefferson, the white culture's Prey, whose last cry is "Let 'em pass by."

Sackler provokes the final question: At what cost to prop up this sham in continued ritual? At what cost to ourselves? Sackler is correct to invoke the carnivalesque throughout his hurtling play. The Great White Hope maintains the culture's necessary ritual in a communal coming together and through a victory and defeat of great import. In the Havana fight, the referee is the play's Jim Jeffries figure, Frank Brady, whom Jefferson defeated for the title. Cap'n Dan muses on Brady's giving the count to a downed Jefferson: "Whole world's gonna see him take [the belt] in his hand again, and hold it up and pass it on like the Kid'll pass it" (239), as if there had never been a black champion. Continuity, stability, erasure, and psychic restoration are all ritualized in this succession, although Cap'n Dan is more correct when he cracks, "You'd think we just organized the Second Coming" (239), which perfectly realizes the unrealizable status of the Great White Hope in this century of white sports insecurity and guilty nightmares.

No such psychic baggage comes with Rocky Balboa, the first fictional sports hero to absorb the actual sport he practices and the latest Great White Hope shift to be articulated in American culture. Almost all the heroes in boxing's cinematic pantheon had been losers or ironic winners, compromised by every sort of either individual or societal moral weakness from Joe Bonaparte in *Golden Boy* through a fictionalized Jake LaMotta in Martin Scorcese's *Raging Bull* (1980). The films had been gritty, tough, and cynical for decades. Sylvester Stallone changed all of that. With four *Rocky* films (1977–85), Rocky has had as many championship fights as have many actual champions and contenders. Stallone has played on all the contradictions of the boxing hero while conveniently voiding most of the consequences. He has an uncanny knack for dramatizing popular practice. The *Rocky* films, for example, have featured the "getting in shape" saga so near to the current middle-class obsession with fitness. Rocky's dawn work-outs and runs were memorable dramatic centers to *Rocky I* and have been invoked in each successive film by keyed music and quick-cut action.

Rocky is a free agent, not tied to any gangster element. He is neither young nor old. He can slug it out with Apollo Creed or Clubber Lang or Ivan Drago, take hundreds of blows, win or lose the heavyweight championship bouts, but remain with brains unscrambled and dignity intact. Stallone's blinded, pummeled, and defeated Rocky is the actual winner in *Rocky I* because he has shown that he can "stand," that he can "take it," that even Prey can have its victory. In *Rocky II,* Creed is finally vanquished after a sensational fifteenth-round double knockdown. The white champion has been crowned. In *Rocky III,* Creed now trains Rocky for his title bout against Clubber Lang, an even more menacing black challenger and a pure Predator who has taken his title. Thus some wished-for scale has been restored with Creed as retainer. To complete the portrait, the film was partially shot at Ali's estate in Pennsylvania. Clubber Lang is played by "Mr. T.," Ali's former bodyguard and a television adventure hero. In *Rocky III,* the white champion must now learn how to stick and move like a black fighter. To defeat the brute Lang,

Rocky improbably must dance like Ali himself. *Rocky IV* provides a Predator trained by computers and steroids, the nightmare Russian, Ivan Drago, who has killed Creed in the ring. Rocky adds a truly American victory to his credit by defeating Drago in Moscow in a Cold War battle of white supermen.

The championship fights in the four *Rocky* films have functioned as the true heavyweight championship bouts of the last decade. So dazzling and dramatic has their action been, so overt and satisfying their symbolic content, that a potential real life Rocky and Creed such as Gerry Cooney and Larry Holmes seemed most uninteresting by comparison. The fictional Rocky had triumphed in the void left after the dismantling of Muhammad Ali. A white fighter had again become the Great White Hope. Larry Holmes' graceless criticisms of the Marciano family after his loss of the title to Michael Spinks in 1985 damned him to the white boxing public. The "real" Rocky's memory could not be sullied by a bitter veteran who was frustrated at never receiving his due as undefeated heavyweight champion. To Holmes, the power of the Great White Hope was perhaps a last galling reminder of what plagues a black champion.[7]

Such a diminished ending is not covered by Stallone's theatrics. Stallone appears sincere when he says that he has not made fight films, really, that the difference is that in his films the viewer really cares about the fighter, not about money or mob connections. As Stallone solemnly points out, money is never mentioned in the Rocky series. Finally, what Stallone is proudest of is that Rocky is someone to care about: "You wanted him to win. And he does. . . . How many times can you stand to get involved with a character and then see him die or something?" (Choice 13). Cap'n Dan in *The Great White Hope* would agree: America can't *stand* it. Death is harsh, and Stallone, obviously no tragedian, would spare us its starkness. With his disclaimers of character complication and mortality, Stallone has exposed the optimistic yearning of his conception. Rocky Balboa fits the culture's requirements for the Great White Hope as He evolved beginning with London's *The Abysmal Brute*. Rocky has become the Heavyweight Champion for millions of spectators. Fictional sports narrative has achieved its first complete factual takeover. The Great White Hope reigns in the imagination which has captured the actual ring to America's delight.

With his gruesome victorious icon borne aloft, Sackler's play provided a final chilling image to the Great White Hope stereotype. No such figure plagues Stallone. In actuality, the only two fully imagined figures who soared from the stereotypical conception in narrative were Pedro Romero and Muhammad Ali—a Spanish bull-fighter and a black boxer. Hemingway and Mailer re-invented culture heroes in sport to fit their sense of aesthetics and personal courage. Their figures are the most encompassing representations of the individual sports hero in our culture. They are ritualists and artists in the commercial arena. They represent each author at his most optimistic about male dominion in and through the body and its transferral through the male artist at work on his book. Their heroes will remain young, will be immortal, will be inventive and imaginative in the kill, and will not be victimized. They will not dissolve into the economic, social, and sexual contradictions that almost all boxing tales array over and against their Ritual Sports Heroes. The Great White Hope, who never truly existed, is a transcendent figure and personally utopian for the artist within the culture who may fully create him.

Every boxing narrative follows at some remove Mailer's instinctive urgency about the seed of murder at boxing's core without Mailer's intellect and transference to his own inventive form. Most boxing narratives remain in the province of an environmentally determined naturalism that thrives on the anger, resentment, and isolation of the individual fighter. Potential sacrifice of the individual fighter is always implied and often realized. The boxer's passage is coded in cultural form in the dilemmas of Youth and Age, in the biological form of Predator and Prey, with the horizon figure of the Great White Hope representing a potential conceptual break-out from the corners of this arena. The boxing narrative's terms are either murder or humiliation. Fighters perpetrate one or suffer the other; in the boxing narrative, it is that stark. Every sports contest truly represents fragments of these elemental terms but they are softened through regulation and resultant sublimation. Also, there are team members among whom to distribute triumphs and defeats, responsibility and blame. Boxing edges close to primary physical facts all the time, traversing its contraries in a ceaseless flow from nature (the individual body) to culture (the collective's ritual) and back again.

Mailer creates the most extreme version of the individual sports hero. He is always immersed in the sensible, the material world where violence is unmediated by play, where dominance and submission are the only states. In ritual sport as depicted by Dickey, McGuane, Mailer, and Kesey, something is *always* consumed: land, resources, people. In play, such consumption is neutralized without a final destructiveness, as Kesey attempts to show. Predation is the compulsion that ritual sport formalizes where a system of practices in a prescribed form or manner expresses the truth of our competitiveness. Play would shatter that competitiveness and open a new space. Boxing is utterly opposed to the possibility of that space and remains a matter of life and death, of potency and un-manning. Ritual Sport does not play.

PART II

Individual Sports Heroism: Responses of the Play Spirit

5.

Play, Sacrifice, Performance: Kesey and Coover

IN RESPONSE to crises of individual sports heroism, authors consider alternative strategies to extreme male self-definition in sport. The play spirit activates much of the resistance to sports pressures and rigid roles. Part II looks at this resistance in playful alternatives to the determinism and sacrifice of the body: Kesey and Coover who play obsessively with the agonies of ritual and sacrifice in great inventiveness (chapter 5); female athletes and players who must find their own language and place within the male dominant of sport (chapter 6); the last School Sports Heroes "playing back to" the time of their heroism to deny the present (chapter 7); anti-heroic witnesses to sports heroism who abstain from heroic action to play off their differences from the larger culture through their control of language (chapter 8).

The Dynamics of Ritual and Play: Kesey's *One Flew Over the Cuckoo's Nest*

MCMURPHY IN *One Flew Over the Cuckoo's Nest* is a "natural," an individual hero who battles society's rites by creating his own. How Kesey positions him as both a ritual sacrifice and as a life-enhancing player makes for a unique combination in the fiction of sport and play. Kesey's McMurphy is one rejoinder to the intimation of ritual fragmentation voiced by Mailer in response to Hemingway's death (see chapter 1). Almost contemporaneous with Hemingway's death, Kesey's 1962 novel began with Mailer's feared technology and depicted a hero neutralizing it by going on the offensive, by accepting nothing from the "hospital" but countering it in the very free play that Hemingway had mistrusted. Furthermore, McMurphy left his followers with a legacy rather than the "curse" Mailer saw as Hemingway's bequest. That there were valid and intricate small rituals to stave off mortality's pull—Mailer's "breath of the beast"—had been Hemingway's great sporting lesson and the artistic triumph of his fiction. Mailer inherited Hemingway's dread but Kesey worked through to resolutions in fiction that countered that dread.

Kesey portrayed an individual sports hero in both *Cuckoo's Nest* and *Sometimes A Great Notion* (1964) but he also portrayed a play spirit akin to the powerful and creative play response to the collective domination that had been a vital lesson in American fiction from Hawthorne to Faulkner. As with ritual, play had been a means of psychic survival, more isolated and lodged in conceptions of the imagination. Play as well as ritual attempts to break reality into meaning. Both ritual and play are transcendent. Ritual validates and regulates play even as play functions to counter-balance ritual solemnity (Blanchard 53).

Hemingway "shout[ing] down the corridors of the hospital" ironically defines how and where McMurphy takes his stand as first a player and finally as a ritual sacrifice. To construct an allegory of ritualized experience, Kesey begins with the ward as arena and with McMurphy as a master player who energizes the men while the final ritual yields a somber meaning. Whereas Dickey renders murder in concealment and confusion, Kesey concludes with a correct sacrificial ritual. Whereas McGuane ends with the exposure of madness, Kesey *begins* there and uses ritual and play to counter the madness.

Kesey's McMurphy plays to bring a society back to health. In Kesey's ward as world, the men have lost any sense of rebellion against Nurse Ratched and the Combine and possess no sense of joy or freedom. McMurphy swaggers onto the ward with all his competitive instincts intact; his battle for the ward is nothing less than his attempted subversion of authoritarian mechanisms. McMurphy's exuberance clearly counters all systems where men are regulated into prior humiliating postures without possibility of growth.

Kesey, like McGuane, practices exposure in his depiction of the true relations of power on the ward. The ward is a pitilessly open arena, its citizens constantly monitored and regulated in a parody of a public square in which a community's external life might be conducted in health and sharing (Bakhtin 132). No concealment is possible. McMurphy employs a living creative laughter as he attempts to make a travesty of the high languages of control that Nurse Ratched speaks on behalf of the Combine. The Combine, which is a mythic source of power for Chief Bromden is, at every level, hostile to dialogue and to openness, as its maxims and rules are naturalized. McMurphy's annihilating laughter would open the "natural" relations of power to comic scrutiny.

McMurphy's play between the physical and the spiritual allows the men on the ward to understand how they can be "other" and still survive in their solidarity. A full range of play is Kesey's tool to depict the anatomy of relations on the ward. In effect, McMurphy has been given his scarlet "A" by the Combine and, like Hester Prynne, he must embroider all around it to be sane, to become, in his own phrase, the "bull goose loony" (19). Furthermore, McMurphy's competition with Nurse Ratched utterly absorbs him and the ward, and his skill, strategy, and pacing of the drama are what drive the novel forward. Yet Nurse Ratched holds final sway over his energy and creativity. After one McMurphy victory, Kesey writes, "the fight would go on as long as she wanted, till he made a mistake or till he just gave out, or until she could come up with some new tactic" (193). McMurphy's infectious creation of illusion dominates while "she waited without comment" (194). McMurphy "ran up and down the hall blowing a nickel-plated ref's whistle, teaching Acutes the fast break from ward door to the Seclusion Room at the other end, the ball pounding in the corridor like cannon shots and McMurphy roaring like a sergeant, 'Drive, you puny mothers, *drive!*' " (193–94).

When McMurphy is playing monopoly or poker or betting on whether he can hit the wall clock with a pat of butter, he is educating the ward to chance, to illusion, to wonder. His agility in transforming the base of the play is most evident in his crusade to allow the ward to watch the World Series on television, what McMurphy considers to be an inalienable right/rite. When, in a test of wills, Nurse Ratched cuts the power and makes the screen go blank, McMurphy pretends not to notice and just sits, feet up, watching the empty gray screen in great contentment. Soon, to Nurse Ratched's fury, all the men pull up chairs and join him.

These lessons in play prepare the men to deal with the awful trauma of McMurphy's lobotomized body which is trundled back to the ward as a lesson about the Combine's power. As discussed in the introduction, Chief Bromden and the men act decisively to deny the reality of the body itself; they refuse in the name of McMurphy's play spirit to accept the death of that spirit. Their illusion, their play, is to deny the Combine its victory. The men sustain a vision of McMurphy's inviolability by calling his body a store dummy, by saying it could not be him: they could "do" tattoos and broken noses but "the arms? They couldn't do those. His arms were *big*" (308). McMurphy's arms gave the illusion of great power so that the men had believed in their size. McMurphy takes on the stature of Faulkner's John Sartoris in *The Unvanquished* (1938), of "doing bigger things than he was"; he attains culture-hero status.

Martini, the ward's minor illusionist, tells McMurphy about the imaginary enemies he bombs from imaginary planes: "They need you to see them" (176). In the end, it is McMurphy, cruelly deprived of all creativity, who needs the men to see him, not in broken body but as overarching presence. He has taught them the "flow," the sensation of total participation where they could discover meanings by playing them into creation. When the Combine ravages McMurphy's body, the men re-cast his body as a semiotic blank and construct a re-affirmation of McMurphy's spirit and meaning. They "re-signify," re-affirm, which is the purpose of any sustaining play.

Suzanne Langer has noted, "long before men perform rites which enact the phases of life, they have learned such acting in play" (Langer 155). McMurphy instructs the men in the possible which they then use out of psychic necessity to perpetuate him. They embroider around his abused body and establish him through denial as spirit, as anti-hero rather than as flesh, as individual hero. Thus what began in play can finally become the foundation for a proper rite.

Ritual and Play: The Good Death of McMurphy

KESEY'S COMMITMENT through *Cuckoo's Nest* is to the power of play. Yet the novel's conclusion has an extraordinary ritual sacrifice that relates it to the fiction of Dickey, McGuane, and Mailer. The climax of the sensual, liberating festival that McMurphy holds in the ward is the sacrifice of himself. His final attack on Nurse Ratched stipulates that he is the surrogate victim for the whole ward community, in Girard's terms, the dangerous insurgent who must be symbolized as sacrifice. McMurphy's exposure of the nurse's sexuality is close to murder before he is pulled off her. Then

> he let himself cry out: A sound of cornered animal fear and hate and surrender and defiance, that if you ever trailed coon or cougar or lynx is like the last sound the treed and shot and falling animal makes as the dogs get him, when he finally doesn't care any more about anything but himself and his dying. (305)

McMurphy is the animal sacrifice in the Combine's ritual hunt. The Combine believes McMurphy is both dangerous and expendable and therefore must act against him. The Combine suppresses him in a "bad kill" that is shocking and reductive and must be countered. But the ward as positive community regenerates McMurphy's sacrificial meaning. Chief Bromden's final act of mercy killing is Kesey's transfiguration of murder-buggery that momentarily redeems the male love from Mailer's fury and Dickey's muddle. McMurphy becomes the *correct* sacrificial victim at the hands of an adept who knows why he is killing, what he is sacrificing, and the meaning of his act.

Although McMurphy's life and death are most often seen in a Christian allegorical pattern of suffering and transcendence, Kesey's current passes from play to incorrect sacrifice to proper rite. Faulkner usually progressed from rite to play, from constraint of a formal procedure to the pursuit of freedom, as in the "Spotted Horses" section of *The Hamlet* (1940); Hemingway had Santiago kill correctly in *The Old Man and the Sea* before the sharks ravaged the dead marlin's body. Kesey places the sacrifice correctly for his concerns by recoding Hemingway's language articulated by Santiago: "Man can be destroyed but not defeated." The Combine intends to defeat McMurphy by leaving him as the nominally breathing record of how they would like all men on the ward to be: defeated but not destroyed, living matter without spirit. Chief Bromden defeats the Combine by destroying McMurphy and pushing out into the moon-lit night to salvage what might be left of his own life. He has grown back into his physical body, capable of a ritual murder and the hurling of the control panel through the plateglass window; he is capable of doing things as big as he *is*. Previously, the primary configuration of ritual sport in fiction was described as *the sanctioned killing to obliterate sexual terror, with another male, the killer brother, for the team*. To defeat the Combine, Chief Bromden commits an unsanctioned murder of a brother already defeated by the collective. In an act of love, he extricates them both from the collective. The sexuality that Mailer deflects toward murder in *Why Are We in Vietnam?* and *An American Dream* fuses with murder and love in the Chief's smothering of McMurphy. Kesey's redemption of murder-buggery in a moral act is a daring, life-enhancing contrast to Mailer's continual heroic cruelty, climaxed in *Ancient Evenings*.

The primary emphasis on the body's fragility and sheer survival is what *Cuckoo's Nest* comes back to again and again. The ritual sports story returns once again to origins of male physical fear and insecurity before the collective's forces. This male insecurity about being male is omnipresent in McMurphy's duels with Nurse Ratched, in her control of the men's guilt, most notably that of Harding and Billy Bibbitt. Mailer's vision of the astronauts in *Of a Fire on the Moon* as "virile" but "done to," "subjected to a pharmacology of stimulants, depressants . . . tranquilizers" (*Moon* 48) describes the life of the men on Kesey's ward where the body is inert and passive in technological violation. Technology indeed "fills the pause" in *Cuckoo's Nest* as it attempts to control the men chemically and electrically while it defeats a great "living romantic." Kesey has proven that play can be a powerful element in neutralizing or suspending the normally oppressive relationships between authority and the dominated. Play initially appears licensed by Nurse Ratched acting for the Combine as she sanctions a continued, permissible rupture of ward routine. To this extent, play can be labeled enervating and not a truly revolutionary force in that it blurs signification into merely pleasurable flow. Play becomes containment rather than change.[1] Nurse Ratched is neutralized, but there is no change in power, merely the momentary exposure of it.

Yet McMurphy finally teaches the men how to respond to their bondage through play. By the novel's conclusion, almost all the men have signed out of the ward, corroborating Nurse Ratched's terror of McMurphy "forever ruining any other look she might ever try to use again" (305). McMurphy's playfulness and imaginative control have achieved this, not his sacrifice. No doubt Kesey's strongest analogue for McMurphy has been as a Messiah figure with disciples. *Cuckoo's Nest* is a blueprint for the growth of a religious figure, one who falls into sacrifice after fully allowing himself to be used by the flock; He submits to a crucifixion yet leaves a part of himself everywhere. Then, too, the novel has uncomfortable tendencies.[2] It identifies oppressive hegemony too literally with a distorted female presence while McMurphy's male body is that of a "truly strong man" so blindingly charismatic without contradictions or the possibility of material seduction. Such bodies are in line with an authoritarian imagery and lead to passive following by the men. McMurphy and the men versus Nurse Ratched and the Combine is a polarized opposition that collapses any dialectical truth into versions of the "other."

Yet to position play and ritual in a text so hostile to an authoritarian world is to inscribe difference and archaic practice into the contemporary narrative between the oppositions. Play humanizes and retrieves small victories for the McMurphy forces. They act in a realm that defies normal transactional relationships of production and consumption. Their satisfactions are what survive in corners of the larger domination. Finally, McMurphy's sacrificial crisis re-grounds these illusions in consequences for the players. The hero teaches and suffers in direct contrast to the heroes of Mailer, Dickey, and Mc-Guane. In McMurphy, the figure of the hunter-priest fuses with that of the player and the figure of the ritual sacrifice, which stipulates a heroic life and an equally heroic death. Ths fusion suggests the roles that sports heroes in school stories and in professional sport combine in most contemporary sports fiction while Chief Bromden is their exemplary witness recording the victories and defeats.

Play and ritual are intimately connected. Both seek to control the real. Play dismantles signifiers, both material and spiritual, re-consti-tuting them in configurations to underscore a relativity of actions. Play produces temporal and spiritual illusions that may become the basis for ritual, either that of competition or cooperation. Ritual is then a pull toward formality in that it makes the re-constituted signifiers rigid and orders the new reality into a similarly extra-real state. Both play and ritual have the same desire: to shape material reality, the one in greater freedom, the other in greater discipline. Play underscores differences while ritual searches for "same" and "like." The imaginative, a-temporal play—when the ward views McMurphy's lobotomized frame—exposes and reverses all the power relationships, while the Chief's act of murder is physically rigidify-ing, stiffening McMurphy's powerful frame in rigor mortis and confirming in piety the sacrifice brutally begun by the Combine. The Combine would reify McMurphy into a lesson; however, the Chief has free will to complete the sacrificial act. What begins as an act of predation in the collective's desire to "make everything [them]," ends with the Chief "making McMurphy other" as an inspiration and spirit.

The description of ritual as an unusually full semiotic flow with no unassimilated elements is clearest here. Play, then, is willful mis-reading and denial of McMurphy's body on the part of the men on the ward and perhaps the only imaginative way to smash the untruth of his living death. McMurphy has been fragmented into each of their texts of potential liberation. Yet it takes the Chief's ritual mur-der to complete the redemption. In ritualizing McMurphy's death even as his life had been exemplary of play, Kesey wrests some grace against heavy odds and provides some of the few transcendent scenes of play and ritual in contemporary fiction. Play defies and defines while ritual re-grounds play in consequence.

Kesey's *Cuckoo's Nest* reduces the sacrifice of the individual sports hero to the novel's climax. He articulates a way in which the ritual may survive in contemporary narrative as the resolution of the individual hero's sacrificial crisis in the school and team world. The fall out of illusions into the glaring truth of power relationships in the collective, the moment in which play is no longer a sufficient challenge to the authoritarian structures governing and influencing behavior, is the very definition of the sacrificial crisis of the natural inserted into civilization. The individual hero who labors in play of the most healing sort or who attempts a timeless state in ritual comes to his reckoning in the moment of sacrificial crisis. Such a moment survives in different sports fiction narratives where the individual battles the collective in a very controlled competitive setting. The ritual purification of sacrifice and/or transcendence is longed for. Time and again it is addressed in incomplete or reversed terms in sports fiction's imaginative efforts to make violence regenerative. The excluded individual is often dismembered as individual sports hero in the contemporary school and professional sports stories where his sacrificial crisis is softened but still recognizable in his history within the collective sports establishment.

Kesey has ranged so far among play and ritual situations and conflicts in *Cuckoo's Nest* that he allows us to construct a series of competitive, playful, and transcendent responses that may stand for a panoply of relations in the fiction of sport and play.[3] The male relation to the body is the fundamental subject of such fiction. The inscription of the male body is written in five separate but related narratives, from complete absorption of another's body in totemic response to complete abstention from competition and trauma. As ever, play is the fulcrum on which the narratives may turn.

"Make Everything Me" – The most extreme response in ritual is to "make everything me," to reduce all warring or extraneous elements to the subject's body. Such a response is ego-dominated, predatory, sacrificial. It is the most devastating and violent of individual heroisms. It does not partake of symbolic victories and losses and knows no rules. Here is blood sport with a survival ethic at its core. Heard here is the cry of Mailer's Sgt. Croft, the anxiety in Lewis Medlock's

survivalism as well as the arrow murders in *Deliverance* and Stephen Rojack's rituals of mayhem in *An American Dream*. In *Cuckoo's Nest*, the Combine's lobotomy is the vicious collective response to end McMurphy's power and cease his play.

Victory Over Others – The less extreme codified expression of domination would be to achieve victory over others in competition, to simulate within the rules a "death" that stops short of sacrifice. Here play masters terminal contest by an ordering to "win" or "defeat" where the sacrificial logic of an end point is resisted. The individual hero becomes a collective hero in order to win. Here play provides a sure substitution of rules for chaos, of winning and losing for life and death. Some agreed-upon decision grants life to the adversary. Here is the model of regulated competition in sport. *Cuckoo's Nest* shows McMurphy battling Nurse Ratched and the Combine and working with the men on the ward both playfully and within the rules. Less stark than ritual sacrifice on the one hand, rule-bound competition stops short of the freedom of play on the other.

Play – The most capacious strategy to survive intact is to retain the play space between "self" and "not-self," to control the possibilities for movement toward the sensual and competitive as well as toward the spiritual and cooperative. Here difference reigns in the play between. McMurphy teaches the men on the ward to veer away from their capture through laughter, uncertainty, simulation, and a joyfulness.

Work With Others – A less individual encounter of self and not-self is in the decision of the individual to work with the other(s), to give up some essential self for the community in a dialogue. Once again, the play is a sure substitution. Cooperation, growth, and self-sacrifice for the community are stressed. In sports logic this is the maturation of working with and for the team, of identification with the other for potential authority and reward. This remains the most fraternal and social of the sports heroisms. Working with others may range all the way from self-sacrifice to/for the group to a revolutionary impulse to change events in historical time. McMurphy labors so hard for the men on the ward that even the Chief senses his utter weariness. Kesey's frame does not allow McMurphy or the reader to grasp how much McMurphy plays for his own liberation and how much for the men on the ward. It is clear, though, that he moves toward his self-sacrifice by teaching the men and inhabiting a community with them. Such will be Kesey's role with his Merry Pranksters.

"Make Me Other" - The final category is that of self-sacrifice into an abstention from the sensual, the competitive, the communal. Here is a transcendence in the reign of the sublime. The resolution of *Cuckoo's Nest* through the Chief's killing of McMurphy works on this level. So does D. J. Jethroe's awe-filled description of the "unfucked" Alaskan wilderness. This sacrifice may also be involuntary and negative in the extreme. Ritual reigns here, as in the sacrificially-dominated realm of "make everything me" of which it is a polar opposite.

The final truth of play's lack of control at these poles is that one cannot play predation or the sublime. One can only sacrifice or be sacrificed, master or be mastered. However, the dance of play as performance holds off these terminal responses into competitive and communal narratives that characters may live in and learn from before being claimed in one sacrificial paroxysm or another.

This range of narrative may be schematized by the following:

"Make Everything—Victory Over—Play—Work With—"Make Me
Me"   Others   Others   Other"

Ritual Sport and Play: *Sometimes a Great Notion*

IN SOMETIMES *A Great Notion* (1964), Kesey creates Hank Stamper, a McMurphy adept in a natural landscape that is also society's work environment. Hank Stamper is an Oregon logger who is a strong athlete and complex competitor. He is an individual hero who survives his own sacrificial crisis to instruct his brother Lee in heroic survival. In his portrayal of the Stamper brothers in *Notion,* Kesey draws on all the narrative conventions of the Ritual Sports Hero from Cooper onward while carrying the violent drama of the "killer brothers" in a more affirmative direction.

Notion provides a competitive arena that is also an organic work environment. Kesey renders the Oregon coastlines of ocean and river with enormous attention to the details of weather and topography, to scenes of nature's power and unyielding bounty. The Stampers are an incorrigible and intransigent third-generation clan of individualists who are ornery enough to wrest a hard living at a tough job. As in Hemingway's Michigan and Faulkner's Mississippi, Kesey's men in Oregon *belong* in the natural environment. Their rituals and play grow out of their work roles. Their drama with the collective is over a union strike that the town of Wakonda desires to perpetuate against a major lumber company. The Stampers battle throughout the novel to retain their right to cut and ship timber on their own terms. Such a struggle has central reference to the debates over land use and the rights of the individual. This struggle has been a central subject of ritual sports narratives from Cooper's *The Pioneers,* where Natty Bumppo battles Judge Temple and the townspeople (including the comic woodchopper, Billy Kirby), through Faulkner's "The Bear" in which Major DeSpain sells the hunting grounds to a Memphis logging company

Notion has multiple narrative viewpoints and styles with which to render this environment. Characters such as old Henry Stamper, Joe Ben Stamper, and Boney Stokes call to mind Southwestern Humor tradition in their language. They are raw, playful, comic, naive, and physically explicit. At the other extreme in narration are Kesey's italicized chapter openings and several key interpolated passages that are quite contemporary in their philosophical and aesthetic questioning. They not only define an author and metaphor-maker at work but herald the Kesey who would so soon be identified as a culture hero by Tom Wolfe in *The Electric Kool-Aid Acid Test* (1968). Between these two viewpoints of naive humor and metaphysical knowing, the majority of the novel is related through the very different sensibilities of the Stamper brothers, Hank and Lee. *Their* notions in *Notion* and their ultimate competitive struggle have reference to all other ritual sport competition heretofore described as well as to the battle between individual heroes.

Hank Stamper is a sports hero who can cut it. An all-state high school football player, he has also held several swimming and track records, so many in fact that the Wakonda High Sharks Sports Records lists "the same name all the way down" (176). Hank can hold a "double-edged ax" (312) straight out in his hand longer than any other logger. He takes on all comers in bar room brawls. For years he trained for swim meets "swimming steadily into the river's current. . . . Hours and hours, swimming steadily, doggedly" (65). Such is the sports emblem's equivalent for Hank's endurance and stubborn courage. Lee remembers Hank's "long sinewy body diving into the river, naked and white and hard as a peeled tree" (65). For most of the novel, Hank is just this indomitable male, hard and erect, a strong man without the survival anxiety of a Rusty Jethroe, Lewis Medlock, or Vernor Stanton.

That anxiety is displayed by Lee Stamper, Hank's half-brother who is twelve years his junior. Lee's mother, Myra, had an affair with Hank when Lee was a small boy. As the novel begins, Myra has committed suicide and Lee is an unhappy literature graduate student at Yale. Lee's fury about Hank's affair with his mother and his male insecurity at having to live in Hank's immense shadow move him to an unsuccessful suicide attempt of his own. When Hank summons him back to Oregon to help in the family battles with the union, Lee vows to bring Hank down by any means he can.

Kesey frames Lee's resentment within that of the witness's animus toward the truly strong man. Hank's motto is "NEVER GIVE A INCH," the phrase painted on a garish, crudely-lettered sign that Henry Sr. had placed over his son's crib. The voice of Lee's recurrent admonition to himself is "WATCH OUT"—for other people and their machinations against him, for weakness in his own resolve to *win* through weakness even as Hank always wins through strength. Lee retains the suspicion of Mailer's D.J. Jethroe toward Tex Hyde and Rusty, of Dickey's Ed Gentry toward Lewis Medlock, of Mc-Guane's Quinn toward Stanton. Once again in *Notion,* the ritual sports narrative continually posits the anxious male witness who feels defective before the acts of the sports hero. The battle is thus framed for the killer brothers. Lee wants Hank down; Hank wants Lee to fight back.

These viewpoints within competition are reconcilable only as Kesey plays off the differences between them. It is at the level of his own mediation that Kesey's play is evident in *Notion,* for neither Hank nor Lee countenance play. Lee is an aesthete, nervous, allusive, literary, ironic. For him, action is only a tentative possibility. Hank is straightforward and bluntly defines himself through action. Yet Kesey gives him an aesthetic as well: "I know, for an instance, that if you want to play this way, you can make the river stand for all *sorts* of other things. But . . . making it more than what it is lessens it. Just to see it clear is plenty. Just to feel it cold against you or watch it flood. . . . And the best way to see it is not looking behind it-or beneath it or beyond it - but dead at it" (105). Hank is a Hemingway empiricist who is committed to encountering the reality he meets in the present. Lee looks everywhere but in the present. When he was a child, Hank taunted him with the tall tale of an animal Hank called the "Hide-Behind," a perfect creature to define Lee's paranoia, a creature never seen but always about to pounce (WATCH OUT).

Lee's despair at Hank's power reaches a crescendo when he imagines himself on his first day of logging in a work contest with Hank, only to find out Hank has been up a more perilous tree, without the gloves which he had loaned to Lee: "He'll always be running ahead for me to catch up. He keeps changing the rules for the run, or the run itself" (181). Lee finds no coherence in rules or contest. He can never stop his self-reflexive commentary. Hank sees only the unflinching terms of competition. The method by which Lee vows to beat Hank is through the seduction of Hank's wife, Viv.

This battle with Hank lies latent in Lee's consciousness throughout most of the novel. Kesey flares it into the open in several striking scenes. An evening fox hunt contains not only a central parable of brave and cowardly dogs, a menacing bear, a poisonous snake, but also two additional tall tales of hunts related by a garrulous old Henry Stamper around a campfire while Lee strokes Viv and whispers that he loves her. The hunt's action swirls around them all. Hank and his cousin Joe Ben return from following the dogs and discuss Lee's inertia: "He acts like . . . *he don't have any reason, ever any reason to fight*" (259), just as Molly, the most courageous of the dogs, returns to the edge of the firelight, distended and dying with a huge snake fastened on her belly. The tale's meaning is complete. Hank's individual bravery in fighting forces larger than he is will be subject to Lee's undermining. Kesey's vivid hunting sketch continues in the ritual sports fictional tradition of memorable scenes in Cooper, Hemingway, Faulkner, and Mailer. Tall Tale and hunting parable are mixed with skill. The various competitions between dogs and fox, dogs and "blue tick bitch," Molly and the bear, the snake and Molly, all comment on the central Hank-Viv-Lee triangle and reverberate throughout the novel in localized language and description.

Hank is revealed at other junctures in *Notion* as a sudden, decisive fighter. Joe Ben recalls when Hank as a high school football player fought and destroyed a new pretender to greatness on his own team. Hank whips Big Newton, a logger who outweighs him by more than fifty pounds, in a match that even turns Lee's animosity toward Hank to wild cheering. However, all of Hank's prowess and Lee's frantic attempts at making some sort of impression on Hank come down to a final brawl between the brothers after Lee seduces Viv. In the novel's penultimate scenes, Hank has been defeated by the awful tragedy of Joe Ben's drowning and of old Henry's losing an arm in a crushing logging accident. Injured himself, Hank cannot save Joby's life, rushes his father to a hospital, and then goes to the Wakonda bar where he is beaten further by toughs who resent his anti-union stand. Hank returns home, swims the raging river, and upon entering the Stamper house, spies Lee and Viv together. He drops to his knees, violently ill, and while hurt and grieving, thinks, "Weakness is true and real. I used to accuse the kid of faking his weakness. . . . No, you can't ever fake being weak. You can only fake being strong" (503). Hank's provisional defeat is a preliminary climax akin to McMurphy's defeat by Nurse Ratched in *Cuckoo's Nest*. The individual hero is a nominal sacrifice; Lee believes he has "won" in their battle, but his victory is severely compromised by Joe Ben's death and old Henry's injuries.

With Hank's defeat, the town goes flat. The ritual hero's weakness is enervating for the tribe. Hank goes into a decline and loses all of his resolve. In a real sense, Hank's unmanning resembles the Combine's lobotomy on McMurphy as the culmination of its determination to stop his power. Lee is the individualized, fraternal agent of the society's displeasure. Yet rather than the transcendence of Chief Bromden's sacrifice of McMurphy and the Ward's playful embroidery around McMurphy's body, Kesey settles in *Notion* for a willful, overdramatized reassertion of Hank's strength and masculine ethos. It is a distressingly un-nuanced and rhetorically shrill conclusion to a varied account of competition and its attraction/repulsion. *Notion* finally appears as a more conventionally Oedipal narrative with clearly defined gender poles in which the strong men bond together.

Hank and Lee do battle as the killer brothers in a brawl. Lee fears he is "it" in a sacrificial crisis: "YOU KNOW YOU CAN'T BEAT HIM. IF YOU KEEP FIGHTING HE'LL KILL YOU. LIE DOWN!

STOP!" (586) but this only enrages Hank further because he is convinced that Lee wants only to receive sympathy from Viv who is watching. When Lee counters his *own* voice of "WATCH OUT" with retaliation in fighting back, he to his own wonderment thinks, "My brother and I finally, totally *wholeheartedly* embraced for our first and last and oh so long overdue dance of Hate and Hurt and Love" (585). After they are spent, he and Hank together defiantly take the logging boom down river on Thanksgiving Day in front of the whole town. Hank and Lee have moved through and past Viv to physically unite in the brawl. Having been bloodied by Hank, Lee restores Hank's resolve and discovers his own. Hero and witness unite and, unlike McMurphy and the Chief, both live to battle again. Hank instructs Lee as they move on the dangerous carpet of logs, "Keep on the bounce. . . . It maybe don't look it, but it's safest to keep on the bounce" (598). In the competitive setting, Lee has been initiated into power and he submits to Hank's authority. Hank has regained his perfect athlete's balance and will need it, while to Viv as she leaves town and her bus pulls away, they are "two tiny figures leaping foolishly from log to log" (598). She now reasserts the irony that would have belonged to Lee at the beginning of the novel.

Viv has been sacrificed as the suitable other before the male imperative. Hank has come to her only in strength, Lee only in his weakness. Having sought to eliminate Hank by any means, Lee now may carry his resentment over against the collective, feeling at one with self, with Hank as powerful adversary, and with nature: he is a Stamper and a logger. Lee played with his notion of his difference from Hank for many years. He played his vengeance game to defeat Hank. Finally, in their ritual, they become "like" and "same." Hank passes through a sacrificial crisis but survives the worst that nature, the collective, and Lee have to offer. Lee, too, survives Hank's attack to become his equal. As in *Cuckoo's Nest,* Kesey transfers the male power to a witness–narrator. The very controlled competitive setting of the killer brothers that dominated the conclusion of Mailer's *Why Are We in Vietnam?* has here, too, made violence potentially regenerative, as in the Chief's murder of McMurphy in *Cuckoo's Nest.*

This male fellowship is not the whole story for Kesey in *Notion.* As in *Cuckoo's Nest,* he posits a very strong play spirit that both underscores and conflicts with ritual and male competition. However, unlike *Cuckoo's Nest,* the play in *Notion* is not fused with the ritual, making the play both easier to isolate and less a potential source of power. The play spirit specifically is present in three areas in *Notion:* in the scene of Joe Ben Stamper's drowning, in Kesey's recurring metaphor of the dance in human relations, and in the language of Kesey's interpolated passages.

One of the strongest intimations of Hank Stamper's impending weakness is his failure to free Joe Ben from beneath the giant log that has pinned him in the rising waters of the Wakonda River. The logs and the river are the powerful natural forces throughout *Notion* and Hank's authority stems in large part from his hard work and respectful mastery of their danger. However, Kesey transforms log and river from economic relations to metaphysical ones, from work to the play of cosmic forces. Joe Ben Stamper has been the novel's merry squire and Hank's faithful lieutenant. Mirthful reaction is his signature. Likewise, the flowing water of the river has been just as capricious. Lee is menaced on the ocean shore by Wakonda townsmen while a car is trapped in the sand as the tide rises: "In five more minutes the foam would be chuckling against the differential. In ten, laughing against the door" (294).

Likewise, as the water rises over Joe Ben, Hank attempts to save him by mouth-to-mouth resuscitation, darting below the water line repeatedly to blow air into Joby's lungs. But Joby begins to laugh at the awful futility of Hank's action, whereas Hank thinks, "as long as the little fart is *laughing* under there we'll make out. I can carry him air all night if it comes to it. As long as he's got faith enough to see it's funny" (487). Hank must accept the literal death for the heroic time "for doing something full-size had long gone" (486). Now the laughter appears to come from outside Joe Ben as well, "a black laughing cancer trying to take over the shell of him" (487). Joe Ben's last interior monologue before death is another series of comic cliche exclamations *about* laughter to match the "black cancer": "Don't you laugh it ain't funny"; "Don't make me laugh"; "Whosoever believe that he don't laugh"; "What's so goddam funny" (488). Joby's last expelled breath is a "bubbling of hysterical mirth," at which point his mouth then becomes the "black laughing cancer" itself, "open in the dark there, open and round with laughing. And huge like an underwater cave" (488). However, the spirit has fled.

Hank and Joby had constructed a playful game in the face of Joby's certain death. Such is their brave challenge to fate cast in a relation to a laughing dance of death, the spirit trying to keep matter alive. Such play resembles the Ward's re-casting McMurphy's lobotomized body in *Cuckoo's Nest* in playful denial of his living death. Such play also invokes a first principle in *Notion* akin to Faulkner's "Prime maniacal Risibility" in *The Hamlet*. The laughing god in *Notion* is alert and sensitive to the ridiculous, the incongruous, and the absurd. Risibility is a first principle that refuses to allow primacy to tragedy or comedy in death in any higher re-combination but rather, in a brilliantly playful mimesis, allows the modes to play themselves out in difference at the very moment of death itself.

Notion is largely dominated by a competitive sporting ethic but Joe Ben's death is Kesey's playful alternative voice to the "truly strong man." Another metaphorical bow toward play and performance in the novel is Kesey's repeated invocation of the dance. The last battle between Hank and Lee is modulated in play as "the dance of Hate and Hurt and Love," cyclical with no final defeat or death; appropriately, Lee narrates and casts their battle as "clinging to each other in a paroxysm of overripe passion we spun the fight fantastic" in "the high whirling skirl of adrenalin that always accompanies this dance" (585). Mailer's intentional line of sex and murder does not dominate in Kesey nor is gender definition ever part of Kesey's agenda in *Notion*. Instead, the duration of the dance is male display, not final contest. Hank and Lee "reeled" and "shuffled," "rocked" and "rolled" and, having regenerated each other, bonded as brothers at last. Boxing serves the dance, agon serves mimesis. As Lee believes, "the dance between my brother and me was not finished . . . It was just intermission. . . . when the partner is equal there exists no end, no winning, no losing, and no stopping" (593). Sport is encapsulated within ritual which for Kesey will always be repeated and which has its base in the dance as play.

One of Kesey's most suggestive interpolated passages sets the largest frame for dance, and, by extension, for play in *Notion:*

> Which brings to mind one more notion to add to the bit about Singers of echoes and Echoers of songs: the notion of dance. Not the weekend dance in the Saturday-night sense, where you two-

step to music you've heard before and always know—even if only in a cellular way—just about where your two-step is headed . . . but the Daily Dance with the wilder step, to a tune as soundless as the eelgrass tune, to an echo of a song or a song still unechoed. A dance where you can never really have much notion where you are headed. You can trip off to places so wild and so wiggy that you don't know where you are until you get back.

And sometimes not even know you tripped off at all because you never get back to know that you've left . . . (306–7)

Kesey renounces the sure substitution of music heard and known in favor of an uncertain play that "plays beyond" in a dance where the outcome—existential, absurd, open—cannot be foreseen. Almost all of the novel's male competitive ethos, including the rather stereotypical ending of Hank and Lee bloodied and pulling together, argues against this dance conceit. Yet "so wild" and "so wiggy" are the places to which Kesey tripped off while writing *Notion* and in the immediate aftermath with the Merry Pranksters that one must read the interpolated passages in *Notion* as the playful discourse straining to be heard in Kesey, even as he was writing a giant of a book with modernist narrative voices, a socially realistic theme, and a frontier individualist hero. Within *Notion*'s play, in *Kesey*'s risibility and its new great notions (sometimes), the "play beyond" cracks through, grinning at death and competition, trying on masks and voices, subverting both Hank Stamper's hard masculine heroism and Lee Stamper's nervous aestheticism.

Very early in *Notion* as he begins gently to introduce the reader to the shifts in point-of-view that determine the novel's style, Kesey writes, "STOP! DON'T SWEAT IT. SIMPLY MOVE A FEW INCHES LEFT OR RIGHT TO GET A NEW VIEWPOINT" (14). Such a stance presupposes the author telling the reader to play between Hank's macho "NEVER GIVE A INCH" and Lee's paranoid "WATCH OUT," as well as to watch for Kesey's own play. Such a relaxed relativity is part of Kesey's enormous versatility and narrative charm, but it presents a problem in an author of major gifts. Seemingly able to write almost any scene, in any narrative voice, from a variety of philosophical approaches, Kesey was also the contemporary American writer best equipped to write of individual male competition and imaginative play. He was both killer athlete and magician, strong male presence and masque-master. For Mailer, his body was the warring ground, a space for battle as ritualized warrior. For Kesey, bodies do die in sacrifice to society or nature (Mc-Murphy, Joe Ben), but the body is more play-ground, a space for ritualized play. A prime example in *Notion* occurs when Hank has fastened his father's severed arm, middle-finger extended, to a pole in front of the Stamper house. Kesey thus uses the phallic arm (a log erect?) in a positive transformation of McMurphy's body brought back to the ward. The Risibility is in charge of the scene in *Notion*.

For Mailer, form is a war. For Kesey, form is a journey. His versatility in play precisely dictates that he will play with all viewpoints of competition and communality, including the brutality and solemnity of ritual sacrifice and the possibilities of transcendence. Tom Wolfe wrote in *The Electric Kool Aid Acid Test*, "Kesey's saving grace was that he never got serious where he could say it just as well with a cosmic joke" (192–93). Such a statement says much about Wolfe's preferences as well.[4] The fact remains that the "cosmic joke" is a major weapon in the arsenal of Twain and Faulkner. It was Kesey's work in this frontier metaphysical tradition of Tall Tale realism and tragi-comic bitter mirth that made him an important voice in contemporary American fiction.

Kesey's complexities of form in *Notion* derive centrally from his own diverse notions about form at this time in his development. As a high modernist with his "big" novel about heroic male individualism, he nonetheless was playing with new conceptions that had scant corresponding sense impressions with the Oregon logging world of *Notion* and its characters. Kesey would have preferred, one suspects, to present in *Notion* the unity of some differentiated whole according to some synthesis that he could have articulated. Yet such an aesthetic was not to be in *Notion*. NEVER GIVE A INCH and WATCH OUT, as well as the defeat of these maxims by the heroic Stamper brothers, would prove to have little application in the world of the Merry Pranksters except as initial states to be overcome in play. *Notion* tantalizes as a station on a longer journey by an author playing several games at one time but already in the service of the goal that Kesey would paint as the destination sign on the Prankster bus itself: FURTHUR.

The central instance of Kesey going with the "flow" in play was his appropriation of chemicals and technology to, in effect, become the "book of Kesey" in 1964, becoming a McMurphy to his Pranksters. Kesey by 1966 (when he was interviewed by Wolfe for *Acid Test*) appeared to have renounced all sure play of substitution as he had intimated in the interpolated passages in *Notion*. He had become McMurphy and was "playing beyond." The Ward was now the whole straight world. His canvas was nature and human nature; his palette and brushes the rich colors of drug-induced fantasy. Kesey finally was playing with the Pranksters toward a way to "be" it, to be "like" or "same" without murder or violation. The erratic, private-public careers of writers such as Kesey, Mailer, and McGuane have placed a constant strain on them to become themselves as texts, to be publicly tested flamboyant ritualists in their own myths. Fiction has not really sufficed for any of them, but rather the testing and reshaping of the body's limits and always the flirtation with the ritual sacrifice of themselves.

Ritual Performance: *The Public Burning*

THAT NEED for control through performance is thematized within the novel form itself in Coover's *The Public Burning* (1977). Coover's novel is a bravura performance in which *everything* is ritualized. No normative reality exists beyond the ritual itself. The dark saturnalia of the 1953 Rosenberg executions provides him with a degraded American historical pageant, one in which the individual and collective roles in ritual are thoroughly dialogized and controlled through Coover's narration. The American social ground and the individual body become a unified whole. If Mailer had conceived of the "body as arena," then Coover writes of the ritual arena as the American national and political body, a living, wounding, violent organism, in which both myth and historical memory feed the compulsive desire for performance.[5]

Coover is the contemporary American author most concerned with the collective and public ritual. His performances are true public events, rich with popular and mythical accents, yet always tuned to the versions of history that are energized by such sources. As such, he is the metafictionist most captivated by American team sport, seeing in football and baseball very suggestive, mimetic rituals that nonetheless have extreme agonistic and aleatory possibilities. Coover's brilliant conceptions of football, the sport of the American reality, in *Whatever Happened to Gloomy Gus of the Chicago Bears?*, and of baseball, the sport of the American imagination, in *The Universal Baseball Association,* will be dealt with in chapters 9–10 (Fictions of Football) and chapters 11–12 (Fictions of Baseball). Here his use of ritual will be discussed to gauge the possibilities for the collective representation of the extreme sexual and psychological rites that have heretofore been examined as the province of individual characters.

Coover's ritual arena in *The Public Burning* is Times Square which he imagines in June 1953 as the setting for the Rosenberg executions. He works in ritual modes that have direct reference to the greatest of American ritualists in fiction, Hawthorne and Faulkner. In his prologue, Coover's narrator writes, "No, friends, America has not arisen: *it has been called forth!* It's like the Divine Hawthorne once said: 'There is a fatality, a feeling so irresistible and inevitable that it has the force of doom' " (9). The "Electrocution Day" has reference to Hawthorne's Election Day in *The Scarlet Letter,* a day of public sport and revelry by hearty Elizabethans that is grudgingly sanctioned by the Puritan theocracy, yet a day that ends in Dimmesdale's manic confession and death.

Coover, like Hawthorne, portrays America as a land caught in a quest for revelation. Electrocution Day, the "burning" day, is glossed by Vice President Richard Nixon, the hapless hero and narrator of segments in the novel. Nixon as Dimmesdale skids miraculously onto the stage in Times Square, pants down, after his assignation with Ethel Rosenberg in the death house at Sing Sing. His "scarlet letter[s]" are the words, "I AM A SCAMP," painted in lipstick on his rear by Ethel. He then proceeds to improvise a speech to extricate himself from one of his "crises" by using rhetoric to persuade everyone in the crowd to drop their pants for America! This energy field of humiliation and feints toward buggery and rape set off the executions themselves as Uncle Sam completes the sacrifice of the Rosenbergs.

Coover's darkness is always richly played, allowing for no other reality. Hawthorne conceived of play as the great contrast to his

146

world of the Fall. His Dance of Death was consistently invoked to underscore the American contradictions in both individual psyche and cultural event. *Everything* in Coover's text is inside the ritual and subject to its control. The control is achieved by Uncle Sam, a Tall Tale and Faulknerian figure, close to Faulkner's concept of a "Prime Maniacal Risibility" in *The Hamlet* but here a narrator as well as a historical character. In contemporary mythos, Uncle Sam is a super-hero who "shazaams" his way into American historical figures, instilling in them the text of his creation. Uncle Sam calls Faulkner in *The Public Burning* "our Nobel Prize-winning mythomaniac" (420) and Faulkner delivers a paraphrase of his Nobel Prize address about "Man—simple, unfrightened, invincible men and women" who will defeat the "ancient Dark Spirit." Uncle Sam knows better and cries " 'WHOOPEE! you gotta be born and reared up in the swamps to think 'em up like that' He gives a puff and the smoke halo over Faulkner's head disintegrates with a little tinkle into a sprinkle of gold dust" (421). Coover pays tribute to Faulkner in his use of Tall Tale narration and in the trope of a master player as controlling creator. Yet Uncle Sam banishes Faulkner for his individual human-ism. Where Coover differs from Faulkner is that he never allows any individual character a victory, nor will he allow rhetorically or dra-matically for a conception of freedom through play for an individual character. Coover's commitment is to the fiction-making process itself, as firm as is Wolfe's commitment to the nonfictional social ground as subject.[6] Play suspends no oppressive relationships in *The Public Burning;* it simply performs them.

In *The Public Burning*'s best sporting scene, Coover portrays Nixon and Uncle Sam at the aptly-named "Burning Tree" Country Club where Sam "shazaams" out of President Eisenhower to confront Nixon with questions as to his knowledge about the true meaning of the Rosenberg affair. Nixon is awkward in reply and as plagued as Rabbit Angstrom on the golf course in *Rabbit, Run.* He muses, "I turned back to my ball, dug my feet firmly into the turf. Times Square, the circus atmosphere, the special ceremonies: form, *form,* that's what it always comes down to! In statesmanship get the for-malities right, never mind the moralities" (91). Nixon's pragmatism is also, on another level, Coover's aesthetic as well. In novels, get the rituals right, provide the performances, and the rest will follow.

All must be approached in the energy of forms. Uncle Sam exults, " 'Fer pleasure or pain, fer weal, fer woe,' he roars, walking softly but swinging a big bat, 'tis the law of our bein', we rips what we sew' " (64).

Uncle Sam's power is control to express and carnivalize the American reality. What Kesey portrayed as McMurphy's play to enhance the possibility of freedom in *Cuckoo's Nest*, Coover portrays as total control. Uncle Sam has a canvas to work on that is much larger than McMurphy's ward in *Cuckoo's Nest*. Uncle Sam creates his super-adversary, the Phantom, to stand for world communism, the threat of ultimate darkness. Uncle Sam creates his own Combine, his own collective evil. He is myth-maker of the Darkness and the Light: writer, director, and ritual hero. His overriding sense is that of motion and energy leading to renewal. His narrative is maniacal as he jerks his participants around in the play of his world. Coover relentlessly practices exposure, as in McGuane's burlesque of ritual sport in nature. "PANTS DOWN FOR DICK" carnivalizes Mailer's instinctive fears, Dickey's intense description, Kesey's transformations, and it politicizes buggery and violation into a transmogrified American violation, one that is willingly accepted in participation by the crowd.

Coover is the laureate of the American national body. His imagination makes Mailer's Hemingwayesque tension and individual violation seem solemn and restricted in comparison. Sam demands sacrifice; his role *is* his core. He shazaams into historical figures themselves, taking them over to commit predatory acts. McMurphy's living, creative laughter is malignant in Uncle Sam whose high languages of control are precisely the low popular languages of the community. Far from becoming a player who combats power, Uncle Sam creates the representation of American power itself in the Times Square ritual. The "truly strong man" of American ritual sport has shazaamed into the creator at play who is also the dreaded male other.

The full range of relations between ritual, competition, and play are also evident in *The Public Burning* as well. Uncle Sam desires to *Make Everything Me* by collectivizing the atavism in his creation of ritual, in which the Rosenbergs are used as sacrifices, and in his seduction of Nixon. Everything in *The Public Burning* is generated through his ego and domination. His publicly constructed battle with the Phantom is his own imagined *Victory Over Others,* the American "sporting" competition that he simulates, orders, and carries to a symbolic victory. *Play* is the control retained rigidly by Coover himself, casting the whole novel as performance in private and public spheres, which he plays between in his own freedom. Nixon preaches *Work With Others,* grudgingly giving up any essentials of self to Uncle Sam and to America in return for a share of power. He is a reluctant self-sacrifice to the team, identifying with Uncle Sam as a powerful "other" to influence events in historical time. Finally, *Make Me Other* is Nixon's cry as well, a desire to be incarnated, even in sexual humiliation. *"I . . . I love you, Uncle Sam"* (534) is an exclamation that might also contain "make me your son," "un-man me," and, with historical foreshadowing, "make me President." The most negative sublimity of personal obliteration is the necessity. Finally, Coover's dance of play as performance holds these violent ritualized responses in a tension in which Uncle Sam reigns.

Uncle Sam's power is unassailable in *The Public Burning.* Other Coover ritualists, including football's Gloomy Gus and baseball's Henry Waugh, are brought to grief in their quests for control. Coover totalizes what Mailer, Kesey, Dickey, and McGuane had exposed: the deep need for male control, most often expressed in the characterization of the "truly strong" males in ritual (Stephen Rojack, Lewis Medlock, Vernor Stanton, McMurphy, Hank Stamper), who want to make the natural environment or individuals or society "same" with or "like" themselves through ever more extreme physical testing and performance. Likewise, Coover's Nixon is a male anxious and paranoid about true strength and violation, a living rejoinder of WATCH OUT to Uncle Sam's NEVER GIVE AN INCH, and desirous of Uncle Sam's incarnation into himself as an American hero. Nixon calls to mind similar males in ritual sport texts: Rusty and D.J. Jethroe, Ed Gentry, Quinn, Chief Bromden, and Lee Stamper. Nixon's fate is to suffer violation by Uncle Sam himself, the necessary "anointing" to begin his incarnation. Nixon and Uncle Sam have been "killer brothers for the team," choosing the Rosenbergs as correct sacrifices to defeat the Phantom and once again save the American venture. Now Sam takes his pleasure by completing the double acts of murder and buggery so familiar in ritual sport narratives. He tells Nixon, "E pluribus the ole anum, buster, and on the double" (530) and "you wanta make it with me . . . you gotta love me like I really am" (531).

The last line is Coover's truth about America itself in all its contradictions but also true for Coover *himself* as novelist. Coover experienced a traumatic few years in the publishing and critical reception of his ambitious American mythic-historical text. He found it had been much safer and more critically acceptable to write of American ritual and history through the performance of American team sport than through the "performance" of the Rosenberg electrocutions, which he also saw as a "team sport," a performing of our nature as a nation. What Mailer attempted to explain through the violent sexuality of the individual body in its compulsive testing, Coover shifted to the national patriotic body, playing with the sacrifices. Few cultural agonies have called forth more ideologizing in the seemingly naturalized "body" politic than the Rosenberg affair where the stakes of interpretation are so very high for both the old and the new left, as well as for all varieties of Cold Warriors. This public passion of both the left and the right was not to be made into a performance, suggested Coover's critics. A last residual criticism of play as inadequate to portray American seriousness came crashing down on Coover.

Coover leaves little room for sympathy or identification in *The Public Burning*. The reader, too, is caught in the overdetermined ritualization of all the novel's elements. Only *authorial* play reigns in Coover, never play at the level of the characters' active control. All that possesses freedom or free will is the novel itself as a living organism, one so fully caught up in performance. The novel itself is the ritual where performance may be devastating and comic at the same time. Uncle Sam's last words to a raped Nixon, rolling on the floor in pain, are " 'Always leave 'em laughin' as you say good-bye' " (534), a familiar signature of closure in contemporary American metafiction from Barth to Coover to Pynchon.

Conclusion

MAILER, KESEY, and Coover are deeply drawn toward ritual process in writing of individual heroes. The ritual itself in their conceptualization and writing is most often a substitute for an American social ground. They respond with a need for ceremony in a country always making itself up. The lament of Hawthorne and James in the nineteenth century over a true definition of American society still haunts American novelists at the end of the twentieth century.

Within their use of ritual, different precursors and emphases prevail. Mailer feels the tension of Hemingway's need to dominate death and sexual anxiety. His rites are clearly sacrificial and predatory. His goal is to keep from becoming a victim, to return to the tribal fire with the luck, talent, and essence that he needs to do his work. Kesey, too, would bind experience toward himself as an avatar of synchronization and control. His obsession is to ride out the trip as far as it can go. Whatever it is, take it further through a psychic intuition rather than a predatory act. Coover desires control through the *author's* performance, through the audacity of the play that American ritual performance appears to totalize.

Mailer's imperative is terminal contest, sacrifice—the impulse to kill it. Kesey's goal is realization, illumination, representation—the impulse to become it. Coover's goal is realization, energy, creation —the impulse to perform it. Each author demonstrates an enormous competitiveness and a need to possess the stage with himself. Kesey had a more varied talent than Mailer and a playful relation to all his masks that re-contained his competitivness. As a writer exploring so many vantage points on ritual, competition, and play, he appeared to have played these vantage points to a stand-off. Coover, with the gifts of a powerful ceremonial and mimetic drive, a social historian's eye and ear, and the male extremity of a Mailer, willfully sets himself against all character identification and reader expectation: "You gotta love [him] like [he] really [is]" in the performance of his games.

Perhaps the sport that dominates each of their sporting experiences is most useful to explain their relation to physical competition. Mailer's first love in sport is boxing, which demands a concentration on predation within an enclosed space and a public display of victory or humiliation, often a life-and-death battle (see chapter 3). Kesey, the Olympic-calibre wrestler, works patiently to get a hold on you. He is binding, compelling, mesmerizing, always changing positions on the mat, coming at you from different angles with many holds, strongly masculine but no killer. How much, finally, is the physical act of the Chief's daring sacrifice of McMurphy an extension of Kesey's sports passion of wrestling? Coover's fascination with baseball and football shows his interest in the American collective's patterns and popular aesthetics, its myths and its histories.

The exaggerated maleness of the sport discussed in chapters 1–5 stems from the facets of ritual that demand a freezing or making rigid of all signifiers, over and over again. This continual image of erection in repetition is the dominant male performance principle that consumes so many of the characters in Dickey, McGuane, Mailer, Kesey, and Coover. This rigidity is a quest for male control over nature, over physiological process, over other people by domination or seduction. The fiction of ritual sports and play is rule-bound and encounter-ridden, with the freedom of play making only a small challenge to the body's need for self-definition.

Three specific modes or impulses are evident in ritual's attempt to deal with the power of nature and the pressures of society on the individual hero. The first, exemplified by Mailer and by characters such as Kesey's Hank Stamper, Dickey's Lewis Medlock, and Coover's Uncle Sam, is to dominate through terminal contest, to become the other's body through a ritual consumption. The second impulse is dissolution into the sublime, signifying "like" or "same," to "become the woods," or be "synched in" to another's moods and psyche, as Kesey is described by Wolfe in *Acid Test* (218). Finally, in the tragi-comic mirth of McMurphy and in major passages of *Notion*, Kesey suggests that the ironies of the mind may subvert the sublimity that *we* introduce into nature and society. Mailer creates no figure other than the truly erect male, Dickey and McGuane collapse this figure in despair. Kesey tries to present a dominant male figure along with laughter, role-playing, and fluidity. Unfortunately for fiction, this attempt did not achieve the synch and control of his vision itself, whereas Coover *did* achieve this vision in *The Public Burning*. Uncle Sam is Coover's fictional creation whereas Kesey in a silver space suit high in the Pranksters' "Tower of Control" at the Trips Festival (Wolfe 232) is in pure performance. Kesey lacks some final pessimism, some sense of original and historical sin born of grave metaphysical error or historical outrage, the marks borne by a Hawthorne and Faulkner. The desire to "make everything me" defines Kesey's move away from fiction and also Mailer's admitted difficulties with plot and characterization while, ironically, it defines Coover's aesthetic very well in the intensity of his fictional control. Control is the imperative at every level: competitive, performative, thematic, narrational.

The narration of ritual sport and play in contemporary American fiction becomes a pattern whereby the needs for competition, for victory, for domination are set against the pleasures of performance, of interaction. Wherever ego-mastery and male anxiety dictate the necessity of a final decision, competition defeats flow and ritual sport masters play.

6.

Women in Sports Narrative:
The Strategies of Mimicry

Because it's not such a simple thing when we say that whoever bears a masculine proper name, is anatomically male, etc., is a man. This feminine voice can pass through trajectories that are extremely multiple and altogether interior. Well, "interior" . . . Not really "interior." And it's reciprocal, since the same thing is going on on both sides of what can be thought of as a mirror. In other words, on the women's side, and even in the most feminist women, the masculine voice is not silent.

Jacques Derrida[1],

Ya just let a pussy beat ya, ya dumb asshole.

Terry Tingloff, Personal Best

THE EMPHASES on killing it, becoming it, performing it in the varied strands of individual male sport and play narrative portray a strong need for victory in competition or for control of the game and its rules. For the most part, the women in such texts are not foregrounded except as adversaries to some aspect of male physical self-definition. Such relationships abound in Mailer, Kesey, and in boxing fiction. Women never truly belong in any male ritual sports narrative except as problem, prey, or potential sacrifice.

Yet this is not the whole story by any means. A strong emerging representation of the individual sports hero is that of the female competitor and player in American sport. The volume of fiction concerned with women in sport and as players is still scant, but so far it is a narrative of varied strength that alters and plays with the traditional male domination in sport while remaining largely determined by it. Women in sport and play are "innocent" and "natural" at their peril, having known these assigned roles as subjugation in their own education. The contradictions of power and how to get it are at the heart of the inscription of women in sports fictional narrative.

It is in this place of contradiction about utility and non-utility, innocence and nostalgia, romance and the control of time, that the active role of women as competitors and players may best be seen. The social and cultural roles of the individual sports hero are similar to female roles. Like a male individual sports hero (but with less primary physical anxiety), a woman is separated from the dominant, conceived as a strong natural force, and idealized by society. The extension of the individual sports hero as hero-ine prompts speculation about the role of women in sports narra-tive through the conventional female roles of mate, mother, and commodity as well as on the competition and play that counter these roles. Such competition is the re-appropriated central fea-ture of the dominant male society while play once more attempts to break the competitive ethos, this time in the service of a posited feminine "elsewhere."

The Strategy of Mimicry

CONTEMPORARY FEMINIST theory provides several concepts with relevance to the role of women in sports and play. Such theory is emphatic that there can be at present no privileged place for female rhetoric beyond a masculine imaginary. All writing by and for women is thus forced into an "irrelevant grid" (Showalter 33). Almost no subject seems as irrelevant to women as that of sport-in-American society with its male-dominated, aggressive, competitive coming-of-age tales. American sports fiction has featured frontier roarers, ritual hunters, school sports leaders, publicly acclaimed heroes, and team members. These figures have been presented in martial rhetoric and in all varieties of male bonding, often precisely in reaction against the male fear of and fascination about the feminine. Yet women have competed successfully and brilliantly in sport from the heroines of both classical myth and record to the modern-day female Olympians. It may be precisely here, within sport, in the extremity of the masculine, that the feminine may best be presented in its difference. I suggest the importance of the female subject in sports narrative by referring to several texts—*Cat on a Hot Tin Roof* (1955), *The Hotel New Hampshire* (1981), *Personal Best* (1982), and *Water Dancer* (1982) —texts that are clearly related to the subject of the individual sports hero but that speculate more centrally on women's relation to sport and to play itself.

Sociological research into the play of girls, as to how it may differ from the play of boys, yields perspective on women's sport and play narrative. Brian Sutton-Smith stresses the aspect of narrativity itself, that girls have a commitment to staging their play, whereas boys are the action-oriented players. Girls' socio-dramatic episodes are more involved than those of boys, have more imaginary objects, and are more inter-active and cooperative (Sutton-Smith 239–40). Girls in play tend to avoid direct competitiveness and model the nuclear family in small groups bound together by love and rejection of outsiders. Such involved dramatic episodes, cooperative and family-centered, well describe Albee's dynamic in *Who's Afraid of Virginia Woolf* as well as the narcissistic rituals and play of the Berry family in *The Hotel New Hampshire,* which is dominated by both female violation and female play. Sutton-Smith describes an "affiliative" rather than an "achievement" orientation to girls' play (244). He stresses that girls frame play as a fairy tale with images of hearth, family, and marriage set against boys' play, which is framed in myths about the larger society, about enemies, fate, and mortality (244).

The potential for the clashes of difference in girls' and boys' play is enormous. The boys' play as myth propounded by Sutton-Smith certainly describes the activities of the male individual sports hero (chapters 1–5) in his wariness about body, "others," pain, and death. Girls' play is more representational and mimetic. The ritualization of this play is not primarily agonistic (the basis for competitive games), nor is it sacrificial (the crisis point in male ritual sport); rather it is *mimetic* in complex ways. This description of girls' play appears to underscore the findings of sociologists such as Nancy Chodorow who in *The Reproduction of Mothering* (1978) states that a key difference between the identity formation of boys and girls is that girls never have to transfer their original bond of identity with the mother in order to love the father or another man. Girls may continue to identify themselves with the relatedness to the mother while adding other roles.

Such empirically based research, helpful as it is to describe female play, is still playing off its differences from the male dominant. More radical feminist theory opposes the whole relation of female identity to the masculine and finds play as one potential response to it. The work of the French psychoanalyst and philosopher-linguist Luce Irigaray is most important in this regard. Her analyses are cogent for a discussion of the individual sports hero-ine in three separate areas: female body image and tactile sense, women as commodities in an exchange market, and women as potential players.

In *This Sex Which Is Not One* (1977; trans. 1985), Irigaray posits a feminine style of writing that would be tactile, simultaneous, and fluid, one "that is never fixed in the possible identity-to-self of some form or other" (79). She metaphorically creates this style from her image of vaginal lips ceaselessly caressing each other: "As for woman, she touches herself in and of herself without any need for mediation, and before there is any way to distinguish activity from passivity" (24). Woman's writing imagines as woman's body experiences and is opposed to the male's blunt intrusive phallic economy of hardest, biggest, most erect, "coming once," etc. Hence Irigaray's woman's modes of experiencing are of ceaseless flow, spontaneity, and touch. The male look or gaze is supplanted by the female touch. The female acceptance within self of an "other" counters the male terror of "other." For women, self-touching and self-affection are an inter-play within themselves.

Women both "are" physically and are inscribed in a socio-cultural process (A. R. Jones 363). That process is explained in Irigaray's chapter "Women on the Market," in which she states that men make commerce of women in a phallic economy but do not enter into any exchange with them (172). Women as commodities have two essential characteristics, a "matter-body" and "an envelope that is precious but impenetrable, ungraspable" (176). Such categorization well describes the defining characteristics of the sports natural as well. How can these characteristics survive together in one image, either in that of the male sports hero or heroine?

They survive together because they define both the desired physical body and the idealized romantic body. These bodies are both ravished and aestheticized; in each case, the image is of hoarding and possession. This possession is never exhausted even as the "golden moment" of some athletic triumph is always already past, yet desired again. Over and over, the experience of the women in sport and play narrative re-creates an Irigaray maxim: "the economy of exchange—of desire—is man's business" (177; emphasis Irigaray's). The body ravished/aestheticized and then exchanged is, for example in Vladimir Nabokov's *Lolita* (1955), a concise description of the alternate currents of Humbert Humbert's self-loathing and artful writing, as well as his rage and revenge over Claire Quilty's abduction of Lolita.[2] Women as commodities portray in the most intense fashion the marginalization, utility, and fetishizing of the individual sports hero-ine. Women in sport and sports fiction do not achieve the vantage point of anti-hero-ines since women always have a matter-body that must be represented. As collective sports hero-ines they may achieve competitive fame while remaining commodities that are exchanged, as are male sports heroes. The coding of women dictates that, as matter bodies, they are constantly described and written about in a language that is not their own. They are dictated into becoming no-voiced beings, in sports fiction's most convenient representation, as naturals.

Irigaray has also added an important dimension to the scope of play and its relation to a thematics of freedom by designating a feminine mimicry as the appropriate path to a true woman's discourse. The passage bears quoting in full:

> There is, in an initial phase, perhaps only one "path," the one historically assigned to the feminine: that of *mimicry*. One must assume the feminine role deliberately. Which means already to convert a form of subordination into an affirmation, and thus to begin to thwart it. Whereas a direct feminine challenge to this condition means demanding to speak as a (masculine) "subject," that is, it means to postulate a relation to the intelligible that would maintain sexual indifference. To play with mimesis is thus, for a woman, to try to recover the place of her exploitation by discourse, without allowing herself to be simply reduced to it. It means to resubmit herself—inasmuch as she is on the side of the

"perceptible," of matter—to "ideas," in particular to ideas about herself, that are elaborated in/by a masculine logic, but so as to make "visible," by an effect of playful repetition, what was supposed to remain invisible: the cover-up of a possible operation of the feminine in language. It also means "to unveil" the fact that, if women are such good mimics, it is because they are not simply resorbed in this function. *They also remain elsewhere:* another case of the persistence of "matter," but also of "sexual pleasure." (76)

Here is a familiar rhetoric of liberation through the play of representation, one associated with the projects of Marcuse and Jameson as descended from Schiller. Play within the dominant holds off its oppression and opens a space, an "elsewhere," while exposing the truth of power relations. The male individual sports hero will complacently stop at the place of "exploitation" in the physical act, in the separateness there with his desire fulfilled. He has no text beyond this point whereas a woman has a political agenda in trying to recover the place of exploitation in order to expose it. In this case, the male dominant's transactions are mimed while the reserving of a persistent residue of pleasure is one of the woman's tasks in play. Such play is always oriented toward the creation of an authentic female language, as much of a "not-yet" as in any conceptual community in Jameson or Marcuse. Irigaray's play in her feminist analysis has direct structural relation to a Marxist appropriation of play as both "a repetition" and a "staving off" of oppression.

However, Irigaray's play is most essentially Derridean. Her play that makes "visible" the ideas "elaborated in/by a masculine logic" recalls the Derrida of "Structure, Sign, and Play" who stipulated that the "play beyond" must pass beyond man, "the name of man being the name of that being who . . . has dreamed of full presence, the reassuring foundation, the origin and the end of play" (292). Such a "name" and "foundation" is the certainty of male power that female mimicry would confront. Irigaray's disruption of presence is the play that converts "subordination into an affirmation," a double reading of play that re-creates Derrida's gloss of "Structure, Sign, and Play" with "Differance" (see introduction).

Irigaray's identification of re-presentation as a fundamental female strategy has been seized on by many of her commentators. Mary

Jacobus lauds the identification and, in analysing the above passage envisions that woman would "find herself on the side of everything in language that is multiple, duplicitous, unreliable, and resistant to binary oppositions" (40). Within the masculine extremity, a certain hysterical re-presentation would identify the female voice while retaining the critical power to attack it. Domna Stanton has written that the emphasis on female difference in Irigaray is the latest articulation of the philosophy of difference that has permeated philosophy since Heidegger and that has been expressed most prominently by Derrida (Stanton 158). In his recent writings Derrida has consistently referred to the play of difference as feminine, what Alice Jardine has named *Gynesis:* "The putting into discourse of 'woman' as that process beyond the Cartesian Subject, the Dialectics of Representation, or Man's Truth" (Jardine 58). In *Spurs,* Derrida wrote, "She who, unbelieving, still plays with castration, she is 'woman.' She takes aim and amuses herself [*en joue*] with it as she would with a new concept or structure of belief, but even as she plays she is gleefully anticipating her laughter, her mockery of man" (61). While Derrida believes that "the feminine distance abstracts truth from itself in a *suspension* of the relation with castration" (59), he concludes that "woman remains nonetheless within the economy of truth's system, in the phallogocentric space" (97).

Stanton has similar reservations about the ability of difference to remain other when uttered/written in the male economy/language. In its "miming of phallocentric scenes and semes," different always risks the "traces of same," of being re-appropriated without alternative voice. Thus a maternal metaphor, for example, of the unrepresented/unrepresentable feminine is "recuperated into scenes of representation that this maternal discourse aims to shatter" (159–61). As discussed in chapters 1–5, the male aim in the ritual sport narrative is to make everything "like" and "same," especially in Mailer's work. To play against that aim would be, in feminist terms, to be different, to be other, to be feminine itself. The essence of metaphoricity is, logically, to be masculine, while the essence of metonymity is to be feminine. The hypotheses for the heroes and heroines of sport and play fiction are as follows: that the individual sports hero in his desire for "like" and "same" space is fundamentally signifying masculinity; that the individual sports hero in his or her desire to be "other" and "different" and to control time in making it "like an-other time" is signifying a desire for difference, for uniqueness that leads to a fetishization akin to that of the female's inscription in male-dominated discourse. For example, the School Sports Hero (see chapter 7) is not often female but shares much of the feminine coding, which is why "he" upsets mightily the desiring imagination of males such as Gene Forrester in *A Separate Peace* and Proctor in *The Huge Season* in the sublimated elements of homoeroticism in the novels.

However, exposure of the present and change in the future are central to any feminist agenda for play. Stanton concludes with a criticism of Irigaray's mimicry analysis, that the "adoption of the mimetic function . . . may freeze and fixate the feminine at the mirror stage, rather than lead to a difference beyond the same old binary plays" (172). Here is the familiar scepticism toward play theory in the question of what is the play playing *towards*? In the service of whose interest? Towards what definition of freedom? The leftist suspicion of play as a licensed vent for excess energy that only re-writes in the dominant economy/discourse is a spectre raised here against the intense feminist interpretation of the play mode. Stanton concludes in a pointed challenge to all the rhetorics of play that "sameness permeates all attempts to speak difference" (173). We now turn to specific examples of men and women at play and in competition in sports fictional narratives as they play out the opposition of "same" and "different."

Cat on a Hot Tin Roof: Maggie Re-Gendered

CONTRADICTIONS OF "same" and "different" surrounding the role of the female player can be seen in the conflicts of Maggie the Cat in Tennessee Williams' *Cat on a Hot Tin Roof*. *Cat* features a vintage individual sports hero in Maggie's husband, Brick Pollitt, an ex-college and professional quarterback, who is fixated on the death of his teammate and close friend, Skipper. Brick is cool and self-contained in the false repose of despair about his relationship with Skipper. His guilt is massive over the love offered by Skipper and his failure to respond to it. His emblem of school sports perfection is the memory of throwing long, graceful passes to Skipper with no complications and no physical contact. Here is the origin-al state Brick would remain in if he could. Brick and Skipper found it easier to be symbolic killer brothers for the team than to have sex with Maggie or with each other.

The drama of *Cat* centers on Maggie's attempt to reclaim Brick through her sensuality, to recall him to life. However, this drama also features a series of transactions that involve economic power struggles for the Pollitt estate in the certainty that Brick's father, Big Daddy Pollitt, is dying of cancer. All of Maggie's ingenuity and play will recall Brick both as lover and as potential new patriarch. Her power is never hers alone to wield for herself. The power lies in continuance of the Pollitt male line through Brick.

Maggie's struggles are those of a heroic player and nominally appear to alter power relationships. For much of the drama, Brick is the passive sex object, reclining on a bed with his liquor, "still slim and firm as a boy" (Williams 17), whereas Maggie's "voice has range, and music; sometimes it drops low as a boy's and you have a sudden image of her playing boys' games as a child" (18). Her frustration with Brick's "cool air of detachment" (17) leads her to struggle for a new definition. Unloved, she feels she's "gone through this—*hideous!*—*transformation, become*—*hard! Frantic!*—*cruel!!*" (22; emphasis Williams'). Assuming a more dominant role, she concludes, "But one thing I don't have is the charm of the defeated, my hat is still in the ring and I am determined to win" (25).

Maggie's aim is once again to place both Brick and herself in the phallic economy. To do so, she desperately announces that she is pregnant to the assembled family on Big Daddy's darkest night when he learns the truth of his death sentence from cancer. She counters with her play, the lie that may save Brick's position within the family, counter the death-dread, and win Brick back to her bed. She plays to win Brick his rights of inheritance. In effect, she on her own has created the unborn child. Brick as individual sports hero has two doubles in *Cat:* the dead Skipper and his child-to-be-conceived. Maggie has inserted herself between Brick and Skipper, who had been mortified into making love to Maggie to prove his heterosexuality and, having failed, began his decline toward death. Now Maggie asks Brick to share responsibility in new life as well as in Skipper's death.

Yet rather than suppplying the male witness's response to demand the sacrifice of the individual sports hero, Maggie manipulates the hero in order to play for his humanity; she competes for Brick and his paternity and wins him through touch. In her singularity, Maggie battles the ghost of Skipper for Brick. She must compete by willing her role as exchange object to keep the Pollitt line intact and she does so by the power of *naming,* traditionally denied to women. With regard to Brick and Skipper's love, she says, "I'm not naming it dirty! I am naming it clean" (44). Finally, she names her pregnancy: "A child is coming, sired by Brick, and out of Maggie the Cat. I have Brick's child in my body an' that's my birthday present to Big Daddy on [his] birthday" (153).

Maggie's play-child is a gift on the altar of male supremacy. Her victory has been (or will be) to restore Brick to that supremacy. Maggie's maternal metaphor, doubly metaphorical since she is only "like" pregnant through language, would restore "sameness," the established order, through her traditional role as wife and mother. Her play has been a temporary assertion of power, to ally herself with it. In Sutton-Smith's terms of girls' play, she has avoided direct competitiveness but has confronted her deprivation through an imaginative pretense, one that would model a nuclear family and save a marriage and line through the assertion of maternity. The individual sports hero is potentially saved, not sacrificed, by the multiple roles of the female player who may cease play when and if Brick assumes his phallic role. At the conclusion of *Cat,* however, male "sameness" permeates all attempts to speak female "difference." Maggie has "recovered the place of her exploitation." Brick has been retrieved from "elsewhere." Maggie's power is firmly in the male dominant. Ultimately, her "residue of pleasure" is dependent on Brick's compliance and Big Daddy's approval. In staging the scenes of Brick's recuperation, Maggie has mimed "phallocentric scenes and semes" and has heroically re-presented the feminine and the maternal.

The Hotel New Hampshire: Tough Girls at Play

JOHN IRVING has contributed a bizarre addition to play fiction as well as to the school sport and hero-witness tradition in *The Hotel*

New Hampshire (1981). The novel is obsessively family-centered and its heroic models are female. Through the characters of Lilly and Franny Berry and Susie the Bear, Irving has identified all the subjects of woman's relation to the male dominant—rape, incest, commodification, and control. He has played fast and loose with these subjects and has been both complacent and sensationalized in recognizable postmodern modes. He effects a yearning for the simple securities of domestic life in what may be construed as a neo-realistic fairy tale, while he assaults that mode through the violent, erotic action of the blockbuster melodrama. These plot actions are presented in a didactic narration heavily controlled by authorial metaphor and manipulation. The female players so ostentatiously featured by Irving within this drama are finally absorbed in their difference back into the "same" of heterosexual male society.

At the center of *Hotel* is the Berry family. The novel is narrated by John Berry who is hopelessly in love with his sister, Franny, the hero of the family and of the novel. The Berry children, including John, Franny, Lilly, and brothers Frank and "Egg" attend Dairy School in New Hampshire, a prep school more out of Evelyn Waugh than John Knowles. Father Win Berry teaches English and grandfather "Coach Bob" coaches the football team. The uniforms are brown and gray; "shit and death" are the school colors, says Franny. Everything in *Hotel* is domesticated to the opinions and sensibilities of the Berrys who are so winning as to rival contemporary American fiction's other cutest family, Salinger's Glass family. It is probably no coincidence that we have Franny Berry (Glass).

Irving lets overt sexuality dominate the school narrative as he did in *The World According to Garp* (1978). His schoolboy quarterback, Chipper Dove, is a rapist, while Franny Berry—innocent, natural, heroic, romantic—is the victim-heroine. Franny as natural is raped in chapter 4, "Franny Loses A Fight," in which Coach Bob's backfield on Halloween night takes revenge on John, Frank, and Franny Berry for prior school battles. Franny is attacked and John is humiliated in his attempts to save her. Liberation is provided by Junior Jones, a huge black lineman, whose "Black Arm of the Law" (consisting of the school's few black students) seeks out the offending backfield and brings them to justice in a dark night of slapstick and violence.

John Berry's passion for Franny is only exorcised in a day-long bout between them that they hope will annihilate their passion for each other. Here, Irving returns to wrestling, the individual sport central to his earlier novels, *The 158–Pound Marriage* (1974) and *Garp,* in which violent and murderous climaxes occur in the wrestling arena, including the murder of T. S. Garp. In *Hotel,* Franny herself proposes and dominates the ritual love-making during which she and John physically grapple with each other beyond endurance, their sex organs worn raw and bleeding. A new sexual science is born: incest aversion therapy. The scene is one of the most banal and unpleasant in recent fiction with Irving determined to utterly demystify incestuous relations into trivial fantasy as his smug, knowing children fuck themselves into exhaustion. The incest scene is one in which the act itself is reified through the ugliest of commodified terminology. Franny, as always, speaks in the most macho language as Irving appears determined to re-gender her linguistically into the toughest of guys by having her try to convert a repellent form of subordination into affirmation. After several hours, John whispers that they had better stop: "'We better *not* stop,' Franny said fiercely. . . . 'I want you a *lot* sore,' Franny said. 'Top or bottom?' she asked me grimly" (333).

Franny is consistently referred to as the mother to all the characters in the novel, or as Irving has her put it with typical charm, "From now on, I'm mainly a *mother* . . . I'm going to take care of you fuckers" (233). Franny without question becomes what Irigaray has called the "nourishing phallic mother" of male discourse (Irigaray 77). Within this role, she talks dirty, takes on responsibility for the family's development, and controls the action. Franny is the mother to them all, the "family star" (383) who winds up in Hollywood playing herself in an adaptation of Lilly's best-seller about the Berry family. Franny is Irving's author as mother, where in a family-dominated tale, the novel is incest.

Lilly Berry described her family's life as "a fairy tale" (335), a sentiment seconded by John Berry. Again, the play images in the novel surround home, marriage, the family, in direct counterpoint to male myth. The most important play scene in this "fairy tale" is the reenactment of Franny's rape trauma in New York City when Lilly directs and writes a pageant designed to terrify Chipper Dove, one that features every member of the Berry menage. Here again are identifiable characteristics of girls' play: deprivation, family, sociodrama, a model of a nuclear family, and a uniting against outsiders.

The rape play is performed within a female parlor setting with recognizable roles of brides and hotel maids. The drama includes vivid costumes and make-up. The scene is dominated by a mode that can only be described as "hysteria." Indeed, Julia Kristeva suggests that women describe as hysterics, as those who are outsiders and marginal to male-dominated culture: "Their semiotic style is likely to involve repetitive, spasmodic separations from the dominating discourse, which, more often, they are forced to imitate" (A. R. Jones 363). The Berry family rape pageant both simulates the violation and keens against it as it attempts to bring Franny into "control" of her rape. It is clear that Irving counts it as a dramatic and therapeutic success. However, the scene also suggests that, far from being a feminist victory for the Berrys and their role players, the rape pageant is still only an uncomfortable exercise in simulated male aggression.

A central performer in miming the madness of Franny's rape is her staunch friend and lover, Susie the Bear. Bears have been shamans and talismans for Irving since his first novel, *Setting Free the Bears* (1968). In *The Hotel New Hampshire,* Susie the Bear is a young woman in a bear suit whom the Berry family meets in Vienna. She is an insecure Sarah Lawrence drop-out with "dark damp hair," a "pale pock-marked face," and "haggard nervous eyes," a burly woman whose only authority comes when she dons the bear's head and suit and performs activities such as rooting around crotches with impunity. She is totally alienated from her own female body, consumed by its supposed ugliness and inferiority (Gardiner 190). She thus joins Franny and Lilly in this regard, Franny as rape victim and Lilly as dwarf who writes obsessively, "trying to grow" as a novelist.

Irving, however, is not interested in allowing Franny and Susie's love to have any dominion in his tale. Susie is a grotesque, albeit a plucky one, and Franny is destined by Irving to confront heterosexual desire in her brother, John, and in a simulated reunion with quarterback Chipper Dove. It is in the rape pageant where Susie stars in one final bear's bravura performance. She acts out the menacing violation of a terrified Chipper Dove in the Berrys' hotel suite while

Franny dressed as a spectre bridegroom watches with Lilly, Frank, and John dressed in appropriate character roles. Irving clearly suggests that this rape pageant brings Franny into "ownership" of her rape, of both her anger and her pain. Even Susie is described as never having to put on her bear suit again. Irving has correctly shown the miming as a female response to the male dominant and has championed the control achieved by the Berrys. And yet, we may ask, in line with Stanton's analysis, how this mimesis does more than mirror the domination itself? What can "owning" a rape possibly mean? Do the women—Lilly, Franny, Susie—gain any control by their play other than another simulated domination through fear?

The answer is that they do not. Lilly is a suicide, not big enough or strong enough to match her literary promise with literary production. Then again, perhaps she kills herself because she cannot take one more repetition of Irving's "trying to grow" metaphor. Franny is always brave and strong, a serious romantic inflation of an individual sports heroine. She ultimately marries Junior Jones, past his NFL career and now a militant black lawyer. As a final gift to John, her brother/lover/son, she "wills" him her and Junior's child to be raised by Susie and John. Susie's post-bear heroics include running a rape crisis center and finally becoming the wife and lover of John Berry, who convinces her that she does not have a "face like a hatchet, like a chisel with a bad complexion," a body "like a paper bag full of oatmeal" (386). In Irving's last truly tasteless metaphor, Susie fears giving birth, for "I might not even *have* a baby—I might give birth to a kind of *banana!*" (389). The excessive violence done to and described by female bodies in *Hotel* is finally unrelenting.[3] Never has a novel purportedly sympathetic to women tried to persuade the reader that a requisite amount of male obscenity and aggression should convince us that tough women are possessing their own language and actions. In Irving's hands, play in female mimicry appears to give the control to become a good domestic heterosexual.

Susie and Franny are calmly and resolutely won over to heterosexuality and maternity. Any difference that may have concluded their narratives is collapsed back into "same." Like Maggie the Cat, their heroic play has been in the service of male domination. This final restoration of a masculine norm in a novel so self-congratulatory on its liberation and celebration of women is, one suspects, a pattern beyond Irving's imagining. His attempt at a fairy tale is more of a male myth of phallic power—of enemies vanquished, fates secured, and mortality countered by the imagination. "One must assume the feminine role deliberately," writes Irigaray. Irving has done so but with little control or knowledge of his own re-contained outcome which is controlled by his dependence on metaphor. Women's role in play and sports narrative awaited texts not so obsessively manipulated by male domination.

Personal Best: Nurture and Competition

ROBERT TOWNE's film *Personal Best* is cinema's most sympathetic portrayal of female athletes in competitive and emotional relations. The film strives mightily to accord personal and athletic dignity and seriousness to the female athlete. There is no more intimate record of women in sport. As writer and director, Towne cares enough to present women working hard at their sport as vocation and the film's photography graces the female body in the agon as the track and field performers go through their training and meets. Towne also depicts a female sports culture that includes locker rooms, parties, and individual relationships. However, it is Towne's narrative that is of most interest here, for *Personal Best* rehearses the familiar problems of women in sport and play, to wit their necessity to perform and compete within a very powerful and extreme example of male discourse. Here, the sports arena is a site of revelation where the representation of sport through female participants underscores the familiar male dominance at the same time it raises the possibility of authentic female difference in competition and cooperation.

Torey Skinner (Patrice Donnelly) and Chris Cahill (Mariel Hemingway) are the young competitors and lovers whose evolving relationship is the primary subject of *Personal Best*. Torey is the older athlete, dark, aggressive, more powerful. Chris is more the innocent, psychically fragile natural in the state of becoming. Torey is the more mature runner who at the film's outset makes the 1976 Olympic Team while Chris fails at the trials. Soon after the trials, Torey and Chris become lovers in a long and tender scene that physically begins with playful arm-wrestling; for three years, they live and train together. Torey arranges for Chris to practice with her own excellent track team and helps her toughen up to believe in herself as an athlete. The shifting roles in the relationship are signaled at an international competition in Colombia when Chris eats bad fruit and is seriously cramped and nauseous the night before the pentathlon. Torey nurses her through the night; in the next day's competition, Torey is ragged while Chris does well. The middle section of the film is primarily about understanding their training and successes. It includes memorable visual scenes of running uphill in sand during work-outs and of slow-motion high jumps.

After Torey provides Chris with a new approach-run technique in the high jump, Chris badly misses her take-off mark and dislocates and shatters her knee. Their male coach, Terry Tingloff (Scot Glenn), instinctively decides that Torey had, out of jealousy, moved the mark so that Chris would be injured. He sets up the wedge that separates Chris in her physical agony from Torey who is in mute bewilderment and pain over the incident. It is at this juncture that the male coach's plot line takes over *Personal Best,* and Torey and Chris lose their alternative relationship and status. Coach Tingloff constructs an account of Chris's injury that features Torey as villain, with Chris as her enemy. He portrays victims, aggression, and competitive obsession. His discrediting of the women's relationship reveals most clearly the male dominance. The coach's narrative of events is the male competitive anxiety tale that will master all of Torey and Chris's affiliation and love and will compel them to live in it. Coach Tingloff conceives of the "killer sisters" to match his idea of male adversaries in wary competition. Such a dark narrative closely resembles Gene Forrester's own initial version of his moment in the tree with Phineas in *A Separate Peace* when the limb moves and Phineas comes crashing down.

Personal Best is suffused with images of patriarchy and the language of a competitive ethos from the outset. Towne conceives of no other phrasing and framing for his female athletes. The very first words in the film come from the male voice on the public address system at a track meet: "If you're not competing, please clear the area." Next we hear, "I'm sorry, Daddy," as Chris apologizes for losing a hurdles race. Then comes Coach Tingloff's opening question to Torey, "What the fuck you think you're doin'?," as she watches

Chris in another race. The terms of *Personal Best*'s competitive language are set. When Torey and Chris meet and speak about their lives, Torey muses about a male lover-pole vaulter, "If the son of a bitch could have cleared 17'6", we'd still be together," a rueful and knowing comment on male need for self-esteem in the athletic sphere transferred to the sexual sphere with an already sports-successful female partner. When they arm-wrestle, Chris exclaims, "I'm gonna whip your ass!" Before love-making, Chris says to Torey that she is *like* her, according to Chris's brother, "a carpenter's dream, flat as a board and easy to nail." The boyish body image, the sexual slang, and the naming itself come from the male. Such is Chris and Torey's only common language about the body.

That language has its strongest representation in Tingloff who not only sees competitive advantage everywhere but who is personally involved with Torey and Chris and who uses Chris's injury to punish them both. The film makes clear his attraction to Torey and his pain when she cannot reciprocate and chooses to live with Chris. When Tingloff becomes Chris's coach, he pushes her to become a pentathlete by placing her in direct competition with Torey not only on the track but also for his favor, that of the coach-father. Even before Chris's injury, Tingloff challenges Chris, "What scares you more? Beating Torey Skinner or getting beat by her?" Towne keeps us distant from Tingloff's motivation most of the time; but suggests Tingloff is as confused and contradictory about his relation to female athletes as they are toward him as coach-father.

Torey herself assumes Tingloff's dominant role for awhile. Chris: "Why would Tingloff want to coach me?" Torey: "Because I said so." Torey later appears jealous of Chris and Tingloff. Towne suggests an alternate reason for Torey's coaching Chris and urging her to move her starting mark. It's not simply Torey's fear of track competition but fear of competition for the favor of the coach-father. Towne makes us believe that in the male-female clash in the sports arena, no action is clear-cut in regard to the characters' motives and feelings. All transpires in an uncharted territory where traditional male power is vied for, compromised, and asserted again.

Tingloff puts both Torey and Chris through a bad trip. After her injury, as he imposes his paranoid view of Torey's action, he exposes his own frustration at coaching women in sport and reveals a frac-

tured male perspective in a very funny monologue. Tingloff's movement around his apartment provides mixed images of his domestic
and paternal roles. He's shown doing his own ironing; his refrigerator is stocked with many flavors of ice cream for his "patient." Chris
is buried in blankets and snuffling, in great physical and emotional
pain. Tingloff as male coach-father-lover alternately sympathizes with
her and rails at her about the incomprehensibility of the female
athletic and sexual "other." He militantly asks, "How can you be
more frightened of me than of being hurt?" He then adds, "All
you're worried about is your fucking girl friend" and "She's crippled
you"; he rips the phone out of the wall when Chris anxiously hopes
a call is from Torey. "I could've been backfield coach at Oregon
State," he says, shifting his speech to the more secure male terrain of
"same." Then, musing about the life of a professional men's coach,
he wonders, does Chuck Noll have to worry that Franco Harris is
gonna cry 'cause Terry Bradshaw won't talk to him? That Lynn
Swann is pregnant? That Rocky Bleier forgot his tampax?

Chris attempts to apologize for her display of emotion but once
again her behavior is incomprehensible to him. Her tears make him
furious as they undermine his edge, his truth. He sneers at her, "Go
home, kiss, fuck, eat each other, whatever the hell you do," the
visceral male challenge to the unknown and traumatic (hence unrepresented) male vision of female love-making. He wants to see her
express real anger. As he continues to strive for a reaction, Tingloff
tells Chris a joke about a passive gay male and then challenges her,
"I wish ya had the balls to hit me." Whereupon Chris gives him a
strong punch in the jaw, and he grimaces, "Do ya always have to do
what I tell ya to do?" When he attempts the almost obligatory
seduction of Chris, knee cast, ice pack, and all, he whispers, "Don't
worry, babe. We'll watch the knee." She stops him with: "Sure.
Make sure I have magnesium, calcium, whatever else you think I'll
need." Her anger is directed toward the coach-father, not simply the
seducer. She has read the male's line and countered it.

Through this reflexive scene of the male athlete's language applied
to the role of the female other in sport, Towne reveals the gaps, the
hostility, the differing modes of male-female response to career, to
competition, to separation. If Tingloff can instill his narrative in the
girls, he can make them become like him in his patterns and defeat

their otherness. To answer Coach Tingloff's berating, his witty transposition of female troubles into jock bravado, Chris has her silence and her tears—and finally a good straight right, though even that is at Tingloff's behest. Towne provides her with no alternative language to brave the laws of sportsworld, no phrasing of her own beyond his obscene casting of body parts and sexual acts, except for her instinct to make Tingloff more comfortable, which is equally enraging to him. Towne gives Tingloff in his frustration an intimation of his own absurdity and Chris is a fine dramatic foil. This scene at the heart of the film's narrative shows the male athlete's language and culture are irreconcilable with the female athletic response within that domination.

After this scene, *Personal Best* wanders off toward a more conventional recuperation of Chris Cahill's knee, her growing maturity, and her reclamation as a suitable heterosexual partner. During her rehabilitation, she meets and is attracted to an ex-Olympic swimmer named Denny (Kenny Moore). She and Denny are more equal. They trade training suggestions and he is not in the primary competition. Towne provides more comic visual representations of "innocent" male desire. Denny bumps his head on the pool edge as he gazes at Chris' body underwater; he blows up her crotch as she spots for him while he lifts weights; she holds his penis while he pees. Denny finally delivers the film's athletic and competitive moral, that in sports, "all you're tryin' to do is whip your own ass," Towne's most encompassing truth for both male and female athletes.

Torey Skinner is almost banished from *Personal Best* during Chris' recovery. Hurt, bewildered, she is now the athlete struggling to make the 1980 Olympic team in the pentathlon. Coach Tingloff, still writing the narrative, cautions Chris about Torey, "Don't kid yourself. You're here to kill anybody who gets in your way. The rest is bullshit." Chris, however, ignores him, wishes Torey good luck, and in the second day of competition, way ahead on points, runs herself out as rabbit in the 800–meter run so that other runners will be exhausted and Torey can get enough points to make the Olympic squad. After the race, Chris beams at Tingloff who, for once, has no male line to hand her. Her cooperative action defeats his language.

Ads for *Personal Best* asked "HOW DO YOU COMPETE WITH A BODY YOU'VE ALREADY SURRENDERED TO YOUR

OPPONENT?" Such a limited casting of the central drama has everything to say about the anxieties of the male competitor but little to say about the realities of Chris and Torey's relationship. *Personal Best* has shown how women can battle for and with women, taking turns in competing and nurturing without losing sight of their bonds with each other on the track. Torey and Chris take turns in both desiring and maternal roles. Just as pointedly, Torey vies with Tingloff in the paternal role while Chris *and* Torey compete for his coach's favor. The imperatives of girls' play are seen to coexist with the male coach's view. The women focus on deprivation, the coach on competitors' villainy. The women stress affiliation, the coach sees enemies and plays the women against each other. The women stress a sensitivity to a particular other, the coach values duty to the organization, the team, the competition. From beginning to end, from their locker-room banter, brave obscenities, stoic resistance to pain, and hard-earned sweat, these athletic women have been deep within the masculine ethos.

With Chris claimed by Denny, Torey is left alone at film's end without even the heterosexual partner Irving gives Susie the Bear in *Hotel*. Hollywood and sports narrative in general still have no continuing role for an unregenerate lesbian to play. Even as Torey has come from nowhere, with no family and past (unlike Chris), she has no future. On the public level, *Personal Best* shows us no lesbian community nor even any censure from society (Straayer 42–43).[4] The film's last lines serve only to lighten everything back to surface banter. As they wait on the victory stand, Torey allows to Chris that Denny is "awful cute for a guy." Chris' last words copy her initial naivete about most everything in the film: "Are you shittin' me?" This lame question underscores a truth about *Personal Best:* Its sporting heroines give lessons in integrating cooperation with competition but their language together has always been that of the male sports world. They are Irigaray's "good mimics." Towne has no language for them as desiring women beyond the one scene of arm-wrestling that segues into love-making and suggests multiple touch but actually stops quite chastely in foreplay. The scene stands for the entirety of their desiring relationship; we do not see them again as lovers. Their physical definition will continually be through athletics, not in bed.

The truth about the presentation of female athletes is that it is always eroticized by the fact that within the male gaze, *any* movement of the female body is erotic. Even without athletic movement, the female body always presents a diffuse, multiple eroticism of limbs and torso, face and hair. When the subject of the gaze is women in athletics, a violently contradictory set of signs applies. Male bodies in competition are precisely the deeply sublimated erotic bodies in culturally coded and acceptable combat and touching within the rules. Women in sport are always and directly erotic within a male symbol system of physical competition and rules designed to sublimate the erotic. Men in sport displace their eroticism onto the activity whereas women display it. HOW DO YOU COMPETE WITH A BODY YOU'VE ALREADY SURRENDERED TO YOUR OPPONENT? would be a forbidden question actually to ask males in sport. To "surrender to an opponent" for a male means defeat, violation, and death. To "surrender to an opponent" for a female within a male discourse is a seduction, a victory as defined by that discourse for the male. The lines are drawn. Women in sport have entered an exceptionally volatile gender-coded arena of signification. The conception of mimicry, of female play, is vivified in the sports arena because it impinges upon fundamental male defenses. For women to continue a relatedness toward each other in competition is to retain an autonomy (in Chodorow's terms). For women to remain "elsewhere" in Irigaray's terms, while acting out their own domination is, in sport, a complex role. On the one hand, the sporting culture is willing to accord them competitive victor's status, the spoils of the system; on the other hand, it wants to deny them any alternative voice within the system.

Personal Best earns a mixed scorecard. It deserves high marks for showing possibilities of athletic competition for women while softening the explosive clash of sexualities in sport. Yet the film provides no language for Chris Cahill and Torey Skinner to strike beyond their status. Are lesbians finally just good jocks? Is that enough? As Irigaray observes, "Feminine pleasure has to remain inarticulate in language, in its own language, if it is not to threaten the underpinnings of logical operations" (77), the logos of which as represented in sport is an entrenched male practice of controlled eroticism within power relations where winning cannot involve losing.

Water Dancer: The Multiples of Touch

JENIFER LEVIN'S *Water Dancer* (1982) is women's sports fiction's most singular achievement to date.[5] Levin writes of heroic marathon swimmers who endure tremendous pain and exhaustion during isolated competition. She has not found a way out of the binds of male-dominated competition and discourse in sport, but she suggests a very important role for women within that competition. Levin attempts to explain the constituent parts to their competition and how they are realized. Her characters and relationships demonstrate great possibilities for the women's sports fiction narrative as she writes positioned by what Irigaray calls woman's *"intimacy of that silent, multiple, diffuse touch"* (29; emphasis Irigaray's).

Water Dancer features a familiar framing from school sports fiction, the death (sacrifice) of the young boy hero. Sarge Olssen is a former record holder in marathon swimming who had trained his son Matt for competition. Matt dies during a record attempt to swim the San Antonio Strait off the coast of Washington with Sarge in the boat next to him. Sarge and his wife, Ilana, begin the long grieving period for their dead son, one tormented by Sarge's guilt that he had underestimated the cold and danger to Matt. *Water Dancer* opens with Sarge's recurring nightmare: "The kid's lips were blue-gray. . . . Stone-gray waves slammed against his shoulders, broke over his face. Daddy help! he screamed" (7). The son, the sacrificial sports figure, haunts all subsequent action.

Within this frame, Dorey Thomas, a crack young female swimmer who had broken down competitively, approaches Sarge for training and enters into the Olssen family grief and compensation. Thus *Water Dancer*'s sporting heroine is initially a replacement for the dead son. Dorey will, in Sarge's hands, attempt to complete the swim that killed Matt Olssen. In this drama, she attains multiple relations to Sarge and Ilana as lover, daughter, and surrogate son. The development of these roles confirms the complexity of Levin's knowledge of female bodies, their relation to each other, and to the male. The competition within the water becomes the maternal-paternal itself, bringing Dorey to birth.

Sarge's role in Dorey's training is to make her "a very strong lady. . . . Better than any man or woman in that water. . . . You'll be the strongest lady on earth" (144). Sarge wants Dorey in super-human condition to take on the Straits. He refuses to lose another child to that water. Swimming's pain to him had always felt like dying (35). He is ready to subordinate everything to Dorey's attempt—his personal feelings for her, his faltering marriage, and, finally, his own hurt and isolation when Dorey and Ilana become lovers. Ilana's relation to Dorey is initially more confused and multi-dimensional. Levin creates Ilana as a mixture of maternal and desiring impulses that have little contour or boundary but which flow into one another in the continuous female identity posited by Chodorow. Dorey's own needs and desires are similarly diffuse and undefined. She remains more of a personal mystery than Ilana, as Levin finds it almost impossible to inscribe a desiring imagination in Dorey Thomas, a female athletic champion in an exhausting competition. Such an imagination is always denied to a sports "natural," who conventionally can never explain his or her heroism. Dorey Thomas is *imagined in* the maternal plot, the paternal plot, the Oedipal plot, the Big Game (Swim) plot. The novel is seldom imagined through her.

Such a truth of Levin's narrative problem about the stability of an inner life to a sports heroine becomes a problematic strength in the novel. Dorey is a blank riddle who is written upon. Ilana's first glimpse of her outside the Olssen's door occurs when "the body pressed dark against the screen and she couldn't tell at first if it was male or female" (15). Later, another swimming champion, the strongly female Anne Norton, describes Dorey: "she's really not very feminine, not at all. But on the other hand she's not masculine either. She's just. . . . Just a *swimmer*—as if she's underwater all the time. Everything, all her movements, are at this very *measured* sort of pace and so are her reactions. . . . So whatever there is, really is, inside there, you just don't catch a glimpse of it when you're with her" (238). To be non-gendered is to lose sexual representation, to frustrate the very workings of difference, but Levin gains a fictional sports heroine by the ploy.

Dorey Thomas is approached by a number of characters who want to define themselves through her while helping her toward birth and representation. Sarge is the male/father/coach who wants vindication and a paternal closeness. Ilana has no goal for Dorey or herself, only not to lose another child. She had been a competitive diver years before: "On ground she seemed to glide" (14). Now with Matt's death heavy upon her, she has turned inward. She correctly sees Dorey "like [Sarge] . . . in some way obsessed, or wholly preoccupied with the constant doing of one particular thing. Swimming. And Ilana could offer nothing to compare. She'd spent her life without an obsession. Never having had one, she could not feel any lack" (34). Ilana sees Dorey's ambition as firmly male, in line with that of the "father." She herself does not want to participate in the obsession and does not want to be included in any male "lacks" and to be driven by goals. Ilana has never "written upon."

Ilana's desiring imagination opens to a conflict of motives toward Dorey. Levin has Ilana dream maternally of offering her breast to Dorey. On the facing page, Levin cuts to Sarge chastely easing Dorey's tired body into a warm bath where he croons to her of her potential strength (142–43). The female and male parenting roles are stressed. Ilana and Dorey are exploring each other's bodies after Ilana's timid question, "Do you like being touched by anyone? Anyone at all?" (184). Ilana's hands move slowly over Dorey's tensed body: "Her hands were shaking but she guessed that was all right" (188); "She'd forgotten how much Dorey herself was invested in the purely physical" (189). As they finally make love, what Dorey felt was "Ilana holding her, or rather holding on to her, as if afraid she'd vanish" (190), whereupon Dorey says, "Don't cry Ilana, I won't die out there. I'm not a boy" (190). Dorey's intimation catches in one phrase her roles as a child replacing Matt, and as a lover full of concern for Ilana as grieving mother. Levin cuts between the two women in love-making to stress the importance of their equal reactions. In the morning, Ilana rides a "full crest of the tenderness" that "poured out through her encircling arms" (192). Dorey sums up their experience, "I'd like to touch you perfectly. Just touch you every way, then I'd see you-I don't know! I can't explain exactly" (193).

Levin's complex seduction scene ends with a perfect evocation of "silent, multiple, diffuse touch" as female signature, a womanly writing that is a quite different economy from the male singularity. For Irigaray, that male project is "linear," the "goal object of a desire . . . toward a single pleasure" (Irigaray 30). Indeed, Dorey rises from her bed already conflicted between Ilana and her own goal, which she sees as a choice with "a cold dry edge of despair. To swim. She had to swim and that meant Sarge. . . . how could she be with them both together anymore?" (195). Such a choice is, along with *Personal Best*'s banner query (HOW CAN YOU COMPETE . . .), a very contemporary version of the traditional "choice" offered to young female athletes throughout the history of sports in fiction: love and desire or competitive sport? (J. G. Messenger 54–55). The rest of *Water Dancer* deepens and gives drama to this quandary: female pleasure in touch versus goal-oriented, single-minded activity? How does Levin resolve the conflicting claims on her characters and on their roles as men and women? What sports ethic emerges?

Levin creates fine emblems of the male and female worlds of *Water Dancer*, the ways in which they remain separate as well as those in which they achieve communion, both sexual and sporting. Sarge had a brief glimpse of Ilana and Dorey entwined together. The next morning he is in the kitchen with them, not knowing what to say or do. As he, Dorey, and Ilana have tea and toast, he looks at them both and feels complete estrangement before the female. He overturns the kitchen table in frustration and Dorey instinctively moves in front of Ilana, shielding her. Levin writes of Sarge's confusion, of "many things, most of which he didn't read, he couldn't. He was so outside of it all. He just stepped over broken plates on the floor, then was out the door" (197). "I wasn't going to tell you, but he saw," Ilana says. And then, they clean up the mess. Sarge has felt totally irrelevant in what Annette Kolodny has called a female sex-related context, the kitchen, where the desired-desiring females retain power (Kolodny 155). The male look ("he saw") of the night before is continued in the morning, and what he sees, he can't "read," "outside" a female text. He futilely attempts to overturn it and the women bend to the traditional task of restoring order to the table.

Sarge's wounds come from male frustration. Expecting "Ilana for him alone," she'd "shared herself without his consent." He wonders if he hadn't always isolated her, "straitjacketed her with his own pain. Since Matt died. Maybe before. He'd held her, somehow apart from Matt, and Matt from her, kept them separate, each, for him alone" (274). In his self-scrutiny, Sarge recapitulates a traditional male economy of possession and manipulation. Ilana's metonymic expression of her roles to Dorey is more fluid and tentative: "I think

it's all right if you're my child sometimes, that's just part of the way
I feel although not all of it or even most of it. But a significant part,
yes. Is that all right? Is that all right with you?" (228). Ilana allows
for serial selves, for becoming both mother and lover, and includes
concern for Dorey's acceptance of these selves. Such simultaneity is
part of her diver's knowledge. Her most "perfect" dive had been one
in which "she recalled no pause between the sequential movements,
it was all a long fast graceful flash of motion through air" (214).
Levin records the honest confusion of her women's roles and finds
the sporting images to punctuate them.

Sarge, too, desires Dorey and wants to be inside her, but she
refuses him. Rather "he came into the nothing her cupped hands fed"
(276). Dorey then slowly rubs the sperm over her body. They drift
toward sleep, coach and athlete, father and daughter–lover. Finally,
Ilana and Sarge agree to work together for Dorey and for her training. Sarge will make her hard and ready for the water. Ilana will
relax her body and tension and allow her to accept the punishing
regimen. Levin never dodges any of the issues pertaining to sexual
multiplicity in her major characters but rather portrays how they
contribute to the complementary roles in training Dorey as a competitor. Rather than feature the strongly gendered clash of males and
females within competition, she achieves narrative momentum by
concentrating on Dorey Thomas as *swimmer,* the role in which Levin
conceives her as containing all gender contradiction within univer-
sals. *Water Dancer* is a fine, informative sports novel where all details
of marathon swimming, its tradition, training, strategy, and dangers
are thoroughly explained and dramatized. The last swim across the
San Antonio Strait is the riveting Big Game so central to sports
fiction. At that time, the sports climax contributes to the characterization. Sarge is in control of Dorey's swim with Ilana as ghostlike
nurturer. Will they lose another child? Each other? Will Dorey come
into possession of herself?

For a sports frame in which to ask these questions, Levin has
chosen marathon swimming, in which women do compete successfully with men because of their endurance level and ability to with-
stand cold. As Dorey thinks, "Women. They're made more for the
water. We just fit it somehow, I don't know" (227). Anne Norton
knows swimming to be isolated, "If you're the swimmer, you're

really alone. . . . It all belongs to you and there's no one else to share it with" (288). Sarge watches Dorey stroke with pride: "The swimmer in there was not his son nor daughter and would never be his lover. Still she was a swimmer—and in that, the most essential sense of that, she was his. He'd nurtured the part of her that would survive" (358–59).

The swimmer as individual is challenged by Levin's multiple uses of "touch" as a controlling metaphor within the sexual encounters as well as within the swimming rules. Touch or tactile sense is of primary importance to feminist rhetoric as it counters the male look or gaze with another way of knowing. In *Water Dancer,* touch is what Ilana and Dorey tentatively achieve in a variety of roles. Part V (321–68) of *Water Dancer* is simply entitled "TOUCH" and is the account of Dorey's final swim. Within the rules of marathon swimming, "touch" is forbidden. The distance must be crossed without any human touch from coach, trainer, pacers, or people in the accompanying boat. Dorey "was the swimmer . . . the world she occupied now could not be touched, it was surrounded by water" (359). She awaits a new birth. Sarge in his heart urges her on through the cold, pitch-dark waters: "Stay awake lady, stay awake baby, stay awake now champ come on kid stay awake come on" (360). The dissolution of her role boundaries are clear here as he, in effect, exhorts lover, child, sporting hero, and his son.

The heroism of Dorey's swim also evokes sharp male and female responses in Sarge and Ilana. To Sarge, the beauty of her effort is the striving for a goal, "that reaching for something. It was his way of moving through the world" (363). Whereas Ilana is most concerned for Dorey's survival: "what was it but a capacity for some incessant kind of behavior. . . . As if the instinct to survive lived deeper in them than desire itself . . . this instinct as base as blood" (363). Ilana had triumphed in a maternal role: "She'd done it all by instinct . . . opened arms, given a breast when instinct said it was needed" (361). To Ilana, this is the miracle of what Dorey had accomplished, that she had persevered without "the relief of being warmed by touch" (363).[6]

Finally, touch is what Dorey *feels,* the sand under her fingers, signifying her victory, burrowing in deep: "It was the sense of touch that distinguished her from fish, that set her apart from the water she had been in" (367), the sense of touch that Ilana had given back to her (320). She has been driven along by Ilana and Sarge, her arms propelling their strokes, "One stroke a lover. One stroke a giant" (364). She arrives on shore alone, "stripped, therefore different" (364), both from them and from her former self. The last images are of her birth, "She looked just about dead. She was dripping water, and alive." She rests in Sarge's arms "and his touch became gentle. Did it, she said" (368).

At conclusion, Dorey is fully born and a human child, born out of nurture and discipline from Ilana and Sarge. She is born, too, out of her and their sexual confusion, pain, and error, and, finally, born of her own enormous effort. In her delirium near the swim's end, she had exulted to herself, "I —am a water dancer" (341) and Levin has proven her own claim to that title as she has found a metaphor for women in simultaneous roles in blood, tears, salt water, amniotic fluid. The conclusion of *Water Dancer* gives us Sarge and Ilana's potential reconciliation but no hint of Dorey Thomas's future sexual nature. All we know at sports narrative's end is that the swimmer has "touched." Dorey had been an inhuman stroking machine. Now she is a human stroking machine. Levin stints neither on the nurture nor on the achievement. *Water Dancer* suggests that within extreme goal-oriented competitive sport (coded as masculine), something like the flowing calm of touch and relaxation (coded as feminine) is necessary to attain the emotional balance and discipline needed to achieve anything.

In this regard, Levin, by her intense interest in women's role in sport, shows, not without great pain on the part of her characters, that masculine and feminine narratives may be complementary rather than polarized, oppressive barriers to love and work. Loneliness is countered. A record is set. A daughter replaces a son. A child is born. The relentless flow of the sea in *Water Dancer* is an example of what Helene Cixous has said in conceiving of images of the mother and water, that the sea floats her and ripples her, that the water, "the unceasing movement of the sea [is] the very symbol of the feminine elsewhere" (Cixous in Stanton 169). Such language is as much a meta-rhetoric as that of male erection and violence. Levin would close the rhetoric and ground Dorey Thomas again on the land. Yet Dorey's relentless passage across the straits echoes Cixous own statement about woman's sexuality and woman's language that "her writing can only keep going, without ever inscribing or discerning contours" (Cixous in A. R. Jones 366). All her bodily drives (oral, anal, gestational, vocal) are in strength of multiple libidinal impulses (A. R. Jones 366). In effect, Dorey Thomas' muteness stipulates that while she as yet has no language, she *is* a language. In this regard, we come back to the essentially wordless description of the individual sports hero, whose physical experience in sport speaks her excellence and grace. Levin has pioneered in wedding the female symbolic in its multiple roles to the language and culture of sports competition in its most tantalizing conception, the sporting natural.

Levin's second novel *Snow* (1983) cast her heroine in another familiar sports fiction genre, the ritual sports story. Raina Scott is an internationally acclaimed adventuress with a public persona: "It was the Raina Scott show—every year or so something different. Mountain climbing. Exploring underwater caves. Bow hunting. Endurance treks through deserts, through blizzards. Spear-fishing for Great White Sharks. . . . She was, in fact, a household word" (59). Not only does she seek competitive mastery in blood sport, she also evinces the strong Hemingway-Mailer drive to face her own death and defeat it again and again: "She'd been blessed with the opportunity to see close up and in living color, the cold-eyed embodiment of what she feared. Having seen it, she knew it. She set about to study it. She set about to encounter it, to put herself closer to it. The ability to do this—to set yourself face to face with each obstacle that might destroy you . . . it was the mark of greatness" (131). Thus Raina Scott's initial coding is strongly in the most masculine of sporting rites. Here Levin faces a major contradiction since by creating her mythic ritualist, she has coded her in all the male activities of testing, competitiveness, manipulation, and performance. Her metonymic roles are, however, re-contained in the largest of maternal metaphors.[7] The power of the mythical feminine is such that Raina Scott in *Snow* is the riddle whom each character desires to *write upon them*. Her potential narrative dominates.

Levin balances this ritual sport compulsion of Raina with an additional yearning: the warrior who cries out to be a lover. Within this need, Levin constructs a wonderful romance at the center of *Snow* between Raina and Karlen Adams Zachary (Kaz), another adept female athlete. But by far Levin's most suggestive conception is in the transformation of Raina Scott into a goddess of a fertility religion in a small war-torn central American country called Bellagua. *Snow*'s great quest in romance time is for Kaz to be reunited with Raina, her human lover, now a figure of mythical dimension in a political cause.

The plot of *Snow* is a blockbuster, a violent, heavily rhetorical cinematic sweep of revolution, international business, primitivism, romance, and adventure. With its large cast, exotic locales, and headline issues, *Snow* hurtles on like the scenario for a T.V. miniseries. Yet Levin somehow thoroughly and honestly explores themes familiar from *Water Dancer:* woman's endurance, woman's power, woman's desire. *Snow* re-works these subjects within a collective frame of politics, war, and economics—three hugely male dominants. *Water Dancer* was tightly locked in on the nuclear family and self-definition and worked through the male competitive ethos in sport. Levin adds a second powerful urge in ritual sport: to "become nature" itself. The role of "goddess" set against that of "lover" provides Levin once more with the opportunity to dramatize women in multiple, if extreme, roles with ritual and competitive sport their catalysts.

Snow's stage is really set for some current Western feminist agendas: an anthropologically based speculative drama of maternal deity, a lesbian romance, an anatomy of what power and desire might mean in these contexts. Levin seeks out the largest issues for her female characters and then animates them through fictional drama. As goddess, Raina Scott has shifted her commodity status from "Amelia Earhart" to the most bizarre and contradictory assumption of both power and bondage. With the frame of "Goddess," Levin may comment on the ironic extremity of a dominant figure who is nonetheless a nurturer. Raina has her body painted and her breasts ritually scarred so that her blood may flow as sacred milk in ceremony. She suffers for the tribespeople, "assuming the role deliberately" in a play that has great consequence. Raina teaches Kaz that "women had always known that survival was a social event" (179), as she invokes female divinities embedded in polytheism, who gave back to the earth and its people. At the center of Levin's metaphorical conceptualization is "reciprocity" (141), which is at the heart of the natural cycle of fertility but which also must be practiced between lovers, among peoples. Such reciprocity recalls questions that Ilana asked Dorey Thomas in *Water Dancer:* "is this right for you? what do *you* want?" Kaz feels that in making love with Raina, "there would be no dramatic surge of difference, no disintegration. . . . All discovery would hold the promise of being mutual" (125). The mutuality of giving and receiving is everywhere the similar impulse in both novels between the private sphere of Levin's lovers and her vision of cooperation (*Water Dancer*) and liberation (*Snow*) in the public sphere.

Water Dancer had been imagined on the concept of touch in all its permutations. In *Snow*, the extension of touch has a similar grounding, the inter-play between the profound rootedness of the goddess and her human need as a lover. Raina says that the Bellaguans will follow their goddess, not "socialist dogma . . . because She weds them to the earth" (203). Levin describes nurture in a radical and sensational frame, Raina as least-free, in constant demand, constantly speculated about, living a *Golden Bough* tension of the royal figure's power on the edge of ritual sacrifice. Yet Levin uses the same imagery to describe Raina's need to forego the ritual role and survive as solitary human: she must "do battle with herself" and "come through at the other end, whole and sane, and walk on the earth again . . . no warrior now, but a lover" (180).

Raina is a super-heroine and Levin's task is to validate the mythical feminine and to celebrate the desiring feminine. The mythical feminine possesses all the power traditionally coded as male, the desiring feminine still seeks a place and a language "beyond." After all Raina's public sporting exploits and heroic nurturing in Bellagua, will there be a residue of pleasure left over for the women? Yes, says Levin, in a final scene beyond the power plays of metaphor and metonymy. *Snow* concludes deep in the jungle, in a candle-lit cave of feathers and incense where Raina ceremoniously (with Kaz as attendant) washes off the paint from her role as goddess and "in love called out a single name" (4). Romance has won a very traditional victory in a very quirky and untraditional ideological text. The adventuress and the Goddess, the sportswoman and the ritual player, are, first, human lovers. The marketing of "snow" [a defoliant], the future of Bellagua, the role of Goddess, and all the desiring imaginations of Levin's males in the novel (Lee, Connery, Pablo, Zachary, Gabriel) are canceled or suspended in favor of romance time at the heart of darkness in a room of their own.

Conclusion

THE WOMEN'S experiences in sport and play discussed here end with real competitive victories and some personal triumphs. Whatever the degree of re-containment in male narratives practiced by Williams, Irving, Towne, and Levin, the consensus is that women achieve heroic victory. This is not the tale of isolated adept boy-men in sacrifice familiar to the male individual sports narrative. The women discussed have come through to birth, to nurture, to victory, to multiple roles. They aren't fixated on past glories. The rhetoric is of liberation within certain narrative constraints.

The most striking of these constraints is the fate of those women who struggle hardest to love other women. The woman's sports narrative does not know what to do with these characters. Neither does the contemporary historical pageantry of *Snow*. Irving's Susie the Bear, Towne's Torey Skinner, and Levin's Ilana Olssen have all nurtured the nominal individual sports hero-ines—Franny Berry, Chris Cahill, Dorey Thomas—and enabled them to triumph. However, the women who battle for and on behalf of these victor-women are themselves denied both the object of their desire and a continued female desiring role. They are recuperated for heterosexuality, "suitable for exchange among men" (Irigaray 180) and/or a senior maternal status or are simply banished as desirers(ees).[8] For example, Ilana Olssen gives everything to Dorey Thomas as mother and lover. As Dorey is about to achieve her goal, "Ilana let her head sink tiredly to her hand. She was older physically and irrevocably. Hair all gray. Too old to bear children. Too much of that water inside had dried up by now" (363). The novel concludes with Ilana and Sarge about to attempt a reconciliation. With Dorey safely born and a winner, *Water Dancer* gives no clue as to what her future sexuality will be. Only Levin's *Snow,* by hurling Kaz (heiress) and Raina (goddess) into romance time beyond politics, history, and their male desirers, achieves the space for female pleasure.

It is interesting to note that *Personal Best* has two token gay male shotputters, *Hotel* has only the minor character of Frank Berry, and *Water Dancer,* while candid about the desire of Dorey and Ilana, is only cryptic about the sexuality of Dr. John Gallagher who had his face smashed in fury by his rowing-sculls teammate and now only competes alone. Such absence and evasion, including the forbidden subject of Brick and Skipper's love that dominates Maggie's play in *Cat,* points all the more sharply to the sublimated eroticism in male sports competition that may never be coded as desire without paroxysms and violence. Women touch and are regenerated within the originally eroticized female sports narrative, in the differences and multiplicity of roles. Men may "touch" only with objects (bats, balls, helmets, padding, equipment) that regulate violence. These objects are manually manipulated phallic, vaginal, and clitoral substitutes. A male ball player may have "soft hands," but he cannot touch other men with them. In contemporary culture, the male athletes, while candid about drugs to the point of reader overdose, have still treated discussion of homosexuality in sport, for the most part, as an ultimate taboo.[9] This silence further confirms buggery and a resultant anti-heroism as the unacceptable state of male defeat and humiliation.

The fixation on the past moment in male sports narrative may also be gender-coded through physical response. The male sexual experience consists in building up to a single pitch of excitement and then falling off into a chaotic present that is momentary, urgent, and then lost. The recapturing of the "golden moment" in school sports fiction is very apt. All must be sought again to make the present "like another time" with no assurance that it will come again. Women's sexual experience is slower, more expansive in the present moment and built in time on known returns of cycle (twenty-eight days, nine months). Such return dictates the female relationships in all the narratives under discussion here, especially Maggie's belief in Brick's return to the marriage bed, Dorey Thomas returning to land, and Kaz and Raina's reunion in the jungle. Such "return" may structure "romance time" itself. We have only begun to inquire as to how physical sexual response determines male and female attitudes toward competition, toward the mental structuring of the orgasmic and competitive moments, and toward the recovery of the past.

However, the female sports world remains one of constant eroticization in the popular media. Tennis is the popular sport most competed in by women for the sports dollar and the television audience. Tennis has offered an unrelenting series of sports hero-ines in radical desiring roles. Billie Jean King and Martina Navratilova have made headlines with disclosures of bisexuality and King has been sued by a female ex-lover. Navratilova lives and travels openly with a female companion and with an entourage dubbed "Team Navratilova," her "family," including several dogs.[10] The transsexual Renee Richards (a real-life version of Irving's ex–NFL player Roberta Muldoon in *Garp*) was Navratilova's sometime coach. The greatest public drama in women's tennis remains the challenge of Bobby Riggs to the women pros, in which he defeated Margaret Court and then was vanquished by King in the Astrodome in prime time in 1973. Finally, when Chris Evert, divorced her first husband, John Lloyd, one of the reported reasons was that he refused to be competitive enough in his own tennis career.

The sports narrative has always been the place to speak *excessively* about the physical body. In the case of the inscription of women in this narrative, the always-already eroticized female body is thus the site of the clash with all the male coding of compensatory aggression and competition that banks down on the eroticism, heterosexual and homosexual alike. Raina Scott in *Snow* has no language to explain her ritual sport obsessions but only the extreme representation of her practice. Within what feminists call "phallocentric dogma," sports narrative is Exhibit A. Its disruption by female presence in its subject roles leads to clashes such as play versus competition, delight in flow versus possession of the moment, and desire for a multiple, receptive present versus a desire to repeat the past in performance. The women's sports narratives by both men and women have really yet to be written. However, they will contain the conflicts between the world of fairy tale and myth in play, between the worlds of family, sex roles, and nurture and the world of the larger competitive society, and, most visibly, the world of enemies, fate, and mortality in the collectively coded activity which is sport.

Some speculation on the male and female variants of the sports tradition are in order in light of recent literary history and practice. The American school sports story lacked the strong association with male homosexual relationships in the English school tradition. The question might be: At what point did the American school sports narrative turn toward what could be construed as a more feminine coding of its hero in non-utility and unattainability? Perhaps the confused portrait of Christian Darling in Irwin Shaw's "The Eighty-Yard Run," a character both threatening and passive, aggressive and physically perfect, is a starting point. An isolated novel such as William Maxwell's *The Folded Leaf* (1945) dealt simply and effectively with male love in a school sport setting. Yet the presentation of male athletic heroes as dreamy amateurs, lost in their natural innocence, out of the competitive dominant, led to the chaste and fetishized naturals in *A Separate Peace, The Huge Season,* and *Seymour: An Introduction* (1959). These novels drove the sexual subject in school sport into sublimated male coding (see chapter 7). The brilliance of *Cat on a Hot Tin Roof* and *Who's Afraid of Virginia Woolf* featured potentially gender-skewed characterization through play and competition. A young Tennessee Williams might have written a very different *Cat* in the 1970s or '80s. However, the school sports narrative did not, except for Patricia Nell Warren's dizzying sex reversals in her tedious *The Front Runner* (1974), treat the potential male desirers with any more candor. It remained for works such as *Personal Best, Water Dancer,* and *Snow* to achieve both candor and artistry in their presentation of female subjects.

Part of the issue, but only part, may lie in the gradual turning away after the 1950s from the modernist preoccupation with the unique, charismatic hero, the super-subject of inscrutable character, the legacy of Fitzgerald's Gatsby and Conrad's Kurtz. "Was I never fated to see him clearly?" is in some part the agony of the male gaze, the frustration of non-possession where males were unavailable, physically and narratively, to other males, including authors. The fury at the other male's intactness is the cross-coded fear of virginity, the rage at the school sports natural's self-delight. The males in *Snow* need to break into that self-possession with all the latent sexual charge of that act. Raina Scott, so radical a desiring super-heroine, is, at one level, the unconventional re-introduction of a female ritual Hemingway hero who assumes a rule-bound, obsessively competitive existence. Modern fiction has seen and deciphered the figure before.

The quintessential modernist novel of sensibility is eclipsed in postmodernism along with much of the sublimated gender coding. The cry in Wright Morris' *The Huge Season* about his tennis hero, Lawrence—"He isn't human. How can you copy something like that?"—is no longer a problem in much postmodern writing where copies of copies are an artistic strategy, where "multiples" also connote a variety of heroic roles, and where a perpetual spatial present is an aesthetic construct more congenial to woman's experience of time. Future texts may yield contemporary sports heroines who play without that urgency for possession of time and the past that so obsessed the modernist male masters and their apprentices. The mostpointed example of this obsession in contemporary fiction was in Humbert's repeated violation of Lolita to possess the one time of his own sexual innocence.

Sublimated gender coding often becomes an invisible issue in the inscription of male athletes within power relations. Within the competitive dominant of sport, men also seek a space for their individuality and desire. For men do not only subjugate women in sport but also, and most often, other men, both on the playing field and in the front office. The resultant male avoidance of competitiveness and a seeking of space is often cast in terms of the male athlete becoming, in his own strategy, multiple and duplicitous. The male athlete or player seeks a suspension of domination and/or the "rules," as in the examples of Malamud's Roy Hobbs, Updike's Rabbit Angstrom, and Kesey's McMurphy discussed in the introduction. The athlete as player becomes a mime of no small accomplishment telling the sports establishment (the team) what it wants to hear, purporting to be ready to kill any opponent, yet all the while undermining that rhetoric in private rebellion. Such is the rhetoric of much football fiction, for example, where the competitors are portrayed as exchange-ridden wage-slaves in a brutal physical business in which they attempt to hold on to their humanity. They do so by affiliation, by nurturing their teammates in loyalty. Often the team itself is portrayed as the family arrayed against patriarchal coaches, general managers, and owners. Such coding partakes of the reciprocity and interaction of relations among the oppressed.

When males in sport practice such behavior, they are seen to be recovering their "humanity," and learning "tolerance" and "cooperation." They are never said to be undergoing a feminization. In the obverse of obsessive competition, the male language grants the freedom to try on these roles in a social context as long as the sexual element is sublimated. "Humanity, "tolerance," and "cooperation" become universal ideals, "natural" in their desirability. Women have no such space in which to become "aggressive" and "competitive" without extreme male approbation and anxiety. For example, "male supremacy" may be uttered as a complacently natural term for "the way things are." If "male supremacy" is re-written as "phallic economy," it is placed within a specific feminist critique of sexual and capitalist oppression. This critique mimes by converting a form of domination ("male supremacy") into an affirmation that makes ideas elaborated in/by a masculine logic retrievable in language ("phallic economy") that is still masculine but politicized.

On a private and personal level, Irigaray's "intimacy of that silent multiple diffuse touch" is unacceptable to males in sport. For Irigaray, the play of vaginal lips is involuntary, perhaps the final, improbable evidence that anatomy is destiny. Men's "touch" or "touching themselves," or any sort of self-delight would be a forbidden masturbation with external stimulation accomplished without gaze or exchange. The flow pattern of play that counters competition is a self-delight. When invoked by males, it is in abstention from competition but again is sexually sublimated. At its most negative, it is buggery or "playing with yourself," the shame and futility of sexual failure. For men to fail in sport makes them a target for sexual violation. Towne catches the full force of this rhetoric in *Personal Best* when Tingloff yells at a male runner who has been lapped by Chris in practice: "Ya just let a pussy beat ya, ya dumb asshole," the former a female external secondary sex characteristic—what is seen by the male gaze. In another transposition of this rhetoric, the sublimated male horror of "being beaten by a girl" is to lose to a feminized male.

The pressure to sublimate is evidenced by the language of antiheroism. Men who rebel from competition through play are on a "personal quest" in "self-definition," which presumes they have subjecthood and the language. They may manipulate the rebelling individual roles from the dominant into heroic postures. Women who compete in the male dominant through aggressive competition are "castrators" and "ball-busters." Furthermore, in the most negative presentations, phallic women are highly dangerous and feared beings whereas feminine men are merely derided and loathed by other men who do not wish to exchange, ravish, or aestheticize them. Nor are feminized men seen as threats to women. Men or women signifying an intense masculinity are em-powered positively or negatively. Men or women signifying extreme femininity are in subjugation.

The complex coding of Gender-Power-Language-Representation in sport and play finally stipulates that (1) to play is in response to powerlessness; (2) to compete is in the male dominant mode; (3) to play as a man is to begin to strike through the mode of powerlessness; (4) to compete as a woman is to strike through the mode of power. For a man to play is, in some ways, to simulate feminization for potential "self-definition" and "rebellion," yet he is only playing that role in his language and self-assertion as one of his choices. He is "playing at play." A woman has no choice but to play, for her only language is not really her own and she is always eroticized within it. Her miming within that language is as involuntary as her self-touching. To be "multiple" is not, in the realities of power and powerlessness, a choice, but the absolutely necessary mode of being for women.

The initial sampling of a woman's fictional sports narrative suggests a voice for women within a cultural activity inimical in many of its associations to the deepest of female physical responses and hence all the more potentially revolutionary. Levin in *Water Dancer* writes of Anne Norton in the frigid dark water pacing a heroically exhausted Dorey Thomas: "Anne dropped into the mirror, went through its other side. She surfaced and looked at a reflection of herself. Something has happened, though, the glass warped. This face staring sightlessly back at hers was swollen and not quite her own. In all other respects they were the same, like two similarly colored stones smoothed to matching dimensions by water" (350).[11] Anne Norton experiences what readers male and female alike may yet glean from an understanding of male and female sexual and competitive roles when "dropped into the mirror" of self and other and forced to confront same and different.

7.

The Decline of the School Sports Hero

THE DECLINE of the School Sports Hero in contemporary American fiction is a palpable one, his strengths altered and qualified in a society that has less and less use for him. The school sports story has had difficulty withstanding the assaults of technology and professionalism as it struggled to remain the most popular genteel American coming-of-age experience. The school sports story had endured as the *Bildungsroman* of sports fiction at the same moment it referred to a prior moment of innocence. The past was central to the School Sports Hero: he never possessed the present which he denied or fled in a number of strategies. He was, in Fitzgerald's words at the conclusion of *The Great Gatsby*, "borne back ceaselessly into the past," away from society's preoccupations toward a moment of excellence, uncomplicated and free, that could not be forgotten.

The School Sports Hero always attempts play back to his heroic moment where he stood uncomplicated and free. The anxiety he feels is in his inability to make that *individual sports heroism* last or cohere into a lesson for the spirit. He pursues an *anti-heroism* that will liberate him but all that occurs is a drive back into innocence where he plays to find the fullness that once was his. Thus the missing term of the Greimas square comes to the foreground of the School Sports Hero's search: the search for the form of a knowledgeable *anti-heroism*. He cannot connect the material to the spiritual.

The anxiety of the narration of sport in fiction described in chapters 1–4 was about the death of the body and its power, a sublimated Hemingway anxiety. With the narration of the School Sports Hero, the anxiety is about the death of youth's spirit and hope, a Fitzgerald anxiety. The ritual sports story is about the hero seeking a "like" space that he will absorb or that will absorb him. The School Sports Hero desires a "time" to return, the time of his great deeds.

The school sports story is not as violent as the ritual sports story. It is a reflective fiction, obsessed with the education of the heart and spirit, at times a text performing duties closely akin to those of the novel of sensibility. The school sports story promotes values which strive to engage love and tolerance, that attempt to conquer lust, fear, and prejudice rather than to ritualize them. Yet often the school sports story bears the grim trace of a sacrificial crisis with the School Sports Hero in the role of surrogate–sacrificial victim. The hero in school stories is, like Kesey's McMurphy, a natural imprisoned in the collective, an excluded hero separated from society because of his great skill. He is consistently at odds with a society that re-affirms the mediocre norm in the face of his brilliance.

At present the school sports frame has split in two with the advent of the hero who is already a young professional when practicing his sport. He is paid and lionized by society, which views the school experience as mere preparation for professional sports, not in the traditional lexicon as preparation for a leadership role and for life itself. This legacy of the school sports subject was already an anachronism controlled by Fitzgerald and Hemingway in *The Great Gatsby* and *The Sun Also Rises* and has been presented with irony ever since. I deal with the school athlete in his professional guise in chapters 9–13 on the fiction of the major American team sports. Here I am concerned with this residual figure, an ambiguous survivor of a different era of sporting heroes and values, the last amateur desiring a dreamy personal autonomy and privileged time.

The dwelling on a past moment of achievement became a cliché of the School Sports Hero through Tom Buchanan's "acute, limited excellence" in *The Great Gatsby*. Prior to Fitzgerald's most influential coding of the School Sports Hero, this figure had been represented since the Civil War by the sons of American privilege and power who competed in preparation for assuming leadership roles in society. Such was the institutional ideology priming the narrative. The prototype for the School Sports Hero was Thomas Hughes' Tom Brown in *Tom Brown's Schooldays* and *Tom Brown at Oxford* in the 1850s. The most famous American descendants of Tom Brown were Gilbert Patten's Frank Merriwell, Owen Johnson's Dink Stover, and the heroes of Jesse Lynch Williams and Ralph Henry Barbour. Beginning in the 1890s, American readers identified with the youth coming of age in a private academy and eastern college. Competitive sports was the central determinant for heroes in the school hierarchy. The convention of the Merriwell era was that the school athlete's experience, grounded in the values of the academy, prepared him for later life. This convention was overturned in figures beginning with Fitzgerald's Buchanan and Hemingway's Robert Cohn, heroes who are caught in *past* heroism and who do not evolve as they age or, alternately, have embraced a vision of time in which they may be suspended. Deluded and psychologically cloistered, they find it impossible to live in the present.[1]

The Last Amateurs

IN THE classic school story, the hero did not have an aesthetic sense or a vivid imagination, but rather a competitive drive coupled with an iron will and a sense of fair play. This figure moves into professional sports and is a most potent individual sports hero in sportsworld. This chapter chronicles those left behind in nostalgia or illusion, the angry or sad or fragile ones. Contemporary sports fiction yields the aggressive, wistful ex-school athlete and the innocent, fragile natural, always in the process of becoming. This fiction is more lyrical and metaphorical, playing toward a nostalgic center of unity that is, of course, a presence denied in temporality. The School Sports Hero cannot convert the material success of individual sports heroism into a spiritual victory; the ability to stand apart in some anti-heroic self-knowledge is denied him. The spirit remains unsatisfied.

Fitzgerald's probing of the figure produced two distinct school sport avatars, those of Buchanan and Jay Gatsby, a lost bully and a heroic romantic. Fitzgerald made Buchanan the physical hero with no utility, possessing nothing but aggression without an acceptable outlet. Buchanan, like Cohn, is no natural. They both learn to use their hands and bodies as weapons and struggle with ideas. The School Sports Hero at the turn of the century was not terribly bright but rather an earnest synthesizer of ideas, solid rather than creative, all in the dutiful shadow of Tom Brown, who frequently had trouble with Latin, but not with cricket. Jay Gatsby is as evanescent as Buchanan is solid, as imaginative as Buchanan is literal, though they both share a credulity and a narrowness. Gatsby's enormous desire to re-create the past with Daisy is a more creative counterpart to Buchanan's seeking "wistfully to recover the turbulence of some irrecoverable football game." Buchanan and Gatsby both want to recover a past moment; both have eyes resolutely on prior triumph. The passage from school to society is arrested and reversed. The possession of time is the goal in the denial of difference. The School Sports Hero wants to structure the present to be like another time in the past when he was "un"-like anyone else. Through play, he seeks a state prior to play. Possession of the golden moment was always nine-tenths of Fitzgerald's fictional law and absolutely elusive.

After Fitzgerald's suggestive Tom Buchanan and Jay Gatsby, the 1930s produced fewer School Sports Heroes than might have been imagined, primarily because the decade did not lend itself to genteel coming-of-age narratives, even in satire or criticism.[2] Fictional sports heroes in the Depression were more viscerally aggressive and deterministic. Hemingway's Francis Macomber, while not specifically a school athlete, certainly partook of the mystique of a Buchanan—burly, fit, a sportsman, thirty-five—but Hemingway gave him other imperatives in the ritual sports arena. At the end of the decade, Faulkner's Labove, the reluctant rural Frank Merriwell of *The Hamlet,* brilliantly combined strains of Washington Irving's Brom Bones and Southwestern Humor heroes with collegiate gridiron heroics.[3]

The Fitzgerald conception of "limited excellence" and the allied, intensely symbolic brief heroism did inform the 1930s two most prominent fictional School Sports Heroes: Thomas Wolfe's Jim Randolph in *The Web and the Rock* (1939) and Shaw's Christian Darling in "The Eighty Yard Run" (1942). Both Darling and Randolph are inert and one-dimensional characters who are used simplistically by their authors. Wolfe's Randolph is George Webber's senior idol when freshman Webber arrives at Pine Rock College in 1916; Randolph is the football star, the "Olympian," the "magnificent creature" (Wolfe 201). He is a "legend" by dint of a list of accomplishments, not the least of which is his 57-yard run to beat Monroe and Madison: "That was the apex of Jim Randolph's life, the summit of his fame. . . . Nothing could ever equal it" (211–12). The "limited excellence" stereotype is adumbrated by his subsequent heroism in World War I where he is wounded in the Argonne and returns with a cane and serious spinal injury. As war hero, Randolph completes the picture of Fitzgerald's Princeton All-American Hobey Baker, dead in France in 1918; Wolfe strove to put the School Sports Hero in an appropriate martial context. Randolph is last seen as a disillusioned New York journalist at age thirty where "his legend still clung to him" (257) but could do nothing to energize him.[4]

"The Eighty Yard Run" is perhaps the best known of all sports fiction short stories but so flatly conceived and programmatically executed that perhaps it is remembered *because* of its sketchiness: the outline of the halfback who has made one great run in practice, whose girl waits for him in the convertible outside the stadium, but whose life never approaches that moment again. The aptly and derisively-named "Christian Darling," an impotent ex-halfback, watches the 1930s unfold all about him as Shaw awkwardly runs the decade past Darling's bewildered, truculent conservatism. As his New York executive sinecure falls apart, Darling's wife Louise takes a job and begins to entertain a potpourri of social "types"—artists, labor leaders, Jewish "free" thinkers, "free" women—all of whom are anathema to Darling. Shaw fragments the 1930s into a washed-out montage of the changing world that the School Sports Hero cannot grasp. As a jock pea-brain, Darling can talk only sports and money while Louise's guests eagerly debate Picasso and Trotsky. Darling declines to attend a performance of *Waiting for Lefty* which might have aided his "schooling."

Shaw reads out a whole bill of resentments against Christian Darling who is a timid, graceless, neutered man. He becomes the sports hero conventionally identified with prejudice, inarticulateness, and a uselessness, but he is nowhere as alive as Tom Buchanan. Darling "hadn't practiced for 1929 and New York City and a girl who would turn into a woman" (438). Darling is no natural, no competitor; he has no desire. He's simply Shaw's idea of a WASP football hero, as much guesswork as Patten's "Yale men" in the Merriwell series. The School Sports Hero, adult unemployed variety, becomes as didactic a cut-out as the victimized fighter in boxing fiction. His "time" has gone. Shaw props up a rather crude chronicle of social change in the role of women, in politics, economics, and art to show how mystifying it is to the WASP center. The School Sports Hero in the 1930s is enlisted in the most genteel of naturalisms.

Both Wolfe and Shaw put their School Sports Heroes in a historical setting, making them emblems of World War I "ghosts" and irrelevant during the Depression. Temporality is their true enemy. As long as they were inert referents to a frozen moment that itself had no collective resonance, they had reference but no representation. Continual references to the "frozen moment" appear in school sports fiction of the 1950s. Babs H. Deal's *The Grail* (1952) is a college football re-telling of the Camelot legend with its high anxiety about the ideal and innocence. As one might guess, School Sports Hero Lance is in love with Coach Arthur's wife, Jenny, with the inevitable collapse of the Castle University team and their lives.[5] Robert Wilder's *Autumn Thunder* (1952) depicts the confused Larry "Big Six" Summers, a southern small-town boy and college football hero c. 1930, who never graduated or left the college town and who experiences a mid-life crisis of identity and spirit.

A last rearguard attempt to sum up the meaning of the elite private school and its effects on generations of American youth was contained in Louis Auchincloss's *The Rector of Justin* (1964). His rock of a headmaster, Frank Prescott (b. 1860), is a character steeped in American mandarin and popular associations. A relative of the historian Francis Prescott, he comes with the best Boston connections. He marries a great-niece of Emerson, but he is also an orphan, a self-made man, a heroic prep school boy in the tradition of Merriwell and of Merriwell's era. He literally creates Justin Martyr Academy in the 1890s with his own vision and strong hands. He is described at age eighty in 1939 by life-long associates, old boys, new acolytes, and his own daughter, archly named Cordelia. Prescott is fierce, upright, "manly," but possessed of a cold heart. He fights harsh battles for his own vision of the forms of things but not for the love of the people involved.[6] Charley Strong (Justin Martyr '11), football captain, a Jim Randolph or Hobey Baker, is a shrapnel victim in World War I and is literally shamed to death by Prescott when he commits the multiple sins of desiring Cordelia, living in Paris, and cultivating an aesthetic sense. Strong is "sincere," "naive," and "charming"; Cordelia accuses her father of turning Strong into an "adolescent robot on the playing fields of Justin" (181, 199). However, as Auchincloss systematically devalues most of Prescott's narrator-antagonists, we are left with the author's approval of Prescott as a rigid, staunch defender of continuity and form.

The temporal intensity of the school sports rite, the strong and damaged heroes thus produced, have been central to a surprising number of modern and contemporary American plays.[7] Two of the finest American dramas of the contemporary era, Arthur Miller's *Death of a Salesman* (1949) and Tennessee Williams' *Cat on a Hot Tin Roof* (see chapter 6) have centered on intense images of the School Sports Heroes to make their deepest points. In *Death of a Salesman*, Willy Loman's son Biff is a tragic extension of his father's dogged belief, in his striving to be well thought of, in form over substance. Willy exhorts Biff as if he is the ghost of the Merriwell past. He tells him that scholarships go to those boys who look like Adonises, that Biff has "all kinds a greatness" (67). Willie and Biff remain fixated on one great school football game at Ebbets Field when Biff was seventeen and an all-city player, but "after seventeen nothing good happened to him" (92). Biff steals from a sporting goods store where he works, flunks math, and cannot attend college. When he finds that Willy is an adulterer, his life becomes an eerie dream, his father's praise filling his head like a tumor. His father's son, he fails at one job after another, refusing to accept any second-rate position. At thirty-four, his accusatory words to Willy are, "You blew me so full of hot air I could never stand taking orders from anybody" and "I'm not bringing home prizes any more and you're going to stop waiting for me to bring them home" (131–32). Willy is both Biff's exhorter-coach and deluding spectator, driving Biff through his years of arrested development.[8] The pressures collapse Biff, who becomes the failed instrument of Willy's wounded pride and yearning for success.

Willy Loman is questing for the uncomplicated and free excellence that the turn-of-the-century School Sports Hero provided. He wants to prepare Biff as a leader through the Merriwellian virtues, including being "well-liked"; the popularity of the School Sports Hero among his peers was never to be in doubt in the Merriwell years. Furthermore, Willy is at the tag end of an American success story that for him never took place. He champions all free enterprise aggression with competitive sport as its leading tenet in the educational environment. Willy values the sharp operator, yet he is one of the last real amateurs who moves further and further from the present as he reminisces about the old days and heroic salesmen who covered the territory.

Finally Miller splits the school sports figure into Willy *and* Biff Loman. Willy is the aggressive, wistful father who has conceived Biff as the innocent, fragile natural. When the myth of Biff's heroism dies, Willy cannot live; Willy, not Biff, is seen to be the romantic whose bluster hides his vulnerability. Biff rudely breaks the fantasy of his heroism for he has always been slack and compromised. He knows who he is at play's end and will not allow pity for his father. Willy becomes the ritual sacrifice.[9]

The language of aggressive competition is the religion in *Death of a Salesman* and is continually invoked by Willy and his sons Biff and Happy. They deride the anemic Bernard, Biff's childhood friend, who winds up running his father's company. Willy idolizes his brother Ben who has become rich on the Alaska frontier. Their dream dialogue is framed by sporting cliches and capitalist dreams. Biff even asks Happy to go west with him: "Maybe we could buy a ranch.

Raise cattle, use our muscles. Men built like we are should be work-ing out in the open" (23). Biff would repeat the Theodore Roosevelt rhetoric of 1900 and wed school sport to manly development. Happy Loman expresses his frustration in the business world through his sports image of himself. The language of competition and the body is constant: "Sometimes I want to just rip my clothes off in the middle of the store and outbox that goddam merchandise manager. I mean I can outbox, outrun, and outlift anybody in that store, and I have to take orders from those common petty sons-of-bitches till I can't stand it any more" (24). Happy's answer is for Biff and himself to sell sporting goods while putting on sports exhibitions. Sadly, they could be traveling sports salesmen, caught once more in their father's commodified world and sports dreams. *Time* is an unbeara-ble burden for all the Loman men. They stitch it together with the threadbare dreams that the collective world has demanded they try on.

The Sacrifice of the Natural

THE CLASSIC strain of the contemporary School Sports Hero is the study of the gifted, isolated hero who wants to stay free of encumbrances. Once again, the *natural,* the romanticized, idealized youth, more of a Gatsby manqué than a Buchanan, is highlighted. This hero refuses to prepare for any role and is "uncommon" in a series of abstentions from public heroism. J. D. Salinger denotes "amateur" as a maddeningly officious purity which Seymour Glass exhibits in *Seymour: An Introduction* (1959).

Salinger's goal with the School Sports Hero in *Seymour* is to envision him as an education within himself, the living lesson of an adept. In *Seymour,* rapt witness Buddy Glass recalls his Zen master brother, Seymour, the saintly hero of Salinger's Glass family cycle and a mesmerizing natural athlete. Salinger concludes Buddy's por-trait of Seymour by a lengthy section of vivid memories of the boy Seymour at play—stoopball, curb marbles, pocket pool—where he is sure, spontaneous, and above competition. Buddy self-consciously braces the reader for his picture of the "Aesthete as Athlete," hoping to do it "without excessively irritating anybody who hates sports and games" (103, 192). No one could really play *with* Seymour because of his maddening, inventive form. Salinger emphasizes Seymour's artist's love of self-mastery when Seymour's games come closest to pure play. He tells an earnest Buddy at curb marbles, "Could you try not aiming so much. . . . If you hit him when you aim, it'll just be luck" (202).

Seymour has no competitive nature at all, only a saintly sweetness. He refuses to move out from his status as natural where nothing is at stake. Seymour *is* Buddy's schooling. His is a coy, precious amateurism that cancels itself without conflicts, growth, or any sort of engagement. There is no hint of pathology in Buddy's witnessing, simply a worship. In Salinger's refusal to connect Seymour to any circuits of competitive sport can be seen the drift of his late fiction as a whole: attractive, witty, gentle folk saying wondrous things on an empty canvas. Seymour's play, unlike that of Kesey's McMurphy, energizes nothing and no one. Seymour has a need to attain a state of grace where play will cease. The play toward an origin or innocence is where he will perfect himself and abolish play through his suicide.

A Separate Peace

SEYMOUR CAN do anything (except live in this world) with the solitary blessing of play-full genius. Phineas in Knowles' *A Separate Peace* is more earth-bound, more limited to mere physical skills, yet no less captivating to his witnesses and no less doomed. Knowles focuses on the disorder of the hero-witness relationship within the boys' school sports story. He writes a throwback tale of private school boy heroes, nominally in the Merriwell-Stover tradition. His narrator, Gene Forrester, walks out whole, but at a cost, the death of Phineas, the natural School Sports Hero. Phineas blazes in all his simple glory like a young Greek god. The painful, dark overtones to his injury, the intense male bonding, and Knowles' rhetorical emphasis on the education of the human heart shade this novel closest to the bittersweet school narrative that E. M. Forster evoked in *The Longest Journey* (1907).[10]

The love and respect between Phineas, the hero, and Gene, his witness, turns on a single incident. In an almost involuntary moment of jealousy, Gene jogs the limb of a tree in which they are both balancing and sends Phineas crashing to the ground. His leg shattered by the fall, Phineas retreats into a world of athletic dreams and attempts to live through Gene who is appalled by the tragedy and fearful of his own impulses. He binds himself ever closer to Phineas as his caretaker, brother, and double. Phineas begins with, in Nick Carraway's phrase about Gatsby, a "Platonic conception of himself," but ends as a physically degenerating power. He is human and vulnerable, killed by his own bone marrow. In Phineas are the contradictions of the natural. At his sport, he is masterful, a thrilling sight. However, in repose, he cannot explain his gifts to his witnesses or present himself in human terms. Instead of providing a representative model, he is a freak of nature. He can never convert the physical into the spiritual as Knowles squarely identifies the perennial plight of the School Sports Hero.

Phineas and his great prowess are riddles that none of the other boys at Devon can fathom. Nonverbal, he expresses himself totally through his physical ability as do Roy Hobbs and Rabbit Angstrom. Like a prep Dick Diver, Phineas is a creator, making up rules for the games he invents and totally masters in mid-play. Knowles portrays him as a supple and inventive player within sport. In his account of Phineas making up "Blitzball" as he goes along, Knowles stretches rules and conventions of known games to achieve an innocent structure that quickly becomes both a martial and then an anarchic paradigm. Beneath the civilized facade at Devon is a primitive battle for maturity. Blitzball catches the boys in revealing poses:

> "Knock him down! Are you crazy? He's on my team!"
> "There aren't any teams in blitzball," he yelled somewhat irritably, "we're all enemies. Knock him down!"
> I knocked him down. "All right," said Finny as he disentangled us. "Now you have possession again." He handed the leaden ball to me.
> "I would have thought that possession passed-"
> "Naturally you gained possession of the ball when you knocked him down. Run." (30)

Phineas in this limited but total sphere of authority acts as the complete governing force of the boys' game which is truly a conception lodged inside his head. The passage contrasts rules, logic, and fair play with Phineas "naturally" dictating the next play. "Since we're all enemies, we can and will turn on each other all the time" (30), says Phineas in an innocent burst of Social Darwinism. Gene stops the flow in order to reason out the next move while Phineas is merely impatient to begin again. Gene becomes suspicious that the whole game might be an elaborate ruse to humiliate him. He can't play and mistrusts the sure, swift motions of the hero. Phineas also possesses grace and gifts not unlike those of Seymour Glass: "He created reverses and deceptions and acts of sheer mass hypnotism which were so extraordinary that they surprised even him; after some of these plays I would notice him chuckling quietly to himself, in a kind of happy disbelief" (31). Phineas lives to play and Blitzball is his finest game creation.

Through Gene, Knowles relates the dilemma of the witness's all-too human desire to destroy perfection. At Devon in the idyllic summer session during World War II, military overtones to campus life are everywhere. The masters attempt to keep the junior class (that of Gene and Phineas) as sheltered as they can while the seniors prepare to enlist. The boys' school sports story at the turn of the century had been permeated with preparedness rhetoric, martial training, and lessons to be converted to the battlefield. Knowles uses and then overturns the convention through Gene who feels after Phineas' accident that he is a killer. He no longer trusts himself in games and feels he should enlist where violence could be sanctioned. Instead, he stays at Devon, does penance by caring for Phineas, and perceives his own nature. In the war, Gene says, "I never killed anybody and I never developed an intense level of hatred for the enemy. Because my war ended before I ever put on a uniform; I was on active duty all the time at school; I killed my enemy there" (196). Their confrontation "on duty," in Gene's terms, is reminiscent of the relation to war and deflection of sexuality between D.J. and Tex in Mailer's *Why Are We in Vietnam?*. Knowles re-aligns "the sanctioned killing to obliterate the sexual terror," not with another male as a "killer brother," but perpetrated against him. However, instead of Mailer's mute pair of murderous boys, Gene and Phineas work through to mutual understanding. Gene's battleground had been the playing fields of Devon: "I was ready for the war, now that I no longer had any hatred to contribute to it. My fury was gone. . . . Phineas had absorbed it and taken it with him" (195). Here is the antithesis of Mailer's boys, who would turn their fury to the war and let it rage. In any event, neither Mailer nor Knowles is seconding the Duke of Wellington in any conventional sense. Working with "limited excellence" and "arrested development," Knowles believes both in Phineas' innocent creativity and Gene's commitment to the tolerance of himself and others that is formed at Devon.

Yet that humanism could be less evasively decorous. Ultimately A Separate Peace does not live, pregnant as it is with emotional possibilities, and the fault lies with the narration. Knowles gives no hint of his narrator's present life or specific emotional circumstances. Gene Forrester is too controlled, too credible, too vulnerable in his school days and too secure in the present, unlike, for example, Kesey's Chief Bromden. Gene is absolutely positive of what everything means in his past while his present is a blank. The almost complete absence of women in the novel is tantalizing but never meaningful. The reader leans heavily on the rote-learning of Gene's catechism as he must when listening to Buddy Glass. The sympathy and interest one feels for a Nick Carraway, a Chief Bromden, or the fascination with a D. J. Jethroe is denied the reader as he measures Gene Forrester. Knowles freezes the tale to the page. By his failure to construct a living narrator, he consigns his novel to the conventional schoolboy genre that he strove to enlarge.[11] Failure to transcend the time-bound life of the School Sports Hero is made explicit in the failure of contemporary American authors to construct a vital witness to the demise of the sacrificial natural. No Nick Carraways or Chief Bromdens in the crowd.

The Huge Season

IN THE Huge Season, Wright Morris has the largest ambitions for the School Sports Hero, desiring him to be a literary-historical benchmark for the 1920s and captivating enough in style to permanently enthrall and bind his witnesses. Through an elaborate layering, Morris attempts several narrative surfaces that the School Sports Hero frame controls. Irwin Shaw pointed out that Christian Darling "hadn't practiced for 1929." None of Morris' characters had "practiced" for 1929 either, nor for the long decades thereafter but their fates had already been determined by their intimate relationship to Charles Lawrence—millionaire, charismatic tennis champion, and a 1929 suicide. Lawrence stands as the galvanizing force behind the mystique of "the Huge Season," Morris' conception of the 1920s, not only because of its towering sports heroes and other pop culture heroes, but also because of its literary giants, specifically Fitzgerald and Hemingway. *The Huge Season* is about dead heroes and their surviving witnesses, a novel that pays deep homage to an era, its athletes, and its artists.[12]

The Huge Season is narrated past and present by Peter Foley, professor of classics and Lawrence's college roommate. The other witnesses to Lawrence's heroism include another roommate, Jesse Proctor, a socialist, novelist, and screen writer, and Montana Lou Baker, a woman of letters, confidante, and mistress to men of letters. Each witness has for years been writing a novel about Lawrence but none of them can finish their work because none can confront his relationship to Lawrence's life and death. Only Foley eventually comes to terms with Lawrence's compelling heroism. Lawrence had been a tennis champion without groundstrokes, hitting every ball before it bounced, either netting it, hitting it out, or putting it away. This grand style that defied tennis logic and, by extension, gravity and mortality as well, sets Lawrence's character for the reader.[13] The novel transforms the elements of tennis into fundaments of character, the "groundstrokes" of the novel itself.

Lawrence is a tainted natural, certainly modeled in part on Big Bill Tilden,[14] who by a sheer act of will has made himself into a champion. He has been left with a permanently stiff right arm as the result of a skiing accident and works hard to disguise the fact, to effect a lordly posture of instinctive grace. Yet he is also a helpless boy hero, terrified of getting syphillis, unable to do his class work, obsessed with style.[15] He is an heir to an American founder's "barbed wire empire" and creates barriers to real intimacy with his witnesses. As Foley says about a faded photograph of Lawrence at tennis, "You can see that he takes the game seriously. I do not mean that he takes it professionally" (6), a fitting description of a School Sports Hero where the stakes are always more desperate than a job well-done, yet less concerned with mere winning and losing.

In the novel's climactic tennis match when Lawrence falls far behind the star from USC, Foley thinks, "Everything we had admired about Lawrence began to look like something simple-minded, a flaw in him really, and not something admirable. A granite-like, sub-human pig-headedness" (154). Yet Lawrence makes an impossible comeback in Merriwell fashion. When he comes into the college mess hall that night, "all the boys that were there stood up. There was no hollering or cheering to speak of; they just stood up. Lawrence put up his right hand, gave them that smile, then Proctor and I took the boy with the clap down the long row of tables to the one near the door where he liked to sit" (157). Morris juxtaposes the champion and his acclaim against his youth and sexual vulnerability. Lawrence's will had triumphed this time "and we all knew that the man with the finest game in the world was not the same as the world's finest tennis player" (157).

Colton, Morris' college in *The Huge Season,* is a fictionalized private school outside Los Angeles based on Claremont, which Morris attended in the late 1920s. Colton is a western re-creation of Fitzgerald's Princeton and romantic brightness. Not only are Fitzgerald's characters and conceptions of school heroism on Morris's mind but on the minds of his created characters as well. On Proctor's desk next to *The Sun Also Rises* is *This Side of Paradise,* suitable readings for a character entranced with the schoolboy hero. Foley tells us that "whenever Amory Blaine made a clever remark, it was underlined" (122). If *Stover at Yale* had been "something of a textbook" for Amory Blaine and Fitzgerald, then Morris makes it clear that the tradition had lived through the next generation as well.

However, it is Foley who writes of the *cost* of school heroism through references to *The Great Gatsby:* "Every day some Tom Buchanan, modern version, man whose last big moment had been in the backfield, shoulders hunched from invisible goalposts he had never put down" (106). Morris fuses the figures of Buchanan and Gatsby in Lawrence who has the arrested development of the School Sports Hero and the mystique of the gifted romantic. "Lawrence had something too, but I don't think we felt it was going to be tennis. There was a limit to what you could do with that sort of will" (152). Lawrence's tennis achievements had no human scale: "It was the same game from the start. It was always a killing game, and he never let up" (156).

The "killing game" is what defeats not only Lawrence but Proctor, his most rapt witness, as Morris creates a sophisticated double witnessing frame whereby Foley witnesses Lawrence and also witnesses Proctor witnessing Lawrence. This remove enables Morris to have a central witness define the complete hero-witness dynamic and yet remain free for commentary. Proctor is more caught in Lawrence's wake than Foley, a Gene to his Phineas. Proctor is caretaker for Lawrence's self-destructive nature. After Lawrence has attempted to maim his own hand, Proctor binds himself ever closer to him by shooting himself in the foot, thus ending his own track career. Proctor does not learn how to live in the present and is victim to his fierce overidentification with Lawrence. What began as a neophyte author's interest in material coupled with a New York Jewish boy's obsession with an Anglo-Saxon establishment hero ends in his own obsession in which he becomes an itinerant idealist and world socialist. There are no conclusions to the novels of Foley, Proctor, and Lou Baker. Lawrence's death has ended their narratives of him unless they would follow the last denial of his narrative/life and kill themselves and/or their texts. Foley's novel is entitled *The Strange Captivity* and he burns it at novel's end, passing the benediction on "Saint Lawrence, the self-slaughtered martyr," and "Brother Proctor, the self-styled martyr" (299), but Foley, too, has run out of text.

Morris' novel is often too precious and knowing of its past materials, running the exact risks of his characters' narratives—hermeticism, stasis, a fixation on past artifacts and style. There is an unhealthy symbiosis among characters in *The Huge Season* that Morris fully described but did not find a way to master—akin to Knowles' problem in *A Separate Peace*—any more than did his writer-characters. Morris can only repeat their litanies. He searches for the driving force that shaped the popular culture of the 1920s and suspended the huge heroes as models that prevented men and women from evolving in time. Foley writes of the perfection and style of 1920s heroes, mixing Babe Ruth, Charles Lindbergh, Jack Dempsey, Juan Belmonte, Albie Booth (a Yale post-Merriwell hero), and Jay Gatsby. But as an anguished Proctor cries, "Why does [Lawrence] make it so goddam hard? He isn't human. How can you copy something like that?" (284). Within this schoolboy frustration is also the veneration of what cannot be copied, a tenet of high modernism in its distancing and detachment. Such perfection and style on the playing field is converted in the late modernist texts of the School Sports Hero to the perfection and style of the narratives.

The present frame of the novel is the early 1950s and the politically extreme McCarthy investigations. Will Proctor and Foley "bear witness" before a committee? If they cannot bear witness for and among themselves, how can they give public articulation to the meaning of their lives? What have they all been after Lawrence? Morris' not altogether satisfactory answer is that Foley has been "a witness to the power, the glory, the terrible risks of art" (189). This cry of mandarin modernist angst seems appropriate when applied to the captivity of the schoolboy tale and underscores the inability of the tale to speak of history or politics. Proctor's frustration is that of Morris as well: not only how can a hero copy his own past but how can a School Sports Hero be represented by an author? The limits of the physically perfect hero who cannot mature, the natural who will not come into adulthood, created a barrier to fictive complexity in the school sport text until the witness (see chapter 8) was successfully made the center of the narrative in a lived relation to the School Sports Hero. This Salinger, Knowles, and Morris could not really do. Perfection and style dominated the reality of their mystical heroes and blanded out their narrators.

Conclusion

THE SCHOOL Sports Hero may be judged finally as an avatar of excellence who retains little currency in an overly professional and technological sportsworld. The inertia of an aging Christian Darling, the frieze of the crippled Lawrence about to serve the ball, portray a loss of energy and confidence in the vitality of the figure who shifted from public leadership to private excellence and finally to a denial of time and of mortality itself. As a pure figure, he shades toward becoming a martyr-sacrifice. Most of the School Sports Hero's contemporary relevance is as a hybrid Popular Sports Hero in team sport where his professionalization and relation to the collective is complete (see chapters 9–13). In this emergent culture of professionalism, the School Sports Hero still represented, as Raymond Williams in

Marxism and Literature describes ideologically, "areas of aspiration and achievement which the more dominant culture neglects, undervalues, opposes, represses or cannot even recognize" (124). Thus the School Sports Hero could still powerfully embody physical perfection, a playfulness, a creativity, a renunciation of competition but at a cost: the extreme displeasure of his coaches, managers, and owners, to whom he is a commodity.

As the pure form of the School Sports Hero is exhausted, he cedes his central role in the narrative to his witness who has been growing increasingly powerful in the School Sports Hero's life and destiny. The conclusion of *The Huge Season* is most graphic on this point and is almost a paradigm of the form. *The Huge Season*'s fractured tale is finally lodged not in the dead Lawrence but in his three balked author-witnesses, Foley, Proctor, and Baker who would be copyists. Their dying manuscripts and moribund relationships are what remain. Thus did Morris write presciently of the shift from the one detached perfect hero to the representational dilemmas of his survivors. All these blank pages and impacted texts reveal a contemporary order: the spectator is now at the center and heroes are fragmented all over the arena. This late modernist re-writing of the School Sports Hero plays with this condition. The shift is from the high modernist novel of sensibility, with its privileging of sight and roots in James and Conrad, to the ironic confessional narrative of the witness which chapter 8 will examine.

8.

Anti-Heroism:
The Witness at the Center

T HE WITNESSES to victories and defeats in sports fiction appear frustrated beyond measure as they labor to get a reading on the meaning of the heroic figures. However, what happens to the witness who would create his own text with no real sporting hero at the center? The most private and expansive individual sports narratives are those of the spectators who can perceive no heroes at the center, who cannot even define the game they might participate in, who come through to no victories. Yet these witnesses counter the blank arena, the empty stage with a comic tenacity, a wry energy that will not admit defeat. They are the witness heroes at the center.

The voice of the spectator is most often an intelligent and vivid confessional voice, richly dialogized with accents acquired through rueful experience. The *individual sports heroes and hero-ines* have been characters who played through physical acts. The witness hero under discussion here plays through language. Taken together, these heroes and their play of acts and play of words comprise the broken halves of the sacred for Benveniste and constitute original plenitude for Schiller. The ritual and school versions of the *individual sports hero* express something "inexpressible," "natural," mythical, while the witness hero, no less a seeker after schooling and knowledge, and deriving from the same search, expresses fully and knowingly his frustrations in a freedom and subversion of order and experience following a realistic fictional impulse. For the witness, the major anxiety is his inability to affect the material or the sensual, his inability, in short, to become an individual sports hero. He remains in the wisest of expansive anti-heroisms, defining quests, reflecting on his defeats and isolations, in flight from both the collective, which he deems as dangerous and absurd, and from the body, which he deems an alternate source of frustration. Veering sharply away from capture by the sensual or by the collective, he celebrates his own uniqueness and difference, desiring neither the binding space of the Ritual Sports Hero nor the temporal dream of the School Sports Hero. The witness hero as male has the *word,* the language which is denied to female athletes and players as well.

The witnesses described here position themselves with reference to the competitive sports world. The spectators have no real way to excel in this environment but have all the yearnings of heroes. They do not have heroic naturals such as Phineas, Lawrence, Dorey Thomas, and Raina Scott with whom to interact; instead, the athletic adepts are fragmented into emblems and corners of the sporting experience: Ty Cobb's uniform pocket in Morris' *The Field of Vision* (1956), Frank Gifford's career with the New York football Giants in Frederick Exley's *A Fan's Notes* (1968), the mystique of homecoming and college athletics in Philip Roth's *Goodbye, Columbus* (1959), the athletic subjects of sportswriter Frank Bascombe in Richard Ford's *The Sportswriter* (1986).

Thus, there are traces of the heroic athlete in these novels but the witnesses are hard pressed to locate heroic presence at all in a crisis of sensibility. The truly representative figure becomes the alienated witness who articulates an unceasing adversary position to any terms of the collective experience by actively or passively assuming an *anti-heroism* which may shade toward play. A strong minor strain in sports fiction cannot locate a heroic individual presence yet has not ceded anything over to the collective team world of the larger society. Such a strain is comic, renunciatory, thoughtful, *literary* to a great degree, since all it possesses is its account of various abstentions and cancellations. These novels articulate the play of desire and the obstacles to it (Jameson, *The Political Unconscious* 142; Hassan, *Radical Innocence* 179). They discuss the constituent literary form to bring about that play even as they inhabit that form. Thus the neutral antithesis *play - anti-heroism* is traversed endlessly in a frustrated relation to the engaged positions of *individual and collective sports heroism*.

The signification of the witness hero is of personal insight informed by impotence and frustration, but the creative dance, almost masturbatory as it feeds on self drives, defines the pride and fierceness of insight. For what can these spectator-figures do but perform in a confessional mode and locate presence within self? They do so by reacting sharply in contact with the world of individual and collective sports heroism. By extension, these witnesses refuse to possess any commodity value. They write a brief against competition that is most valid when filed within its sphere. Compelled to contemplation of their own estrangement, what they are able to produce is a record of a life that they would like to bring to birth.

Heroes and Witnesses: A Brief Literary History

IF THE witness-spectator has become a representative man in one version of American sports fiction, what can we learn from Emerson and the nineteenth century about this figure? How does he appear in earlier eras of sports fiction and in light of modernist fictional conventions?

In nineteenth-century America, the most popular concept of heroism was that set out by Emerson, who was greatly influenced by Thomas Carlyle's maxim that great men should rule and others should revere them. In early essays such as "The American Scholar," "Heroism," and "Self-Reliance," Emerson was most interested in calling for the democratic hero who would define himself through his instincts and realize his great potential for both thought and action. The democratic hero would make himself up in fundamental ways and become the figure who, as William James observed, would be the man "from whom our majorities shall take their cue." The emphasis on the individual driving figure who would through vigorous self-discovery become an American ideal was tempered by Emerson's later, more passive search as a refined witness to identify history's great men. Nowhere is this shift better exemplified than in Emerson's *Representative Men* (1850). As the American sports culture and its fictions both reach middle age, they appear to recapitulate Emerson's phases in working through the problem of identifying heroes. His early vitalist writings called for men who would be heroes, while his latter prose works called for informed witnesses.

Earlier sports rituals were often captured through the narration of intense witnessing. Southwestern Humorists contributed tales of half-civilized roarers and backwoods athletes through a witness-narrator, very often the gentleman outsider to that culture. Natty Bumppo commented on the spectacle of the pigeon shoot in *The Pioneers* while Huck Finn witnessed the Grangerford-Shepherdson slaughter as well as the shooting of Boggs by Colonel Sherburn. "Ahab's quenchless feud seemed mine," says Ishmael in *Moby Dick* (150), assuming the burdens of the hero as witness in describing the combatants and contest and summing up the final score. Billy Budd, the innocent natural hero, kills his witness-tormentor, Claggart. In *The Red Badge of Courage,* a novel much in debt to aggressive American sport and its reporting, Crane continually shifts Henry Fleming's perspective between confused, terrified participant and deluded romantic hero to detached witness of other companies in battle. The perspectives are multiple and the interplay is between heroism and witnessing. The reporting of battle scenes or of grim urban vistas—which Crane, Norris, London, and Richard Harding Davis all knew so well— provided new angles of narration and emphasis on physical aggression and war. At the same time, these writers all reported and were part of American sporting culture. Finally, a cynically comic and supple style was crafted in turn-of-the-century sportswriting by writers such as Finley Peter Dunne and George Ade.

In modernist fiction, the narrated novel was the novelistic development that richly partook of the hero-witness tension. Narrators such as Conrad's Marlowe, Ford's Dowell in *The Good Soldier,* Fitzgerald's Nick Carraway in *The Great Gatsby,* Hemingway's Jake Barnes in *The Sun Also Rises,* and Faulkner's Ratliff in *The Hamlet* all looked at heroism from the vantage point of the witness. They are spectators for whom traditional heroism is closed for a variety of reasons—temperamental, psychological, historical, circumstantial. Lardner, though he professed to be simply a working sportswriter, nevertheless wedded the reporter to the author's conception when he created his gallery of fictional narrators as teammates, umpires, managers, sportswriters, and fans. The frame narrator has been exhaustively studied as the character created to express the modern author's disbelief in a heroic center.

The sports story itself had always been witnessed and recorded. Competition, aggression, and play all had to be transformed into and by language. Furthermore, physical heroes in sport could not tell their own stories without awkwardness. How does an athlete record his feats at the moment of performance? How can the impossible hero take time out to describe his heroism? Witness-narrators vividly re-create the aura of the heroes while they describe the heroes' ability to move men. In contemporary American fiction, these would-be heroes move to the witnessing center of the narrative, approaching heroism as quixotic or absurd, in isolation, paralysis, or fantasy about power. They are, for example, the comic outcasts of Saul Bellow, including Tommy Wilhelm, Augie March, Henderson, and Herzog, or an underground man such as Ralph Ellison's narrator in *Invisible Man* or Salinger's Holden Caulfield or Robert Penn Warren's Jack Burden in *All the King's Men,* a reporter-witness dragged down by his connection with a powerful hero. The witness became the center of the narrative in much contemporary fiction. There are few models of conduct. Rather, life is a search for a viewpoint, the proper commentary on a denied heroic action.

A central text that validated the witness as hero in relation to sports culture was Bellow's *Dangling Man* (1944) which immediately engaged concepts of modern American heroism. On the very first page of his first novel, Bellow wrote,

December 15, 1942

There was a time when people were in the habit of addressing themselves frequently and felt no shame at making a record of their inward transactions. But to keep a journal nowadays is considered a kind of self-indulgence, a weakness, and in poor taste. For this is an era of hardboiled-dom. Today, the code of the athlete, of the tough boy—an American inheritance, I believe, from the English gentleman . . . is stronger than ever. . . . To a degree, everyone obeys this code. And it does admit of a limited kind of candor, a closemouthed straightforwardness. But on the truest candor, it has an inhibitory effect. Most serious matters are closed to the hard-boiled. They are unpracticed in introspection, and therefore badly equipped to deal with opponents whom they cannot shoot like big game or outdo in daring.

If you have difficulties, grapple with them silently, goes one of their commandments. To hell with that! I intend to talk about mine, and if I had as many mouths as Siva has arms and kept them going all the time, I still could not do myself justice. (9–10)

Bellow's manifesto contains the seeds of a new way to approach athletic heroism through the eyes of the witness who does not compete or play and who freely expresses his vulnerability. What is being explicitly criticized here by Bellow is the configuration that later came to be known as the Hemingway code hero and that figure's supposed stoic acceptance of pain and danger, the emphasis on violence in his personal life, and the absence of an interior life. Bellow also defies Hemingway's literary progeny, the Tough Guys. He champions the vulnerable anti-hero who is in pain and admits it.

Bellow correctly identifies the inarticulate, physically dominant reality of the athlete. But his major interest is in the frustrated witness. As Joseph, the narrator of *Dangling Man,* continues, "The hard-boiled are compensated for their silence: they fly planes or fight bulls or catch tarpon, whereas I rarely leave my room" (10). Joseph is the witness watching a world off to war while he waits for his draft number to be called. Bellow's witnessing to pain and impotence marked a new confessional strain in American fiction that was highlighted by a generation of Jewish American writers, including Malamud, Roth, and Mark Harris in sports fiction. These second-and-third-generation sons of immigrants had no stake in reporting the decline of Anglo-Saxon heroes such as Tom Buchanan or spending time reacting to Hemingway's WASP vision of a Robert Cohn. Instead they reported sport as outsiders who would be assimilated, seeing it as an American comic myth, a popular and collective presentation of athletic heroes and their witnesses, their foibles and disasters.

Bellow took on a Hemingway at his peak and pointedly wrote out from under that influence. At the very outset of his career, he questioned the American individual sports hero and opened a space for the anti-hero in renunciation. He subverted Hemingway through a criticism of Hemingway's own language game, that of the Ritual Sports Hero and the sporting "gentleman," both of whom became material for the articulate comic witness. This play of/on words is further literary commentary on the Hemingway anxiety, this time in the realm of fictional aesthetics rather than physical conduct.

The wise-cracking, self-aggrandizing tone of the pain in Bellow's closing words suggests the comic thrust of the witnessing. Lost as the hero may be in self-deprecation, his narcissism is triumphant in the search for his own freedom. His bitterness is often masked by the absurdity of his yearnings, the desire to array and display himself to the world in a manner surely designed to bring on defeat (Hassan, *Radical Innocence* 180–202). The spectator-witness is a closet performance artist, shaping small rituals that he ruefully understands as his own repetitive games of defeat. The witness is a kind of natural as well, maintaining his innocence from the collective competition. He practices a comic deflection of mortality toward failure. He indulges in the willful patterning of the quixotic which replenishes the confessional self while damning the collective world and its possible victories.

This patterning would not be possible without a strong commitment to a vision of plenitude and spontaneity. Eugene Goodheart has written that when a player has a conviction of the fullness of life that overflows beyond the game, the game is an occasion for personal expression. When that conviction disappears, the game "becomes instead a mechanism to be disassembled and examined with detachment" (Goodheart 137), as perhaps in Frederic Henry's speech about cosmic rules after the death of Catherine in Hemingway's *A Farewell to Arms*. Thus witness heroes are vintage de-constructors of both competition and play. The heroes of Morris, Exley, Roth, and Ford swing in an arc between the affirmation of plenitude and the denial of the rules of the game. To adapt Goodheart's phrase, their emphasis vacillates between "the playing of the game to the arbitrariness that initiates the constellation of rules that constitute the game" (137). Goodheart does not trust play as a first principle. His argument is always for something cohering past play at a true center while the "arbitrariness" actually heralds a play that is unceasing. The only way for heroes in witnessing texts to endure is never to cease the game of playing the rules for their meaning.

The search of the witness heroes is the imaginative search for promise of unity that lies beyond a language that can never fully express it (Goodheart 142). The natural in sports fiction has only the repeated physical motions to express that plenitude. Language is always inadequate to his genius. The witness has *only* his language, has only his act of "see-ing" to describe, and it takes priority through language. The witnesses must play in and through language in what Derrida calls the very essence of play, the discourse that is the "field of infinite substitutions in the closure of a finite ensemble" ("Structure, Sign, and Play" 292). Through playing the differences, the witness dismantles gesture and life of the body into discourse that, as Goodheart comments, "wants to dispel naive illusions about plenitude" (144). Exley wants to scream at Gifford at USC, "Listen, you son of a bitch, life isn't all a goddam football game! You won't always get the girl! Life is rejection and pain and loss" (Exley, *A Fan's Notes* 63).

The witness moves to supplement the theatricality of gesture with that of language. Without an active hero that he un-self-consciously learns from, he consistently is driven to gestural parody and rueful reflection. He binds himself to undertake the hero's quest and reflects on it in an assumption of an uncommon heroic role with sports framing everywhere the signature arena for his experience.

Fleeing the School as Arena: The Witness "On the Road"

THE VALUE of school has always been mistrusted in American fiction. The school environment had been more limited in scope than the experience of existential engagement. In Faulkner's "The Bear,"

Boon Hogganbeck disputes young Ike McCaslin's right to stay at Sam Fathers' camp after Lion, Ben, and Sam have died in the epic battle: "You're damn right you're going back to school . . . or I'll bum the tail off of you myself. . . . Where in hell do you expect to get without education? Where would Cass be? Where in hell would I be if I hadn't never went to school?" ("The Bear," part 3, 250). In Boon's case, the answer should be "no comment!" Faulkner's questions through the hulking comic Boon point to the traditional mistrust of education in schools bound by walls that American authors have been writing about for 150 years. The anti-school *bildungsroman* is the great American tradition, as Faulkner knows. Sam Fathers' camp in the woods holds lessons that it will take Ike a childhood to learn and a lifetime to qualify. Melville stated that though Ahab had been in universities, a whaling ship was his Yale and Harvard (Melville 102). A line of heroes from Huck Finn to Henry Fleming to Nick Adams fled the schoolroom and domestic society to learn the lessons of the river, the woods, war, and the city in varying combinations.

The two most famous witness-narrators of contemporary American fiction, Salinger's Holden Caulfield in *The Catcher in the Rye* (1951) and Ellison's narrator in *Invisible Man* (1952), both begin their journeys in nominal school sports frames that are overturned in favor of quests on the road. In their singularity and pursuit of knowledge, these narrators must first establish their own difference from the cultural institutions of education, as they are "expelled" into the world. The openings of *The Catcher in the Rye* and *Invisible Man* provide the examples of the literal shift from the school sports milieu to the individual's emotional development in the witness narratives.

Holden Caulfield could not stay at school but did make education his calling and commitment. Holden is the most humane adolescent in contemporary American fiction but not a character generally associated with sports or athletic heroism. However, Salinger uses the boys' school sport stereotypes precisely in the service of a wider vision of anti-heroism. At Pencey Prep, Holden confronts the full force of the athleticism of the typical prep school environment. Salinger gleefully provides Holden with perhaps the lowest status position in the annals of school sport: manager of the fencing team! Holden rooms with a sports star, the center of the basketball team, with whom he has a fairly good relationship. Furthermore, Holden is no athletic misfit. He tosses a football around for fun and plays tennis and golf.

However, Holden confronts the prevailing mores of Pencey by criticizing the conventional school wisdom about athletes and the way they define school structure. He quotes from the school brochure: "'Since 1888 we have been molding boys into splendid clear-thinking young men.' Strictly for the birds. They don't do any damn more *molding* at Pencey than they do at any other school." Holden begins his narrative on the afternoon of the football game with arch rival Saxon Hall, and "you were supposed to commit suicide or something if old Pencey didn't win" (6). Holden suspects the Merriwell rhetoric and criticizes the concept of fair play. He counters an aged master's statement that "Life *is* a game, boy!" with his instinctive critique of competition: "Game, my ass. Some game. If you get on the side where all the hot-shots are, then it's a game, all right. I'll admit that. But if you get on the *other* side, where there aren't any hot-shots, then what's a game about it?" (ll).[1]

Ellison's imaginative use of ritual, boxing, and school sports frames informs the brilliantly hallucinated opening scene of the Battle Royal in *Invisible Man*. In Ellison's major difference, the sacrificial victim is expelled into a larger education rather than dismembered. Furthermore, Ellison's hero has language as his great tool and the only real source of his power as he moves into isolation playing the differences. The narrator of *Invisible Man* has made a ringing valedictory speech at the black high school. Now one day later he is to repeat the speech before the town's leading white citizens at a male "smoker." Before he can speak he must participate in an awful, staged boxing match where he is blindfolded and must flail out at nine of his classmates to the laughter and cries of the white audience. Here Ellison presented the first of many scenes in the novel in which black is set against black by the white authority. The boxing scene has direct reference to ritual sport. It is a rigged spectacle mounted by the power structure of the collective in which the town leaders are mentors and the boys are initiates. The educated black must be marginalized and sacrificed because he is a threat. The boys must battle it out for they cannot be killer brothers for a team they are not even allowed to join, for a priesthood that does not include their fathers. All they can negotiate is a parody of a commercial boxing fix and payoff.

Ellison torments "school" and "sport" into a new configuration in the mind of the narrator, initially a last true believer, a boy who wants only to rise on the power of his eloquence to become a real Emersonian, if not Merriwellian leader. Ultimately, he only posesses language in the novel and first senses the thunder of language's power in verbal play at the Battle Royal. He substitutes "social Equality" for "social responsibility" in his speech and gauges the stillness of fury in his audience. His play-full insertion defines his only freedom in the controlled ritual, the only human note sounded in subversion. His oratory, which will be his true talent in the North, is first tried out here. The instant's flash of power is his real intimation, as he mis-reads the standard southern "text" on subservience. He inserts his *own* language, making the town men "choke" on it, per his grandfather's advice. He learns the power of difference in the play of the substitution of "equality" for "responsibility"; the difference defines his racial role as other. He desires with all his being to be "like" his mentors but their ritual has the contradictory goal.

When he is given a calf-skin (fatted calf) brief case and a scholarship to a black college, he dreams that inside it is a note: "To Whom It May Concern. Keep This Nigger-Boy Running." All of schooling is a game, as the narrator learns when he is passed on to new mentors and new rites in the North. Ellison had the insight to posit education as the great American search for self and national identity. Schooling soars beyond the artificial time-spans and locations for the narrator who takes to the road as did previous generations of American fictional seekers. The early school and ritual sport fiasco is where the narrator begins to seek his true nature. He finally seeks future time and space at his narrative's conclusion, understanding that his education will never cease. The witness hero always looks toward the future. Ellison's narrator concludes, "I whipped it all but the *mind*," as clear an emphasis on the primacy of spirit and knowledge of the witness hero as we possess in contemporary American fiction.

The Field of Vision: Witnessing and Reader Response

IN MORRIS'S *The Field of Vision,* the subject is the current of belief and sustaining power between the hero and his witnesses. Morris brings together a group of characters in a Mexican bull ring and moves the narration back and forth among them to highlight both their vivid and their buried memories. The hero or "natural born fool" of the novel is Gordon Boyd, despairing ex-playwright, roustabout, and almost everything in-between. In Mexico he meets a group of vacationing Nebraskans that includes Walter McKee, Boyd's best friend in childhood; Walter's wife Lois; Scanlon, her aged father; and McKee's grandson, Gordon, who has been named for Boyd.

Morris' use of the bullfight and the arena is radically different from Hemingway's conception. Morris deflates the ritual in the arena through comic realism. To delineate the pull of the past he must twist and contradict the bullfight ritual to which none of his American characters have a sustaining relationship. He creates Gordon Boyd as a Gatsbyesque projector-player in a Hemingway arena narrated through multiple Faulknerian perspectives as in *As I Lay Dying.* Boyd works his dreams as diligently as Gatsby and is in fact pointedly from the same class of '16 or '17, not consumed in romantic melodrama but rather drifting on in comic realism past middle age.

Boyd is a self-proclaimed professional failure who has been obsessed with the hero's role for more than forty years. As a teenager he had caught a foul ball off the bat of Ty Cobb when the Detroit Tigers were barnstorming in Omaha, Nebraska. After the game, he ran onto the field along with the other boys to get the ball autographed, but Cobb kept moving away from the crowd. Boyd reached out after the retreating figure and tore the uniform pocket right off Cobb's trousers; Cobb never even turned around. The soiled, torn pocket becomes Boyd's talisman in good times and bad. Morris imagines it in many guises: a piece of the true cross, a fig leaf, a bullfighter's cape, a bull's ear, a coonskin cap (17, 68, 102, 109, 155).

The pocket "was the only thing he hadn't lost his grip on. Everything else he got his hands on . . . he dropped" (17). Boyd had dropped the ball as he chased Cobb, the ball he wished to have "transformed": "To get it transformed. And this had occurred. A stranger transformation than he had thought. Not merely a foul ball into a pocket, but a pocket into a winding sheet where the hero lay cocoon-like for the next twenty years" (109). Such a quotation underscores the temporal quest of School Sports Heroes. Boyd learns that no transformation is ever complete because the hero's role must be appropriated again and again. Mere possession of the object (the pocket) leads to personal paralysis, the famous "arrested development" of School Sports Heroism. Boyd is moved to risk everything in mock heroic gestures to hold on to the transformation. The life that always brims over in Boyd is transmitted through a series of gestures: the pursuit of the pocket, his kiss of Lois McKee on her front porch (the only true flowering of her life at age seventeen), and his boyhood attempt to walk on water with McKee as rapt witness. At the bullfight, he continues in character by squirting the bull with a bottle of Pepsi Cola, then squirting himself. These are acts at once heroic, comic, and desperate by a man more alive than anyone else in the arena.

Boyd attempts to hold the center of the arena but what Morris records is the impossibility of holding that center. Boyd's parody takes command of play as an artist while he denies any control over the seriousness of ritual. He rather expands the self-conscious frame of the player. Morris gives Boyd the freedom to express his helplessness in self-deprecation (Hassan, *Radical Innocence* 123, 178). But that is his limit as he becomes his own witnessing commentary, his own cancellation. Boyd has the freedom to gesture toward the heroic but the narrative is not under his resolution or control. The arena for Morris is where all the spectators see according to their vision of plenitude or its absence. Hemingway and Faulkner allowed their witnessess to observe sporting scenes of great significance in *The Sun Also Rises* and "The Bear." In *The Field of Vision,* Morris stresses not the scene before the witnesses, but the witnesses themselves and how each spectator might come predisposed to see through his or her generation of desire, his or her own otherness. What is produced by McKee or Scanlon or Lois McKee is each one's fragment of Boyd's signification, a piece of the "pocket."

Morris' fragmenting of perception underscores the textual production of the aesthetic object in an overtly reader-response-oriented text (Iser 16). *The Field of Vision* is a novel that highlights the "perspectively formed" reality of any text (Metscher 36). Morris explicitly remarks on the reader-response issue: "This crisp sabbath afternoon forty thousand pairs of eyes would gaze down on forty thousand separate bullfights, seeing it all very clearly, missing only the one that was said to take place. . . . In all this zoo, this bloody constellation, only two men and six bulls would be missing. Those in the bullring. Those they would see with their very own eyes" (159). Fiction about the bullfight has a double ordering, a combination of the already altered symbolic world of the bullfight and its textual representation. The virtual position of the text is somewhere unlocatable between the novel and the reader's perception of it, but *The Field of Vision* makes us acutely aware of the dynamics of such positioning. Our knowledge of Boyd's actions depends on the prior ability of McKee, Lois, and Boyd himself to "read" Boyd. The spectator becomes the competitor for Boyd's meanings.

Boyd has the conviction of plenitude, of individual lives reproducing themselves in a coming of age. The ending of the novel with the Mexican children swarming the bull ring, with another young McKee trying his wings, shows what is accessible to striving. This vision is not only that of the young. Old Scanlon recounts a prairie tradition where settlers traveling west in wagons had to lighten their loads by dropping goods, only to have them picked up by people in other wagons. Then "they would see ahead on the trail, what they had put down themselves a day's ride back" (96). In a fine sustained metaphor, Morris comments on the appropriation of someone else's vision, about our conservatism of wanting our past even as we move into the future, but finally, along the way, picking up someone else's vision or fantasy and occasionally meeting our past further along the route. Witnesses all have their own particular bullfight or baseball hero and conception of heroism in the mind's eye. The spectacle in the arena gives back what they need. What witnesses see in the arena is what *is* for them and they act accordingly, heroically, foolishly, but always in human desire for some revelation. *The Field of Vision* reveals no present other than that defined by the past for the future.

Boyd's life is running out but Morris suggests the problem for contemporary hero worshippers is how to keep alive and open to new experience: "The problem? In an age of How to-do-it, the problem was how not. How *not* to be embalmed in a flannel pocket, how *not* to be frozen in a coonskin hat. . . . To keep it open, to keep the puzzle puzzling, the pattern changing and alive" (155); in short, to preserve the freedom of playing the differences. Boyd stands halfway between comic hero and renunciatory witness as Morris deconstructs his sober natural, Lawrence, from *The Huge Season* into a figure of language. What was fixed, serious, natural, and nostalgic in *The Huge Season* is in *The Field of Vision* fluid, comic, natural, and questing. The individual sports hero has become the anti-hero.

The age of "how to do it," of mass-produced coonskin hats, of the goods continually dropped and picked up again on the frontier, shows *The Field of Vision* to be pointedly commenting on the commodity exchanges of middle America. In this sense, Morris reconstitutes the depth perceptions of *The Huge Season* in *The Field of Vision* as a study of horizontal surfaces, in a popular culture that cannot be escaped but that must be the subject matter itself.[2] As *The Huge Season* sounded a death rattle of late modernism's quest for perfection in style, so did *The Field of Vision* preface a postmodern eagerness to revel in the icons and artifacts of the quotidian. The novel asks, "How does it look from here?": a question that literary criticism would finally raise as the study of reader response but one that sports fiction has always known as the problem of the witness's relation to heroism.

A Fan's Notes

FREDERICK EXLEY's memoir, *A Fan's Notes,* is a deeply American book, an eclectic narrative of great feeling and comic wisdom. *A Fan's Notes* rests somewhere between a confessional autobiography and a novel as Exley's major character, "Frederick Exley," bears witness to, in his words, "that long malaise, my life." Exley's attempt is to make sense of his quest for literary fame in the context of "life's hard fact of life's famelessness" (70). His consistent reference points are football and its attendant glories and heroes. As Exley tries to break into the monolithic American success myth, he chronicles the life of himself as spectator, ennobled and alternately overwhelmed by what he sees on the field before him. Although he can never locate the center of American heroism for himself, he nonethe-

less can position *himself* as the locus for heroic yearnings and cancellations and reach a triumph. As Dickey wrote of Exley's book, "This
is the horrible and hilarious account of a long failure which turns
into success: the success that this book is."

Exley has utilized many of the conventions of the school sports
story. He is life's witness searching for models of conduct that will
sustain him. He has a deep and lasting attachment to his father, a
School Sports Hero in his own right. He identifies most strongly
with the heroics of football star Frank Gifford who is Exley's Lawrence, his Phineas, beginning with undergraduate days at USC in the
early 1950's and continuing in Gifford's years with the New York
Giants lasting through 1964. Finally, Exley is the perennial adolescent in his own dreams of glory where athletic and literary fame are
equated time and again, but, more fundamentally, he is the spectator
complete in himself.

In chapter 2, "Cheers for Stout Steve Owen," Exley works a
series of denials of a father figure while coming into full possession
of his own obsessions with fame and death. Exley's father had been
a superb small-town athlete in Watertown, New York, a hero to all
the boys, such a well-known figure that his son is amazed: "Doors
opened before his growing legend, and through the one into the high
school games he took not only himself and me but every scrawny-
kneed, matty-haired, nose-running, jug-eared, obscenity- prone kid
in town" (34). The pressure of being only *one* of Earl Exley's many
"sons" is intense. Exley must rise from this mass submission to seek
recognition from his father and from a hero-worshipping society;
"Other men men might inherit from their fathers a head for figures,
a gold pocket watch all encrusted with the oxidized green of age, or
an eternally astonished expression; from mine I acquired this need to
have my name whispered in reverential tones" (35).

Exley links the death of his father with the professional death of
Steve Owen, Giant football coach from 1931 to 1953. Owen, who
also functions as Gifford's father with the Giants, provides Exley
with his first image of his father's vulnerability. Earl Exley had
dragged his embarrassed son to meet Owen in the late 1930s. Earl
had hoped absurdly to arrange an exhibition game between the
Giants and his semi-pro team. When Earl introduces his son, Owen
growls, "Are *you* tough?" and Earl calmly answers, "It's too soon to

tell" (53). When Owen gracefully ducks aways from the Exleys, Exley recalls, "I did not dare look at my father. It wasn't so much that I had ever lived in fear of him as that I had never before seen any man put him down. . . . At the same time I had yearned to emulate and become my father, I had also longed for his destruction. Steve Owen not only gave me identity; he proved to me my father was vulnerable" (56–57).

Exley thus grows into his desire as other from his father, separate but also in his thrall, as he balances vulnerability and immortality, famelessness and fame. Fame is "an heirloom passed on from my father" (30); Exley vows, on the other hand, that fame will "come to [him] on [his] own terms" (44). However, as he attempts to launch his writing career in New York, he suffers "the inability of a man to impose his dreams, his ego upon the city" (70) and spends the latter part of the 1950s in and out of mental institutions. In New York, Exley continues his long identification with Gifford, much as Steve Owen doubles as his father. Exley first encounters Gifford at his peak of school sports heroism at USC. Upon seeing Gifford in a campus malt shop, Exley can hardly contain himself. He gives a "hard, mocking so-you're-the-big-shit? smile" which Gifford politely and innocently returns to Exley as a stranger, "as though he were having difficulty placing me" (63) and walks out the door. The graceful exit duplicates the way Owen extricated himself from Earl Exley years before. Similarly, Exley turns this incident into a real lesson: "With that smile, whatever he meant by it, a smile that he doubtless wouldn't remember, he impressed upon me, in the rigidity of my embarrassment, that it is unmanly to burden others with one's grief. Even though it is man's particularly unhappy attitude to see to it that his fate is shared" (64).

Here is the traditional heroic lesson of a sports hero such as a Merriwell or, in a more complex way, a Jake Barnes. Like a Nick Carraway, Peter Foley, or Gene Forrester, Exley wants some external corroboration of his existence. However, Gifford provides an innocent sober hero for his flighty imaginative witness, thus reversing the terms of the individual sports hero–witness confrontation. The effect here is to lodge the life and spirit within the witness-spectator. Exley's skill lies in the fact that he never diminishes Gifford in any way but allows him to retain a legitimate jock dignity, to age gracefully in "manly" style. The scene at the malt shop is vintage Exley. He is capable of suggesting heroic discipline within scenes of comic pathos and then concluding with a rueful universal that the prose has earned. The space that Exley forges for himself is that of verbal play. He uses it to maintain his dogged anti-heroism.

The "success that this book is" depends upon Exley's equation of writing and football, of sport actualized as an endeavor like writing, then compared to writing: "Where I could not, with syntax, give shape to my fantasies, Gifford could, with his superb timing, his great hands, his uncanny faking, give shape to his," and "my yearning became so involved with his desire to escape life's bleak anonymity, that after a time he became my alter ego, that part of me which had its being in the competitive world of men" (134). This transference is a testament of faith to Exley and not reductive at all. Gifford "had possessed the legs and hands and the agility, tools of his art—I had come to New York with none of the tools of mine, writing" (231). When it is suggested that he must dislike Gifford intensely, he replies, "But you don't understand. He may be the only fame I'll ever have!" (232). The bond between Exley and Gifford, so one-sided on the spectator's part, is validation of the witness at the center. Such validation is also Exley's acknowledgment of the "other's" difference and the necessity for it.

Exley has several of the most impressive scenes of spectating in contemporary sports fiction. He witnesses Gifford in many different circumstances over his years in New York. The first incident finds Exley sitting in the Polo Grounds next to a scrubbed-clean-and-cheerful American family of "snub noses, orange freckles, and sparkling teeth" who provide Exley with "the most uncomfortable afternoon of [his] life" (66). Gifford plays "superbly" and Exley wants to "jump up and down and pummel people on the back" (67); it is Steve Owen's last game as Giant coach and Exley has a deep need for Gifford, the son, to bequeath a last gift of victory to Owen, the father. Exley pummels the family's stiff father on the back and screams, "Oh Jesus, Frank! Oh, Frank, *baby!* Go! For Steve! For Steve! For Steve!" (68). When Exley begins to weep after the Giants lose the terribly close game, the father sniffs at Exley, "Look here, it's *only* a game" (70), whereupon Exley gives his standard retort: "Fuck you" (70), at which the family practically faints. In Exley's view, the bad form of the father and his failure to understand what the game had meant fill Exley with rage. "Anything you really care about, old man?" asked Lawrence in *The Huge Season*. For Exley, that question is classically answered in the affirmative: quality, endurance, discipline, feeling. Here it is answered in the brave hope that one son will consecrate the symbolic death of a father and thereby redeem Frederick and Earl Exley as well.

Exley creates the opposite environment in a 1954 game at the Polo Grounds. In a wonderful scene of a community of fans, Exley and a regular standing room group "found we enjoyed each other so much that we decided, quite tacitly, to stand the entire game" (133). Exley has nothing in common with the working class men, except the knowledge of the difficulty in any sport and appreciation for the art of its perfection. Like so many jewelers dazzled by fine stones, they appraise fairly and even humor Exley in his partiality toward Gifford. A knowing fan solemnly tells Exley about Gifford, "He's a pro. *He is a pro.*" (134). These are words Exley would wish to hear as a writer, yet he must begin, lovingly, with his acceptance by his peers in the stands. When he weeps at the judgment on Gifford, "we all roared at my sentimentality and roughed each other affectionately with our hands, dancing round and round in the cold winds of the Polo Grounds" (135).

Such a positive current of feeling is fostered among the witnesses that it is clear Exley has a different intent from writers working the hero–witness material in the ritual and school sport narratives. He is not interested in the ritual sacrifice of the hero but in the hero's survival. Gifford must live at the center of Exley's heroic identification, although Exley does not allow himself any personal intimacy with Gifford. The public Gifford is enough for Exley. When Gifford is seriously injured in a 1960 game against the Philadelphia Eagles, Exley fully expresses his special relationship to this hero: "For the first time since the beginning, when so many autumns before we had had the common ground of large hopes, we were in our separate ways, coming round to the most terrible knowledge of all: we were dying" (349). Exley learns from Gifford that he himself is vulnerable, even as Steve Owen had given Exley that knowledge about his father. The sports hero shares the bond of mortality with the witness. Exley learns in part to assuage his madness by making a truce in his deep struggle to impress himself upon American reality. His reluctant perception is, "It was my destiny—unlike that of my father, whose fate it was to hear the roar of the crowd—to sit in the stands with most men and acclaim others. It was my fate, my destiny, my end to be a fan" (357).

Exley's memoir is punctuated by repeated references to the American literary tradition, particularly to Hawthorne, in whom he sees a kinsman probing into the nature of moral acts, writing of outcasts and the pressure of psychic distress. He has a keen sense of quality and in the second volume of his three-part fictional autobiography, *Pages from a Cold Island* (1975), Edmund Wilson replaces Gifford as heroic model. Exley is a wise fool, an expansive writer who is shrewd enough to be restrained and overwrought by turns. The tension in his work is most deeply felt when the book we read is the struggle to shape his battle with his own excesses to the fullest degree. He won't be anyone's victim but his own and there is a simple courage in that. He is the artist of his own depression, inflicting his own wounds while choosing the anti-heroism that enables him to create. He ducks becoming any sort of commodified object and in a series of abstentions plays himself most fully into creation.[3] Exley is as resilient as Gifford, whose comeback in 1962–63 enables Exley to rise again. Upon Gifford's miracle one-hand touchdown catch that put the Giants in the NFL title game in 1963, Exley may exult one last time, "Oh, good, Frank! Good! Very good indeed! I mean, swell! *Really swell!*"; The next line belongs to Exley as writer as surely as to Gifford: "One had to hand it to the guy, his gift for living out his dreams" (376).

Goodbye, Columbus: Suburban Games

PHILIP ROTH creates a witness hero at the center of *Goodbye, Columbus,* a novel that also includes original interpretations of the individual sports hero and heroine. Roth keeps the center of the novel open and fluid by his witness Neil Klugman's fastidious avoidance of the terms of heroism. In addition, Roth creates a comic School Sports Hero in Ron Patimkin and a tenacious competitive heroine in Brenda Patimkin.

Goodbye, Columbus is a contemporary Jewish American version of *The Great Gatsby,* squarely in the tradition of the American success story and quest myth. Neil pursues Brenda through the new suburban green world of Short Hills, New Jersey. He chases a dream that promises rich rewards only if he can win the golden Patimkin girl. Neil is both Gatsby and Nick Carraway as Roth plays out his quest through Neil's satiric, anti-romantic sensibility. The controlling series of metaphors that define character relationships in *Goodbye, Columbus* are always those of competition and play.

Sports images best symbolize the tensions and competitive way of life among the Patimkins. Their backyard features what Neil calls "the sporting goods trees" beneath which "like fruit dropped from their limbs, were two irons, a golf ball, a tennis can, a baseball bat, basketball, a first baseman's glove, and what was apparently a riding crop" (15). The "fruits" of these sporting goods trees are in constant use by the Patimkins. Contrasting with the trees is the Patimkins' old refrigerator brought up from Newark. It resides in the basement and is filled with every imaginable fruit, a rich cornucopia of plums, nectarines, peaches, grapes, and cherries, from which the competitors select their prize. Neil marvels, "Oh Patimkin! Fruit grew in their refrigerator and sporting goods dropped from their trees" (30). The dislocation makes it clear that Short Hills is a tropical paradise of deep freezes where Neil's journey coincides in the novel with the imaginary trip of the little black boy gazing at Gaugin's prints of Tahiti in the Newark Public Library.

In the three decades of his career, Roth has created in two major styles, the one characterized by seriousness and attention to realistic detail (*Goodbye, Columbus, Letting Go, When She Was Good, My Life as a Man, The Professor of Desire*), and the other by satiric invention through sustained comic power (*Portnoy's Complaint, Our Gang, The Breast, The Great American Novel*). The Zuckerman cycle of recent (1979–86) novels (*The Ghost Writer, Zuckerman Unbound, The Anatomy Lesson, The Counterlife*) appears to have finally synthesized Roth's two dominant creative impulses.

Roth has attempted to explain the progression of his work, an explanation that makes *Goodbye, Columbus* seem sober and restricted in its satire. Roth has said that in the 1950's, his early sense of fiction was "something like a religious calling" ("On *The Great American*

Novel" 77). Roth recognized his dilemma in balancing high seriousness and low comedy. He wrote, "One of my continuing problems
as a writer has been to find the means to be true to these seemingly
inimical realms of experience that I am strongly attracted to by
temperament and training—the aggressive, the crude, and the obscene, at the extreme, and something a good deal more subtle and,
in every sense, refined at the other" (82). This balancing also contains
two oppositions familiar to a study of the School Sports Hero. Roth
retains the desire to write a novel of depths and stylistic perfection
akin to those of high modernism while the confessional narrator's
relation of the surfaces of middle class Jewish American life pushes
him closer to Exley's outrage and posture of the wise fool. *Goodbye,
Columbus* contained traces of the stately School Sports Hero but its
anger and confusion of roles now appear as vintage 1950s frustration
with American suburbia. Within *Goodbye, Columbus,* then, were both
the attention to narrative perspective as in *The Field of Vision* and the
comic confessions of *A Fan's Notes.* Neil Klugman exhibits these
tensions in Roth's first longer fiction. He is the repressed and irritated
Jewish son who can neither embrace Patimkins as they appear to him
nor endorse a vision of something beyond them. Roth refused to let
his witness-narrator gain any control over his own contradictions,
for he himself was only beginning that internal debate, one that he
immortalized as that between Henry James and Henny Youngman
("On *The Great American Novel*" 80–82).

Neil Klugman as narrator vacillates between two extremes. At
times he shows the tolerance and understanding of a Nick Carraway
or a Peter Foley, complete with their sense of history. At other times,
he shows the hurt, cramped disgust of an angry critic who is caught
in a round of social games and unable to envision any alternatives, a
critic much like the narrators in Lardner's stories such as "Champion," "Alibi Ike," and "My Roomy." Neil Klugman is twenty-
three years old and a librarian in Newark, New Jersey in the mid-
1950's. His parents have fled New Jersey for the medicinal desert
climate of Arizona, leaving Neil to live with his aunt and uncle in
Newark. He is restless but not ambitious, wary of commitments and
goals, and fundamentally bored and irritable. Adrift in a world where
everyone appears to be on a competitive course, he remains incapable
of choosing a life of his own. When Neil meets Brenda, it is his

desire that motivates him. *Goodbye, Columbus* recounts his summer as a young Jewish knight-errant from Newark in pursuit of a Radcliffe girl from the suburbs.

Brenda Patimkin: School Sports Heroine

THE HERO-WITNESS relationship in *Goodbye, Columbus* is actually that of Brenda and Neil with Brenda as the sports competitor as well as the person who sets the rules of the game. The novel begins with Neil's words, "The first time I saw Brenda she asked me to hold her glasses" (2). Neil obliges and spends a summer sampling the view from her Patimkin world. He attempts to push through to a vision of his own but he is continually balked. As Neil watches Brenda play tennis at dusk, he says, "All I could see moving in the darkness were her glasses, a glint of them, the clasp of her belt, her socks, her sneakers, and, on occasion, the ball" (7). The darker it gets, the more aggressively Brenda rushes the net. Neil is doomed to perceive only fragments of Brenda in motion, never quite getting the feel of the game or learning where the ball is, a paradigm for their summer of love. He is always anxious about the difficulty of establishing his *own* "Field of Vision."

The conclusion of the opening tennis scene in *Goodbye, Columbus* is similar in effect to the scene in *The Great Gatsby* when Gatsby first kisses Daisy on a moonlit street in Louisville before leaving for World War I.[4] Neil is entranced by the same image of climbing when he embraces Brenda:

> I tugged her towards me, too violently perhaps, and slid my own hands across the side of her body and around to her back. I felt the wet spots on her shoulder blades, and beneath them, I'm sure of it, a faint fluttering, as though something stirred so deep in her breasts, so far back it could make itself felt through her shirt. It was like the fluttering of wings no bigger than her breasts. The smallness of the wings didn't bother me —it would not take an eagle to carry me up those lousy one hundred eighty feet that make nights so much cooler in Short Hills than they are in Newark. (10)

Both Gatsby and Neil Klugman are consumed by the promise of a kiss in the dark; both embark on quests to hold the moment. Fitzgerald invoked whiteness, brilliant light, and romantic flowers and Gatsby became Daisy's prisoner for life through visual and aural images. Roth's narrative begins in muted tones and is marked by resentment. Neil's dominant sense is touch; once more he is blind in relation to Brenda, having no "view" of his own. He experiences no pleasure here and gives none. Rather he expresses an economic and cultural dissatisfaction in the expert lines of a resculptured nose, Roth's contemporary counterpart to Daisy's musical voice, and evocative of Fitzgerald's emancipated heroines with their bobbed hair. The only Patimkin nose retaining its identifying ancestral bump belongs to Ben Patimkin, on whose strong back (as opposed to tiny wings) the family has moved to Short Hills from Newark. As Neil pulls Brenda toward him, he says, "Let me see if you got your money's worth," his anger expressing Brenda as an object "on the market," and coveted in exchange with the Patimkin father.

Not since Jordan Baker in *The Great Gatsby* has an American fictional heroine been characterized so fully through sport as Brenda Patimkin of Radcliffe. Brenda is an athlete in a family of athletes. Her brother Ron is a college basketball star, her mother "had the best backhand in New Jersey" (18). Little sister Julie tries for every advantage at ping pong. At one point, an exasperated Brenda tells Neil, "You can't hear anybody move around here. They all creep around in *sneakers*" (47), a wonderful oxymoronic image of stealth. Brenda's daily uniform is polo shirt, bermuda shorts, sweat socks, and sneakers (uncommon for women in the mid-1950s). Neil is amazed and somewhat jarred when he finally sees her in a dress.

Brenda has been taught to press for every competitive advantage. When asked why she rushed the net only after dark, she answers that she has just had her nose remodeled and wouldn't dare come up so close to the ball if she expected it to be returned. Similarly, when asked about her nose, she explains, "I was pretty. Now I'm prettier" (9). Brenda will not come into focus, always controlling the play with Neil who is often a wary participant. Brenda asks him, "Where did you get those fine shoulders? Do you play something?" Neil replies, "No, I just grew up and they came with me" (12). His wariness extends to their romance on which he casts a serious appraisal: "We whipped our strangeness and newness into a froth that resembled love, and we dared not play too long with it, talk too much of it, or it would flatten and fizzle away" (13).

When Neil is a Patimkin house guest in Short Hills, she decides the two of them should run every morning before breakfast. He reluctantly agrees and they arrive at the high school track reincarnated as boy and girl athletes. Brenda remarks that they look alike and Neil thinks, "We were dressed similarly, sneakers, sweat socks, khaki bermudas, and sweat shirts, but I had the feeling that Brenda was not talking about the accidents of our dress —if they were accidents. She meant, I was sure, that I was somehow beginning to look the way she wanted me to. Like herself" (50). Neil moves helplessly into the contest for Brenda against the forces of Mrs. Patimkin, the family money, and their materialism. However, he remains the outsider who can't learn the Patimkin rules. On one morning run, Neil relates, "When we approached the half mile Brenda suddenly swerved off the track onto the grass and tumbled down; her departure surprised me and I was still running" (50). Brenda controls the play during their "race." Neil never knows when to stop and this scene prefigures her eventual calling a halt to the sexual game while Neil is still running after her.

The game in which Neil is a play-thing is in the competition for female supremacy in the Patimkin household. Mrs. Patimkin, a former tennis champion, resents the youth and freedom of her daughter and never ceases to drag down Brenda's confidence. Neil becomes the recipient of the fall-out from this competition. When Brenda finally succumbs to his pleading and is fitted for a diaphragm, Neil waits for her outside the doctor's office. When she comes out, he anxiously asks her where it is: "My answer at first, was merely that victorious look of hers, the one she'd given Simp the night she'd beaten her, the one I'd gotten the morning I finished the third lap alone" (72). This latest victory for Brenda is really a triumph over her mother. On her return to Radcliffe, she leaves her diaphragm at home for her mother to find (Neil thinks) and to learn about Brenda's sexual relations with Neil in the Patimkin home. Thus Brenda neatly steps out of Neil's life and deals her mother a shock. At considerable cost to herself, Brenda remains a confused and unhappy winner.

Brenda is cast as the surrogate victim whose expulsion is impossible for her family, but Neil is a clear sacrificial victim with no real ties to the Patimkin community. His last exasperated conversation with Brenda in the Boston hotel provides a final acknowledgment of how he is still indentured to her vision. When she asks if he can picture them all around around the Patimkin table at Thanksgiving, Neil's reply is a weak "I can't if you can't and I can if you can" (95). Their play ends when Brenda calls an end to the game, when she can no longer "imagine" Neil in her vision. The witness is resigned to a world void of play. Brenda and her mother declare war and run right over Neil, the convenient battleground, who wishes to be more than just a witness in the Patimkin competition but ultimately reverts to that. A "date" on a college weekend, he leaves Boston musing on his own contradictory and self-wounding nature.

It is clear as well that Brenda's nominal control over Neil is really control at the behest of the father. She is the competitive prize. Neil's "victory" at persuading her to get the diaphragm for his pleasure and her tentative victory over her parents are replaced in the larger male dominant discourse when the diaphragm becomes the key artifact in the competition. Brenda has tried "to recover the place of her exploitation" by "making visible" the diaphragm. The symbol of Neil's oppression then may be used to wound the phallic mother. Brenda mimes her role as sex object to slip that role and force her father to affirm his love. Roth manipulates Brenda Patimkin into considerable self-loathing here. Her unhappy status within the patriarchy will continue. Her triumph of "I'm wearing it" becomes the latter triumph of banishing Neil as lover and Patimkin. Her action is half-consciously perceived, according to Neil, and achieved through play that is "multiple, duplicitous, unreliable" (Jacobus 40) to be sure, but play that leaves Brenda with no residue of pleasure or liberation. Since we are never allowed into her narration or inside her motives, we must trust Neil as a weary analyst at novel's end. Clearly, her female power signifies Patimkin domination to Roth, her femaleness more that of the king's frustrated daughter, her desires finally meant to frame Neil's desire, which Roth was much more interested in. Neil Klugman has the *language* that allows him continued abstentions and questions in the narrative, while Brenda has only desire's artifact (the diaphragm) to play out her own oppression.

Ron Patimkin and Neil Klugman: School Sports Hero and Witness

IN THE Patimkin bridegroom, Ron Patimkin, Roth has created a very funny School Sports Hero in a genre not generally known for comedy.[5] Brenda's older brother is a genial boob of a college athlete. He could have stepped out of a number of Lardner stories with his non sequiturs and repeated ineptitude. He is a benign comic counterpart to the violent nativist, Tom Buchanan, in *The Great Gatsby*. The "acute limited excellence" of Ron Patimkin was as a basketball star at Ohio State. Jovial, uncomplicated, and banal, with a loose-jointed muscular presence that unnerves the tense Neil Klugman, Ron is heir to the Patimkin sink empire: a comic rejoinder to Phineas or the distant Lawrence or Brick Pollitt. Ron has been certified from a midwestern heartland school. If the Patimkins have climbed out of Newark to Short Hills, Ron has explored even stranger western American lands in aptly named Columbus, Ohio. He has returned from the New World of fraternities and sports events unable to supervise even the unloading of a Patimkin truck. The novel's title nominally refers to Ron's commemorative record, a sentimental trip through his years at Ohio State, which he reverently plays for Neil. When Ron hears the narrator describe a homecoming football victory led by one Herb Clark, he "closed his eyes" and "tightened" on his bed; there was "goose flesh on [his] veiny arms" (73–74). His ecstasy at the recital of a banal, surface world of college events climaxes when he hears the crowd roaring for him: "Here comes Ron Patimkin dribbling out. Big Ron, Number 11 from Short Hills New Jersey. Big Ron's last game, and it'll be some time before Buckeye fans forget him" (74). The narrator on the record concludes that all the members of the class of 1957 will leave Columbus on graduation day, "the most stirring day of their lives" (74). "Till then, goodbye, Ohio State, goodbye red and white, goodbye Columbus . . . goodbye, Columbus . . . goodbye" (74).

Roth plays on many resonances in this burlesque of school sports sentiment. *Goodbye, Columbus* is concerned with movements in American history as well as in personal history. It is less lyrical than Fitzgerald's vision of the Dutch sailors arriving in the fresh New World at the close of *The Great Gatsby,* but Roth's satire gives the

School Sports Hero's nostalgic sense of innocence and loss an original and comically diminished quality. The new Columbus exploring American suburbia and midwestern fraternity life is the Jewish son and basketball star. Neil Klugman is the intellectualized double of this explorer, hoping to make the trip from Newark to Short Hills. Brenda at Radcliffe might explore yet another version of the American school dream, but Roth is not as interested. In *Goodbye, Columbus*, Roth provides a most varied adaptation of school sports in his tight patterns of migration and frustration which are as deftly constructed as the reverse patterns of all the midwesterners in *The Great Gatsby*.

Neil looks deeply through Harvard's Lamont Library glass at himself after leaving Brenda for the last time in Boston, Roth provides the novel's final comprehensive sports metaphor: "I wished I could scoot around to the other side of the window, faster than light or sound or Herb Clark on Homecoming Day, to get behind that image and catch whatever it was that looked through those eyes. What was it inside me that had turned pursuit and clutching into love, and then turned it inside out again? What was it that had turned winning into losing, and losing—who knows—into winning?" (97). Neil's catechism to himself is his bewildered attempt to describe his own fragments of sexual nature; as Michel Foucault states about sexuality, "We demand that sex speak the truth," the "general and disquieting meaning" that presents us with "a general signification, a universal secret, an omnipresent cause" (69). However, Neil has not become Herb Clark, has not possessed his own nor the Patimkin vision, and his "homecoming" is Newark on the first day of the Jewish New Year, the first day out of his Patimkin captivity. Not "see-ing" has been his continual state: Brenda can't see without glasses, Neil can't see through her eyes, can't see her in the dark or at the swim club. Brenda can't see him at the Thanksgiving table, nor can he see himself through the library window. The "Field of Vision" may be there but no character can accomplish heroic seeing, least of all the desiring male through the nominally powerful male gaze.

Neil's mixture of desire, resentment, and self-disgust is vintage witnessing in the sports framing. *Goodbye, Columbus* points to the ease with which sport and competition come to be at the center of a secularized suburban family. Roth reveals the ways in which we compete, hurt, and hide from each other. Neil is terrified by this life because he can envision himself paralyzed by grudge ping-pong matches, by the seductive branches of the sporting goods tree, and by dawn runs with his love on high school tracks. As the black boy in the library would put it, "Ain't that the fuckin life." The ghosts of Lardner's narrators as well as the ghost of Nick Carraway would join the chorus in mordant affirmation.

Roth commented in 1973 that his career had been a zig-zag: beginning with *Goodbye, Columbus* in 1958, "each book veer[ed] sharply away from the one before, as though the author was mortified at having written it as he did and preferred to put as much light as possible between that *kind* of book and himself" ("On *The Great American Novel* 84). Roth himself had been a Herb Clark in the open field, eluding tacklers and reversing directions. In the vacillation of witness Neil Klugman between helpless desire and revulsion at the Patimkin lives and objects, in the problems of his own nature, one sees to the roots of Roth's literary problem on the cusp of late modernism's breakdown into competing voices: to criticize through comic vulgarity or through more traditional moral seriousness. Foucault also comments on this split in the sexual subject who has come to "a knowledge not so much of his form, but of that which divides him, determines him, perhaps, but above all causes him to be ignorant of himself" (70). Roth has identified himself as a "redface" in his typically witty play with the terms of Philip Rahv's famous essay on American authors as "Palefaces" and "Redskins," but he contends that the problem for American writers now is a "feeling of being *fundamentally ill at ease and at odds with both worlds*" ("On *The Great American Novel*" 83; italics Roth's). This authorial state of discomfort has haunted all of Roth's protagonists, including Gabe Wallach, Alexander Portnoy, Peter Tarnopol, David Kepesh, and Nathan Zuckerman, but Neil Klugman's love/hate affair with the Patimkins and himself is its first created analogue. As such, it describes the witness's attempt to define himself through his education in competition and play and suggests the deep division between them in American life.

Roth kept the center of the sports narrative open with Ron, the nominal hero turned comic foil; Brenda, the nominal "golden girl" turned unhappy sports heroine; and Neil, the quester turned unhappy witness. Within these turns of tradition, Roth has shown the Patimkin sportsworld as the constant lure. Brenda and Neil live within the illusion of love for a time but with the anxiety of no trust or knowledge of the other. Neil's last harsh glimpse at himself in the Lamont Library window pushes through his shadow "to a broken wall of books, imperfectly shelved" (97). Roth's final image is of the frustrating literary ordering that is his, of heroes and heroines skewed out of place, players on wrong fields (shelves) who will not play a single authorial game of "individual sports hero" or "confessional witness" for an author divided and playing the differences within his own talent.

The Sportswriter: Epiphanies without Cause

LITERARY ORDERING is a challenging task for all authors of fiction. Richard Ford's The Sportswriter finally undertakes a fundamental inquiry of the relation of sports writing to fiction writing. Ford does so through a vintage witness hero, Frank Bascombe, a writer who in his rhetoric about his art intends to explain why he is no longer attempting to write fiction after a promising early career. He is now a working feature sportswriter, not a heroic novelist. Ford's examination of Bascombe's estrangement from fiction and from all heroic pose purports to write a brief against fiction itself. However, Ford's literary game in the guise of a negative critique of fiction is actually to champion the sort of fiction he himself believes in and writes. The Sportswriter gives evidence that the "novelist" *is* a sportswriter if he writes according to Ford's aesthetics.

Ford shrewdly reverses the nominal direction of the sportswriting-fiction debate. American sportswriters have always been faced with the elite criticism of their calling, to wit, that sportswriting is not a serious artistic endeavor, that fiction makes more complex claims on writers in the realms of theme, style, and narration. When they have attempted fiction, sportswriters such as Lardner and Dan Jenkins have adopted the protective coloration of the working journalist, deprecating their own achievements, deflecting all artistic judgments of their fiction, and in general hedging their bets against censure and failure while wearing their successes very lightly. Lardner's reputation in particular has always suffered from the judgment, best and most positively expressed by a regretful Fitzgerald, that Lardner never attempted a long and complex work. However, novelists have long appreciated, as Fitzgerald and Hemingway did about Lardner, the strengths of the deft sportswriter that may be applied to fiction: concision, a feel for dialogue, a clarity of representation, a commitment to present action.

Ford's Frank Bascombe joins this debate and tradition from the stance of the sportswriter who has chosen his craft in preference over that of novelist. He is a writer and a man whose crisis is that of the witness *in extremis*. He wants to work out for the reader and himself what is to be valued. He writes, "In the end, this is all I ask for: to participate briefly in the lives of others at a low level; to speak in a plain, truth-telling voice; to not take myself too seriously; and then to have done with it. Since after all, it is one thing to write sports, but another thing entirely to live a life" (Ford 209). Bascombe's writing life consists in writing of competitors, yet he himself has given up competition in every sphere. He writes simply of wife, family, and emotional openness, yet he is divorced, his eldest son has died at thirteen, and he is effectively isolated. Ford places Bascombe in a familiar arc for the witness hero, between the affirmation of a plenitude, an abundance of life, and a de-construction of the rules of society's games to which Ford adds the game of fiction itself.

Bascombe has only his act of see-ing to describe. At the same time, he quietly wants to affirm certain illusions that he maintains about his field of vision, how firmly attached that field is to the quotidian. Bascombe believes, "If there's another thing that sportswriting teaches you, it is that there are no transcendent themes in life. In all cases things are here and they're over, and that has to be enough" (116). He denies an emphasis on the past which he sees as "death-dealing" and "overworked," championing instead "the tug of the ever-present" (24). Transcendence "is a lie of literature and the liberal arts" (16) which, Bascombe says, is why he failed as a teacher and put his unfinished novel in the drawer. Ford cancels the school sports nostalgia and all frames of playing back to origins. His is a cool rendering of anti-heroism in a command of the present in mimetic commitment. Bascombe's witnessing was intuited by him even as a boy on the baseball diamond: "I could always see myself as though from outside, doing the things I was told to do. And that was enough never to do them fully. An inbred irony seemed to haunt me" (27), what he calls his "dreaminess," a "state of suspended recognition" (42).[6] Here are Bascombe's temperamental links to Morris' Boyd in *A Field of Vision* and to Roth's Neil Klugman in *Goodbye, Columbus*.

How do Bascombe's choices and preferences relate to his vocation of sportswriting? He casts the "limited excellence" of athletes as a virtue, not as a problem. He believes that "athletes, by and large, are people who are happy to let their actions speak for them, happy to be what they do" (62). Athletes "make literalness into a mystery all its own simply by becoming absorbed in what they're doing"; they avoid "contingency and speculation" (63). Variously presented individual sports heroes such as Lawrence, Gifford, and Ron Patimkin all give testimony to this state. Such commitments of the athlete are, in Bascombe's opinion, a virtue that he would like to practice. The "mystery of literalness" is Ford's fictional subject, what he would himself make into literature if only he could conquer his propensity to "see around the edges" of what he feels and describes. The trick for Bascombe-Ford is the translation of "personal recognitions into the ambiguous stuff of complex literature" (42–43) which involves a merging "into the *oneness of the writer's vision*" (64).

Though Ford "sees around" the corners of both sportswriting and literature, he looks squarely at the aesthetic problem of see-ing at all. He does so by supposedly playing the differences between sportswriting and fiction writing. Bascombe's commitment to the present, the literal, to the representation of it, is constantly jarred and challenged by the witness's ability to feel many different ways at one time, to "see around" an action, a feeling, a person. To "stay within yourself" as a good athlete must, may be, in emotional terms, a cruel and defensive isolation. Yet Bascombe counts as a virtue the fact that "athletes probably think and feel the fewest things of anyone at important times" (120). Here is the fundamental problem in extrapolating from the drama and performance of sport and athletes into more complicated life situations and choices. Bascombe's aesthetic collides with his crisis of see-ing during Easter Week in encounters with his ex-wife, his girl friend Vicki and her family, a crippled ex-

NFL lineman who is his interview subject, and a casual acquaintance who commits suicide. How can Bascombe live his life in minimal reaction, avoid "seeing around," and still succeed in establishing some human contact and commitment?

Ford places his fictional markers along the route. In his commitment to plenitude, he writes, "The world is a more engaging and less dramatic place than writers ever give it credit for being" (209), that "literature's consolations are always temporary, while life is quick to begin again" (223). Yet he also states, "I simply found out that you couldn't know another person's life and might as well not even try" (229). Ford's minimalism raised to maxim expresses a common recent trend in postmodern American fiction toward the bare essentialist rendering of emotion and relationship. In Ford's aesthetic, Bellow's confessional witness has come back full circle to a voice that criticizes introspection itself. Ford creates a voice that is straightforward *without* expressing a Hemingwayesque tension, without defining the edge of heroic action. Such a voice seeks a grace without pressure. Furthermore, Ford cares nothing for the grand comic effects of confessional witnessing in Morris, Exley, and Roth. Ford is earnest above all and could be called existential in the tradition of Walker Percy's *The Moviegoer* (1961), but in wearing religion and philosophy so lightly, he achieves a limited humanism and general tolerance.

All first-person narrators are better at knowing themselves than knowing anyone else. The witness's text will always achieve self-scrutiny. What is longed for by witnesses and never easily achieved is communication within a community. Ford's vision of a possible plenitude is sharply limited, an expectancy without much consequence and without dialogized relation. Bascombe is consistently rebuffed in his simple outreach. Ford portrays him at novel's end waiting in a darkened office building for a new girl friend. He is in his favorite state ("nothing gone wrong, all potential" [365]) when he begins to wonder about a man staring down at the street below from a window in the building across the street. For once, Bascombe questions like an inquisitive author: Who is he? What is he looking at? What is his past, his future? Such questions appear positively Jamesian in their suddenly aroused interest. Bascombe concludes, "And I step closer to the glass and try to find him through the dark, stare hard, hoping for even an illusion of a face, of someone there watching me here. Far below I can sense the sound of cars and life and motion. Behind me I hear the door sigh closed again and foot-steps coming. And I sense that it's not possible to see there anymore, though my guess is no one's watching me. No one's noticed me standing here at all" (365). Ford's witness allows himself this one fictional impulse and hopes for his *own* witness, someone who will ponder *him*. Yet his reverie is canceled by a greater potential in the fictional gospel according to Ford, the sound of the girl's footsteps come to reclaim him as an actor in the sensual present. Ford imagi-natively completes Roth's last sense of Neil Klugman's skewed vision when he peered through the library shadows at himself. For Bascombe, "literature" is "seeing around" in the "dark" whereas plenitude is the "footsteps coming," a present-ing where personal recognition and the literal will replace speculation.

The above scene is, in effect, the real conclusion to *The Sportswriter* and the best example of what Ford might call the ethos of sportswrit-ing, the quickening of the present favored over speculation and qualification. In an epilogue entitled "The End," Bascombe relates the succeeding year of his life, which is more of his moving across a horizontal field; as in croquet, he says, "I am a side-approacher by nature" (255). Even in such summing up, which essentially goes against his grain, Bascombe ends in a sort of epiphany-without-cause, a postmodern reductive state where "you suddenly feel pretty good" and wonder "how long it's been since you felt this way" (374):

> a feeling of wind on your cheeks and your arms, of being released, let loose, of being the light-floater. And since that is not how it has been for a long time, you want, this time, to make it last, this glistening one moment, this cool air, this new living, so that you can preserve a feeling of it, inasmuch as when it comes again it may just be too late. You may just be too old. And in truth, of course, this may be the last time that you will ever feel this way again. (375)

Caught within the thrall of this intimation, Ford allows Bascombe to conclude with a fine bit of athletic description, one of physical sensation and mastery cut by the knowledge that past and future must deal for themselves, that the flow of plenitude without loss or regret is perhaps the best we can do. This last paragraph is one of the few places in the novel where sportswriting is actually in the service of physical sensation and action. Ford's conclusion earns the novel's title so well-dissected in the preceding witness commentary. The "glistening one moment, this cool air, this new living" is an ecstasy in which the witness always hopes "to preserve a feeling of it," which is why witnesses traditionally need sports heroes to play out the feeling for them.

This preservation is what the witnesses in their own texts are after in whatever comic, ironic, or cynical deflection of their own pain. They hope to unite time past ("the way it was once in my life) and time future ("you want this time to make it last"): Ford's present-ing as a "light-floater" is his playing of these differences. Sports fiction with Ford has reached its minimal presentation in the current neo-realism, not in the possible recovery of a heroic moment but in the prolonging of a pleasant moment for the witness. Frank Bascombe has no football tucked under his arm à la Christian Darling or Frank Gifford but has accomplished his task through justifying his use of language. He has described time in his own present without seeing around the edges of his field of vision.

Conclusion

THE OBSESSIVE running after heroism in the anti-heroic witness texts has many emblems: Boyd clutching at the pocket, Exley's final image of running after fame, Neil's desire to scoot around behind Herb Clark's eyes, to shelve the "imperfectly shelved" text, Bascombe's desire for his own witness in the darkened building. There is a great pressure in witness texts to continue speaking, as in Bellow's angry opening cry in *Dangling Man,* because witnessing presupposes all heroism reduced to utterance and text. Morris summed it up for all the characters in *The Field of Vision* by having Boyd conclude, "The proof was not in the pocket. Had it ever been? The proof from now on was in the telling" (232–33). The absent center is filled by the witness's language. The males in the witness narratives have the language that women and "naturals" never have. It is an excess of language, a power that the anti-hero turns into a limited capital.

The de-construction of its own see-ing is what the witness text finally accomplishes. It goes beyond the phenomenological basis for the role models of individual heroes and their spectators. Morris, Exley, Roth, and Ford seek the "original plenitude" of an organic heroism. Yet they write a supplement in its place, a re-appropriation of heroism itself in lieu of the default of the sports hero as a coherent entity for reference and representation. This crisis in late modernism, so well-captured in the energy of *The Field of Vision* and *Goodbye, Columbus,* becomes the given condition for postmodern writers such as Irving and Ford. The witness's desire here is finally not to be "like" or "same" but to find out what is different, what is not them: to continue to play differences rather than to end the play. Their specific alienated consciousness of being "un-like" is their glory. They mistrust spatial identification and temporal dreams.

Throughout the school sports and the witness narratives, heroic play is both nostalgic and visionary at the same time. Here can be placed the projects of a Gatsby, a McMurphy, a Boyd, what Skipper and Brick wanted to achieve through their long passes in *Cat on a Hot Tin Roof,* Rabbit in his great golf shot, even Ron Patimkin in his reverence for campus heroism. Deciphering anterior truth is a witness's conjuring while affirmation is a hero's calling. The witness's text is that of a survivor who avoids the sacrificial crisis, whose transcendental consciousness dominating the text is a phenomenological ruse. Morris best shows us the empty arena animated only by the text of various spectators. Exley inscribes marginalia and graffiti; he is the court wit observing the kingdom of the collective and its inconsistencies, its blind inhumanities. Roth's voice is the most intricate because Neil cancels as he creates, draws us to Patimkin competition, and pronounces it defective. "Columbus" is an origin that recedes. Ford's voice lays bare the present as the proper temporal frame for all sports writing. As arenas, Boyd has the bull ring, Exley has the Polo Grounds, and Neil has "Homecoming Day," the perfect sports referent of return to origins.

In summary, the individual paradigm in sports fiction as related in chapters 1–8 can be seen in very different configurations. The hero's body *is* the arena in the ritual sports narrative, in Mailer's variations, and in fictions of boxing (chapters 1–4). Only in the inscription of heroic players by Kesey and Coover (chapter 5) and in the inscription of heroines in sports fiction (chapter 6) is there the rhetoric of positive sports and play achievement in the service of an emancipation from male domination, even if often re-contained knowingly and un-knowingly by authors. Individual women in sport and play may be said to have a *collective* agenda and need for victories unencumbered by male nostalgia and irony about the collapse of the center. They practice affiliation rather than isolation or renunciation. They are competitive but they also mime the aggressive language of physical sport and seek a space within the dominant for their own play. Narratives about the School Sports Hero are more about narrative problems in general; they speak of an isolated hero with no language who desires a prior intimate relation to heroism as he searches for perfection (chapter 7). Finally, the subject becomes the witness hero who cannot perform as an individual sports hero at all (chapter 8).

The individual paradigm in sports fiction may finally be glimpsed at its male behavioral poles by two late 1950s texts of physical anxiety, Mailer's "The Time of Her Time" and Roth's *Goodbye, Columbus*. Mailer's Sergius O'Shaughnessy is the coolest of competitive sexual athletes while Roth's Neil Klugman warily shuns the final engagement in that arena. The ironies and dilemmas, the victories and defeats of the desiring imagination are everywhere controlled by sport and play. Within the arc of these texts, between the compulsive sexual scorer and the inhibited desiring witness, is the full range of narratives of male anxiety. These narratives are also played heroically by the female antagonists, Denise Gondelman and Brenda Patimkin, who may compete only within the strictures of their own oppression and whose priorities must be divined from the obsessively male narration. The work of Towne and Levin in *Personal Best* and *Water Dancer* suggest that in the near future female players and competitors can and will be heard.

Mailer strove to hold the hero-witness split together in a last Promethean attempt to shout down the corridors along with Kesey's McMurphy. Yet the majority of authors working seriously within the individual paradigm of sports fiction could portray the hero-witness split only through naturalistic pessimism or in comic deflation, through the ritual or school sports narratives. In my concluding chapters, I want to turn to another authorial strategy in sports fiction, the chronicling of the American team sports experience, where authors attempt to defeat the terms of the individual sports hero's isolation and open a vision of sport that has full correspondence with the widely lived and shared collective heroism of American team sport. However, the splits and contradictions of the hero-witness narratives follow the individual sports hero into the quest for the very center of American achievement and recognition where, once again, play becomes the free alternative.

PART III

Collective Sports Heroism: Fictions of Team Sport

9.

Fictions of Football:
Between the Lines

CHAPTERS 1–8 have focused on the individual paradigm in contemporary fiction about sport and play. The hero embodying that paradigm has been discussed in relation to the body, to a single opponent, to nature, to schooling, and to witness-spectators. Chapters 9–13 will posit the collective paradigm of sports fiction by describing the result of the interaction between the individual sports hero and the reigning American team sports of football, baseball, and basketball. The fiction drawing on our three major team sports places the individual sports hero with all the previously discussed crises of gender definition, self-definition, and courage, in the collective's power and organizational apparatus.

The contemporary team sports hero truly dominates the fiction of the collective paradigm of sport. The Popular Sports Hero who would become the team sports hero was born on the frontier in the almanac tales of Davy Crockett and Mike Fink and in the Southwestern Humor narratives of outlandish physical heroes and confidence men. By 1900, the figure had been scaled down to become a player for a team in an urban setting. Ring Lardner was the great early portrayer of the Popular Sports Hero, crafting that hero's language and persona with such skill that novelists coming to professional sport as subject matter are still working in Lardnerian forms three-quarters of a century later.[1]

The Team Sports Hero: A Man for Our Season

AMERICAN TEAM sport developed as a record of both our working-class and middle-class leisure-time preferences as well as our elite and mass educational philosophies of competition and group athletic endeavor. Team sport has histories of its own, but these are continually intertwined with the development of American industrial capitalism. Team sport duplicates structures and levels of the macrocosm and has its producers and consumers in the world of collective sports heroism. Team sports heroes have all the strengths and weaknesses of other heroes and of the society that produces them. The Popular Sports Hero is commercialized as part of the organization of spectacle in collective sports heroism. He begins in individual sports heroism. However, in that role, he speaks from inside an apparatus which accords him recognition and financial reward. How his play forms and how individual achievements are adapted to the collective sports world and the transactions between the hero and the collective form the tension of the fiction about the team sports hero.

What perhaps pushes the team sports hero toward the limited vision he can faithfully inhabit is his contradictory stance as a mythical figure within a nominally realistic enterprise. Bakhtin flatly states, "A sealed-off interest group, caste, class, existing within an internally unitary and unchanging core of its own cannot serve as socially productive soil for the development of the novel" (*The Dialogic Imagination* 368). To adapt this premise, the team in the collective paradigm fights any dialogization of team members, any interaction off the field where they have functioned as mythic figures. Team sports heroes must live the great majority of their lives away from their sport where their "unitary" language will not suffice in situations of personal complexity and a variety of social pressures. This contradictory realistic world has always provided the problems for the fictional team athletic members from Lardner to the present.

One contemporary gauge of the potential of mythical and realistic figures in the collective paradigm is the usage of the "natural" in sports fiction. When a mythic formulation in sports fiction is "the hero is a gifted physical natural," we may see that popular sport has given expression to the culture's mythic feeling about individual sports heroism and its relation to physical prowess. The athlete's play embodies physical grace, beauty, and power while it reinforces his primary relation to a mystifying perfection beyond the reach of the popular audience. "The hero is a gifted physical natural" has been encoded in a large number of contemporary sports fiction texts, including *The Natural, The Huge Season, A Separate Peace, One Flew Over the Cuckoo's Nest, Rabbit, Run,* and *Water Dancer.* Yet the natural's mythic tale is almost always subjected to realistic deflation. The hero arouses envy and mistrust and is confronted with the collective's pragmatic and material goals which draw off the hero's initial power and grace.

The natural's destruction is carried out in two ways. The first is a mythic, naturalized response by witnesses to his stature in an Iago-like "motiveless" denial of grace and beauty. The realistic response is to submerge the natural in sportsworld's power structures. In both the mythic and realistic formulations, society is seen to challenge the power of its greatest sports heroes. The team sports hero is often the classic American failure, initially posited as a mythic natural and then ironically inscribed in the American success story with its deterministic denouement. The team sports hero thus trods the path that American sports heroism may symbolize to the fullest extent in contemporary society.

Although the *play* of the *individual sports hero* is both a beginning of his awakening to himself and oftimes a rueful end point glimpsed after the fall into *anti-heroism,* play must not be viewed as an absolute in sports fiction but rather as a dialectical point that is most vital when charging or "playing off" its opposite of team sport. In the end, there is always a transaction in which the *collective sports hero* barters away the freedom of play for external reward. He then may realize that he has compromised himself to a degree and desire to move back toward his freedom in play. However, these routes must lead through a renewed individual sports heroism or through an anti-heroism that are both inimical to the collective.

The collective sports heroism at its conceptual point provides the contradictory challenge to play's utopian freedoms while not denying its generating powers of difference. The autonomy of play and of the "natural" are both illusory and ultimately meaningless without the animation of history, temporality, and fiction. In a very real sense, sport and play are destined to inscribe the battle between fiction and myth itself, with the caveat that play *is* subversive, potentially revealing, and an aesthetic exercise in self-mastery. To the extent that play leads out to a development of human energy, it will never be an end in itself; but if, in a materialist ethos, it is re-invested in history and temporality, we may begin to appreciate its power in human behavior. The fiction of this embattled opposition of team sport and free play is incarnated in the figure of the collective sports hero.

Between the Lines

SINCE ABOUT 1960, football has made a concerted challenge to baseball's position as the reigning American popular sport. Football appeals to very different sporting impulses and encompasses different American realities than baseball. Reul Denney identified football as fitting perfectly the patterns of our industrial society and summed up, "American attitudes toward football demonstrate a forceful need to define, limit, and conventionalize the symbolism of violence in sports" (114). Michael Novak sees that "football's ritualized, well-controlled violence is a more accurate picture of the actual experience of American life than the pastoral peace of baseball. Baseball may be the longing, football is the daily reality" (77). Of his fictional treatment of sports in *Cut 'n Run* (1973), Frank Deford remarked, "A few years ago I could not have treated them at all—because pro football, sports generally, had not entrenched themselves in society to this degree (*Sports Illustrated* October 30, 1972, 5). Deford spoke for the many contemporary American authors who have perceived the team sport patterns in American popular sporting culture as the basis for material in fiction.

Football is a sport with little backlog of heroic song and story. As Kevin Kerrane points out, football has no equivalent to "Casey at the Bat" and most contemporary football novels deal with the game as if it were invented in the 1960's (Kerrane 89). That game is perceived in fiction as raw, direct, literal, and dominated by metaphors of force, possession, and acquisition of territory. The players are aggressive, specialized, and fixated on the team as a unit. Football novels as a group deal with what are pessimistically believed to be American maladies of the late twentieth century: racism, superabundant wealth, love of violence, regimentation—all the subjects coded or sublimated in football for a society of spectators thrilled by gladiators in a spectacle.

James Dickey's poem, "For the Death of Vince Lombardi" (1970), articulates much of what football fiction would attempt to capture. Dickey addresses the dying coach as spokesman for his millions of witnesses ("I never played for you. You'd have thrown/Me off the team on my best day") and hurls him his charge: "You are holding us/Millions together: those who played for you." And now, around his death bed, "We are held in this room/Like cancer." Dickey has Lombardi's disciple, guard Jerry Kramer, say, "I wouldn't be here/If it weren't for the lessons of football." Dickey as the collective's witness cries, "Coach, don't you know that some of us were ruined/ For life? Everybody can't win. What of almost all/Of us, Vince? We lost." Dickey concludes by linking the dissolution of Lombardi's body to the wastes of the football witnesses: "Too late. We stand here among/Discarded TV commercials:/ Among beer cans and razor blades and hair tonic bottles,/Stinking with male deodorants: we stand here/Among teeth and filthy miles/Of unwound tapes, novocaine needles, contracts, champagne/Mixed with shower water." After this catalogue of detritus mixing artifacts of fans and players, the cry of Lombardi's witness is that Lombardi, who told us all that we were tough beyond measure, is dying, a betrayal of great magnitude, for he had told us we could deny death by controlling it behind football armor. Dickey unites Lombardi, players, and witnesses in the fact of mortality in his last lines, "We're with you all the way/ You're going forever, Vince," a fine turn on one of football's most prevalent cliches, "We're going all the way."

Dickey personalized with emotional rhetoric the fact that football is now the largest of all sports empires at the college and professional level. Its structure is perceived as one part military machine, one part corporate empire, and one part media circus. Football appears to embody all of the collective's power and pressure on the individual sports hero, who is nowhere else so severely circumscribed in a sports unit. With the exception of boxing, no sport is perceived by its authors as less playful or more constrained by the unit. Baseball similarly may be big business but its ethos and mythos work to mask the reality, while in football, the organizational structure is always foregrounded and lived as the individual sports hero's greatest problem. His only real alternative as a collective sports hero is the fall into anti-heroism which for the football hero is often abrupt and painful.

The real protagonist in football fiction is the game itself which fascinates and appalls, which obsessively claims its warriors and sets them in submission to the collective order. Football fiction produces numerous anatomies of the team, its hierarchies, and its spectacles. The game itself is omnipresent and determining in its power and control and carries with it a cluster of associated meanings in which I believe much of the authorial interest in football is lodged. The categories are:

I. FIELD STRUCTURE AND SYMBOLISM
II. FOOTBALL AS EDUCATION: THE SCHOOL SPORTs STORY
III. FOOTBALL AND THE CONFIGURATION OF THE BODY
IV. THE TEXAS CONNECTION
V. THE PROFESSIONAL PLOT
VI. "WHY WE ARE PLAYING"

Since football divorced from the school sports story is a recent subject for sports fiction, the following time line lists a representative catalogue of football fiction proper over the last two decades (irrespective of residual school sports football fiction which will also be discussed):

FICTIONS OF FOOTBALL

1967 - Robert Daley, *Only A Game*
1968 - Gary Cartwright, *The Hundred Yard War*
       Frederick Exley, *A Fan's Notes*
1969 -
1970 -
1971 - James Whitehead, *Joiner*
1972 - Dan Jenkins, *Semi-Tough*

       Don DeLillo, *End Zone*
       Noel Gerson, *The Sunday Heroes*
1973 - Peter Gent, *North Dallas Forty*
       Frank Deford, *Cut 'n Run*
       Elliot Berry, *Four Quarters Make a Season*
       Alan S. Foster, *Goodbye Bobby Thomson! Goodbye John Wayne!*
1974 - Jack Olsen, *Alphabet Jackson*
1975 - Robert Coover, *Whatever Happened to Gloomy Gus of the Chicago Bears?*
                 [re-published in expanded form, 1987]
1976 - Sam Koperwas, *Westchester Bull*
       Gary K. Wolf, *Killerbowl*
       Robin Moore, David Harper, *The Last Superbowl*
1977 - Lloyd Pye, *That Prosser Kid*
1978 - Peter Gent, *Texas Celebrity Turkey Trot*
       Jay Cronley, *Fall Guy*
1979 -
1980 -
1981 - Frank Deford, *Everybody's All-American*
1982 - Douglass Terry, *The Last Texas Hero*
1983 - Peter Gent, *The Franchise*
1984 - Dan Jenkins, *Life Its Ownself*
       Pat Toomay, *On Any Given Sunday*

Of the twenty-four novels listed, nineteen are about pro football in some form, suggesting that pro football is the dominant subject in the two decades of football fiction. However, the three recent novels of Pye, Cronley, and Terry focus on college football while the quite recent second football novels of Deford and Jenkins and Gent's third football novel all look at the football phenomenon in total—college, professional, and the traumas of life after football.

The greatest output of football fiction was from the early-to-late 1970s. This may have been because the social and political climate in which football was lodged contained real contradictions between an authoritarian team structure and a drive toward individual freedom. The variety of viewpoints on these issues was offered by three very different and popular nonfiction football books from the era—George Plimpton's *Paper Lion* (1966), Jerry Kramer's *Instant Replay* (1968), and Dave Meggysey's *Out of Their League* (1970). The emphasis on American aggression in Vietnam sparked an enormous debate about our "aggressive nature" as a nation and fostered a sense of alternative "natures" that might be lived. Also, in a time of greatly increased drug use in society, revelations about drug abuse in football made football a microcosm of the society's quandaries. This suddenly expanded dialogue between authority and freedom, between the individual and the collective, situated at the time of the Vietnam conflict, coincided with the full flush of pro football's challenge to baseball as America's national game. If that challenge has by now largely been met—on the field, in the box office, certainly by authors in sports fiction—football nonetheless remains prominent as subject matter and societal paradigm for late twentieth century American collective organization.

Field Structure and Symbolism

FOOTBALL'S FIELD structure and resultant symbolism dictate to a large extent what authors see on the field and what sort of fiction they create in response. Football's spatial conception is relentlessly linear and chronological, traversing the field back and forth, always moving in acquisition and defense of territory. The dominant mode is collision. This movement is one of a short burst at the line of scrimmage, a regrouping, and more short bursts. The long bomb notwithstanding, the short passing game to the contrary, football is earth-bound. This earth-bound state influences football fiction to be almost exclusively realistic with almost no flights of fancy, no break-up of points of view, no alteration of linear plotting. Baseball, in contrast, fits easily into myths of return and regeneration, while basketball has "upward space," transcendence, and flight. Baseball possesses a mythology, a driving back in time to approach its own origins, its own skewed histories of itself. Football has the scrimmage line and the *end zone*. The ball is repeatedly touched down.

Football is not only an earth-bound sport but time-bound as well.

Quarterbacks "work the clock" in the "two-minute drill" in which teams take on time as a direct opponent to be mastered by strategy. The dominant mode is repetition. Coover in *Whatever Happened to Gloomy Gus of the Chicago Bears?* makes a structural principle out of repetition. Gus lived in a time tunnel: "Every minute of every day he lived was completely used up in working on his skills"; "after he scored, he only knew how to score again" (96–97). Similarly, football fiction simply stops and reaches an end point where time runs out. In baseball fiction, the team could theoretically remain forever at the plate and defeat time. In football fiction, the crisis for the hero is almost always an end point, the closure of renouncing the sport.

Loosely depicted, if baseball is a sport with a strong past referent and basketball a sport of transcendent future, football is squarely present in orientation with little memory or history. Football converted into football fiction is neither experimental in technique nor fanciful in conception. To a great extent, football fiction is as roughly, harshly prosaic as the sport itself. The goal for the author and his players is to find redemption in violence and/or beauty, as Michael Oriard has suggested ("Professional Football as Cultural Myth" 34).

This insight is driven to its ultimate potential by Don DeLillo in *End Zone* when he equates fascination with football's collisions with fascination about atomic warfare. For DeLillo, the curve of the mushroom cloud and the clean emptiness of a burned area seduces as does the order of the advanced technology and its language. The portrayal of football in fiction reveals a certain guilty and ominous gratification on the part of the individual player, a sense of "God help me but I love it so" and a fear that "it's all there is." Characters in football fiction sense being in thrall to violence and destruction without being able to come to a resolution about them.

The most talented novelists meditating on football's violence and potential for destruction have done so by imaginatively commenting on the line of scrimmage and the moment of football's release of energy as the ball is snapped. Characteristically, Hemingway and Mailer focused on the intimate male body in positions of loss of control and release of sexual energy, respectively. DeLillo and Coover, their more consciously cerebral postmodern descendants, abstracted the line of scrimmage and its released energy into statements about the structure of freedom and language.

The vulnerability of the lineman at the line of scrimmage was described by Hemingway in *The Torrents of Spring*. As a high school center, Hemingway had loathed the line of scrimmage where the defense could blast him just at the moment he hiked the ball. Within the rules, his opponent had all the advantage. For Hemingway, loss of control was built into the very structure of the center's role. Hemingway could express his pathology about physical entrapment and ultimate illogic through the unfair game he felt football to be. Three decades later, Mailer attempted a hipster's analysis of football in *Advertisements for Myself*. Both visceral and cool in his appraisal of the T-formation, he concluded, "let us be brave with the fact [that play began] like men in the classic pose of sodomy. The ball instead of being passed was handed back between the legs." The T-Formation he wrote, "is closer to the sexual needs of the team, and so liberates more testosterone," thus combating passivity, which Mailer believes to be the greatest male danger. Football is "as is true of all wars . . . a study of energy and entropy" (383–84), and the football "war" between Rusty and D.J. Jethroe on the Dallas front lawn in *Why Are We in Vietnam?* is Mailer's fictionalization of his theory.

While Mailer wanted to speak of a hormonal liberation of energy at the line of scrimmage, Coover in *Gloomy Gus* suggests that the line of scrimmage is a fulcrum in which a sudden burst of freedom might occur (70–71). Coover sees football from the eyes of his radical sculptor-narrator. The issues are aesthetic and political, as they usually are when "freedom" is invoked through sport and play. Such sporting freedoms were never possible for Hemingway and Mailer. Coover's football hero Gus is a nightmarish, *imbalanced,* anal possessive who releases sexual energy at all the wrong moments, whose pile-ups are absurd. Coover reforms Hemingway and Mailer's sober opinions in satire. For DeLillo in *End Zone,* the scrimmage line is explosion—that of language, bodies, and, ultimately, of atoms. DeLillo states that football is not about warfare but about language (90). Language precedes and sets the burst into action. Football is what language sets in motion. Nuclear warfare is DeLillo's ultimate subject, the purification of language his goal. Football is the game to bridge content and form here, the play-space in which language and nuclear war will meet.

All four authors re-create the scrimmage line and the violence there. Hemingway sensed the collision as de-individualizing and frightening, while Mailer saw it as sexual and powerful. Working with these insights, Coover and DeLillo added their sense of football's ironic potential for aesthetic satisfaction, which further comments on the author–reader–spectator's continuing validation of the player's cry of "God help me but I love it so." Both Coover and DeLillo take as one theme the morality of aesthetics. Football fiction moves both knowingly and unknowingly through the intimations of the inherent terrors and satisfactions of football's perceived structure: violent, sexual, de-individualizing, apocalyptic.

Three final aspects of football's structure influence its fictional use. First, no other team sport has so many players or so much on-the-field anonymity because of uniforms, helmets, and masks. The game is structurally de-individualizing as Hemingway knew; hence the battle is so very strong in football fiction for individual self-definition. Secondly, football has a poverty of weather-related lore and thus little organic growth in and of itself. Baseball begins in the spring with the earth and dies into winter with its commissioner sitting shirt-sleeved in snow squalls. Baseball has a coherent, rhythmic relation with the earth. Football has only the unyielding ground (and synthetic turf) of the dead fall and winter, a factor that, in the fiction, strongly influences the "no-growth" pattern of many of its protagonists. Football cannot be lived with day-by-day in a "growing season."

Finally, football takes place solely between the lines. No structure of return to origins or home inheres in its spatial universe. No prior reference point may be imagined. Players may only repeat the dogged march they have recently undertaken. Likewise, there is no "play beyond" the lines, no individually free motion; all is coordinated with a unit. Liberation within the rules is not possible, nor is return to innocence. Caught in the "play between," football yields only the illusion of subject-centered play space: to play, one must actually step away from football itself. Authors then confront a sport inimical to imaginative play that they nonetheless must transform by imaginative play. Such a tension defines football fiction's consistent stance: suspicious fascination with football's domination and a wary depiction of its play-less structure by its lesser novelists. Football fiction's most talented novelists attempt to re-work an aesthetics to counter that play-less structure, and they conclude with their own criticism of an aesthetics of violence that itself becomes the problem (see chapter 10).

Football as Education: The School Sports Story

FOOTBALL NARRATIVES were embedded in school sports stories from the 1890s through the 1950s. The schoolboy hero played football to prepare himself for leadership in an aggressive American society. The Frank Merriwell and Dink Stover tales in the early twentieth century had always portrayed football as a lesson in teamwork, command, and grit. In reaction, by the 1920s and 1930s, authors of adult fiction focused on the romantic and wistful ex-athlete who could not convert his football currency in the larger society: Fitzgerald's Tom Buchanan, Wolfe's Jim Randolph, Shaw's Christian Darling (see chapter 7). The emphasis was always on the bewildered individual hero with no real role in society. Such figures were almost always drawn from the elite and drawn melodramatically. As school sports fiction about college football developed, the individual sports hero was depicted in the "problem" tale in which football heroism delineated a larger issue of the school's relation to society. Thus the fictional subject became the sport itself as a powerful institution within the educational system.

The "problem" in the 1940s and 1950s was the commercialization and professionalization of college athletics, a dilemma sensed as early as the 1890s by educators and social critics but one that did not cohere in fiction until after World War II. Many sober fictional discussions addressed this issue. Millard Lampell's *The Hero* (1949) followed an earnest ethnic boy up through the evils of recruitment pressure and big-time college football. Howard Nemerov's *The Homecoming Game* (1957) portrayed the relative failures of morality among university administrators, academicians, and students when faced with the star halfback's probable academic ineligibility and possible exposure for having accepted bribes to throw a game. William Manchester's *The Long Gainer* (1961) strove for an encyclopedic view of the entire collegiate world and its compromised positions in the larger society. The long, slow shift from elite to mass education was presented by Manchester within the frame of the school sports story. In *The Troubled Air* (1951), Irwin Shaw presented a new football variant: the heroic quarterback as dedicated Communist. Shaw's milieu is radio during the McCarthyite paralysis. His hero is a college professor-radio producer whose former student, Victor Herres, was a brilliant college quarterback but cynical and manipulative, never submitting to the rules. Shaw envisions Herres as a real devil-figure, a seductive, powerful, intelligent *quarterback,* full of will and energy and gone over to *them.* Watch out, America!

Politicization of the football story in the 1940s-1950s underscored the current between the school world and the larger society with football heroism as an expression of the power that inhered in the ruling ideology. The collective's practices were set in an anatomy of relationships, and football heroism could not remain at a safe distance from the effective dominant culture. Such heroism is what Raymond Williams calls a "residual cultural element" (123), one reinterpreted by the dominant culture, diluted, and projected into new forms. In the football tales of the 1940s and 1950s, it becomes clear to authors that school football heroism and its "education" were *always* approved branches of the socio-cultural apparatus and subject to its control. School was not the final lesson. Football was a business and its fictions could begin with that fact.

In opposition to this harsher conceptualization of football and school sport was the specifically southern variant of school sport fiction which offered both frontier humor and its antithesis, southern gentility, evidenced through a cavalier heroism. These two strains lived in uneasy coexistence but provided a bridge to football fiction proper. The more physical sporting tale evolved into the narratives of the modern popular team sports hero. Recent southern school sport frames are grittier or more apocalyptic, more in tune with the rhythms of small-town high school heroism without the veneer of college sport. Two excellent examples are Larry McMurtry's *The Last Picture Show* (1966) and Harry Crews' *A Feast of Snakes* (1976).

In *The Last Picture Show,* the real protagonist is the small Texas rural town in which the boys live and where school and sports are two of its major interstices. However, Sonny and Duane, McMurtry's traditional pair of friends coming of age, have little use for the school or for athletics.[2] McMurtry writes movingly of lost innocence and loneliness among all age groups and of an "education" of the heart that never truly ends. The novel begins on the night of the boys' last high school football game. After Sonny graduates, "people he had known all his life were all around him but they simply didn't see him. He was out of school" (205). The novel ends on a note of sympathy and selfless pity for the confusions of youth as Ruth, the coach's wife and Sonny's lover, soothes him and thinks that after all, he was only a boy.

Crews' Joe Lon Mackey is the ex–high school football star in *A Feast of Snakes*. For its pitch of bizarre symbolic ritual cruelty, it is surely the most malevolent of recent backwoods tales. If Flannery O'Connor had ever contemplated football, she would have produced something like Crews' novel. Joe Lon Mackey has been the pride of the Mystic Georgia Rattlers, a team whose nickname derives from the rattlesnake roundup convened in Mystic each summer. Other football players in the novel include Buddy Matlow, a former Georgia Tech All-American tackle, who is now a county sheriff whose knee was blown off in Vietnam and who is castrated in the novel, his penis described as a bloody "toy snake," and Willard Miller, Joe Lon's successor for the Rattlers, who has a "direct lidless stare and tiny ears"—Crews leaves no snake symbolism to chance. The novel begins with Willard's cheerleader girlfriend in her snake letter sweater: "She felt the snake between her breasts . . . coiled, the deep tumescent S held rigid, ready to strike" (3). Joe Lon sinks deeper into madness; the crescendo of the rattlesnake round-up melds with the football violence as Joe Lon finally turns his shotgun on the crowd of snake hunters and spectators, killing several people before the enraged mob pushes him to his death in the snake pit. Joe Lon becomes the sacrificial victim in the rite, expendable by the town in his murderer's role. He is the "host" consumed at their "feast."

Under the strong romantic influence of Fitzgerald, the South provided a different aura to American school sport and football than that of McMurtry and Crews. Fitzgerald's identification with Princeton as the school of lean, wraith-like football heroes imaginatively sounded a note in a shift in the School Sports Hero from the descendants of Harvard's Robert Shaw and Yale's Dink Stover to the descendants of Jeb Stuart and Faulkner's John Sartoris (a Princeton man).[3] Frank Deford, another Princetonian, has drawn on this tradition to fine advantage in his *Everybody's All-American* (1981).

Before Deford, several traditional southern emblems of football heroism existed in contemporary American fiction. In Robert Penn Warren's *All The King's Men* (1946), Governor Willie Stark's son is a brilliant running back for State U. but a reckless, headstrong boy, an adolescent version of his father. Tom Stark's snapped vertebrae in a big game leaves him almost totally paralyzed and Willie raging in grief, for his son had been a partial extension of his pride and authority as Biff Loman would be for Willie in *Death of a Salesman*. In William Styron's *Lie Down in Darkness* (1951), the tragic Milton Loftis wanders over Charlottesville, Virginia on the day of a big college football game in an alcoholic, shame-ridden haze, searching for his star-crossed daughter, Payton, amidst the Fitzgerald-like bright youthful boys and coeds at the game and along fraternity row. Deford's *Everybody's All-American* is a complete account of a southern hero's passage through American college and professional football, not as sensational as the football fiction of Peter Gent nor as broadly humorous as the work of Dan Jenkins, but balanced in its judgments, wise and witty. Deford follows the familiar School Sports Hero line in suggesting that the penumbra formed around the school football hero is encasing and confining, fixing him in a persona he will live in for the rest of his days. This is hardly original news in the wake of Tom Buchanan and Jim Randolph as well as all their descendants. However, Deford is comprehensive in his portraits. His hero, Gavin Grey, is an All-American halfback at North Carolina in the mid-1950s; he has an aura that infatuates his witnesses, intrigues the commercial society which wants to buy and sell him, and frustrates those people who would love him.

Deford's novel comes at a time when all the original turns on School Sports Hero romance and professional victimization of the hero of limited excellence have been made and recorded. The college football material takes up a little less than a third of the novel and Deford foregrounds some unexpected subjects. Part II, "The Mother of Four," is really Babs Rogers Grey's section, about how an All-American girl adjusts to being the wife of Gavin Grey. Deford's Babs is a fine character, spirited, strong, and gorgeous, whose difficult task is keeping the "ghost" alive in the more complex present. Unlike Daisy Buchanan, she is not irresponsible and flighty; like Maggie the Cat, she both threatens Gavin with her sexuality and graces him by bringing him back to the time when he was the "ghost."

Yet Deford is a deft synthesizer and commentator on extant football and fictional football modes. He writes, "If there is any difference now, it is that the great athletes tend to be black and the pretty girls all let themselves get laid at an early age, so nobody takes either quick moves or beautiful faces quite as seriously as they used to" (30). Deford here combines truths about current American athletics and popular romance while acknowledging that he is writing of a residual scene of power that is declining in force. He draws out the graceful, melancholy curve of a great athlete's career in its achievements and final tragedy when a middle-aged Gavin Grey puts a pistol to his head in his burning house on the afternoon of a North Carolina–North Carolina State game in 1980. The "Grey Ghost" whom Gavin and Babs had so nostalgically and sensually attempted to keep alive is really the dead School Sports Hero, the pact between them yet another tale of the athlete's inability to convert matter into spirit. Gavin Grey becomes a bewildered commodity rebelling against time itself in his search to "play back to" his great moments.

While football fiction had strong ties to the nostalgic rhythms of the school sports story, football's new status as a popular sports obsession dictated its assimilation into traditional American popular heroic modes of comic realism. In addition, football's pain and violence dictated assimilation into yet another revival of literary naturalism. Lone victims of the collective were depicted in the ritual sports story, particularly in boxing; the football hero embodied this victimization in team sport. The football player had a more sophisticated double anxiety: fear of his body's dissolution and of the collective's domination, the twin subjects of the first (c. 1900) and second (c. 1930s) generations of American literary naturalism, respectively. Deford's Gavin Grey is plagued by this double anxiety. In a sense, these twin subjects were what the contemporary football hero was to be "educated" about with this difference: football was the "schooling" and the end point with nothing beyond itself but its own contradictions. Thus football fiction reached back to a tradition of the School Sports Hero, partook of the pessimism of the Ritual Sports Hero, but grafted these strains onto the new element of the Popular Sports Hero's commercial team status.

Football and the Configuration of the Body

OF THE three major American team sports, football is the one with the greatest emphasis on the physical body. No sport portrays so many bodies under attack. Since the field symbolism is most often military, it is no surprise that casualties are present in great number. Football fiction sends two dominant messages about the body:

1. that the body is vulnerable, mortal, and always potentially in pain, and
2. that the body is manipulated by the collective in its own interest.

The body breaks down in contemporary football fiction as sheer physical anxiety dominates. The physical outrages perpetrated on the body are extended in narratives of economic and social exploitation. This violence done to the body is reminiscent of the violence done to boxers in sports fiction through the 1950s. Indeed, football appears to have replaced boxing in contemporary sports fiction's most intimate studies of the body. Seen in its most extreme light, football is collective representation of group aggression where a man is subordinated to an oppressive team, rather than as the lone brawler with his fists against one opponent.

The representation of the body is most often extreme and sensationally presented. In *The Last Superbowl,* a quarterback is brutally sacked. His brain simply short-circuits as he is bludgeoned and winds down like the computer Hal in Stanley Kubrick's film of *2001.* When he finally expires on the field, a crippled ex-player turned commentator is shown staring at his own hair spray commercial on his television monitor. In *That Prosser Kid,* a fullback dies when he is tackled over the sideline in practice and pinned in a wire fence by the force of the pile-up. *Killerbowl,* a science fiction football novel, posits the National Street Football League in the year 2010. Games are played for twenty-four straight hours every Sunday in abandoned ghetto blocks of major cities. Players are equipped with clubs and knives; each club's "hidden safety," recruited from prisons or military units, is equipped with a rifle containing one bullet which he can use at his "discretion." Each team is assigned its own medic with a bag of bionic parts (the medic may perform surgery during the game). Television controls the players with implants in their brains; each player has his own cameraman.

Extreme in representation and hardly subtle, these examples are no match for the intimate force with which Gent describes the football body's pain in *North Dallas Forty*. The reader literally watches Phil Elliott come apart: "The first hours of the morning were always the most miserable. Getting arthritic joints, torn muscles, and traumatized ligaments warm took at least an hour. In addition, huge quantities of blood and mucus had to be emptied from my head" (43); "I walked back to my locker feeling that if the tape came loose I would just ooze out on the floor" (158). Even sex becomes painful: "'Don't hurt me,' I whined as I crawled into bed, 'I've been hurt so much lately'" (73). This naturalistic emphasis on the disintegration of the body is delivered in blunt narration in an attempt to show the brutalization of the body in football combat and then to extend bodily abuse to an abuse of the spirit when a player is a commodity. Thus Gent moves from the cry, "We're just the fucking equipment to be listed with the shoulder pads, head-gear and jockstraps" (263), and says, "Football players aren't people who leave home and play football. They are football players who come home and try to play people" (196).

Coaches hound players into desperate actions. Harold Sims in *The Last Texas Hero* is made to run the stadium steps endlessly at Dallas University. In the novel's climax, he is left "stopping on that last step and dangling one leg in the free air beyond the steps of the stadium" (Terry 240); the implication is that he jumped. Terry's hero, Homer C. Jones, experiences a freshman year full of brutal practice sessions in "the pit" where freshmen square off with rubber hoses while an assistant coach screams, "Who wants to be a leader?" (183). The terror of being injured off the working team is intense in football fiction. In *The Franchise,* Gent goes the farthest in extending the results of football pain and conditioning. Simon D'Hanis, a young offensive tackle, undergoes knee surgery that is botched and results in a permanently weakened knee structure. The team realizes that he is damaged goods and arranges a trade with Los Angeles which promptly cuts him. Simon heads home to Texas completely out of control. Taylor Rusk, his teammate and friend, attempts to talk him down in vintage football righteousness: "They lied to you, maltreated and abused you, with no concern for the health of your body. But that doesn't make you a fool. It makes them *criminals*" (326). Here is Gent's continual indictment in his three football novels. The football scrimmage is always between the individual player and the team for control of the body and Simon has lost the battle. He kills his wife and two daughters, then turns the gun on himself. Taylor Rusk remembers Simon's words, "You have to sacrifice your body. Sacrifice your body. Destroy yourself" (327). Destruction in the service of football dictates that no body can survive the physical strain, the emotional conditioning; the players have become time-bombs.

Football fiction vacillates in its extreme presentation of the body between romance and naturalism. Gent describes his quarterback, Taylor Rusk: "There were no soft contours anymore. It was a hard face; the years had changed it. It was not handsome but like a wild animal's. Furious eyes, nose flattened, nostrils flared, he looked tired, beaten down, yet somehow stronger, painfully tempered by his struggles" (231). Gent's portrait is seen through the eyes of Taylor's lover, Wendy Chandler, and could be the romantic vision of a veteran boxer. James Whitehead's *Joiner* furthers that image but in a different vein in the person of Foots Magee, a veteran NFL center whose body had been used up by football and had turned to fat. Sonny Joiner thinks in Faulknerian cadence, "Foots had found the bone-and-marrow hatreds—and I suspect it comes from being left out or dropped, from never having it or from losing it. Or from being close to people who never thought of not having it, and certainly never thought of losing it" (174). Foots Magee becomes the equivalent of a punch-drunk boxer, out-of-control and dangerous, and Sonny Joiner kills him in a Civil Rights confrontation.

A comic vision of the body-as-commodity occurs in *Semi-Tough* when a Minnesota Viking scout happens to see an automobile wreck involving the Viking quarterback. Before seeing how badly he is hurt, the scout rushes to a truck stop, calls the general manager, and tells him to deal the quarterback immediately! Gent provides the best fused image of the physical pain and expendable commodity status in *Texas Celebrity Turkey Trot*. An artificial turf salesman wants to demonstrate his product to the Dallas team in a bus parking lot. An eager rookie volunteers to "cut" on a swatch of it, ruins his knee, and is left writhing on the asphalt, awaiting the ambulance. The players silently drift past him onto the bus, the twin commodities of rookie and plastic turf deemed of no further use.

Coover's *Gloomy Gus* takes the violent football body, its relation to the collective's aggressive material success, and naturalizes the imagery in a comic fantasy that proves Gus doomed to abject, total repetition, a prisoner of his own generated capital. Gus' collisions are awful, for he is in imbalance through his faulty sense of a fulcrum. Coover imagines Richard Nixon as Heisman Trophy winner at Whittier College and rookie of the year for the Chicago Bears in 1934, before his painfully worked-up system of controls goes mad and he begins compulsively to "plunge off-side." As an individual subject, Gus consistently believes himself "in control"; however, he is brought to grief when social contradiction foils his every attempt at individual heroism. In his football training, he takes on every particular linear assignment and attempts to build on a sequence but he is always charging at the wrong moment in a "game plan" that is a parody of over-specialization. He may only add to an ever-growing list of drills and cues. His body is in "horizontal madness" (81), an insane material production, an overloaded system. Coover has found the relation of Gus's body to football a perfect practice of representation for the rigidity and overachieving regimen of an American anti-natural. Gus' plunges off-side are the transgressions of the body ultimately visited by Richard Nixon upon the body politic in Coover's Watergate fable. Coover writes, "We talk about living in the present because we can't imagine actually doing it. [Gus] did it. He was in that sense the perfect realist, the absolute materialist" (97). Coover's intuition was to place Nixon-Gus in *football,* the most present-tense, realistic, and materialistic of American team sports.

Finally, the pain, honor, and sacrifice of the football body and spirit were apotheosized in Herbert Wilner's moving story, "The Quarterback Speaks to his God" (1978), written shortly before Wilner's death from cancer and heart damage. Bobby Kraft, an aging pro quarterback, awaits open-heart surgery with a fierce resentment of doctors who would probe his organ of courage and his physical core. Kraft speaks with enormous pride in his body and honest fear in the face of mortality:

I played in mud to my ankles and in the snows and over ninety in the Coliseum like in hell before the roar My God. Keep this my heart or let me die you sonsabitches. Pray for me again Elfi that I didn't love you the way such a little thing you are, and it was to do and I couldn't, but what could you know of me and what I had to and what it was for me, born to be a thing in the lot and the park, and in the school too with all of them calling me cold as ice bastard, and I wasn't any of that or how could I come to them in the pros out of a dink pussey college and be as good as any of them and better than most of all those that run the show on the field that are Quarterbacks. Godbacks goddammit. The way he's supposed to, this Gottfried with that stare and not any loser. Me? A loser? Because I cry in the dread I feel now of the what? (101)

The Texas Connection

THE TEXAS Connection refers to a constellation of associations in football fiction. More than half the novels in football fiction take place in Texas or have Texans as the central characters. Texas looms over them all as a new sports and financial capital, as seat of frontier and backwoods lore, and as the seat of national violence. If baseball fiction resides in a state of mind shared by author and reader, football fiction resides more often than not in Texas.

In effect, the Texas Connection provides an imaginative bridge or gloss on the unresolvable antithesis between configuration of the body and the professional unit in football. The Texas Connection stipulates that outsized physical heroes may individually dominate their relation to the team unit and live a collective sports heroism without contradiction or loss to themselves. This first premise of the Texas Connection has its roots in comic realism. The outsized sexual giantism of heroes in football fiction harkens back to some of the earliest American sports fiction in the frontier almanacs of the 1830s and 1840s, as well as in the sketches and stories of the Southwestern Humorists where prodigious hunters and boatmen coexisted with sly wagerers and con men.

Contemporary football fiction is most often represented through a revitalized comic realism that is at the same time full of literary naturalism's tints of pain and defeat. "Texas" in this fiction is part body and part commodity heroism, the physical body of power wedded to a powerful sports capitalism. Such a marriage defines the legacy of Southwestern Humor because the riverboatmen were economically powerful as well, symbolizing the growth of an expanding America, even as the Davy Crockett of the almanacs possessed a magical body that could stand for the national patriotic body. The Texas Connection makes legitimate all physical excesses in the service of team and financial excesses. Texas football becomes that utopian dream that allows the powerful body to win and grow rich without contradiction. Yet while authors have felt comfortable working within the Texas environment, they do so in an uneasiness, spies in their own land, where they write in critical reaction to the received mythos while still captivated by it. Their reception and conception of Texas is presented in a guilty love that rivals their guilty love of football itself. Finally, Texas and football so interact together that separation in the fiction becomes impossible.

Any discussion of Texas and football fiction must begin with the fact that the two most popular best-selling authors of football fiction are Peter Gent and Dan Jenkins, an ex-Dallas Cowboy flanker and an ex-Fort Worth sportswriter, respectively. Gent and Jenkins have achieved triumphs of popular writing arising from the sports culture itself, in a most Lardnerian tradition. While Coover, DeLillo, and Whitehead have accomplished much more with the football subject in terms of their aesthetics, *North Dallas Forty* and *Semi-Tough* have shaped America's current view of football heroism. Gent, an adopted Texas son, wrote, "I love Texas but she drives her people crazy. I've wondered whether it's the heat, or the money, or maybe both. A republic of outlaws loosely allied with the United States, Texas survives quite well by breaking the rules. Now there is a new generation of Texans who want to do away with the rules" (*North Dallas Forty* 8). Jenkins, an adopted New Yorker, wrote that when *Sports Illustrated* first began publishing in 1954, "they had some guys from over at *Life* who could probably find the Harvard-Yale game, if they had to, but that's about it. They didn't know anything about sports, especially football, so they had to get a bunch of Texans who did" (Reinert 10). Obsession with and pride of region is always part of their fiction.

Fictional precursors helped prepare the way for Texas football fiction proper in subject matter and form. Mailer had provided a Texas football vignette in Rusty and D.J.'s Oedipal gridiron battle on the Dallas lawn in *Why Are We in Vietnam?* Mailer also dealt with Texas corporate power and sporting violence in humorous and sca-tological presentation. Such expansive subject matter and form moved Mailer to write that in *Why,* "everything [I] knew about the Ameri-can language with its incommensurable resources went flying in and out of the line of [my] prose with the happiest beating of wings" (*The Armies of the Night* 62). A popular success such as McMurtry's *The Last Picture Show* and Peter Bogdanovich's resultant Academy Award-winning film (1971) candidly portrayed the gritty Texas plains small town that is at the heart of the lore about Texas and its love of football.[4]

In the early 1970s as football fiction came into its own, White-head's Sonny Joiner climaxes his Mississippi high school and college football career with a year (1963) on the fictional NFL Dallas Bulls. Jenkins and Gent received major public notice with their Texas pro football novels. DeLillo's *End Zone,* set in an eerie southwest Texas desert with associations to the Los Alamos, New Mexico bomb testing site, achieved a sports fiction first when it was excerpted in *Sports Illustrated* the same week it received the front page review in the *New York Times Book Review* (April 9, 1972). The late 1970s provided yet more Texas college football heroes in profusion, this time of the college football variety: Prosser in *That Prosser Kid;* Ben Elliott in *Fall Guy;* and Homer C. Jones in *The Last Texas Hero.* Gent added two sequels (*Texas Celebrity Turkey Trot, The Franchise*) to *North Dallas Forty.* Even a duplication of Gent as *author* occurred when former Dallas Cowboy defensive end Pat Toomay published his first novel, *On Any Given Sunday.* Finally, Jenkins brought *Semi-Tough*'s Billy Clyde Puckett, Shake Tiller, and Barbara Jane Book-man up to date in his sequel, *Life Its Ownself.*

Much of the creative energy in football fiction was generated by a group of writers associated with *Sports Illustrated* since 1960. Jack Olsen (*Alphabet Jackson*]), Frank Deford (*Cut n' Run*) and Jenkins were all experienced beat reporters who became humorous popular novelists. Hamilton "Tex" Maule, formerly of the *Dallas Morning News,* put an indelible stamp on pro football in *Sports Illustrated* when he called the Baltimore Colts' 23–17 overtime victory over the New

York Giants in the 1958 NFL title game, "The Best Football Game Ever Played" (*Sports Illustrated,* January 5, 1959). Maule's serious, laudatory game reports and his hand in the creation of a new sports genre book, the big, glossy photo-history [*The Pros: A Documentary of Professional Football in America* [1960] with artist-photographer Robert Riger) did much to establish pro football's dominance. Maule stressed *men* at work and teamwork; furthermore, pro football was depicted with harsh, physical beauty. Riger's photographs were gritty and stark black and white. There was an impersonal but lyric quality to Maule's conception as he and Riger worked to educate the fans to the intricacies of each position.[5] Of the conclusion to the Colts-Giants game, Maule wrote, "The tremendous tension held the crowd in massing excitement. But the Giants, the fine fervor of their rally gone, could not respond to this last challenge" (60).

Such language, so traditionally valiant and formal, gave way in *Sports Illustrated* in the 1960s to the inventiveness of Jenkins, a TCU graduate and *Sports Illustrated*'s first-rank college football reporter (with John Underwood) and feature writer throughout the 1960s. In addition, Jenkins' friend and fellow Texan, Edwin "Bud" Shrake, shared the pro football beat with Tex Maule. Jenkins' reportage could not give full rein to his comic imagination but he managed to lace his reports, particularly those from the Southwestern Conference, with enough local color and down-home quotation to make his pieces true popular cultural excursions into a region.

Of his early years in Ft. Worth, he wrote, "I had been born in the football capitol of the universe, South Bend, Indiana, and Tuscaloosa, Alabama, notwithstanding (*Sports Illustrated,* November 7, 1977, 81).[6] He was to convince America of that fact in *Sports Illustrated* and *Semi-Tough.* Whereas Maule had reported on the football team as a unit, seldom highlighting individuals or quoting them, Jenkins thrived on football personalities in his reports. *Semi-Tough*'s linguistic energy was prefaced throughout the 1960s in Jenkins' journalism. Jenkins reported Texas football coach Darrel Royal describing his All-American linebacker Tommy Nobis as "the one without the visible chain on him" and "aside from his super ability, he's just one of those trained pigs you love. He'll jump right in the slop for you" (*Sports Illustrated,* October 18, 1965: 40). As Lardner had listened to the Cubs and White Sox, so, too, did Jenkins listen and reproduce a vital sports vernacular.

Dan Jenkins and Texas Triumphant

JENKINS' VERBAL resources could be indulged in *Semi-Tough* which posited a world where Texas celebrities—country singers, oil men, world-class models, television stars, football players—were themselves eagerly consumed by an America that saw in them a ribald, countrified, albeit commodified vision of the last American frontier. Jenkins, like Lardner before him, debunked any literary pretensions, stating characteristically, "I wrote the book for calisthenics, just to see if I could write a semi-novel" and allowing that the narrative was "a little less complicated than *The Brothers Karamazov*" ("When the Frogs Were Princes" 79). *Semi-Tough* was part professional, technological version of *The Last Picture Show*, part football follow-up to *You Know Me, Al*, and part Huck/Tom/Becky story brought up to date. Jenkins' Texas is a largely benign one, full of bluster and folk wisdom, from which physically perfect, sly Texas children go forth to conquer the sports and media centers of America.

Semi-Tough is also the football fiction counterpart to Roth's *The Great American Novel* in its scatological inventiveness. Jenkins' narrator, Billy Clyde Puckett, is Henry Wiggen or a contemporary Jack Keefe who does not write semi-literate letters home to Al but rather speaks into a tape recorder in his Beverly Hills hotel during Super Bowl week. Presumably, All-Pro fullback Billy Clyde has a tidy six-figure advance on his book. Jenkins is writing a satire on the "instant" sports book, hastily put on tape, the spelling and punctuation to be supplied by a Texas friend and sportswriter—the "Al" of the narrative, one Jim Tom Pinch. Jenkins envisions Super Bowl week as the new total American spectacle, glittering, plastic, raunchy, awash in money and sex, the football game itself merely an ordering center to the carnival demanded by television and the corporation. Super Bowl *Week* is the subject, as Jenkins makes clear when he lets the narrative jump from pre-game to post-game. Only later does Billy Clyde report the game itself which, true to popular fictional form, is a thriller with himself as ultimate hero.

Jenkins has identified the new axes of football power and authority in sportsworld in the New York-Texas-Hollywood triad. Wide-eyed Billy Clyde and his more cynical best pal, Shake Tiller, are steeped in small-town Texas high school and college football heroism. *Semi-*

275

Tough finds them as teammates and stars on the New York Giants in the sophisticated capital of pro football's media center. Billy Clyde and Shake are playing the "dog ass" New York Jets in the Super Bowl in Los Angeles, the fantasy capital of superstardom. In many wry and discouraging scenes, Jenkins suggests that these country boys with an East Side singles bar veneer are quite at home in Beverly Hills which consumes them and packages them for the nation.

Jenkins is a light satirist, skimming the surface of contemporary media sports culture with very attractive and successful characters as spokespeople. Billy Clyde and Shake are joined by their best friend, Barbara Jane Bookman, oil heiress and world class model who is Shake Tiller's but who marries Billy Clyde at the conclusion of *Semi-Tough*. In *Life Its Ownself,* Jenkins continues their adventures. Billy Clyde writes, "Barbara Jane, Shake Tiller and I had known each other since the third grade. It was in the third grade that we had formed our own private club, a society dedicated to laughing at life its ownself" (48). Such staunchness and hermeticism preclude adversary positions, antagonists, or growth. As textbooks of false consciousness, *Semi-Tough* and *Life Its Ownself* contain characters who are quite candid about their complicity in the syndromes that they describe, a facet of postmodern writing itself best expressed by Donald Barthelme in "Brain Damage" when he wrote, "I could describe it better if I weren't afflicted with it" (156).

Jenkins firmly ties his superstar children to Texas and to the power there. Barbara Jane's father, Big Ed Bookman, is a bumptious, walking encyclopedia of American prejudices and material success, a comic reincarnation of Mailer's Rusty Jethroe in *Why Are We in Vietnam?*. Famous country singer Elroy Blunt, a former NFL cornerback, throws an orgy for the boys the night before the Super Bowl game. His songs frame much of the action in melancholy lines about big, virile men and lonely women. Another Texas boy, television Western star Boke Kellum, lingers and basks in the boys' Super Bowl publicity. Throughout his football novels Jenkins suggests that there is no excess a Texan may commit that will not be applauded by America at large.

Billy Clyde is in the tradition of American sly monologuists who attempt to tell truths from behind the mask. He can say about "his" novel, *Semi-Tough,* "I happen to be writing it in my spare time between running over a whole pile of niggers in the National Football League" (3) but continues, "What I'm getting at is that a football player is a football player. . . . Now if a nigger doesn't want to be a nigger in real life, that's something else. But I sure know several who can block and tackle themselves pretty damn white" (4). As Shake Tiller passionately believes, "A sumbitch who don't block or tackle is nothing but a nigger hebe spick with a little A-rab thrown in" (5–6). Jenkins sees players judged by their courage under fire, the cacophony of epithets along the way meant to express a rough, nativist democracy of sport, the sort of humility that football, the most physically humbling of team sports, fosters in its wisest players in football fiction.

Jenkins' language is a supple instrument. An example of Billy Clyde's deadpan moral relativism: "I look at it this way, anyhow. If eight out of every ten NFL games are honest, that's a hell of lot better percentage than you can get in that pro fucking basketball" (164); when a running back keeps asking for a signal check at the line of scrimmage because he can't remember the play, the Giant quarterback points to "Puddin Patterson's butt" and says, *Right* fuckin' through here, you country cocksucker" (181). The Jets' great linebacker, Dreamer Tatum, is the "bad dream" opponent whom Billy Clyde and Shake prepare for all week, who in defeat says to them simply, "What *could* have happened, *did*. That's what I know" (198).

Finally, in "semi-tough," Jenkins found a perfectly-pitched verbal equivalent for jock self-deprecation combined with enormous pride. "Semi" means "super" in an understated and cool terminology that governs naming and response of the players. "Semi-tough" is joined by "semi-hilarious," "semi-massive," "semi-solitude," and the conclusion of Elroy Blunt's lament, "I could halfway fall in love,/For part of a lonely night,/With a semi-pretty woman in my arms" (144). Shake Tiller "lights out for the territory" after the Super Bowl leaving Billy Clyde and Barbara Jane alone in New York without heroic masks and costumes. At the conclusion, Jenkins quietly closes the bedroom door on his semi-married couple and the frantic, sexually-charged atmosphere of Super Bowl week dissipates in their final boy-meets-girl shyness, a semi-sentimental ending that fits the convention of popular novels and their heroes and heroines.

277

Life Its Ownself is fully as genial as *Semi-Tough* but more a book of sketches, of Jenkins wanting to satirize media culture which is now indistinguishable from football culture. Several years after *Semi-Tough*, Shake Tiller is an unsuccessful novelist who turns to writing self-help books (*The Art of Taking Heat*) and exposé journalism about pro football. Barbara Jane has gone to Hollywood to star in a new situation comedy, *Rita's Limo Stop*. Billy Clyde in his ninth year with the Giants has his knee torn apart by Dreamer Tatum and embarks on a T.V. sportscasting career. As a producer tells him, "You still have your Texas accent. Good! It will create an aura of sincerity on the air" (72). In the book's funniest subplot, T. J. Lambert, the crudest of their teammates on the Giants and now a semi-barbaric football coach at TCU, has misadventures in recruiting the two best Texas high school running backs, illiterates Artis Toothis and Tonsillitis Johnson. The description of Artis Toothis shows Jenkins remains in fine comic form in *Life Its Ownself*:

> [Artis Toothis] had wound up at SMU all right, but had dropped out of school. His explanation to the press was that he had been lonely and unhappy in Dallas, which was to say that he had been forced to enroll in a freshman English class, and he had heard a rumor that his meal allowance of $3,000 a month was far below the figure a running back at the University of Texas was getting. Artis had gone home to Willow Neck in the sleek white jaguar he had decided to keep. He was mostly just lolling around the house now, playing with the cur dogs and watching one of the 240 T.V. channels he could pick up from the satellite dish an SMU alum had installed in the yard. (144–45)

Finally, the novel is about a crisis in Billy Clyde and Barbara Jane's marriage caused by bi-coastal job commitments and media publicity. They appear more as tired yuppies caught in mid-career. The novel ends at halftime of the opening TCU game against defending national champion Auburn where Artis and Tonsillitis have rolled to a 42–3 halftime lead. Billy Clyde and Shake receive awards in the heart of football Texas and Barbara Jane reconciles with Billy Clyde, who thinks, "And in the stadium where I'd heard so many cheers, where the scent of winning was in the air again, it occurred to me that I'd scored the greatest victory of my life. Barbara Jane had come back" (316). As in *Semi-Tough*, Jenkins ends as sentimentally as possible with the oldest ending of football and school sport fiction—the guy who wins the girl and the game.

Jenkins sets limits on his fiction by appropriating both the Southwestern Humor and the sentimental romance. The author remains fully in control of the irony in a comedy of manners. The structure of the team and of society remains intact. No criticisms of football's hegemony are extended beyond their comic potential. Jenkins' Texas football children negotiate a world without depth from inside a star system that they know and criticize but that they don't feel compelled to alter or escape from.

Jenkins' fiction is engaged in the quintessential postmodernist popular mode, the copy or reproduction of the already existing media reality, the commodity re-commodified or cycled in a slightly revised form. Eerie conflations of celebrities, fictional characters, and football players collide. A prime example of postmodern simulacra in popular culture may suffice. On September 19, 1977 in the ABC Monday Night Football booth, Frank Gifford had just concluded a promotional interview with figure skater Dorothy Hamill when he turned to Don Meredith and said, "She's no Barbara Jane Bookman but she's a #1 pick." Dandy Don replied, "You tell 'em, Shake," to which Gifford countered, "O.K., Billy." In a blurring of art and life, Gifford and Meredith assumed the personae of the most popular *fictional* pro football characters of their era and, aesthetes that they are, picked the correct masks. This easy sliding of reference between fiction and football reality suggests how lightly Jenkins has reproduced football consciousness; Gifford and Meredith are aware of football fiction even as they have already been fictionalized, Gifford in *A Fan's Notes* and Meredith as model for Seth Maxwell (unflattering) in *North Dallas Forty* and Rylie Silver (flattering) in *The Hundred Yard War*.

Jenkins has said that if Billy Clyde grew up, he would *be* Burt Reynolds, not precisely a limitless horizon. (*Sports Illustrated*, November 7, 1977, 82). It is finally difficult to know any longer whether *Semi-Tough* is a book by Dan Meredith about Billy Clyde Reynolds played by Burt Puckett—and the vertigo continues. Such reproductions of copies show the ultimate reciprocity of icons traded between the sports and media cultures in the Texas celebrity worlds of Gent in *Texas Celebrity Turkey Trot* and Jenkins in *Life Its Ownself.* Jenkins cannot see his way to a vantage point where he can comment from beyond the cultural mythos that sport represents. In this refusal, he has recapitulated Lardner's great weakness, even as he extended the sports fiction tradition of Lardner's deft colloquial narration.

Gent's troubadours in *North Dallas Forty* are not country singers as in *Semi-Tough* but Bob Dylan and the Rolling Stones. Contrasted with Billy Clyde Puckett's belief that the good life will never end for the smart Texas children, Philip Elliott after a meeting with his coach says in deterministic fashion, "He was right. I am immature. I am also crippled and growing rapidly older. And there is nothing I can do about any of it" (49). Gent echoes Dickey's poem about the dissolution of the football player. Gent's negativity is as unrelieved as Jenkins' continual whimsy and packaging of truth in homespun. Yet together, the two novels are the best inside narratives of pro football. Gent *is* the player; we ache with him and watch his manipulation and pain. Jenkins is the witness, both novelist as sportswriter and participant in the total football spectacle. Gent seeks to expose the grotesque characters whom Jenkins creates in comic triumph.

Gent and Jenkins are complementary in their literary production of Texas. Gent's Texas is that of violence, corporate hypocrisy, and a rough frontier to be defended: it is Texas present seen through a radical male determinism. Jenkins' ideal Texas is TCU of the 1930s–40s small towns, best girls, country wit, grit, language, and music; it is Texas in nostalgia seen via New York and Hollywood. For Gent's individual sports hero, Texas is what *is,* the physical reality that wounds and holds him captive in so many ways in the collective. For Jenkins' Billy Clyde, Shake, and Barbara Jane, Texas is their point of origin, what keeps them whole in their life in the professional unit in media America.

Dallas, 11/22/63: "Why Are We Playing?"

TEXAS FOOTBALL fiction contains a specific historicization in the linking of football violence to national catastrophe, specifically to the assassination of President John F. Kennedy in Dallas on November

22, 1963,[7] and, more specifically, to the NFL's insistence on playing its full schedule of games on Sunday forty-eight hours later. The assassination is commented on in the football fiction of Cartwright, Gent, and Pye, and it plays a central role in the conclusions of *Joiner* and *Goodbye Bobby Thomson! Goodbye John Wayne!*.

In the fiction, football is seen to embody both the violence of the murderous act itself and a "business as usual" attitude that captured the corporate profit motive at its worst. *Sports Illustrated* worked to defuse the issue of games on assassination weekend when it commented, "All men are not alike in their sense of fitness. The games that were held were very well attended. It was, in the end, something that everyone had to decide for himself. No act of fiat—one way or the other—would have been an appropriate memorial" (*Sports Illustrated*, December 2, 1963 13). The colleges were truly indecisive. Michigan State and Illinois, playing for the Big Ten title, canceled on Saturday morning; the Ivy League canceled its schedule. The American Football League, led by Commissioner Joe Foss, a Kennedy associate, wiped out its slate and made the games up in late December. Tex Maule was silent on the issue in his pro football report, and *Sports Illustrated* chose to run as its lead article, "The President Who Loved Sport."

Yet when football became a reaction point for criticism of American military aggression and national regimentation in the late 1960's, a retrospective look at Dallas and 11/22/63 provided authors with an event, a metaphor, and a paradigmatic moment.[8] Immediately after describing Texas as a "republic of outlaws" in *North Dallas Forty*, Gent goes on to speak of the West's open spaces, even in the Dallas-Ft. Worth corridor. However, "that was when Braniff's planes were gray. Jack Ruby ran a burlesque house. And the School Book Depository was a place they kept schoolbooks" (9–10). In *That Prosser Kid*, Pye describes how college coaches urge the Cajun State team to vote to practice in a show of aggression on the day of their teammate's funeral after a gruesome practice injury: "'Shades of Kennedy,'" mumbles a player. Foster's Pittsburgh Steeler lineman, Pete Murray, in *Goodbye Bobby Thomson! Goodbye John Wayne!* plays into the second half of a listless November 24, 1963 game against the Chicago Bears and then simply walks off the field and out of the NFL for good, the assassination crystallizing his disaffection; "This was no time for any more violence" (179). Whitehead's injured Sonny Joiner leaves Dallas the Sunday after the assassination. On November 22, his Dallas Bulls' linemate, Morningside Robbins, locks himself in his room in grief. Joiner says, "He stared at that picture of Jackie climbing onto the wounded body of dead Jack, said 'Uh, I ain't playin,' got up and left for good." To the coach's pleas, Robbins retorts, "You tell those fuckahs I'm gone until Monday afternoon" (404). Joiner returns to Mississippi but cannot rid himself of the violence he carries.

Thus the contextualizing of November 22–24, 1963 in football fiction provided authors with a plurality of politicized meanings. Whether fleeing the violent game or merely creating an emblem of it, "Dallas, 11/22/63" has been a repeated minor motif in football fiction, coincidental with the Dallas Cowboys' 1970s incarnation as "America's Team."[9] Even that sobriquet carries in part the connotation of a wished-for normative metaphor to replace the extreme national memory. Football lacks any real scandal to match baseball's Black Sox "Fall" or the basketball fixes. What football fiction offers instead is a variety of responses to one apocalyptic historical moment in a football capital and the "games" that were played in the aftermath.

The Professional Plot

THE BODY in football fiction is vulnerable and in pain as well as subject to the collective's economic interest. These are truths that are masked by the outsized portrayals in comic realism best expressed through the Texas Connection. Football fiction more than any other sports fiction obsessively returns to collective heroism, what it means to belong to a team and to take identity from that fact. The professional unit is situated apart from the society itself. The imagery is streamlined, the language technical. The player's pride is in doing the job while his fear lies in being expelled from the unit.

Thus sports fiction about the collective paradigm features a character bearing the signature of his ideological contract. In football fiction, he is the individual sports hero whose great athletic skill will be tempered and bonded to the institution. The tension in the fiction between the individual and the collective arises when the subject believes himself to be a "point of origin," controlling his "destiny" by his own aspirations and energy (Coward and Ellis 77). This initial illusion of freedom within the ideology is all the more dramatic because of the individual sports hero's sense of physical power and dominance which he attempts to transfer to more socially and culturally-determined spheres of action. The illusion of the subject as origin has been a continual theme in sports fiction, particularly in football fiction where the individual sports hero finds himself an employee rather than an immortal, perhaps an ex-player in the ideological rendering of physical decay in anti-heroism. Thus while the individual sports hero in his hubris sees himself as center, he is most often seen by authors to be worked over by the contradictions of his bondage to the collective. Nowhere is the athlete more compromised as subject in team sport than in football fiction.

The sports hero in his relation to the team fits the "professional plot," what Wil Wright observed in describing Western heroes in cinema. Wright describes groups of heroes working for money as professional men, specialists, "whose skills explain why they are there" (97). The team becomes a working unit that shares affection and comradeship and is isolated from any relation to an outside world. This model fits a corporate profile, a work-place "family." The model is particularly relevant to the football team with its many sharply defined work roles performed under largely anonymous circumstances behind helmets, masks, and padding. Society is unrepresented in this model, although, in fact, it is *everywhere* inasmuch as the model of professionalism is one erected by the larger society in one of its models of a capitalist elite. Membership on the team assures the player of recognition and public status. In the fiction of a team sport such as football, society outside the team is consistently devalued and unpleasant. Such a behavioral model is most congenial to Wolfe in *The Electric Kool Aid Acid Test* and *The Right Stuff*; its closest counterpart in football fiction is *Semi-Tough*.

In football fiction, players and fans have no real relationship. Indeed, Oriard states that football means something radically different to the players than to the spectators ("Professional Football as Cultural Myth" 33). The baptism in pain, in discipline, in commitment to the team appears to preclude any sort of relation to an outside society that creates the team as a model of its own relations. The professional player re-invests his alienation, allowing himself to work for the team and keep at arm's length anyone from outside this unit. Unfortunately, most sports fiction refuses to see that the society generates the team. In a coherent base-superstructure argument, they could not be divorced one from the other. The society excluded by the professional unit is the same society from which the professional unit has been generated. Authors choose to center on the team sports hero in the collective, but seldom control both in any lived relation. This double subject is central to football fiction while baseball fiction evades the plight by more excursions into myth and rebirth.

Athletic heroes in the collective such as Billy Clyde Puckett and Shake Tiller find manipulation of belief an incredibly simple matter as society is primed to be seduced by them because of their skill. The team is a refuge where goals may be pursued and the ambitions of the individual athlete become realized. Professional pride is expressed by Sonny Joiner, who says, "*Amateur* is liking it, loving it, whether you get paid or not, and here in America we pay people for being good" (190). Furthermore, the professional unit in football purports to teach a rough equality analyzed by Billy Clyde Puckett in *Semi-Tough*: "We decided that nobody can help being what he is, whether it turns out to be as black as a cup of coffee at a truck stop, or a white Southern dumb-ass like most of our parents. A man makes himself a man by whatever he does with himself, and in pro football that means busting his ass for his team" (4). Here, the moral complexity of race relations fits into the "game space," the limited model of the team.

In a sense, the skills of the players are all that determine why they are on the team. The men work and pull together and build bonds of respect and comradeship. Yet the team itself is insular. Although it is drawn from a model of the larger society's corporate units, the team is *all there is* in football fiction. Inside the unit, the player is lionized and treated with respect for his contributions. To be "off the team" is the great anxiety in football fiction. The affiliation is total. No valued, privileged society exists apart from the team, and this is a startling poverty in the fiction itself. As a player says in *That Prosser Kid,* "Football has been a major part of my life since I was ten years old. . . . It's the thing I know best and feel closest to. Can't you see? I know how bad it is, but I love it anyway. I get a satisfaction from

it that I just can't explain" (50). In football fiction, the heroes often
have tremendous difficulty in defining a difference between what
they do on the field and who they are in any moral or aesthetic sense.
They cannot play their way to a free relation because they have no
perspective on a society outside the team unit. They cannot play
differences outside the lines. Football fiction promises no transcendence or self-knowledge for its heroes. Lives run out. The fiction
stops. Those players who can, walk away from the professional unit
with great contradictions.

No other sports fiction concentrates so much on the team at the
center of the narrative, certainly a direct reflection of the fact that no
team sport has a more collective identity. The team is really the
protagonist from its managerial class down through its coaches to its
hierarchy of players—quarterback leaders, disaffiliated ends and backs,
huge and wise linemen, black and white subcultures. That the team
is primary subject matter can be evidenced by Cartwright's *The
Hundred Yard War* (1968) and Gent's *The Franchise* (1984) working
obsessively in the same mode sixteen years apart. Cartwright's novel
was and is still overlooked in football fiction, perhaps because he
created no true hero or consistent narrative voice. As an early attempt at a team anatomy, the novel ultimately centered on two
figures, quarterback Rylie Silver and Coach Ward Dandridge. Silver,
a cavalier and quixotic Don Meredith figure, is finally dislodged as
team leader by Dandridge, a ringer for Vince Lombardi. The triumph
of the football organization is complete. Rylie Silver, the team's life-
blood, a sometime winner but genial individualist, must be moved
and the novel simply stops when he is traded in pre-season.

Other novels attempt studies of a bewildered minor league football reject (*Westchester Bull*), intense pro football fandom (*Cut'n Run*),
team executives (*The Sunday Heroes*) or a multiple narrated "big
game" (*Four Quarters Make a Season*). Another *Sports Illustrated* edi-
tor, Jack Olsen, wrote *Alphabet Jackson,* a novel about a veteran NFL
center that labors to achieve Jenkins' colloquial ease in narration.
Olsen mixes genres and conjures up a black militant tight end going
berserk and hijacking the team plane after the Super Bowl. *The Last
Superbowl* and *Killerbowl,* melodrama and science fiction, respectively, offered shrill criticisms of the violent, corporate entity that
they saw professional football to be.

Pye's indictment of college football's dehumanization in *That Pros-*

ser Kid is only a more extreme version of Texas high school and college novels such as *Fall Guy* and *The Last Texas Hero*. In each novel, the evils of rabid coaches, venal alumni, and fans who demand winners are borne by player-victims, those who came to highly organized football with desire and freshness but who are tormented into failure and resentment. Cronley's touch is the lightest in *Fall Guy* while Pye in *That Prosser Kid* brings the resentment to real pitch. Prosser is the aloof, reluctant running back star of the redshirts, a sort of football Robert E. Lee Prewitt in his singularity and reluctance to bend to team discipline. The scrubs and scout team members comprise a rebel underclass that finally indulges in a job action with Prosser as symbolic leader. On the final play of a bad defeat inflicted on Cajun State by Texas, Prosser makes a touchdown on a kick-off return that is a tantalizing work of art. Because of this final touchdown, Cajun State beats the point spread and drives the gamblers mad. Like a western hero dropping his guns in the dust, Prosser then deposits his uniform and equipment on the training table and utters the familiar closure to football fiction: "I quit."

Peter Gent: The Professional and Pain

PETER GENT has now written a pro football trilogy (*North Dallas Forty, Texas Celebrity Turkey Trot, The Franchise*) from the proud standpoint of a warrior who has lived the professional plot and its contradictions. No other comparable sports fiction has been achieved by a professional athlete. For that reason alone, Gent is singular. His blasted lyricism, his shy, romantic loner's voice, is coupled with a taste for the sensational depiction of the sporting empire of which he was a part. Gent was an outstanding basketball player at Michigan State and was signed as a free agent wide receiver by the Dallas Cowboys with whom he played from 1964 to 1968. He presently lives in Texas; the hill country in his fiction is where he hunkers down against the contemporary violence that always seeks out his heroes.

Gent is football fiction's laureate of physical suffering and paranoia. He has also fought hardest in his novels for a vision of the football player as a beleaguered working-class hero, consistently betrayed by coaches, owners, and society. His novels are totally within the pro football world which always pushes his characters to extremes of affiliation and disaffiliation. Life after football seems unimaginable for Gent at this time; he obsessively returns *to* that end point as choice and punishment. He walks all around football's negative implications in his novels in guises ranging from breezy irony to murderous rage. His writing to date is perfectly emblematic of his own persistent subject matter: how to say "I quit" with personal integrity while remaining vital and in control. In describing what he, like Jenkins, is afflicted with, Gent remains a prisoner of football's varied appeals and is half appalled at his fixation.

North Dallas Forty combined with *Semi-Tough* in the early 1970s to establish the subgenre of football fiction. Gent's Texas was outsized and grotesque like Jenkins' but it was almost never humorously perceived and rendered. Gent's Philip Elliot is not wry "country" or engaging, nor is he relating to the spectacle of Super Bowl Week. Although, like *Semi-Tough, North Dallas Forty* is a history of one week in a season, the week begins and ends in violence off the field, with physical trauma and collapse in between. The lives of the players are out of control. Relationships appear impossible; drugs are everywhere to ease pain, enhance performance level, break the tension. *North Dallas Forty* today has the feel of a vintage cultural document from the late 1960s and early 1970s, a time when football was first in revolt against the symbols of the revered autocrats such as Lombardi and Landry, Lombardi reified as a "block of granite," Landry as a "computer mind." These twin images of unyielding physical power and technology were criticized in football's version of a counterculture. Ex-NFL players such as Dave Meggysey, George Sauer, Jr., Bernie Parrish, and Chip Oliver wrote a spate of books on why they weren't marching anymore, linking football's regimentation and aggression to all the ills of the Vietnam era. Indeed, *North Dallas Forty*'s Dallas football owner makes his fortune by manufacturing napalm and the novel is framed by violent death. In the opening scene, huge linemen are out shooting "doves" in an explicit reference to the peace movement. The last scene is reminiscent of the conclusion to a film such as *Easy Rider* when Elliot's mistress and her black poet-lover are massacred at her ranch by a rich Dallas playboy who has been a hanger-on with the football team.

The vignettes in *North Dallas Forty* are gloomy, almost perversely negative. Gent's warrior Elliott is devastated and in constant pain, hoping for some personal salvation from his role as team sports hero but believing that his experience has possibly rendered him unfit for human interaction. His bodily image, his sexual life, and his sport are constantly linked in anxiety. Elliott thinks, "Part of my consciousness remained detached, watching, lest the sex play get too spirited and I suffer a dislocation or serious sprain. On the night we met she had separated one of my rib cartilages" (73). Elliott wants to keep life simple and atavistic: "I am a man who has learned that survival is the reason of life and that fear and hatred are the emotions. What you cannot overcome by hatred you must fear. And every day it is getting harder to hate and easier to fear" (131). Something of Mailer's perception of Hemingway feeding his destructive ape is present in Gent's vision, which also includes a Hemingwayesque obsession with rules and controls and a mistrust of freedom except in the performance of his skill: "There is a basic reality where it is just me and the job to be done, the game and all its skills. . . . That's what's true. That's what I loved. All the rest is just a matter of opinion" (265). Such a brief for the individual sports hero posits an ideal of the athlete's absorption and gratification in private patterns. Such a running present-tense commentary of the athlete's self-delighting in skill betrays Gent's basketball years since his description is squarely in line with basketball's self-transcendence motif (see chapter 13). His isolated stance is thus an extreme complementary position to the collective heroism he fiercely criticizes.

Texas Celebrity Turkey Trot is Gent's tentative exploration of life after football, a novel more similar in presentation to *Semi-Tough* than to *North Dallas Forty;* fittingly enough, Gent's hero, an end-of-the-line defensive back, is named Mabry *Jenkins. Texas Celebrity Turkey Trot* is a study of how everyone in Texas has become a media star, from ex-rodeo cowboys to ex-astronauts. The president of a conglomerate hiring ex-athletes feels, "In this world of personalities they are international heroes. They will cultivate world-wide markets, world-wide allegiances. . . . We think ex-athletes are good, disciplined technicians" (128). Mabry Jenkins makes his way in a contemporary Vanity Fair—that of the electronic circus. All the extras from *Semi-Tough* seem to have found their way into Gent's novel. Mabry Jenkins' life finds him moving from the "Willy Roy Rogers Annual Texas Music Festival" to the "Annual Baja Celebrity Fish Tourney" which has a subdivision, "The Celebrity Fish Tourney Victory Luau and Cockfight"; he also enters the "Midland/Odessa Battle of the Celebrity Sexes Golf Tourney and Charity Telethon." His girl friend, Stormy Claridge, sings "ragtime Cowboy Joe" in gold lamé in the Miss Texas pageant. His journalist pal, Titus Bean, reports on the music festival for *Rolling Stone*.

Behind the glitter, Mabry is drowning in self-disgust. His odyssey begins with a nightmare knee that cannot be repaired. Gent's portrait of Mabry's desperation is more clever than moving: "I'm purposeless. I'm like everyone else and I can't stand it" (112); indeed, the novel is narrated from a slightly embarrassed point-of-view, Gent perhaps feeling that it is humiliating to live this totally false commodified existence without football to make it honorable. As Mabry's teammate tells him, "You haven't got Sunday to make everything all right" (215). Sundays are what he still pursues and, by novel's end, he's back in training for a comeback, exuding the false confidence of the novel's first pages: "Life is a contact sport and I've got a team to make" (239). Gent played the role of *Dan* Jenkins uneasily in *Texas Celebrity Turkey Trot*. Not a satirist at heart but a romantic avatar of literary naturalism, he found the commodity world of *North Dallas Forty* without the football ritual to be doubly insane. *Texas Celebrity Turkey Trot* reiterated a central truth of football fiction: there is no life after football.

The paradigm over and over again for the football novel's conclusion is the litany of "I quit" or "I'm out." Quitting is the only choice in football fiction. You either stay (if you are allowed to stay) and embrace the order, regimentation, and aggression of the professional unit or you renounce and become an ex-player. The choice is a renewed and diminished relation to collective heroism or an embracing of anti-heroism in a distancing where perspective may be achieved but not within the heroic experience itself, except in Dan Jenkins' comedy. Again, there is no way to sustain football heroism at football fiction's closure. Time simply runs out. Prosser walks off the field forever in *That Prosser Kid;* so do Shake Tiller in *Semi-Tough* and Taylor Rusk in Gent's *The Franchise*. Such a "choice" is often wrested from the beleaguered player, however. Duke Craig in Daley's *Only a Game* and Philip Elliott in *North Dallas Forty* are banned from the NFL. A whole roster of players in football fiction are released, injured, or dispensed with. Yet over and over, the cry of the heroes in football fiction is of an irrational love for what they sense is killing their spirit.

The Franchise: The Professional and "Control"

A POSITIVE side to the vision of the individual professional in football fiction does exist: Sonny Joiner's pride in football as "proper labor" (*Joiner* 27); Billy Clyde Puckett's version of team democracy in *Semi-Tough.* For Exley in *A Fan's Notes,* Frank Gifford sustains him through the lasting excellence of his play over time—the very definition of a pro for Exley. However, the negative side of the professional is in his coolness, the dispassionate lack of identification with anything other than the team, the self-defeating comment of Mabry Jenkins in *Texas Celebrity Turkey Trot* that "the real freedom is in keeping quiet and watching it all go by. It's the real power" (239). This sad capitulation, a sort of smug resignation of the warrior in the gray plastic helmet, masks the real fear that, without football, the athlete would have nothing. Yet no control appears possible in the commodified arena. The professional continually barters a potential freedom for the external rewards of victory—fame, money, and power—recreating in the collective the choice of the player who bartered freedom for spiritual rest in the ritual sports story. Football fiction continually hammers at this essential exchange relation in late capitalist society with spiritual wholeness as the utopian goal.

"Control" is what Gent seeks in *The Franchise,* his third and most sensational attempt to portray the professional football world. Here, the subject is the economic birth and growth of the Texas Pistols from an idea to Super Bowl champions in their own domed stadium. The cost of the "Franchise" is measured not only in hundreds of millions of dollars as well as dozens of ugly and squalid dealings but also, by my count, sixteen deaths: fourteen murders and two suicides. Included on this roster of the dead are a wide receiver, an offensive tackle and his family, a sportswriter, three mob hit men, three racketeers, a general manager, an owner, and the head of the player's association. At the conclusion of this carnage, "control" of an insane sort has been achieved. Furthermore, *The Franchise* is a pro football novel for the 1980s. Money in *The Franchise* is what everyone kills for, its power and authority. Everything about *The Franchise* is inflated, its length, sadistic violence, and extremity of situation. Such a novel, a copy of both machismo tales and tough detective tales, is very much in the postmodern popular idiom. At one juncture, Tough Guy quarterback Taylor Rusk says, "I feel like I'm in an episode of *The Godfather*" (341), exposing Gent's own perception that he is caught in copies of popular genres. If Jenkins muses on the similarities of his characters to pop cult figures such as Burt Reynolds, Gent finds his similarities on the level of genre.

Gent's stance is that of Hemingway and of Mailer as well: the testing and probing by individual sports heroes of what is darkest and most dangerous in ever more rule-oriented ritual where freedom does not exist. For Taylor, "All his life he had sought control of situations. He played quarterback so he could call the plays, control the game. . . . Performance and grace under pressure, never losing one's grip on a situation no matter how difficult, frightening or painful"(193). With the utterance of "grace under pressure," Gent has complacently copied the Hemingway credo first identified by Philip Young. Gent climaxes a fourth generation of American male writers (London, Hemingway, Mailer) who show an inability to see beyond the dominance of control in performance.

However, by *The Franchise,* Gent has decided that control is not possible, that life *within* the football world is not worth living. The repeated metaphors are of "crashing," "burning," and "hitting the wall." Taylor Rusk is moving too fast; he is the Franchise itself, hurtling to keep a Super Bowl date beyond the limits of physical capability and moral norms. Taylor is fighting for the player's association, primary target of the mob, which wants to control the enormous pension fund. The melodrama of the situation is in the apotheosis of the football hero as victimized worker, whose various madnesses can be explained by his association with the sport. The money in the pension fund belongs to "everyone who left their humanity in the game" (269). Here is the final, improbable reinstitution of an economic naturalism in sports fiction.

Taylor Rusk throws eight touchdown passes against Denver in

the PistolDome on Super Sunday while mayhem is the order of the day in the owners' boxes and in the stands. Taylor's bodyguard, a half-mad Vietnam veteran and devout Pistols fan, napalms enemy mobsters in retaliation. After the game, Taylor "shut himself down completely": "He was finished. He had delivered. It was over. There would be no more" (394–95). The familiar football paradigm of "I quit" becomes a tentative reality, yet Taylor must defend his child and lover in a final gun battle with the avenging mob.

The battle occurs at the ranch in the Texas hill country which functions for Gent as the Hemingwayesque "good place"; the "chatter of mockingbirds," the "white rush of water," the "stone ranch house." Gent portrays such a sanctuary as always subject to mortal danger. A comparable site in *North Dallas Forty* was the ranch of Charlotte Caulder, whose murder there dashed Philip Elliott's hope at the novel's conclusion. At the ranch during the final siege Taylor knows that "shutting down" is dangerous: "It threw off his timing and execution" (420). "Shutting down" gives fear the edge over hate. Nonetheless, in pure thriller fashion, Taylor survives the assassins with his family intact. The last image of him is in retirement with his wife, Wendy Chandler, now the *owner* of the Texas Pistols, and their children "splashing in the slow running creek" (423). Taylor has secured self and family and has reached a separate peace based on partnership with ownership and after the aforementioned sixteen deaths. Taylor told Wendy, "I'm a player and I don't want my son to be a player *or* owner. I want him to have different, better choices" (269); but these choices are nowhere to be found in Gent's tale of sports insanity and greed.

In the professional plot, the individual hero's illusion is that he can be in control of his life within football. He denies the exchange relation that he makes but will not acknowledge. Sustaining his illusion, he lives as if he could be the very commodity itself and remain in control. It is to Gent's credit that he takes the contradictions of the professional plot very seriously as opposed to Jenkins, for example. Yet Gent produces transactions within football as an ideological institution without any ability to distance his views. His basic disavowal of a conceptualization of freedom makes it unlikely that play wrested from an engagement with sport will ever be an answer for him, either philosophically or psychologically. Football is inimical to imaginative play and Gent has not left football's strictures. As the professional's best chronicler in football fiction, Gent leaves us at present caught between his indictments in the professional plot and his escapist peace (the guy and the girl and the game) without a semantic re-working of football as metaphor in some further novelistic synthesis. For that, we must turn to football in the fiction of Coover, Whitehead, and DeLillo.

10.

Fictions of Football: "Why We Are Playing"

The extension of the question "Why are we playing to-day?," asked by some players in football fiction on a bleak week-end in November 1963, finally becomes the attempt to justify "Why we are playing at all." No other sports fiction, including boxing fiction, really frames the question in such blunt terms. The football fiction examined in chapter 9 stipulates that life within football is almost a separate existence, perhaps a temporary refuge, but often confining and dehumanizing, a problem within itself. Football is *the* defining collective entity in the fiction. The characters in football fiction are captives within football consciousness. Football is what the hero *is*, not just what he does, with the resultant apprehensions that the sport is over-refining some qualities (aggression, competitiveness, adjustment to a unit) at the expense of others (passivity, play, individuality). Describing what its heroes are afflicted with appears to be the conceptual limit of most football fiction.

Three authors—Coover, Whitehead, and DeLillo—manage to go beyond these boundaries. They re-invent football in fiction and balance it with other realities in configurations that finally may stand as "fictions of football." These configurations play with the ideological constraints that football labors under as well as play with football's inherent field structure and symbolism. In *Gloomy Gus,* Coover makes us keenly aware of football aesthetics which he counters with a more deeply held and liberating aesthetics for the artist as he did in *The Universal Baseball Association.* Whitehead in *Joiner* consistently historicizes the football violence within a culture of racial strife and personal violence; he weds the physical and the metaphysical in rough alliance. Football is dangerous but so is history which contains it and is subject-related by individual passions. DeLillo's *End Zone* is also a disquisition on our craving for and fear of violence but is controlled by an inquiry into the nature of the language we use to name that violence. DeLillo plays with our love of pattern and symmetry and their relation to our fascination with nuclear explosion.

Aesthetics. History. Language. Coover, Whitehead, and De-Lillo break football out of the opposition of individual heroism—collective heroism where it is apparently condemned to oscillate. They create their fictions of football within an obstinate material base. They write imaginatively through a sport that is stubbornly realistic, prosaic, physical, and martial, one in which "scrimmage lines" and "end zones" must continually be denied to produce challenging complexities and to articulate why *they* are playing.

Gloomy Gus: Football Aestheticized

COOVER'S 1975 novella, expanded and published as a novel in 1987,[1] is a literary exercise in configuring in which Meyer, his sculptor-narrator, evolves into a vital surrealist. Through Meyer, an artistic counterpart to J. Henry Waugh in *The Universal Baseball Association,* Coover plays off Gus' football misadventures against the strong need of Meyer to celebrate differences. Gus and Meyer meet in the football realm of "collision." Gus will flatten anything that moves if his cues are confused. Alternately, Meyer believes football is about balance and "a sudden burst of freedom," one that is so inimical to football's structure. Meyer uses flattened metal scraps to mold his sculptures, creating a collision of forms, particularly the antithetical notion of depicting motion through an inert object. Collision remains paramount for Meyer; he sees the physical impact of football as "the dialectical prerequisite to participation in the mystery . . . a kind of asceticism, akin to the political activist's frequent punishment, the artist's privation and solitude" (71); Meyer concludes, "in football, as in politics, the issue is not ethical but aesthetic" (71).

Bodies in sport celebrate the "burst of freedom" that keeps Meyer approximating such form in his creations: the living form that expresses speed but is itself inert. Gus may only experience the separate planes of his creations but Meyer wants "to make them collide. It will be uncomfortable, but I want to do this" (93). The power of Meyer's sculpture is to arrest "speed" and mask "weight" through his living form while at the same time expressing it. In such an aesthetic, Coover expresses form's honor of the play of differences, the idea and the mass neutralized and suspended in the form of the sculpted object. The active merging of the forces of speed and weight is preserved in the difference between the forces.

Coover has sought that principle of difference in collision and has countered it with Gus' play-less consumption of time and space. If Meyer loves the freedom of speed and weight, Coover depicts their imprisoning through Gus without nuance or representation. When Gus "lurched out of control," slamming into the opposing line or some poor potential lover, "there seemed to be no motive behind this overeagerness. It was just part of him"; he operated on "a short-circuited stimulus response system" (74–75). Like some primitive computer, he had to be continually re-programmed in each sequence: "Even the offside practice: he got it down to about two minutes a day but he couldn't get rid of it" (81). Gus takes repetition to nightmare lengths, the structure he so painfully recreates as an anti-natural. He is incapable of free motion or any improvisation.

Coover chooses to end his fable with a specific query about "Why are we playing?". When Gus is dying after being shot by the police at the Republic Steel works during the violence of the 1937 Memorial Day weekend strike, he asks Meyer, "Why is it we go on forever, making the first mistake we ever made, over and over again?" Meyer concludes, "'Well, it's probably *not* a mistake, Gus. . . . Probably it's the only_____' But by then he was dead" (110). Perhaps Meyer would have concluded, "Probably it's the only thing that makes us human," in the sense of "the Fall," but Gus has never understood humanity and is human no more. Also, Coover has cited Borges' remark that we go on writing the same story all our lives (Coover, "Interview" 72). Finally, Coover's blank space allows an "open" frame for the reader to fill as did Meyer's flowering appropriation of a swastika that had been painted on his door. This gesture celebrates Meyer's love of "openness" and possibility in life. The riddle of Gus' repetition is not meant to be solved. Football remains between the lines with no reconciliation or return to origins.

Football was sharply segmented aggression to Gus, the great athlete who knows nothing of play: "He was completely metaphor-free. He had no imagination at all!" (98). As a slave to drills, cues, and inhibited reflexes, Gus is the perfect football player: what he *is* and what he *does* become the same. He has no life outside his football regimen. Coover's Nixonian fable is both comic and wise about the Horatio Alger dream gone mad. Gus is a comic robot Jay Gatsby with a schedule whose literary initials ("GG") are most certainly on Coover's mind. *Gloomy Gus* uses the contexts of American literary, social, and political history (the Republic Steel strike) as well as sports history. The Bears really *were* 13–0 in 1934; they *did* have a rookie star, Beattie Feathers, who compiled the highest average gain per carry in pro football history (101 carries, 1,004 yards, 9.9 avg.) and was the first back to gain more than 1,000 yards in one season.

Coover takes repetition and collision as football principles and draws out their aesthetics. Gus knows only rigid schedule and repetition in his rituals. His collisions are determined and brutal, yet finally outrageous and destructive. Coover has only criticism for rigidity and repetition. Yet he manages to re-work collision into the openness to try new combinations, an eclecticism of materials and shapes that make welding and sculpture the perfect material metaphors for Coover's own works such as *The Public Burning*. Meyer is proudest of his created jugglers and dancers which he describes as "sentient bodies at full stretch" (70), a lovely phrase in which knowledge and physical expression are satisfied in the play of Coover's image. Meyer requires the onlookers to supply the ball as an extension of the logic explaining what the figures are doing: "They actually seem to move because without the logic of motion, they make no sense" (70). *Gloomy Gus* finally celebrates creative play as an active, humane principle in life and art. Collision is its fully dialogized force in the service of "reveal[ing] different things at the same time" (109). Meyer's final vision of "multi-faceted pieces" (109) of sculpture is a vision of structural play that is similar to Derrida's description of Nietzsche preserving the play of differences in "this 'active' (in movement) discord of the different forces and of the difference between forces" ("Differance" 149).

Joiner: Football Historicized

WHITEHEAD'S JOINER is the true historicizing of football in an attempt to wed the violence on the field to violence off the field. *Joiner* is rich with insight and speculation about the quality of a life's work. Sonny Joiner is not a heroic back or disaffiliated wide receiver but rather a huge (290–315 lbs.) offensive lineman who has committed his share of sins in the Mississippi of his young manhood but who has never stopped learning what he is capable of as he searches for his true vocation.[2] Sonny quotes Montaigne: "I order my soul to look upon both pain and pleasure with a gaze equally self-contained" (106). More in line with Sonny's wit is this satirical representation of players in the post-football utopia envisioned in the late 1960s: "I'm supposed to finish my Ph.D. in Radical History. I'm supposed to thin down to a skinny two-twenty, and then I'm supposed to SEIZE POWER" (63).

Sonny narrates from his exile in Texas; he has left football after playing one year with Dallas in the NFL. He is teaching grammar school, learning to love a new woman, and aligning his past experience with his new knowledge. One part that football plays in his history is that of "proper labor," for he insists, "the goddamned game is unsymbolical. To hell with the anthropologists who would make it so" (149). He also knows its ugly violence and suffers

"alternating shames and elations" (32) in vintage football consciousness. Sonny kills two football players, one while in high school, one
an ex–NFL player several years later. In doing so, he confronts
central truths about himself and his era. Whitehead refuses to indict
football or the South or Sonny Joiner but inscribes them within a
Mississippi where racial strife is inevitable in playing out the historical realities. Football is violence within the rules, a controlled outlet,
but the rest of our lives remain just as vulnerable to aggression and
pain of loss, says Whitehead. Games don't heal or contain; they
simply portray what *is* and allow pride in work well-done to emerge,
along with the victories and defeats. Whitehead cares little about
exploitation within football; he sees larger issues of suffering in the
American society.

Joiner hurls the huge football body into collision with rednecks,
Civil Rights demonstrators, sheriffs, winsome wives and lovers,
cracked relatives, friends, and teammates. Whitehead seconds Coover:
collision is prerequisite to participation. Sonny Joiner is a serious,
lyrical, sensual young man. The giantism of the football hero's
prowess, generally worked for satire or comic grotesquery by Jenkins and others, here is realigned by Whitehead. The 463–page novel
contains fewer than 100 pages directly concerned with football. Yet
Whitehead gets a lot accomplished. He writes deftly of boys moving
slowly through town to the high school football field on game night
and of the many small rituals that take place on such a night. He is
the actual laureate of high school football bonding though he writes
without sentiment. His characters rival McMurtry's in *The Last Picture Show* but are historicized through more complex narration.

Whitehead also creates the most memorable gallery of players in
football fiction. Each provides Sonny Joiner with insight into "why
[he and they] are playing." They include mean-as-a-snake Billy
Weatherford, the potentially great high school player whose love of
liquor and tonk women get in his way before he is killed in self-
defense by Sonny; Foots Magee, the sad ex–NFL center reduced to
race-baiting and self-loathing as a gas jockey in Bryan, Mississippi;
Morningside Robbins, Dallas' black all-NFL offensive tackle who
rages in grief at John F. Kennedy's assassination and who had previously told Sonny, "We in a crib, man. Nothin' but a crib!" and
"FOOTBALL—IT   SPELL   OUR   NAME—OH,   SON,

I. . .AM. . .SO. . .TIRED. . ." (393); and Bill Wallick, the "Saint of the Interior Line" who was "always studying the calculus of a perfect block" (189). Wallick dies of a heart attack in the shower after an NFL game, moving Sonny to a peroration: "Bill Wallick was a fucking pro. He loved it and he got paid for it, and he wasn't any whore either. He was the best there was at a hard job" (191).

Other Whitehead characters include Bo "Unicycle" Mitchell, Sonny's college teammate, who survives a coach's hazing with dignity to perform flawlessly, and quarterback Royal Carle Boykin, Sonny's high school teammate, a self-conscious player with limited skill but intelligence and grit who represents the New South of sharp operation, business sense, and discipline, against Sonny's instinctive identifications and emotionalism. Boykin is a cool perfectionist even in grammar school, a fact that one day moved his classmates to tie him up and pelt him with rocks. When Sonny shouts at them to stop, he sees "their eyes were innocent. *If* he survives this he's O.K. Let's see how good he really is. Son, it. . .is. . .a. . .pain. . .to follow another boy" (136). Boykin is cut loose by Sonny "and before he is grown he has one way or another done in every last one of the boys that threw at him on that day" (137). As quarterback, Boykin plays to engineer their defeat on the field, calculates it, while hating the game, even as he goes on to play quarterback at Tulane. Whitehead fixes the metaphor of the melancholy quarterback in relation to Sonny's own social passions and pride. Sonny says, "Royal's done some good stuff but he never led the people in a fight, and he never played in the NFL. He never led the People against their cruel oppressors" (141). To complete his success, Boykin marries Sonny's ex-wife, April.

Collision and confrontation are both Sonny's style and his fate, reified through the football imperative and his personal beliefs. Whitehead also works well with another of football's primary properties, that of repetition. His key metaphor for repetition is the running and rerunning of the game films "in slow motion in a dark room, with your peers looking on, the *in*sane coach with his pointer on your position in the line" (193). Sonny believes that "forward agony is bad—but backward agony is even worse" (194). "Reverse the picture" and all the players "seem to be straining foolishly and helplessly against the force that implacably returns them to where they started, you know how perverse recollection finally is" (195).

Joiner mourns much in his past but celebrates as well. To be caught in technology's mocking of football's obsessive drive forward is to know the sadness of a defeat that refuses to honor growth and forward movement where "all things [are] toiling in the slow calculus of error" (194). Like Coover in *Gloomy Gus,* Whitehead celebrates motion and knows of "sentient bodies at full stretch." At the novel's conclusion, from a life beyond football, Sonny Joiner would nonetheless integrate a vision of life that included football in the "calculus of error," not cast as an evil or an obsession but rather as part of what he was and a proud example of what he did in all his—and football's—contradictions.

To be sure, *Joiner* is a prime case of football fiction's pose of over-compensatory "thinking" to help counter the brute facts of the game. Whitehead attempts to establish the sensitive mind atop the huge aggressive body, illustrating the potential of football fiction to dramatize in popular form a contemporary dissociated sensibility of the physical yet intellectual warrior (Kerrane 94). Sonny's radical girlfriend remonstrates with him that football is "*useless* labor and bestial play." Naked, she moves through the room, miming the planting motions of agriculture. To which Sonny thinks,

> But finally I say to hell with her: I was and am a Populist, in spite of the game. It damned well *was* digging and grubbing. Anybody who ever spent an afternoon doing two-one-one drill when it's 101 degrees knows goddamned well about digging and grubbing. . . . The whole world said it was the natural thing to do and a better art than the cornet. Cup them hands and swing them titties, Mary, but in no wise will you ever change my sense of history. The great Vico knows: there is no true wisdom except for the sweet patterns you yourself have made. (27)

Here is the classic historian's commitment to the individual within history. Sonny remains free to range over his desires in a coming-to-consciousness through aesthetics that may be an apprenticeship for a potential political and social freedom. Here, the freedom obtained through the play of Whitehead's images comes closest to matching Jameson's concept of freedom as an "interpretive device" (*Marxism and Form* 84). The novel's last lines herald Sonny's return to Bryan, Mississippi with Mary to collide again with his own history.

Joiner can become precious and knowing, too much in White-head's allusive control. However, the juxtaposed sensual, football, and historical narrative lines are vivid and finally irresistible. *Joiner* does present an intelligent expression of "why we are playing" and underscores what football fiction does well: an honesty, a pride in work well done, a gruff, blunt acceptance of various planes of reality, a commitment to the individual subject, a humility before the body's power and its vulnerability, and the aggression of which it is capable.

End Zone: Football, Nuclear War, Language

IN 1896, Stephen Crane responded to a review of *The Red Badge of Courage* (1894) which had expressed both enthusiasm and surprise at his knowledge of battle. Crane wrote, "I have never been in a battle of course, and I believe that I got my sense of the rage of conflict on the football field. The psychology is the same. The opposing team is an enemy tribe" (Stallman 18l). Certainly *The Red Badge of Courage* has real affinities with football writing; the languages of football and warfare were already inextricably mixed in the 1890s.[3] As always, the issue is the language itself, both that of the sports lexicon and its larger relations as expressive of cultural patterns. A lesser-known anecdote concerns Ludwig Wittgenstein at Cambridge in the 1930s. One day when Wittgenstein was passing a field where a football [soccer] game was in progress, "the thought first struck him that in language, we play games with words. A central idea of his philosophy, the notion of a 'language game,' apparently had its genesis in this incident" (Malcolm 65).

DeLillo's *End Zone,* the most provocative and intelligent of all football fiction, places both the intimation of Crane and the analogy of Wittgenstein into a structure that stipulates the language of football to be the language of our deep cognitive and metaphysical needs for collision and repetition posited as football's representative tropes. DeLillo finally refuses to dissociate the violence on the field from an inhumanity off the field. DeLillo knows, as Coover does, that even with violence and nuclear warfare, the issue is aesthetic. Our love for beauty and symmetry leads us to the darkness of obliteration and pain, toward the "perfection" of a mortality both individual and collective.

For roughly the last two decades, some of the most discussed writers in contemporary American fiction have been those who have brought an intelligent scepticism to the entire fictional process while creating either playful, self-reflexive worlds of extravagant fantasy, or spare, ironic portraits of cultural and linguistic breakdown. For Robert Scholes, they are the Fabulators; Robert Alter believes they practice (in Jorge Luis Borges' phrase) "partial magic"; Susan Sontag, George Steiner, and Ihab Hassan conceive of an entire strain of Western literature that approaches the realm of silence.[4]

American authors most identified with both the play worlds of fantasy and the minimal, reductive zones of silence include Barth, Pynchon, Coover, Vonnegut, Barthelme, and Reed. Whatever else they have been concerned with—the uses of myth, the meaning of history, terminal alienation, irony about that alienation, irony about that irony—they have conceived of language itself as both redeemer and ultimate villain, as the primary tool moving toward order and yet perhaps the universal disorder. Much recent American fiction presents language as the subject, validating both a sense of creative language play and theoretical positions of a generation of structuralists and post-structuralists such as Barthes and Derrida whose work often outstrips the creative capacities of the novelists themselves.

Since 1971 DeLillo has written nine novels that probe the limits of language through the examination of current cultural phenomena and popular forms. Each novel dissects the language of its subject: the inexactitude and commercial banality of television's messages in *Americana* (1971); in *End Zone* (1972), the brute sounds of football, the one sport that is sent into action by language and contains a pervasive appropriation of military jargon (and vice versa); the dilution of meanings and the pure grunt of the rock lyrics in *Great Jones Street* (1973); inspired scientific twaddle mouthed by geniuses in *Ratner's Star* (1976); and the strange discontinuous rhetoric of both terrorists and self-realization movements in *Players* (1977). DeLillo's most recent novels have featured the blunt, clipped language of the thriller genre in *Running Dog* (1978); the ultimate inscription of language itself into its own mystical cult in *The Names* (1982); and the language of the nuclear family in *White Noise* (1984). Finally, *Libra*

(1988) fictionalizes the life and plots surrounding Lee Harvey Oswald. Each novel examines the contaminated "language of the tribe" and identifies crisis zones of communication in which characters begin to search for a way into or out of the language in which they live.

DeLillo's writing has been prolific and uniformly intelligent. He confronts the possibility that there is some root unnameable matter or principle in the universe that resists being named or combined through human consciousness. His work shows the deep influence of Wittgenstein's concept of language games and Wittgenstein's ending to his *Tractatus Logico-Philosophicus,* which stipulated that what we cannot speak about we must pass over in silence. DeLillo is also another American heir to Samuel Beckett in his frightening ability to evoke terminal isolation and self-consciousness. He strips language to the barest and most austere of fictional premises as if he wished to move literally to the center of the riddle of human language and signs. Nonetheless, DeLillo remains a very playful author. He does not revel in cultural and linguistic collapse; indeed, his characters are often the last rational men and women, battling for meaning against silence, yet swooning toward it as if obliteration of oppressed, solipsistic brain cells might be the abstract embodiment of the death wish, both physical and cultural.

In *The Dismemberment of Orpheus,* Hassan has projected a line of development in the novel from Sade through Dada, Hemingway, Kafka, Surrealists, and Existentialists to Genet and Beckett that moves literature close to exhaustion and silence. His metaphor is the dismemberment of Orpheus who now plays on a lyre without strings. Hassan quotes Germaine Bree's term of "aliterature" for the writings of Alain Robbe-Grillet and others as that literature which moves toward a still center and, within that, toward a point even more still: "Aliterature emerges mainly as the language of consciousness at its reflexive task, the creative process giving phenomenological evidence of itself." Hassan points out that such fiction portrays a mind threatened by nominalism on the one hand and by solipsism on the other (*Dismemberment* 161).

Such minds abound in DeLillo's novels. Like Vonnegut and Barthelme, he has examined the level of individual consciousness in a flat, sophisticated comic rhetoric that is in itself a self-conscious style.

His allegiance is to *aleatory* language play, where chance and random combination determine meaning, His writing is playful, capricious, discontinuous, and absurd (Detweiler 59). His language play is not in the deeply mirthful "automatic" style of creating art in the sense that Frank Kermode has suggested that late modernist art is aleatory art (Kermode 19–21). Rather it is a philosophical acknowledgement that all language communication may be akin to accident, even when most seriously conceived and scrupulously implemented.

Aleatory play fiction contains the cold laughter of the reductive absurdist and seeks knowledge through the simplification of both experience and language. It is rigorously analytical below its deceptively flat surfaces. In aleatory play fiction, words are more frightening and real than characters who are reduced to analysts of their own linguistic behavior. DeLillo's characters retreat to the "safe" zones of mathematics, symbolic logic, diagrams, cryptic epigrams, mumbling wordless sex, mute drug trips, pile-ups on football fields, the roaring inside a cave of bats or within a player's helmet, the death-dealing statistics of nuclear destruction or the illusory security of the nuclear family.

The Collision of Differences

FOR DELILLO, language is forged in consciousness, the mind's arena, where words are grouped and the simple naming of things becomes the game. In *End Zone,* DeLillo would "unbox the lexicon," which is "a cryptic ticking mechanism in search of a revolution" (90). That "revolution" is one influenced for DeLillo by the aura of Wittgenstein. DeLillo has commented that he admires Wittgenstein's *Tractatus:* "The language is mysteriously simple and self-assured" ("Interview" 26). However, DeLillo appears even more indebted to the language-game theory of Wittgenstein's *Philosophical Investigations* (1953), since he has called *End Zone* a "book of games" in which characters have "wars of jargon with each other," in which "fiction itself is a sort of game" ("Interview" 21). The Wittgenstein of the *Tractatus* posited a "picture theory" of meaning which at its simplest stated that the meaning of language is that to which it refers: the proposition and its referant have identical logical form and naming has primacy (Keightley 18; Harnack 54).

In *End Zone,* Gary Harkness ponders the classic football cliché, "When the going gets tough, the tough get going," and thinks, "it seemed that beauty flew from the words themselves, the letters, consonants swallowing vowels . . . a semi-self-recreation from line to line, word to word, letter to letter. All meaning faded. The words became pictures. It was a sinister thing to discover at such an age, that words can escape their meanings" (13–14). Gary analyzes a locker room speech: "Men followed such words to their death because other men before them had done the same, and perhaps it was easier to die than admit that words could lose their meaning" (42). Such a maxim is applied not only to football but to nuclear warfare when Gary says to Major Staley, "There's no way to express thirty million dead. No words. So certain men are recruited to reinvent the language." When Staley protests that he doesn't make up the words, Gary adds, "They don't explain, they don't clarify, they don't express. They're painkillers. Everything becomes abstract" (66). The continual language analysis in *End Zone* finally overturns the Wittgenstein of the *Tractatus* in favor of the Wittgenstein of the *Philosophical Investigations.* Words may be used as names but are used in different language games by different people.[5] Gary Harkness and other characters desire to hold a pictorial relation to language. The sinister aesthetics of slippage dictates frames, users, and intentions which Gary strives to integrate.

DeLillo conceives of football as a system that replicates other interlocking systems. Football is "the one sport guided by language, by word signal, by snap number, color code, play name" (90). From this fact, DeLillo sees players moving from assigned positions to a collision of bodies and a pile-up, to a breakdown of the play that language began. He extends the images of language and football as systems to the third interlocking symbol, that of nuclear war, which also possesses atoms seeking collision and which can be launched through the jargon of atomic destruction that DeLillo shows to be strangely similar to that of football.

Language, football, and nuclear explosion all have symmetry and a fascination with order. They all possess root particles of meaning (words, players, and atoms). All have the power to create or destroy.

Language is portrayed in anarchic particles analogous to the football bodies strewn on the field or to the victims in a nuclear attack who so obsess Gary Harkness. *End Zone* finds him an exile at his fourth college—Logos—set deep in a southwest Texas desert. DeLillo's Texas is that of unyielding space—open, harsh, almost unnameable. He continues the violence associated with the Texas Connection but in an original way. Not concerned with Texas money, power, or folklore, his metaphor is the Southwest as a "burn area," a nuclear testing site.

His players are as odd a group as assembled in football fiction. They include a black superstar running back who is moving into mystical withdrawal; a huge lineman who, when injured, stands on the sidelines talking into his wrist, practicing for a sportscasting career; and a quarterback who upon finishing a very hard game, returns to the locker room, takes out a football board game and begins to play. Gary's teachers include a paranoid "exobiologist" named Zapalac who vies for his soul with Coach Creed and Staley, the Air Force ROTC Commander. All the characters are linguistics students who at "Logos" do indeed seek cosmic governing principles that may be imminent in reality. The players are young clerics, training to keep their bodies hard and lean under the quietly fanatic Creed, while their own dialogues constitute a comic *logomachy* as they dispute about words that are used without awareness of meaning.

Trying to name nuclear terror moves Gary to search for order, especially in the austere desert around him, one all too similar, although DeLillo doesn't make the overt reference, to Los Alamos, New Mexico. The fact that the nuclear fission device was developed under Amos Alonzo Stagg Field at the University of Chicago is not lost on DeLillo either, one suspects. The blank desert expands in Gary's mind to encompass a world after destruction. His concept of that void drives him to think, "What we know must be learned from blanked-out pages. To begin to reword the overflowing world. To subtract and disjoin. To recite the alphabet. To make elemental lists" (70–71). Gary begins by naming "The sun. The sky," but his list quickly mutates to horrid abstract destruction as consciousness assumes control and he names, "Blast area. Fire area. Body-burn area" (71). This second list obliterates the natural objects in the areas that are waste zones, *true* end zones. *End Zone* contains three definite "end zones": the numerous conversations and explanations that wind up in some irreducible state of language frustration; the terminal blasted area defined by the bomb's destruction; and, finally, the football end zone itself.

Gary's lists are linguistic rituals of order, Hemingwayesque in their stateliness and seriousness, what DeLillo has in place of bull-fighting or fishing the Big Two-Hearted River. DeLillo is similar to Hemingway in his quest for constraints. He has stated, "People leading lives of almost total freedom and possibility may secretly crave rules and boundaries, some kind of control in their lives. Most games are carefully structured. They satisfy a sense of order and they even have an element of dignity about them" ("Interview" 21). DeLillo would thus join Hemingway in the fear of free play, in the rigor of limits and rules. Such is his temper and that of football fiction, particularly in the novels of Gent. Football is the sport that sets the most violent collisions within the most structured of arenas. The nominal relation that it mimes is that between the wary consciousness and its collision with the forbidding alphabet. DeLillo is an inheritor of Hemingway's intimation of dignity in ritual and of the terror that ritual combats. He inscribes the ritual in the collective sporting practice of football. The terror in nuclear war is not in polarization with football but as expression of the same impulse for order.

DeLillo's vision of football is complex and directly relates to Gary Harkness' longing for wordless states. Language can send football players into action but language sending bombs into action is the unnameable. Thus, at one level, football releases the word into action and breaks the tension. It is the codified substitute for colliding atoms and destruction. Football also provides the simplicity, harmony, and physical sense of being alive that Gary seeks. Once a play is launched, it is a refuge from language and consciousness: "Through my jersey the turf felt chilly and hard. I heard somebody sigh. A deep and true joy penetrated my being. I opened my eyes. All around me there were people getting off the ground" (107). To arise after the collision, to *not* suffer obliteration in the explosion, is the football difference. Repetition of plays becomes an ecstatically beautiful thing to Gary, a struggle against nihilism. Football collision is definite; it is happening to him and there are no end zones except in clearly marked lines.

Security is in the middle of a collision at football's ground zero. In a melee, Gary notes, "The real danger was at the periphery where charges could be made, individual attacks mounted, and I felt quite relaxed where I was, being rocked back and forth" (114). "It was lovely to be hemmed in that way" (159), Gary thinks during a pick-up game in the snow. To be limited in space within collision is his strongest desire in football. Collision is a first principle in *End Zone* and has many emblems. Gary collides with a safety in a freshman game: "He died the next day and I went home that evening" (18); an assistant coach preaches "blowing them out," "popping" them, and "punishing" (96). A player comments about his rhetoric, "That's something I respect. I think it's a distinctly modern characteristic. The systems planner. The management consultant. The nuclear strategist. 'It's all angles' [Gary] said. 'The angles at which great masses collide' " (39). Collision, then, is inevitable from bodies to words uttered to the very letters in combination themselves. Finally, DeLillo makes concrete the language/football analogy when he slyly offers up to all symbol hunters the wisdom of the Logos sports information director, "You got to climb inside their mouth" (145), what an author must do and what football language and nuclear language as invading entities do to DeLillo's characters.

DeLillo deadpans that "commentators have been willing to risk death by analogy in their public discussions of the resemblance be-tween football and war" (89). His own contribution to football combat writing is the account of the Logos-West Centrex game, the most inventive fictional football game yet written. The game is structured as a series of black-outs where players move on and off the field, returning to the sidelines to report on casualties. The lan-guage is basic and primal: "This is footbawl. You throw it, you ketch it. You kick it. Footbawl. Footbawl. Footbawl" (104), or "Then we were going down the runway, the sounds louder now, many new noises, some grunts and barks, everyone with his private noise, hard fast rhythmic sounds" (84).

The sportscasting player on the sidelines recreates the bizarre ca-dences of a Chris Schenkel: "College football—a pleasant and color-ful way to spend an autumn afternoon. There goes five, six, seven, eight, nine ten, eleven yards, big thirty-five, twelve yards from our vantage point here at the Orange Bowl in sun-drenched Miami, Florida. John Billy Small combined to bring him down" (112–13). Other players sound like bomber pilots ruefully describing a botched mission: "I didn't infringe. The coaches wanted optimum infringement. But I didn't do the job. I didn't infringe" (108). As Gary says, "We were all making the private sounds. We were getting ready. We were getting high. The noise increased in volume" (104). As Gary waits to return the opening kick-off, "an awful sound was filling [my] helmet" (85), like a bomb about to explode. Here, language, the "ticking mechanism," is wedded to football. The game on De-Lillo's field gives pattern and regulation to the explosions.

Gary Harkness frees himself once to participate in a football game beyond Coach Creed's control and destruction's thrall. The Logos players have a ghostly post-season football scrimmage in a newly fallen snow in which "the idea was to keep playing, keep moving, get it going again" (158). DeLillo pointedly structures the scene not in free play but in the familiar football search for order and limit: "We were part of the weather, right inside it"; "Certain reflexes were kept slack; it seemed fitting to let the conditions determine how our bodies behaved" (159). Gloves and huddles are outlawed, then passing, reverses, and laterals. Teams must announce their plays beforehand. Gary thinks, "We were getting extremely basic, moving into elemental realms" (159). Football's simplicity is stressed by DeLillo who always strips down his premises and states toward the primes. The game is ultimately reduced to collision, regulation, repetition: "We kept playing, we kept hitting, and we were comforted by the noise and brunt of our bodies in contact, by the simple physical warmth generated through violent action" (161).

Football allows Gary to experience the center of an explosion (the pile-up) without being a victim. Coach Creed:

> Football is a complex of systems. It's like no other sport. When the game is played properly, it's an interlocking of a number of systems. The individual, the small cluster he's part of. . . . Football is brutal only from a distance. In the middle of it there's a calm, a tranquility. The players accept pain. There's a sense of order even at the end of a running play with bodies strewn everywhere. (163)

Substitute "language" or "nuclear war" "for football" in this speech and the zones of intensity in *End Zone* can be seen to overlap. Creed had been a B27 bomber pilot in World War II and his Logos team is nicknamed "The Screaming Eagles." The father of Major Staley was "the school's most famous alumnus," a three-letter man and one of the crew on the Nagasaki mission.

The language that connects man with his football and war experience is a pure system but can be used to wound or kill. The novel while short and deceptively cool in tone contains a number of violent acts with individuals dropping like casualties in a war. A quarterback coach shoots himself in the head and is eulogized by Creed "as one of the best football minds in the country" (55); one player dies in an automobile accident, another goes berserk in a dormitory; the widow of the college president dies in a plane crash; and Creed mysteriously takes to a wheelchair. Gary sees ominous words popping up all over campus such as MILITARIZE and APOTHEOSIS. The systems of military destruction range outward from the calm of ground zero to "bodies strewn everywhere" after the "sense of order" of the uniform explosion on the field. Through it all, Creed is seen as the *aleatory* creator: "This was his power, to deny us the words we needed. He was the maker of plays, the name-giver. We were his chalk scrawls" (110).

Gary, made captain of the team by Creed, continues to move toward his own silence, sifting the received language symbols. As he investigates abstract features of language, he moves closer to his personal end zone through last interviews with Major Staley and Taft Robinson, the black running back who has quit the team and now meditates in his room, all communications having been terminated. Gary looks around Taft's spartan quarters and "took a moment to scan the walls for tape-remnants. Poster of Wittgenstein, I thought. Maybe that's what he had up there, or almost had. . . . Two parts to that man's work. What is written. What is not written. The man himself seems to favor the second part" (192). Here, De-Lillo makes his only overt reference to Wittgenstein in his eight novels and does so in a material emblem of a Derridean trace as Wittgenstein's presence is felt in the *absence* of the poster. Wittgenstein sensed that the *Tractatus* was at bottom an ethical study but that the part that he did not write (on morality, religion, and aesthetics) was more important than the study of the language in which the ethics would be articulated (Pears 89). The trace of Wittgenstein in *End Zone* refers beyond itself to Gary's fierce loves of collision and repetition. Finally, the trace of Wittgenstein shows how Gary can relate collision and repetition morally to violence and death, the "part that he cannot write" and does not want to bring into language. DeLillo's "What is written. What is not written" is a paraphrase of the well-known letter Wittgenstein wrote to his publisher concerning the *Tractatus:* "My work consists of two parts: the one presented here plus all that I have not written" (*Letters* 143).

Gary moves to renounce the language game as he and Taft discover they share fascination with nuclear war and concentration camp atrocities. DeLillo burdens Gary Harkness with the consciousness that he is a sentient representative of the century in love with death. Such a realization gives great impetus to the movement toward silence as George Steiner has eloquently shown in *Language and Silence*. Throughout the novel, Gary has struggled with words competitively, fearing their randomness, their deadly weight which he could not control. How a culture patterns out its deepest fears and loves in a game such as football is thus only part of the novel.[6] DeLillo is telling us that we play language, football, and nuclear war on quests for order within the disorder of the collision of words, of bodies, of atoms. He postulates an organic connection among these states, expressing the tension at first most fundamentally as a longing for order set against a longing for obliteration. Aesthetics, history, and language are repeatedly and fundamentally connected by DeLillo. However, erasure, denial, obliteration, and the not-human not obfuscated by language may *be* the only order that humanity can bear, and that is Gary's awful secret, which he carries into his final silence.

DeLillo writes in football fiction's tradition of making the game itself the subject of individual speculation and criticism. His is yet another voice expressing guilty fascination with football's violence and power. Like Coover and Whitehead, DeLillo's great interest is in the body's placement within the sport, a question of "what is me" and "what is not me" and "what am I capable of" within the football structure. All three writers inquire as to how that structure is emblematic of the political and historical reality that has created it. Within this reciprocal relation of individual consciousness and collective structure, DeLillo has chosen to focus on what may only be called his own idiosyncratic inquiry into differences. DeLillo creates an order that expresses the differences making order possible. In *Ratner's Star,* DeLillo writes, "There is something in the space between what I know and what I am and what fills the space is what I know there are no words for" (370). DeLillo has correctly positioned the play of differences between knowledge and sense to name "the unnameable," to tell the "untellable" between being and knowing.

Language games derived from Wittgenstein thus play the differences in their energy and individual diversity. Wittgenstein observes in the *Philosophical Investigations,* "Isn't my knowledge, my concept of a game, completely expressed in the explanations that I could give? That is, in my describing examples of various kinds of game, showing how all sorts of other games can be constructed on the analogy of these; saying that I should scarcely include this or this among games; and so on" (*Philosophical Investigations #75* 35). Coover, Whitehead, and DeLillo in their aesthetics conceive of football in fresh semantic rows, proving "how all sorts of other games"— artistic, historical, linguistic—"can be constructed" from the basic structure of the sport. Football is placed in a large constellation of meanings and feeds into visions that contain it. Which is, after all, what we finally ask of sport and of fiction in our lives and why we are playing.

Conclusion

FOOTBALL FICTION remains captivated by the game itself, both its potential for violence and its capacity for elemental physical satisfactions. Nothing about football suggests transcendence to its authors. The game may not aid us in transcending *any* state, least of all the mythos in the society which creates and sustains the fascination with football. Football fiction is about power, control, discipline, and vocation. The lessons are learned through the body's collision. Little in the fiction suggests a more traditional hermeneutic of restoration or recovery. Innocence and origins are not at issue.

Likewise, a more radical hermeneutic of playing beyond the game or of extending the game itself to other rules and limits of practice is not seen as a possibility. Both past and future are problematic. Football players crave present realities. Coover's Gus lives "moment by moment, each one cut off from the next" (97–98); DeLillo's Gary Harkness wants "elemental realms" and "simple physical warmth" (159); Whitehead's Joiner seeks the "sweet patterns" of "digging and grubbing" (27). Football fiction stands squarely within the game itself, in the present, at the scrimmage line, within the huddle and the pile-ups, between the sidelines. There is pride in what the body has withstood and endured as well as fear of the cost and misgiving as to the tenor of the satisfactions, the ultimate rationale. The body is torn, the spirit is tested, while the fiction seeks to know "to what end?"

Writers such as Coover, Whitehead, and DeLillo attempt to position a freer individual subject within football, the most constrained of collective sports practices. They get beyond more conventional football fiction's obsession with the false polarization between what a football player is and what he does in the game. They know that in football, as in all sport, we play the differences between offense/defense, line/backfield, run/pass that re-present and codify the deep structural divisions in our own experience between the sensible and the intelligible, between the body and the spirit, between our individual fates and history; as Coover's Meyer remarks, "Between our cells and the informing universe . . . there's a lot of action" (*Gloomy Gus* 65).

Whether the football subject's plight is cast in the more mimetic mode of the individual sports hero versus the collective, or whether that level of reality is only a first pretext for a more metaphorical and metaphysical inquiry of rule and limit, the definition of football is "between the lines." Football by its extreme emphasis on all sorts of boundaries perhaps best models "the play between." Fictions of football become self-limiting studies of differences *within* football.

Fictions of Baseball:
Baseball and Passages

B ASEBALL IS the most enduring of the major American team sports, the one with the richest historical tradition, the greatest backlog of memory, and a homegrown mythology. The mythology of baseball is that it springs from the American folk, from tow-headed boys in green fields in small towns (and more recently from blacks in Alabama and from the "town of shortstops" in the Dominican Republic). Although it easily can be shown that baseball's early organized development was essentially urban, the myth persists that baseball is America's link with its rural past. Baseball is, then, always available for textualization as passage, an American rite bequeathed generation by generation, from father to son. Baseball is our summer game, the only team sport that is born, lives, and dies with the seasonal cycle, which provides both its poetry and its poignancy.

Furthermore, baseball does wondrous things to time and space that make it an author's delight. Baseball's temporal dimension is always in the domain of game time as it unfolds in pure possibility. Played without a clock, baseball provides open-ended drama. One can defeat time and mortality through an endless, rapturous inning. Baseball's differently measured tempos may include, for example, a six-pitch inning or a half-hour inning, a two-hour game or a seventeen-inning game. Such measurements of number and time foster in both players and spectators the expectancy of varied narrative. Innings are chapters opening up into thrilling action or closing down into abrupt summary moments when statistics can be totaled before the next engagement. A rally may quicken the pace of the game and just as swiftly dissolve back into quiescence. The game's pauses offer more opportunities for reflection on what the eye has seen. The pauses in baseball's action are moments for narrative interstices, for telling and re-creation.

Baseball's spatial metaphors are similarly suggestive. The game begins in an inner geometric grid that is logical and beautifully proportioned. The interaction of planes and surfaces, the drama of the pitcher/batter and the basepaths are all capped by the circular horizon of the outfield beyond which a ball could soar endlessly. The inner diamond always contains a journey, perilously begun at "home" plate, and, with a bit of luck, courage, skill, and aid, a return "home" with the object of the quest, the run (Porter 147–51). The game that provides open space within enclosure relates to space in the American psyche. Oriard writes that baseball is an expression of frontier cooperation and individualism, each player protecting his own space, yet working together when necessary, paralleling the dynamic of American democracy ("Sports and Space" 33, 35).

Commentators also attempt to define America's infatuation with baseball in sociological and historical terms. Ralph Andreano believes that the mythical qualities of ballplayers require that they and their institutions be kept separate and distinct from American industrial organization, that the game should naturally predominate over discussion of it as business or work (125). Roger Kahn in *The Boys of Summer* (1972) writes an excellent emblem of this split when he recalls complimenting ex-Brooklyn Dodger outfielder George Shuba on his "natural" swing and great wrists. Shuba replied, "You call that natural? I swung a 44–ounce bat 600 times a night, 4,200 times a week, 47,200 swings every winter. Wrists. The fast ball's by you. You gotta wrist it out. Forty seven thousand two hundred times" (241). Leverett Smith states that baseball changed from a pre-Ruthian, pre-Black Sox identification with the values of a dominant commercial culture to a paternalistic, autocratic, perennially adolescent family image that isolated players from adulthood and baseball from industry (207).

Indeed, baseball fiction, although always concerned with the individual sports hero's relation to the collective, is less likely to center there in crisis, proving to have greater resources of magic and play as it veers away from capture by the commodity drive. Baseball fiction may speak *meta*-physically with more ease than football fiction since there is little physical contact and no true configuration of the body in danger or distress. The players' endless cycling of the diamond by players has reference to the traversal of the semiotic square as well, with *individual sports heroes* moving fluidly from *collective sports heroism* to *anti-heroism* and back to *play,* resisting capture by their imaginative response. Just such a restless pattern provides baseball fiction with its dominant aesthetic: the quest for "home" and origin, matched by a ceaseless wandering, a state of exile in which there is longing for nurture and rest. A venturing out is matched by the yearning for reconciliation, a desire for the imagination in play to at least pattern "return," to narrate and speak of everything. If baseball's heroes are unable to live in historical time, they at least, through the art of the narrative, may "stay at bat forever" in the present.

Thus the three dominant play modes discussed in the introduction—the play toward origins, the play beyond, and the play between—are all prominent within baseball aesthetics. The play toward origins in baseball is always a "coming home," a marker of your presence as you are present there. Tallying a run cancels your absence as well as gives symmetry to what you have begun. Within the rules of baseball, home plate or the space of origin is recoverable in a simulation. In dramatic countering, to be "left on base" or at home plate is to be denied the play toward origins. Likewise, in the play beyond, baseball "dances outside the [diamond]" by liberating itself from time within its rules, and by liberating the space beyond the inner diamond where one may, theoretically, hit a ball as far as possible, to endless distances.

Such evocation of patterns underscores the authors' convictions of the learning capacities of baseball, a curriculum unbounded and perpetually renewed. Thomas Wolfe wrote in 1938, "Almost everything I know about spring is in [baseball]" (*Letters* 722). Mark Harris commented of his own Henry Wiggen that "baseball taught him everything as an art teaches" (Harris, preface to *The Southpaw* [unpaged]). Philip Roth wrote, "not until I got to college and was introduced to literature. . .did I find anything with a comparable emotional atmosphere and as strong an aesthetic appeal. . . . Baseball was the literature of my boyhood" ("My Baseball Years 35).

"What is it you like about this game?" Father asks Little Boy at the Polo Grounds in E. L. Doctorow's *Ragtime* (1975): "The same thing happens over and over," Little Boy replies (195). Little Boy's aesthetic pleasure in replication is the fundament of his role as psychic historian in *Ragtime*. Doctorow provides several striking emblems of baseball aesthetics. First, Little Boy is mesmerized by the repetition of the pitcher–batter drama. However, Father believes that what he sees on the field is his own private history in "the coded clarity of numbers" of the scoreboard, "for his secret understanding" alone (195), the view of an individual capitalist and romantic. Little Boy's alternate perception of history is more subtle and ironic. When a foul ball is hit into the stands, he reaches for it and possesses it momentarily. History has aimed right at him; for one instant *he* is the "record." However, he relinquishes the ball to the Giants' mascot, Charlie Faust, a halfwit who takes it back with an enigmatic smile, the "tale" returned to the possession of the idiot, as history moves on in its irrational course. Little Boy can envision the future in brief mystic images but is doomed to conserve artifacts and images, not to affect events. Charlie Faust is believed by the Giants to be a talisman but is quickly discarded when his "luck" runs out and they no longer see him as influencing the team's "history."[1] Baseball is an intimate aesthetic lesson for Little Boy and has complex historical association for Doctorow.

Ragtime is studded with characters who ponder their relation to history and seek an artistic or mystical release from it. J. P. Morgan, seeking to flee his own era and be reincarnated, spends a discouragingly prosaic night in the Great Pyramid in Egypt. Upon his exit into the morning light, he sees running toward him, hand outstretched, "a squat ugly man in pin-striped knee pants and a ribbed undershirt" (263)—it is John McGraw, manager of the New York Giants. Furthermore, a dismayed Morgan looks out over the Sphinx and sees the Giants in black uniforms "swarming all over her, like vermin" (263) or, appropriately, as scarabs (dung beetles), the Egyptian symbols of reincarnation which thus mock Morgan's quest. Morgan flees at this intrusion of American pop culture that familiarizes the scene and stamps baseball as both timeless and historical, both neutralizing and re-inforcing the Sphinx and its ageless temporal riddle. In a structural antithesis, McGraw would "hand the ball back" to Morgan, even as Charlie Faust had asked for its return from Little Boy. This rhythm of relinquishing/withdrawing from and returning to history is central to baseball fiction's continual dialogue of expulsion and reconciliation. Doctorow's final baseball emblem is of Harry Houdini, the *Ragtime* artist most sensitive to his historical role. Houdini is reading about the assassination of the Archduke Francis Ferdinand while suspended upside down, halfway up the *New York Times* tower. He then rises "past the baseball scoreboard attached to the side of the building" (265). Doctorow catches in alternate motions the clarity of number, the anarchy of history, and Houdini's bold but desperate play to master them both.

Creating the Field/Book

CLOSELY RELATED to baseball fiction's referential and self-referential use of history is its emphasis on "creating," the organic sense that baseball may be played anywhere it can be imagined *sans* schedules, crowds, and organization. "Creating the field" is expressly

linked to "creating the book" in many baseball novels. As Roger
Angell has remarked, an "interior stadium" (Angell 303) exists where
one may defeat time in memory of games and teams, in one's own
personal history in relation to the game. W. P. Kinsella's *Shoeless Joe*
(1982) relates the preparation of a magic ball field. Ray Kinsella
constructs this field on his Iowa farm in response to an inner voice
that tells him, "If you build it, he will come" (Kinsella 4). The "he"
is the shade of Shoeless Joe Jackson who eventually does materialize
along with his Black Sox teammates. Kinsella writes,

> I laid out a whole field, but it was there in spirit only. It was really
> only left field that concerned me. Home plate was made from
> pieces of cracked two-by-four embedded in the earth. The pitch-
> er's rubber rocked like a cradle when I stood on it. The bases were
> stray blocks of wood, unanchored. There was no backstop or
> grandstand, only one shaky bleacher beyond the left-field wall.
> . . . My intuition told me that it was the grass that was important.
> It took me three seasons to hone that grass to its proper texture, to
> its proper color. . . . Three seasons I've spent seeding, watering,
> fussing, praying, coddling that field like a sick child. Now it glows
> parrot-green, cool as mint, soft as moss, lying there like a cash-
> mere blanket. I've begun watching it in the evenings, sitting on
> the rickety bleacher just beyond the fence. A bleacher I constructed
> for an audience of one. (8)

Kinsella creates lovingly, patiently, in response to his vision. To
him, baseball is a ritual as is good writing, as is growing up, "more
deadly than religion, more complicated than baseball, for there seem
to be no rules. Everything is experienced for the first time. But
baseball can soothe even those pains, for it is stable and permanent"
(85). Kinsella passionately explains all this to J. D. Salinger whom he
has "kidnapped" to "ease his pain" (as the voice also instructed him)
by taking Salinger to Fenway Park! Kinsella places baseball and
writing in an equation when he muses, "What does [Salinger] have
in common with a baseball player?. . . He dispenses joy" (85).

Coover's *The Universal Baseball Association* (1968) is a wholly
imagined universe of a board game played by a middle-aged accoun-
tant at his kitchen table. In Coover's novel, the intensity of presence

and its fragility, the enormous imaginative belief in the reality of the fictional "universe" underscores creating and telling. In his baseball-possessed creator, J. Henry Waugh, Coover has given us an "author" who brings us closer to the day-to-day labor of a novelist and his concerns than do all of the novels purporting to have sensitive artists and thinkers as protagonists. Coover solves the problem of how to get a creator/character to *do* something in which we as readers may believe. Henry is visible through most of the novel where his mind churns and creates scenes and characters while he shapes the Association's life. Coover's imagery of Henry Waugh also provides homely emblems for creation and baseball: "Henry turned water on to wash, then hesitated. Not that he felt superstitious about it exactly, but he saw Damon Rutherford standing there on the mound . . . dry, strong, patient—and he felt as though washing his hands might somehow spoil Damon's pitch. From the bathroom door he could see the kitchen table. His Association lay there in ordered stacks of paper. The dice sat there, three ivory cubes, heedless of history, yet makers of it. . ." (18). Baseball's "ordered stacks of paper" can be statistics and game reports but also manuscripts of fate and history. The hero's delicate balance and the author's proprietorship are invoked by Coover's lines, suggesting baseball to be truly a game of the book.

Baseball can be played on the diamond in Kinsella's corn field or on Henry Waugh's kitchen table. The play space is often improvised and therefore more treasured. Tommy Neil Tucker's "The Perfect Garden" (1981) depicts an ancient umpire figure who appears from nowhere to build an exact ballfield by dead reckoning and instinct; he is the spirit of baseball itself who knows "the true nature of the game" (62). As a boy, Harris's Henry Wiggen in *The Southpaw* (1953) "had a regular system. I throwed the ball from out where the clothesline begins, and if I hit the house in 1 certain spot and caught the ball it was a strike. . . . It was all very real to me. Out behind the house was Moors Stadium in New York City, thousands of people and a good deal of cheering. Sometimes the ball would hit the clothesline, and there was no way to explain that, and I did not try" (23) In the intensity of the imagination, "clothelines" are simply ignored or assimilated as a contingency in the larger frame of play. In *The Natural,* Roy Hobbs strikes out the Whammer from a pitcher's mound measured out on a railroad siding next to a country carnival. His catcher, an old scout, wears a washboard as chest protector. They borrow baseball gloves from kids and use a bat and baseballs won at the carnival. No matter how makeshift the game, its outcome is one of epic import. Hobbs strikes out The Whammer and goes forward to meet Harriett Bird and his own baseball destiny.

Wherever Jerome Charyn's fabled hero Babe Ragland in *The Seventh Babe* (1979) plays, *there* is the spirit of baseball. When Babe travels with the Cincinnati Colored Giants, a platoon of diamond magicians creates the field out of nothing: "an umpire, a witch doctor, wandering carpenters and groundskeepers, and fourteen Giants. The groundskeepers set up a baseball diamond in a field across from the bus. They labored like fools with their trowels and their scythes, while the carpenters built a grandstand near first base. They'd turned a stinking field into a diamond in forty-five minutes." (153). Authors perceive that the diamond is imaginatively present in the mind's eye. Baseball is the American team sport always available for sculpting. No sports fiction concentrates more lovingly on the creation of its own play space; authors find something almost sensual there. They revel in the satisfying geometry of its clean lines, the suggestiveness of its open areas. Within these spaces, individual heroes create their passages with reference to baseball myth and history and their roles in the collective history of modern America, the largest field in the novels.

Coming Home: Fathers and Sons

ALLIED WITH the continuing trope of creating the field/book in baseball fiction has been the psychological theme of "coming home" which takes its primary structure from baseball's journey around the diamond. Baseball fiction has provided the strongest of contemporary sports meditations on questing, exile, and return. Always overlaid on the journey is a strong family drama of fathers and sons, potentially a clash in Oedipal terms but just as often negotiated in baseball fiction as a calm and loving transfer of potency and manhood. Baseball also appears as the sport that has bonded fathers and sons, one that ensures the continuity of generations. Only baseball possesses this element to any degree. Baseball is *taught,* handed down as a skill like glass-blowing; its appreciation is readily and eagerly shared. Such a certainty provides the impetus to the use of family throughout baseball fiction, to align experience and its personal moments of growth to the larger collective history.

Roger Kahn writes, "the game begins with sons and fathers, fathers and sons. The theme is older than the English novel, older than *Hamlet,* old at least as the Torah. You play baseball with love and you play baseball to win and you play baseball with terror, but always against that backdrop, fathers and sons" (*A Season in the Sun* 5). Such a "backdrop" has been most congenial to Jewish-American writers who, with the exception of Coover, have been the most influential contemporary authors using baseball as subject. The Jewish baseball novel form, writes Eric Solomon, "must be a special kind of baseball novel, moreover, rich in myth, values, and ideas; a book that will be at once American in subject, baseball, and Jewish in form, parable" (50). Such resonances include the repeated goal of learning in history and the education of the heart to sustain in continuity the wisdom of a home. Jewish American novelists have found in this country a deeply rooted sports sensibility available to immigrants in a democratic and mobile society, the sensibility of a symbolic historical-religious community that, in Solomon's view, is a substitute for both *schtetl* and *schul* (Solomon 48).

While writers such as Harris, Malamud, Roth, and Charyn have enriched baseball as novelistic subject, they drew on the pattern of baseball's development that was already strongly present in the larger American society. They came to baseball sharing interest in subjects that may be identified as those of a Jewish messianic sensibility. Their baseball fiction expresses the sense of a transcendent self, one who finds a way to act in history through suffering and self-sacrifice, one who takes on burdens and grows, who reconciles himself to duties and limits after a wandering and an alienation.[2]

In the Jewish-American adaptation of baseball in fiction, the central baseball characters have been anglicized or at least have not been specifically Jewish, as if to write through the mask of American popular sport is a way to code the tale as a universal one, to draw on traditional thematic material in the contemporary American setting. In effect, assimilation is built into the tale rather than being its subject; therefore, Jewish American authors writing of baseball efface their Jewishness at the same time they draw on it for metaphysical statement in the specific American milieu.

How baseball fiction can provide reconciliation and home-coming between father and son first may be found in the primal scene of pitcher and batter. John R. Tunis' *Young Razzle* (1949) explored the scene in its most sentimental form when young rookie Joe Nugent, Yankee second baseman, hits a home run in the fifth game of the World Series to defeat the Dodgers and his father, forty-year-old pitcher Raz Nugent. Raz deserted the family when Joe was a boy, had a great career, fell victim to alcoholism, but climbed back to the majors. His resentful son wins the Oedipal battle and they are reconciled. In Kahn's *The Seventh Game* (1982), Johnny Longboat, another aged pitcher who has not been an attentive father, quits baseball and chooses his family over his mistress: "Johnny looked at his son and saw his father, dead eleven years; in a sense a boy was his father and his son at the same time" (293). The distraught father in Foster's *Goodbye Bobby Thomson! Goodbye John Wayne!* weeps to his son after Thomson's miracle home run in the Polo Grounds in 1951, "I don't want to lose you, too" (53); he has one dead son in Korea. The father had rooted for the Giants, his son for the Dodgers. Philip F. O'Connor in *Stealing Home* (1979) tells of a suburban father and Little League coach who chooses son and family over flight. In Fielding Dawson's *A Great Day for a Ball Game* (1973), a novelist makes delicate overtures through baseball to the proud, mistrustful eight-year-old son of his lover. Charles Newman's "The Hair Cut" in *New Axis* (1968) portrays a father and son turning homemade bats on a lathe in their basement in an epiphany of craft and loving detail.

In James McManus' *Chin Music* (1985), the narrative journey is a literal coming home of father and son under the grimmest and most moving of circumstances. Ray Zajak, an ace left-hander for the Chicago White Sox, awakens from a coma after his beaning in a World Series game. It is the last morning of earth: nuclear missiles have been launched and Chicago's death sentence can be measured in minutes. Zajak is an amnesiac but "he assumes without question that he's got some sort of family out there, waiting for him to come home" (15). Zajak himself, memory-less, with good intentions, has become the awful buzz of apocalypse. He weaves home through a nightmare city while his son plays a pick-up baseball game at school, falls in love with a girl on the other team, and then moves toward home himself. McManus acknowledges the beanball ("an enormous white blur, eclipsing your view of all else," 143) as baseball's individual analogy to nuclear explosion. However, he is equally interested in baseball's structural rhythms of coming home and fathers/sons that counter death and destruction. Working from the starkest of fictional premises, McManus uses baseball's deep thematics with sentiment and grace.

John Sayles' *Pride of the Bimbos* (1975) provides a fine variant of the father-son nurture in the dwarf Pogo Burns' care of nine-year-old Denzel Crawford. When Pogo dies, the touring Bimbo barnstormers dress Denzel like Pogo in wig and spikes so that the show may go on that night. Denzel's real father, a laconic outfielder on the team, ends the novel, "worried because finally there was no one left between him and the boy, and he didn't know how to handle it. Just didn't know" (248). Denzel now feels that the trip to the next game town "seemed like too long a ride to take alone." Characters bereft of fathers also find ways through baseball to call them home. In *Shoeless Joe,* Kinsella needs a catcher to complete his team of Black Sox shades on the ghostly Iowa field. He summons his dead father, an old minor league player, and tells his frightened twin brother, Ray, "the right chemistry will be there, it can't help but be. You both love the game. Make that your common ground and nothing else will matter" (230). Kinsella watches his father on his own imagined field. He sees him as young, strong, and hopeful: "Think about it. I'm getting to see something very special" and "It should be enough for me, to see him doing what he loves best" (232).

The potentially threatening Oedipal scene of a son supplanting a father is handled in many different modes in baseball fiction. Irwin Shaw's *Voices of a Summer Day* (1965) sentimentalizes the scene into three generations as Benjamin Federov watches his thirteen-year-old son Michael play ball while remembering his own childhood when *his* father, Israel, taught him. Benjamin muses, "The generations circled the bases, the dust rose for forty years as runners slid in from third, dead boys hit doubles, famous men made errors at shortstop, forgotten friends tapped the clay from spikes with their bats" (12). Less sonorous is Harris's flat account without trauma of Henry Wiggen in *The Southpaw* replacing his father on the mound in a game for the Perkinsville, N.Y., semi-pro nine. Henry calls on all Pop has taught him and is triumphant without guilt or epiphany on either side. In contrast, Lamar Herrin in *The Rio Loja Ringmaster* (1977) provides a sad tale of Dick Dixon's father, a bitter former minor league infielder, who takes his ten-year-old son to his first Cardinals doubleheader only to start drinking with an old friend and forget about the boy, who sits alone in the left field bleachers. In an almost deserted Sportsman's Park, Dick wanders out to the mound, a tiny, terrified figure: "He tore out his lungs trying to shout. . . . Yesterday he was propped on his bed surrounded by baseball cards and listening to the near-fabled events that had taken place here, here on this diamond, and today he was at the center of it and everything was gone" (Herrin 57). Abandoned by his father in this ritual arena, he separates from him psychically forever. Baseball becomes a taut pursuit of his selfhood from then on into a successful but unhappy major league pitching career and subsequent flight into exile in Mexico.

In *The Natural,* a book punctuated by Roy Hobbs' substitute fathers—Sam Simpson, Pop Fisher, Max Mercy, Goodwill Banner—the absence of Roy's father only lends urgency to his quest and a furtive quality to his relationships. As discussed in the introduction, the cinema version of *The Natural* thoroughly establishes a father-son frame for the tale from beginning to end. Malamud's novel, however, has only the trace of the father, preserving in difference the figure's authority in non-presence. Roy Hobbs' sudden vision on the first page of the novel is of "this white-faced, long-boned boy whip[ping] with train whistle yowl a glowing ball to someone hidden under a dark oak, who shot it back without thought" (7). The mechanical return of the ball from the hidden figure is literal and not loving. It immediately stamps Roy Hobbs as shrouded and alone and one who will, in his own wandering and regeneration, seek to "shoot it back without thought." His early victory over the Whammer is a primal scene. Spinning himself into the ground, "the Whammer understood he was, in the truest sense of it, out" and "dropping the bat, he trotted off to the train, an old man" (19, 25). An ailing, bitter Roy Hobbs will be struck out by Herman Youngberry, a green farm boy, at the novel's conclusion as Hobbs comes full circle to his own aging and defeat. Malamud in *The Natural* gives extreme definition and drama to the moral and psychological tropes of fathers/sons and coming home through mythic analogues.

Roth in *The Great American Novel* is ribald and grotesque in his rendering of the father-son relationships in baseball. He plays with all mentors and nurturing; the fathers are Polonian drudges, the sons insensitive immortals, and the current of communication or growth nonexistent. Charyn's Babe Ragland in *The Seventh Babe* slays the father by denying his childhood as Marcus Tannehill, heir to a copper empire. Instead, he fashions himself an orphan, in line with the legend of Babe Ruth, and battles all authority for a half century, including team owners and Judge Landis, until he becomes his own reincarnation, an aged boy, the very spirit of baseball: "a baseball baby. Orphan Rags" (167); the "kid dug a home for himself around third base" (220). Charyn cites the suggestive father-son relationships of Ruth and Ty Cobb, which are lesser-known bits of baseball history. Ruth was not actually an orphan but had been placed in St. Mary's in Baltimore as "incorrigible" by a father who could not handle him, facts that Ruth never stressed. Cobb greatly respected his father who was shot to death by Cobb's mother when Cobb was a boy; allegedly, she had mistaken her husband for a home intruder. Such separation and pain is not lost on Charyn. *His* Babe tells Ruth's tale but lives Cobb's fury to a great extent until he passes into exile and ultimate mythography. Thus Charyn contextualizes the powerful father-son thematic by the usage of actual baseball history.

Coover works the most original turn on the father-son theme in baseball fiction. The Universal Baseball Association play is finally brought to grief by the death of Damon Rutherford. Damon is the son of immortal pitcher Jock Rutherford. As a rookie, he pitches a perfect game. In his excitement to see perhaps a second perfect game in succession, something never accomplished in the Association's history, Henry Waugh then pitches Damon out of turn. Henry's action can be experienced by a baseball fan as a serious flouting of baseball's convention, which Coover enlarges into a cosmic flaw or weakness. A series of triple ones on Henry's dice decrees that Damon's time at bat in the second inning is referred to the Extraordinary Occurrences Chart where the decision is rendered: "1–1–1: Batter struck fatally by beanball" (55). Henry is stricken by the death of a player who is a son to him. By letting Damon pitch out of turn,

Henry has tampered with fate. From this moment on, the creator of the Association begins to cheat, to break his own rules, to plan vengeance against Damon's slayer, another of his "sons," a fellow rookie with the Biblical initials and baseball name of Jock Casey. By the equation of creating the field and book with paternity and mortality, Coover has portrayed the creation of history through authorship with the moving father-son tragedy at the core of Henry's aesthetic heroism.

Baseball and Education

OF THE three American team sports, baseball in its passages has always been perceived as the sport that teaches, that provides lessons in art and life. This education is not, like that of the School Sports Hero, buried in a past moment, but is an ongoing journey toward self-knowledge. Lardner's stories had established the convention that lessons were there to be learned through the sports team experience. He did not aggrandize baseball as anything special; he simply felt that character was tested in a public arena. The results in his fiction were mixed. Buster Elliot in "My Roomy" and Jack Keefe never learned anything while Grimes in "Horseshoes" and Frank X. Farrell in "Alibi Ike" came through to knowledge and victory that controlled their neuroses. For Lardner, the team is representative of a collective society that was unfailingly rational and normative. The individual sports hero was at fault if his idiosyncrasies would not allow him to conform and perform. Wise managers, sportswriters, and teammates gave him his chances. For Lardner, it was then all up to him.

Contemporary baseball fiction generally reverses this conservative position. The individual sports hero is most often the focus of attention and sympathy in a battle with the oppressive collective. However, Mark Harris' Henry Wiggen novels continue the Lardnerian convention that the baseball team is a place where one can grow and take counsel from others. For Harris, too, the collective is relatively benign and is where the tests are, where experience with many people allows us to grow, in the collective (secondary) paradigm of the play experience.

What are the key facets of baseball's "education"? What are authors and players educated about? Harris' statement about Henry Wiggen, that "baseball taught him everything as an art teaches," is significant for the "art" that baseball is seen to be. In the aesthetics of baseball, the playing of differences—of bat and ball, ball and glove, infield and outfield, pitcher and batter, ball and strike, safe and out —define the meaning of the game between the lines. Furthermore, the language of the sport itself becomes a temporal substitution. The baseball narrative control begins with the literal negation of time within the sport's play frame. Authors play with this temporal dynamic in affirmation or negation. Witness Harris' affirmation of "baseball teaching" as "art" countered by the assertion of Roy Hobbs at the conclusion of *The Natural:* "I never did learn anything out of my past life, now I have to suffer again" (190).

Both Harris and Malamud are working within a central intimation in baseball that you *can* "go home again" and that by "staying up [at bat]," you may never die. Return and the defeat of mortality are baseball's seductive promises. Baseball simulates both options and within the same structural movement. By scoring a run, the player returns to his origin and retains control in the present as well, to "return" repeatedly to the future. Baseball for authors is the perfect play of possessing the center with continual reference to past (home) and future (the endless, outless inning) without capture by either. A baseball narrative is a substitution for the passage of time which is concealed through individually coded events and disclosed by staying up at bat, the deferral of an ending.

Such an aesthetics is, to be sure, not at the tip of the senses (or pen) for most authors of baseball fiction and their heroes. Yet within limited perspective, baseball in realistic fiction is first validated as a complete life experience, a model for this-or-that relation of the individual sports hero to the team. James Farrell (Studs Lonigan, Danny O'Neill) and Nelson Algren (Lefty Bicek) both described their young Chicago adolescents as neighborhood baseball players, and Farrell wrote of his life-long affection for the game in *My Baseball Diary* (1957). Baseball fiction proper contains a few doggedly realistic studies of baseball as a business. Martin Quigley's *Today's Game* (1965) describes a "big game" from the manager's point-of-view; Eliot Asinof's *Man on Spikes* (1955) provides an anatomy of baseball types but focuses on thirty-four-year-old Mike Kutner who, in the novel's deterministic climax, strikes out in his only major league at-bat. Age is often the vantage point from which the baseball hero describes his passage and what he has learned. Charles Einstein's Stat Hunter in *The Only Game in Town* (1955) is a rookie player-manager trying to beat back time and his dead arm. Such baseball novels seemed closer to deterministic boxing narratives.

Kahn's forty-one-year-old pitcher in *The Seventh Game* delivers his last pitch in the seventh game of the World Series; it tears his weak shoulder, the batter hits it for a grand slam home run to win the game, 4–0. Yet both Stat Hunter and Kahn's Johnny Longboat are reconciled to their wives and families, whom they had previously neglected to follow their careers. A more boisterous veteran, Hemphill's Stud Cantrell in *Long Gone* (1979), is thirty-nine years old and playing on the worst team in the lowest Southern Class D League in organized baseball. When called on to fix a game, he protests, "This game is all I ever had. Now I got to treat it like a cheap whore" (202). He knows, "Baseball's a simple game. All you got to do is hit the ball and run like hell. . . . It's just plain democratic when the best man wins" (185). All Stud Cantrell knows has come through the game he has lived for twenty years. On the other hand, career minor league shortstop Darrel Skaits in Morry Frank's *Every Young Man's Dream* (1984) has learned nothing from organized baseball: "I couldn't get along with those people. They wanted to make a lifer out of me" (545), but he is obtuse and his own worst enemy. More optimistically, baseball is seen to telescope and bond all ages together. Shaw's Israel Federov in *Voices of a Summer Day* was "made into an American catching behind the plate bare-handed in the years between 1895 and 1910" (42). Ace Chicago softball veteran Buddy Barnes is firmly caught in the only game he knows in Tom Lorenz's *Guys Like Us* (1980). William Brashler's veteran pitcher Leon Carter in *The Bingo Long Travelling All-Stars and Motor Kings* (1973) thinks that his great arm talks to him and he listens. When his arm goes dead, he knows it intimately and retires quickly, the truest knowledge having been transmitted.

An alternative to the reconciliation with age, to the final coming home, is to rage against it in perpetual renewal by staying up in the game forever as Charyn's Babe Ragland would do in *The Seventh Babe*. As Young Rags tells his millionaire father's lawyer, "Tell him *this* is school for me . . . the ball feeds me" (152). By the time Rags is in his sixties, still barnstorming with the Cincinnati Colored Giants, "you couldn't have guessed his age. He was like some mad, ancient boy walking in his own fever" (294). The life in baseball has obliterated time. The narrative description in the temporal dimension has replaced Rags' aging as he has divested himself from all organized forms of baseball. Rags cannot go home; he has made baseball his home and thus will never die. Charyn has fulfilled the rich structural possibility of baseball's timelessness.

Malamud in *The Natural* works directly against baseball's timelessness since Roy Hobbs is obsessed with making up for his lost fifteen years. He is always mystified by his inability to understand the terms of his heroism. When questioned about his own ideals and beliefs by Harriett Bird, he is heedless of them. He is "the natural" whom life turns into a bitter, aging, disciplined quester, clock-terrified in the timeless game, no home to return to in the game of return. Malamud voids baseball's deepest rhythms, shows Hobbs replacing them with his own desires, and thereby highlights baseball's education all the more. Rather than reconciliation and acceptance of aging, Hobbs denies time, insisting "if you have leave all those records that nobody else can beat—they'll always remember you. You sorta never die" (125). Here is a quantified "immortality" of the ledger informed by none of baseball's aesthetic vision or knowledge but consistent with mythic stereotype.

Harris: The Education of Henry Wiggen

ONE COULD say that Roy Hobbs was confidently on his way to becoming Henry Wiggen before he was cut down by fate and by Malamud's commitment to myth. With Harris's creation of Henry Wiggen, American fiction finally is provided with a baseball hero who is everything a hero should be—and a winner besides. Harris's *The Southpaw* (1953) and *Bang the Drum Slowly* (1956)[3] suggest that the individual heroic education of Henry Wiggen enables him to come through as a mature man. Henry is seasoned through his striving; he is not torn apart by his desires but rather he is matured by fulfilling them. The novels concentrate on what Henry learns about his own nature and the natures of the people around him. Baseball provides a suitable education for a modern Huckleberry Finn who just happens to be a talented left-handed pitcher. The team and the flow of the season become Henry's schooling and he records it for his readers.

Henry is baffled by books and school teachers in the best tradition of anti-school American boy heroes. He reads pulp fiction about baseball: "There was 1 fellow name of Homer B. Lester that wrote a whole series of 16 books about a pitcher called Sid Yule. . . . There was 'Sid Yule, Kidnapped,' and 'Sid Yule, No-Hit Pitcher,' and 'Sid Yule in the World Series,' and 13 more, and all the books had 24 chapters and run 240 pages and you couldn't skip a one" (*The Southpaw* 34). He tires of these "novels" which are his earliest impressions of what life in baseball is like. In utilitarian fashion, Henry's other reading is the "How To" series ("How To Pitch," "How To Play First Base," and so on, around the diamond). Finally, he reads the "autobiography" of Sam Yale, the Mammoth's star pitcher, a ghost-written tale full of bland aphorisms that purports to tell boys how to reach the major leagues. This predigested wisdom about cleanliness, godliness, and the wisdom of high school coaches is taken as scripture by young Henry who literally drops to his knees to read the text in the town library, then steals the book, and keeps it by his bedside.

Unfortunately, when Henry joins the Mammoths, he meets the real Sam Yale, who turns out to be a sour, disillusioned, foul-mouthed old pro who has no love for the game nor any respect for himself. One day in the clubhouse after a particularly drunken evening, he moans, "Some day I have got to read that book to find out where I done wrong" (86). Henry ultimately learns from the sad, unhappy man that Sam Yale is. However, the early hero worship drove the boy to become an individual sports hero himself. Once achieved, Henry's heroism is tempered by his realistic assessment of the role and his place in it.

Harris specifically links *The Southpaw* to Lardner's work by having Henry remember the boys' sports books in the town library:

> There was also some books of baseball stories, such as those by Sherman and Heyliger and Tunis and Lardner, although Lardner

did not seem to me to amount to much, half his stories containing women in them and the other half less about baseball then what was going on in the hotels and trains. He never seemed to care how the games come out. He wouldn't tell you much about the stars but only about bums and punks and second raters that never had the stuff to begin with. (34)

Although Henry protests, he will come to know of a ballplayer's life as Lardner wrote of it. Slowly he will learn to sympathize with or have pity for the "bums and punks and second raters" and will learn how to avoid being one of them. Hotels and trains will yield relevant information about other people's lives. Women will actually appear and at times dominate his own narrative, to his youthful surprise. Between the poles of his youthful idolatry of Sam Yale and his early scorn for Lardner's ballplayers, Henry evolves his own sense of his duties and tempers his egotism.

Harris' novels are sentimental and deceptively flat. Most of the dramatic situations in the Wiggen books have benign conclusions, the notable exception being the death of Bruce Pearson from Hodgkin's Disease in *Bang the Drum Slowly,* itself a re-telling of baseball culture's most enduring mortal drama, the death of Yankee Iron Horse Lou Gehrig from a form of lateral sclerosis at age thirty-nine in 1941. If "education" is in baseball's line and "staying up forever" one of the game's goals, then Gehrig's death is the intimation of mortality's power in the timeless game, the end point never forestalled and only dimly grasped. All sports literature from A. E. Housman through Mark Harris has had that poignant contrastive potential of the vital young physical star who is cut down, as if to underscore more strongly the universality and mechanistic irony done to those whom death chooses. The death of Bruce Pearson affords Henry Wiggen his final lessons in brotherhood and courage. He is, in his own term, "growed." Henry knows by the end of his stewardship of Bruce that the essentials are not merely game-ridden but the realities of life and death. As Henry's catcher, Red Traphagen, Harvard graduate and team liberal, tells Henry in a burst of narrative strategy, "Stick to death and Pearson." Henry writes, " 'I will try,' I said, and I done so" (244).

He has "done so" through a frame that allows the team to grow into its responsibilities to Pearson, a figure whom they had either shunned or ignored as a "rube" and third-string catcher of no importance. Henry learns, as they do, that Pearson's life and death are intrinsically valuable. Harris plays for these stakes with much sentiment but is squarely within sports fiction conventions. He makes Bruce Pearson a true Lardnerian bumpkin with no self-knowledge or sensitivity, and resists all attempts to make him into an individual sports hero. Instead, Bruce is without any victories, physical grace, or mystical power, a completely de-mystified Georgia farm boy without legend or wit. Harris makes effective use of the hero–witness dynamic of school sports fiction. Henry will be Bruce's witness; he will portray the worth of all dying men. Furthermore, the New York Mammoths, going nowhere after great pre-season hopes, playing for themselves in a listless selfishness, rally through their perception of mortality. They care for Bruce and win the pennant and World Series. For Harris, the collective unit is capable of benign growth, as is the individual sports hero. *Bang the Drum Slowly* shows the players coming together for a sentimental nurturing. The common enemy is natural (death), not economic or social (big business, the team). In *Bang the Drum Slowly* Harris shows heroes and society alike capable of reinforcing each other's potential and sympathy. The players have solidarity but to no radical purpose or change. There is no more optimistic vision in sports fiction of the individual sports hero's passage in collective sports heroism. Commodification and dehumanization exist in Harris' novels but are always effectively countered by Henry Wiggen and his mates by fixing on natural facts.

Henry finally records Bruce Pearson's death, one as abrupt and uneventful as his life had been. Bruce's teammates gently lead him off the field as a pelting rain halts a late-season game and signifies the return of Bruce's clock time. Henry has fought to preserve Bruce's value as a human being and has brought a personal aura to "roommate" and "teammate." In the language of its own conclusion, *Bang the Drum Slowly* "rags nobody" and makes us believe in it.

Baseball and Myth

BASEBALL CONTAINS expansive contradictions that make it so supple for writers. On the one hand, baseball is timeless in its game structure, providing for imaginative re-creation that works with and against that trope. On the other hand, baseball is seasonal and organic, coming alive in the spring and dying out in the fall, a yearly fertility cycle dominated by images of return and renewal. Both its timelessness and its growth cycle suggest mythic potentialities for baseball's rendering. Myth feeds on historical material and abstracts from it large patterns of symbolic human endeavor while, at its source, myth has been traced to the ritual patterns surrounding a culture's sense of its generation and continuities.

The absorbing interest in myth and its potential for energizing fiction and poetry becomes a benchmark of high modernism in the work of Yeats, Eliot, Joyce, Lawrence, and Faulkner. Modernists attempting to control Eliot's "immense panorama of futility" that is modern history or to awaken from Joyce's "nightmare" appropriated forms that were both classic and primitive. Myth was classic in its large mannered motions of stability and cultural explication and primitive in the roots of culture described by James Frazer and his descendants in the Cambridge School of anthropologists at the turn of the century. Thus the literary education of the modernists included a rich folk criticism being practiced by classical scholars. Such a criticism became one weapon in the arsenal of New Criticism which was centrally concerned with explaining and justifying the products of High Modernism.

The Natural became a textbook for modernist myth study. When asked about the genesis of *The Natural,* Malamud said, "Baseball players were the 'heroes' of my American childhood. I wrote *The Natural* as a tale of a mythological hero because, between childhood and the beginning of a writing career, I'd been to college" ("An Interview" 9). Malamud's wit is very apt. Myth and its structural properties of magic and fantasy have been the great suggestive force for academy-trained authors conscious of their heritage and nowhere more evident than in the transformation of the fictional baseball subject.

Such was not initially the case, however. Lardner's success during World War I did not spawn a generation of baseball fiction. Except for isolated minor novels, short fiction, and Heywood Broun's *The Sun Field* (1923), an account of a Ruthian slugger married to a feminist who tries to educate and civilize him in a reverse-sex Pygmalion plot, there was no real sustained advance in form and content be-

335

tween *You Know Me, Al* (1916) and *The Natural* in 1952 with *The Southpaw* touching homeplate with a run for Lardner's team in 1953. For more than three decades, baseball fiction was in the hands of hacks, humorists, sportswriters, and boys' fiction authors, the best of whom, John R. Tunis, educated a generation of American youth about tolerance and fair play. Here is a remarkable drought considering the sustained popularity of baseball itself. Some educated guesses about that drought include Lardner's perfection of comic realism so that copies appeared futile, Lardnerian "boobs," who did not interest "serious" authors; the Depression and its second generation of American literary naturalists, who did not find baseball's verities terribly relevant; World War II's desolation and subject matter; and, not incidentally, a strong high culture-popular culture split fostered through modernism in which certain subjects were simply deemed unacceptable for sustained treatment in serious fiction.

Baseball and American professional sport boomed after World War II with record-breaking attendance levels and the advent of televised sports. Malamud's novel presented culturally acceptable and ancient forms in modern athletic dress, bringing high culture tropes and contemporary sport together in fiction. Authors approaching baseball for fiction have never looked back. If *The Natural* seems somewhat familiar to readers today, it is only because Malamud's descendants in baseball fiction such as Coover, Roth, and Charyn have enriched the magical-mythical baseball fiction tradition, as high culture-popular culture barriers have relaxed into senescence.

Malamud: The Passion of Roy Hobbs

THE NATURAL has a deceptively realistic surface that initially promises the reader a modicum of belief in the daily events on the diamond; however, no scene is allowed to pull its own weight without an overlay of symbolic transparencies, including classical, Biblical, Arthurian, and Freudian archetypes, as well as enactments of the wisdom in Frazer's *The Golden Bough* and a repeated usage of the fund of baseball's popular lore. *The Natural* lives to be interpreted — or did before it was interpreted to death. Harriett Bird herself strains to be an earnest critic as she reviews Roy Hobbs' strikeout of the

Whammer, "of David jawboning the Goliath-Whammer, or was it Sir Percy lancing Sir Maldemer, or the first son (with a rock in his paw) ranged against the primitive papa?" (26). No further attempt to "get" all *The Natural*'s references will be attempted here. Instead, with the distance of several decades since its publication, it is time to look at *The Natural* from the standpoint of baseball fiction's history and as a sort of meta-commentary on the continuing problem of the conversion of sport into fiction.

Malamud's writing a baseball novel *was* novel in 1952 but his method of approaching sport as subject, encasing his fiction in mythical reference and high style, was the old story of an author deeming sport and play not serious enough within themselves. For Malamud to have approached baseball at all was to approach the "chapel perilous." Yet, in his defense, Malamud merely formalized what is evident: the relation between baseball and folk culture-world mythology is in the patterns of season and of return, of baseball's organic connection between nature and the quest. Such patterns have been expressed at length by Denis Porter who linked the narrative of baseball's quest structure to Vladimir Propp's *Morphology of the Folk Tale*. Thus heroes of mythic quests, dangerous journeys, ascents and descents, heroes with a heightened sense of duty and therefore of language, are all suddenly germane to baseball fiction through *The Natural*. Then, too, baseball has its own store of almost-mythic folk references and Malamud re-invents anecdotes surrounding Joe Jackson, Wilbert Robinson, Ted Williams, and Babe Ruth.

Roy Hobbs plays for the Knights and is managed by Pop the Fisher King. Malamud's deepest rhythm in *The Natural* is that of the fertility cycle, seen by Frazer as a tragedy, "for there is no ascent out of it, and as its crimes are the crimes of nature, there can be no blame" (Hyman 262). Here is as firm an explanation as any for *The Natural*'s pessimistic conclusion in which Roy Hobbs strikes out in the wake of an ignominious fix and must begin a new cycle of suffering. Roy Hobbs has cut himself off from the past, from any sense of his own dark passage. He plays against "coming home"; there is no "return" except to personal responsibility and suffering, the continuing theme of Jewish-American fiction in the contemporary era.

Baseball is, ordinarily, an *affirmation* of "coming home," in the passage around the bases, in the redistribution of power from father to son. The affirmation of baseball is told without a death, without a return to the earth to replenish life. Baseball is rather a humanistic re-telling of origins that circumvents the consciouslessness of death. Malamud's pessimism is born of myth's memory of natural cycles that baseball only mimes above the earth's pull, reminding us of the artificial solace of all rule-bound play in its duel against mortality. Roy Hobbs' terror at aging, his flight from Iris Lemon once he learns she is a grandmother, is the instinctive recoil of a priest-god of fertility, who, in one of Frazer's great primal scenes—that of the priest at Nemi—cannot relax his strength or vigilance, nor show any signs of aging, lest he be slain. When Roy Hobbs at nineteen yields to desire and forgets his quest, his vigilance, he is cut down by Harriett Bird:

> She said sweetly, "Roy, will you be the best there ever was in the game?"
> "That's right."
> She pulled the trigger (thrum of bull fiddle). The bullet cut a silver line across the water. He sought with his bare hand to catch it but it eluded him and, to his horror, bounced into his gut. A twisted dagger of smoke drifted up from the gun barrel. Fallen on one knee he groped for the bullet, sickened as it moved, and fell over as the forest flew upward, and she, making muted noises of triumph and despair, danced on her toes around the stricken hero."
> (33)

Although the scene takes place in a Chicago hotel room, the "forest" stipulates we are indeed in a sacred grove. Yet we are also in a comic, slow-motion frame of athletic grace, as well as in an intentionally overwritten little domestic tragedy, starring Hobbs as bumpkin-priest and Harriett as baseball groupie-nemesis. In this passage, Malamud sets the tone for all the magical realism in baseball fiction to follow: a racy rendition of symbolically heavy events, a self-conscious pastiche of high cultural modes and pop culture effects, all in the service of a pivotal moment in the novel. Previously, Roy had struck out the Whammer with a ball like a "slithering meteor" and to the accompaniment of a "banging gong" (24–25). The "bull fiddle," "silver bullet, "twisted dagger," and Harriett's signature as a "twisted [unnatural] tree" are all baseball Gothic. More humorous is Roy, so full of hubris he believes that with lightning reflexes he may "catch" the bullet as it "bounces." He imagines himself, like any instinctive fielder, groping for the ball (Is there still time to catch the runner? To erase the "E" on the board?). The forest flies "upward" as a prop or stage set; he falls and views it prone. Harriett then makes her victory dance in bewildered triumph and despair, one with real affinity for the master sports fiction narrative of heroes and their witnesses (see Chapter 8).

This pagan ceremony/Hollywood violence video/baseball comedy/ sacrifice of the natural quite radically anticipates cinematic slow-motion scenes of shootings, first brought to critical attention in Arthur Penn's conclusion to his film *Bonnie and Clyde* (1967), though Humbert's shooting of Quilty in *Lolita* is the unchallenged playful suspension of clock-time in the representation of murderous violence in contemporary fiction. In Malamud's shooting scene are all the rawness and formality of the novel: "thrums" sound as "silver" bullets "bounce into gut[s]." Such effects have two sources: first, the primitive nature of the rituals and myths that Malamud is most attracted to as a source for the novel and second, a Depression era naturalism that makes Roy Hobbs into a minor league version of a character such as Faulkner's Joe Christmas in *Light in August,* a similarly deeply traumatized isolate of no verbal explanation but a man acquainted with grief. Of course, Faulkner had more ambitious plans for Joe Christmas' background and annunciation. In Malamud's refusal to provide an individual human center to Roy Hobbs, *The Natural* appears cold and old with little beyond its mythic core but a deterministic brutal world; it is decidedly against sentiment or growth. The reader is in an enchanted forest with knights and ladies but also in the degraded modern world of a failed sensual man who has thrown himself away on an uncaring mob. The dissonances of myth and naturalism, while possessing a clear affinity with each other in their denial of history, combine to produce an enormous alienation that is the very antithesis of the effect of most baseball fiction and which Malamud is powerless to redress. Malamud's commitment to the tragic cycles of the fertility myth dominates all other considerations in the novel.

339

Beyond Malamud's interest in myth as an underpinning to the baseball novel, the contemporary uses of myth by writers such as Barthes and Bakhtin contrast myth with fiction and are relevant to a discussion of *The Natural*. Basically, Barthes in *Mythologies* sees myth as speech already "worked on" in advance to make it suitable for communications and says that a conservative mythic discourse is clumsily theatrical in speech and gesture (110, 143). Bakhtin repeatedly stresses that a mythic character speaks authoritatively from language that cannot truly be enriched by dialogue. Indeed, in *The Natural*, Roy Hobbs' world is violently invaded by Harriett Bird when his inability to answer her questions seals his fate. Such inarticulateness is the natural's continuing plight from Phineas in *A Separate Peace* to Dorey Thomas in *Water Dancer* to Rabbit Angstrom in *Rabbit, Run*. The "natural" is also the "mythic." Caught in his or her great skill, the natural cannot be placed in history and yet is subject to all the collective's blandishments and insecurities without knowing how to secure a place in its fictions. Growth, the great element of the novelistic, of the dialogic, according to Bakhtin, is thus never a goal or possibility for the natural. Self-contained, the figure can only radiate "specialness." Rather than brought into a human community, he or she becomes "mythological," something "other": a hero, a paragon, a target, a sacrifice.

Roy Hobbs desires blindly with no vision of integration, only with the urgency of a priest who envisions his certain death. There is no reconciliation for him, only fame held out by the collective at the end of a record-breaking course. Barthes points out that myth transforms history into nature (129). For Barthes in *Mythologies,* the "mythic" has no tragic dimension, it is simply ahistorical, whereas for Frazer in *The Golden Bough,* myth is the response to a tragic sense of nature's death and renewal. Barthes opposes myth to history while Frazer says myth is a response to the deep structures of prehistory. Malamud instinctively blankets both definitions. Hobbs is ahistorical and learns nothing; he also embodies the role of any annointed priest-king.

Malamud intellectualized baseball material to the extent that its own rhythms of renewal and return to origins were lost in the mythic pessimism. He did expose baseball's great mythic potential but he did so in the insecurity of a first novel in which he suppressed his own ethnic and religious background. He refused to allow readers to be honestly moved without sly analogy and high style. Eddie Waitkus as the priest at Nemi remains a bizarre game that despite itself suggested a range of imaginative play for authors who followed Malamud to baseball.

In contemporary fiction the visions of Harris and Malamud through Henry Wiggen and Roy Hobbs—that of baseball as education and baseball as myth—are now generally incorporated in the same novels. What previously resided in separate semantic planes now can be included in the same text, as the works of Coover, Roth, Charyn, Kinsella, Jay Neugeboren, and Nancy Willard have shown. Harris defensively reinstated Lardner's subject and narration while Malamud cautiously launched his career encased in New York Knights armor, ready for charges onto the field by high culture critics who would enter the lists. Together, Harris and Malamud brought baseball fiction, as well as popular sports fiction of any serious intent, into the fictional mainstream at last, providing for professional team sport the sort of novelistic care and invention that Fitzgerald, Hemingway, and Faulkner had lavished on school sport and ritual sport in the preceding generation.

Coover: The Diamond Alive in the Sun

THE MORTALITY of the players is dealt with more intellectually by Coover in *The Universal Baseball Association*. Henry Waugh is caught in a cycle of depression and grief following the death of his "son," Damon Rutherford. The Association's rational structure collapses after his vengeance against pitcher Jock Casey, whom Henry deliberately "kills" by a second rigged roll of the dice. Furthermore, one of Henry's duties at the conclusion of each season is to perform the "death rolls," allowing the dice to tell him what old-timers or current players are to be eliminated. Henry's role as keeper of the books is fundamentally enlarged to include this and other godlike functions, for even as he is the paternal figure, so is he the reaper at life's end.

In *The Universal Baseball Association's* last chapter set on Damonsday CLVII, Coover portrays a culture that has reached a grave crisis

341

in the failure of belief in its own roots. Clearly, he is writing an intellectual cameo history of the twentieth century, turning his ball-players into brooding men with existential questions. They are assigned roles in the Damonsday re-enactment of Damon's death, what has come to be called "The Parable of the Duel," which may end in ritual sacrifice. They sit and argue in the bullpen (suitably enough), muttering like a philosophy quiz section over the meaning of their fate: "He hits a ground ball to third, is thrown out. Or he beats the throw. What difference, in the terror of eternity does it make?" (171). By focusing on Roy Hobbs' decline and fall and Henry Wiggen's stewardship of Bruce Pearson, Malamud and Harris had individualized and personalized the baseball quests for meaning and purpose. Coover wrests the game away from myth and from the lowered eyes of honest sentiment to ask ontological questions with wit and inventiveness.

Coover's goal in the last pages of *The Universal Baseball Association* is to bring the UBA players out of ritual forms and into a fuller relationship with the play spirit itself. To accomplish this final move to play, he must de-mythologize baseball. Coover frees his players from history and from myth's capture by aligning play with creative forces in the present and future. As one conservative player says in response to an irreverence about Damonsday,

"I don't believe in just making fun of things you don't understand."

"No," says the Witness, blushing Raspberry, "but, well, legend, I mean the pattern of it, the long history, it seems somehow, you know, a folk truth, a radical truth, all these passed-down mythical—"

"Ahh, you radical mother's mythical cunt!" sniffs Gringo Greene. "It's time we junked the whole beastly business, baby, and moved on."

"I'm afraid, Gringo, I must agree with our distinguished folklorist and foremost witness to the ontological revelations of the patterns of history," intercedes (with a respectful nod to Schultz) Professor Costen Migod McCamish, Doctor of Nostology and Research Specialist in the Etiology of Homo Ludens, "and have come to the conclusion that God exists and he is a nut." (167–68)

Coover's fiction to date is precisely an argument for "making fun of things you don't understand" as a playful response to existence. The mythic "pattern" that Witness York gropes for is talked out and worn out; we must "move on," not only out of this novel but over the strewn refuse of incestuous speculation and back to the sport itself.

As Frazer had written, the origin of myths was that they arose out of rites distorted and misunderstood (Hyman 239). As Hardy Ingram sensibly points out on Damonsday, "Doesn't make much sense to knock off your best young talent every season, but he knows people aren't always rational" (159). Not only does irrationality rule on Damonsday but the academics appear in control, a bad sign. "Nostology" with its semantic links to "nostalgia" is the study of the senile stages of an organism or race of organisms, a negative casting of the search for origins and home. "Etiology" is the science of causes; "Homo Ludens" is Coover's pointed reference to Huizinga's influential work on the play spirit in Western civilization. Coover chooses to end in play rather than in the spiritual confusion of anti-heroism to which he has nonetheless ascribed great seriousness. Baseball as myth has been given its fullest fictional scrutiny to date by Coover and has been judged as a penultimate ordering before the imperatives of history and play.

Coover concludes by having Paul Trench and Hardy Ingram (playing Damon and Royce in the Damonsday reenactment) see once again the stark beauty of the game, beginning with the round-the-horn ritual before the first pitch. The players then assume their roles in the parable, which is, as Coover tells us, all that we ever do:

> "It's not a trial," says Damon, glove tucked in his armpit, hands working the new ball. Behind him, he knows, Scat Batkin, the batter is moving toward the plate. "It's not even a lesson. It's just what it is." Damon holds the baseball up between them. It is hard and white and alive in the sun.
>
> He laughs. It's beautiful, that ball. He punches Damon lightly in the ribs with his mitt. "Hang loose," he says, and pulling down his mask, trots back behind home plate. (173–74)

Coover ends on a literal diamond where he names hard, bright, well-defined objects, and the game goes on. Here, beyond mortality and its compensatory ritual are the artifacts of baseball itself where the "play between" the lines with definite shapes, textures, and colors dance away from metaphysical capture or from mere content. Coover's play is Nietzschean out of Derrida, "the affirmation of Being conceived without nostalgia" ("Differance" 159). The last message is one of spontaneous pleasure that resists attempts to ascribe meaning to passage. Our modicum of free will depends on our courage and ability to experience joy. The game *is* rather than *means,* the life-and-death grip on history has been relaxed, and life lived exuberantly in the game is a brave challenge to fate.

Coover's metaphor of universe-making casts the widest net for baseball tropes in fiction. *The Universal Baseball Association* is a treatise on fictions, a novel of fictional ideas and dilemmas. No American author has used sport so wonderfully to animate play fiction, fiction as play, as has Coover with baseball. The creation of the Association and the playing of its games are seen to be part of the same function, that of the tension among the familiarization of baseball, the aesthetic roughening of the sport by Coover, and the reader's re-familiarization with baseball and fiction. The reader "comes home."

Coover is knowledgeably aware that play is the space in which to avoid being captured by myth or history, even as play inevitably shapes that myth and history. Coover moves surely all around the diamond—and the Greimas square. The structure is richly fleshed out along every axis. We move from the individual passions of Henry Waugh and his "sons" in *individual sports heroism* to the enormous material responsibility of the Association's history in day-to-day operation, a massive *collective sports heroism,* to the historical crisis and resultant collapse into spiritual rebellion in *anti-heroism* of the players in the Damonsday ritual, where they pointedly desire to "become" their role in ritual, to witness order and to *be* it. Yet Coover then turns from ritual to the *play* that questions and counters inert form with rich verbal jousting. We are led back finally to baseball itself, to objects at the material pole, to a secular ritual of pitch and catch between Damon and Royce.

Myth's memory of natural cycles includes a sacrificial return to the earth. Ritual grows precisely from the seasonal distress about the resultant approaching mortality. Beyond rituals of "resistance and

344

rot," Coover posits baseball itself, a humanist re-telling of return to origin without mortality, an affirmation of being partaking of myth, ritual, and history. Coover combined the "play back to" in our quest for origins with a "play beyond" in speculative fiction—and all accomplished in the "play between the lines," on the diamond, in the novel. Coover is seeking through baseball and play fiction to inhabit that space between matter and spirit that Schiller claimed for aesthetic play, that Derrida claims for the differences of language, that Jameson seeks to fill with the agony of historical form. As a "willing accomplice" to all these "heresies," Coover strove to make limpid the inter-locking planes of imagination, language, and history. As old Hettie Irden says in a different but wholly complimentary sense after sex with Henry Waugh playing the role of Damon Rutherford, "Oh, that's a game, Henry! That's really a *great* old *game*" (31).

12.

Fictions of Baseball: Baseball Historicized

Baseball as education deals with maturation and mortality. Baseball as myth evolves out of history or prehistory but deals with magic and with large mannered motions and is not specifically temporal at all. It is a tribute to baseball's formidable suggestiveness that it may encompass so many different strands of thought and representation. For if baseball passages have the capacity to be quite a-historical, they nonetheless have very detailed and important historical records that are part of American cultural history itself.

Contextualizing the Passages

MOST OFTEN, less ambitious authors simply equate the history of their protagonists with that of their baseball history. Lucy Kennedy's

The Sunlit Field (1950) is a historical novel about the assimilation of
the Irish working class into American life in the mid-1850s at the
dawn of organized baseball, where the original pre-Civil War New
York City teams such as the Knickerbockers, Atlantics, and Excel-
siors compete. Baseball's early history is shown as that of democracy
and community helping to build the larger community. At the novel's conclusion, admission to games is introduced and sport has
become a business, as a historic baseball event reveals a larger historical pattern of American sport and leisure. At the same time, the
novel's recurring dream is of tall men "stretching their bodies in long
beautiful arcs" (30). The poetic imagery is underscored by the fact
that the friend and advisor to the players is the inscrutable and lyrical
"Walt," none other than Whitman himself, whom Kennedy animates with fidelity to his published remarks about baseball and democracy. In a similar vein, Brashler's *Bingo Long* concludes with the
first black players signed for the white minor leagues, a historic event
for American team sport.

Novels may interpolate back into actual baseball history, as in the
compelling "slave narrative" in Neugeboren's *Sam's Legacy* (1974),
rendered by a fiercely proud black pitcher, Mason Tidewater, who
recalls his intimate affair with Babe Ruth. In an eclectic heroic identification, the narrator of Paul Newlin's *It Had to Be a Woman* (1979)
plans to model his suicide on that of Cincinnati Reds catcher Willard
Hershberger in 1940. Other authors equate novel time with game
time. Likewise, from Douglas Wallop's *The Year the Yankees Lost the
Pennant* (1954) to Gary Morgenstern's opposing *The Man Who Wanted
to Play Centerfield for the Yankees* (1983), authors have written of fans
whose consuming dream is to break into baseball history itself.

Shaw's *Voices of a Summer Day* reviews the life and motivation of
its central character as he watches his teen-age son play in a baseball
game. Foster's *Goodbye Bobby Thomson!, Goodbye John Wayne!* resolves a father-son crisis at the Polo Grounds immediately following
Thomson's historic home run to win the pennant for the Giants. The
tension of the "big game" informs Kahn's *The Seventh Game* in
which veteran Johnny Longboat recalls his childhood and rise through
organized baseball interspersed with the progress of his final game.
Irwin Faust's *The Steagle* (1966) takes its central character, a college
English professor, back through a number of pop historical roles,
beginning during a desultory literature class when he snaps and

347

begins a manic peroration on Willie Mays. Baseball history itself yields a fictional narrator when Black Sox's Buck Weaver narrates sections of Harry Stein's *Hoopla* (1983). Malamud in *The Natural* makes reference to a number of baseball's historic moments, including the Black Sox scandal, the Ruthian conversion from pitcher to outfielder, and the shooting of Eddie Waitkus. Herrin's *The Rio Loja Ringmaster* ends with pitcher Dick Dixon on the mound in Mexico, imagining the entire cast of his life—family, ex-wife, lovers, friends, enemies, teammates—as circling the bases around him, his contextualized history regulated on the diamond in a final profusion. Coover in *The Universal Baseball Association* conceives of the collapse of history itself into warring cells of belief, all within the encapsulation of a futuristic baseball ritual that is as primitive as it is profound. Baseball fiction delights in creating counter-histories. Roth's Patriot League in *The Great American Novel* is a paranoid's dream, a third major league beset by political strife and international subversion, an entire world which disappears and is supressed in memory, becoming a comic McCarthyite and Orwellian fable lodged solely within the mind of Word Smith, a ninety-year-old sportswriter.

The strongest way to link the potential of the *individual sports hero,* his desire, skill, and potency to the self-knowledge and spirit of the *anti-hero* is to run him through the collective. The current of heroism would then test innocence and skill by immersion in the collective. There in the glare of *collective sports heroism,* the hero acts and is acted upon by history. In the baseball novel, as already discussed, narrative itself is a substitute for temporality. Time is recorded *as* history. History becomes the sum of differences, assuming the role in textualization that time had relinquished in baseball's open-endedness.

Baseball's deep historical structures relate strongly to its sense of differences. In other words, the preoccupation with journeying, home, and origins is written into baseball's historical master narrative. The specific contextualizations of this narrative are diverse but may be summarized in two large patterns. They are baseball's "Legend of the Fall," the Black Sox scandal of 1919 and its resultant banishments and exile, and the exclusion of blacks from major league baseball before 1947. These exiles and exclusions have fostered an entire counter-history of baseball that limned America's hypocrises and prejudices. Both contextualizations have become important fictional commentary about the collective society's practice toward its criminals and "others."

The Black Sox remain the primal cautionary tale of American sports' ensnarement by money and greed. All the abuses of the economics of sport are in evidence. Of all the representations of the "fix" in American sports fiction—surely the most obsessive plot complication in the collective—the Black Sox have remained the most fascinating villains in American baseball's only open scandal. Baseball *since* 1919 has regarded itself as the innocent game above all compromising scandal. Yet its authors know how to work its dialectical opposite of experience and rueful knowledge. If innocence is the official baseball myth, then experience is the bitter legacy in baseball fiction. Home-lessness (the baseball equivalent is being left on base) is extended to permanent banishment, wandering and severance, so clearly present in Malamud, Roth, Charyn, and Kinsella. From being footnotes to history, players slip beneath baseball's official history. Or they wander in shadow leagues so far below the major leagues as to be invisible.

Unlike boxing and football fiction, which present an anatomy of individual sports hero-collective sports hero relations, baseball fiction tends to idealize its economics into parables and sentiment about exiles, those "caught off base" or stranded. However, this slippage below official baseball history frees authors to create mirror baseball worlds that may be parodic, grotesque, or lyrical. The historical theme of exile is a temporal estrangement, a de-familiarization from the real, the known. Banishment for the author of baseball fiction is thus a "fortunate fall" to subjective perspective and aesthetic re-creation. The author begins an obligatory journey to where/what Ralph Ellison has called the "lower frequencies" of the individual experience—which may "speak" for readers in history as well. Here is where the author *plays* in baseball fiction.

Characters in baseball fiction deal with the crisis of temptation in many guises. *The Year the Yankees Lost the Pennant* adapts the Faust legend to baseball. A middle-aged Washington Senators fan sells his soul to become super-rookie Joe Hardy who will lead the Senators to a pennant over the hated Yankees. Or there are the straight replies of a character such as Kahn's Johnny Longboat in *The Seventh Game:* "I can live without the Porsche and the damn last thing that I could live with is knowing that I'd let crooks into baseball" (217). Stud Cantrell in *Long Gone* is asked to throw a game to save the team's franchise from collapse and he does so, not without great soul-searching. Malamud's Roy Hobbs is completely caught in his urgent ambition, sells out, strikes out, and must begin his bitter journey all over again, homeless and not having scored. Charyn's Babe Ragland begins his odyssey when he is framed by a jealous owner and banned from baseball by Judge Landis. Roth's Patriot League in *The Great American Novel* degenerates into fixed games, chemical alterations, and international subversion: an entire league is disbanded, suppressed, and erased from memory, extending the metaphor of banishment. Coover's Universal Baseball Association falls prey to the cheating of its creator. The players become metaphysical exiles, alienated from self and from the game.

The Black Sox scandal was early utilized by Fitzgerald in the scene in *The Great Gatsby* where Gatsby proudly points out Meyer Wolfsheim to Nick Carraway as "the man who fixed the World Series in 1919" (74). Nick's stunned reaction perfectly expresses his own moral nature and also reflects America's innocence about baseball and about a criminal economic "play" with faith on the part of Wolfsheim. To Gatsby, it was a business "opportunity"; to Nick it is "staggering" (74). Though a symbolic center to fictional representation, the Black Sox scandal itself was not addressed in its specific historical moment again until quite recently, climaxing in Sayles' film *Eight Men Out* (1988), an adaptation of Asinof's 1963 book. Three novels, Stein's *Hoopla,* Kinsella's *Shoeless Joe,* and Eric Rolfe Greenberg's *The Celebrant* (1983), pick up the subject in different ways. Stein is a Lardnerian, Kinsella a magician out of Malamud, while Greenberg writes a legitimate historical baseball novel. *Hoopla* is alternately narrated by a fictional sportswriter, Luther Pond, and by Buck Weaver, the Black Sox third baseman banned for life in 1920. Although Pond is a potential Lardner and Buck Weaver reads *You Know Me, Al* and even sounds like a tepid echo of Jack Keefe, Stein's prose never really comes alive. There are set scenes where Pond interacts with historical icons such as John L. Sullivan, Ty Cobb, and William Randolph Hearst but the novel, while earnest and historically correct, is more of a history designed to flesh out dramatically the life and times of an early twentieth-century sports culture. It is a *Ragtime* in its conception but not in metaphor or execution.

Stein's Shoeless Joe Jackson is illiterate, cantankerous, and dull. In *Shoeless Joe,* Kinsella's Jackson is a dignified shade as are his teammates, the men for whom Ray Kinsella builds his diamond to redeem them from their wandering and give them a place to play. Kinsella does not judge or question the ghostly crew and is satisfied merely to have them there. Neither *Hoopla* nor *Shoeless Joe* is ideologically aware, Stein more a transmitter of history than a transformer, Kinsella a baseball mystic of high sentiment.

Greenberg's *The Celebrant* is a historical novel that re-creates baseball's first two decades of this century, climaxing with the 1919 World Series and Black Sox scandal. *The Celebrant* is narrated by Jackie Kapp, third son of a Jewish family of New York City jewelers, whose life and work cross the path of New York Giant pitcher Christy Mathewson from 1901 to 1919. Until the scandal in 1919, each section of the book is built around a pivotal big game moment in Mathewson's career (1901, '05, '08, '12) that defines his greatness for Kapp and that allows Greenberg, like Stein, to describe early modern sports culture, its mores and habitués. The structure of baseball history punctuates Jackie Kapp's narrative and moves it along. Kapp designs jewelry to commemorate events and ceremony. His art provides Mathewson with keepsake gems while he himself idolizes the pitcher in reserved appreciation. *The Celebrant* is very decorous. Potentially about a vital, growing immigrant culture and the Giants under the brawling John McGraw, it nonetheless takes its tone from Greenberg's vision of the refined, college-educated Mathewson and Jackie Kapp's appropriately dignified response. Almost against its will, *The Celebrant* becomes a sort of school sports novel about an "amateur" hero of great reserve and stature and his worshipful witness. Mathewson quotes Alexander Pope in describing McGraw to Kapp and says things like, "You have an aversion to the man, don't you? I sensed it at my apartment" (90).

Greenberg weaves the baseball scenes so well it is a shame he cannot bring the historical culture and the Kapps to life. We learn in detail of Matthewson's three shutouts in the '05 World Series, of Merkle's "boner" in '08, and of Snodgrass's "muff" in the '12 World Series. The commercialization of sport is a theme laid on rather heavily over Mathewson's classic form but it is a significant development in professional sport. Through the Black Sox debacle in 1919, Greenberg is determined to expand Mathewson into a full-fledged Christ figure. Mathewson comes unhinged at his realization of Black Sox perfidy and shifts from his reserve into a manic keening for his sport. He curses its defilers:

> "I do damn them," he said. "With a mark I damn them. I damn Cicotte. I damn Jackson. I damn Risberg and Gandil and Williams. And if there be others I will damn them as well, I will root them out and damn them for eternity. And I damn the filth that corrupted them, the dicers and the high rollers. They will pay. They will pay in time. I shall not rouse them now, for I will allow them their full portion of loss, and when the corrupters are counting their gains I shall spring upon them and drive them from the temple!" (262)

Here is an Old Testament prophecy wedded to baseball's Fall. Mathewson is obviously dying for the sins of the Black Sox. Jackie Kapp's brother Eli, who has gambled away family company stock on the Series, crashes his car over the ridge of Coogan's Bluff: "It came to rest, shattered and burning, against the black walls of the Polo Grounds" (264). Some middle style of energy and wit between the intensity of Mathewson's final mad scene and the genteel representation of Jackie Kapp and his classical pitcher-hero might have allowed Greenberg to succeed more fully in establishing Mathewson as the wounded historical body of American baseball. Nonetheless, for sheer theatrics, *The Celebrant*'s climax will be hard for baseball fiction to beat.

Along with ballplayers banned or excluded because of crimes, other players in baseball fiction choose to de-historicize themselves in willed exile. Herrin's Dick Dixon in *The Rio Loja Ringmaster* drops out into a Mexican odyssey after winning the seventh game of the World Series. Donald Hays' narrator, Hog Durham, in *The Dixie Association* (1984) drops back *in*. He is an ex-convict released to play for the Arkansas Reds, a lively and disaffiliated minor league team of stoic Indians, exiled Cubans, and young blacks. Their manager is a one-armed, ex-major leaguer of communist sympathies who runs a food co-op for the poor and leaflets the stands with manifestos between innings. The Reds battle a regressive, racist team from Selma. Alabama, display great solidarity, and give positive meaning to "collective." *The Dixie Association* is baseball fiction's ideological counterpart to Whitehead's *Joiner* in football fiction. Sayles' *Pride of the Bimbos* follows a southern barnstorming team who dress as women on the field and take on local semi-pro teams. Sayles' well-crafted sketches are about rural men and women who play out what has been dealt to them, his finest creation being tough guy dwarf Pogo Burns, a figure of dignity and strength. The Bimbos, too, are collectively homeless, a team without a league or a history.

Benign Myth and Demonic Reality: Roth's *The Great American Novel*

THE BASEBALL novel most suffused with the theme of banishment and exile is Roth's *The Great American Novel*. It is also the most consistently comic meditation on baseball and history. *The Great American Novel* grows out of the particular pressures in America during the 1960s and early 1970s when the "official" record of American life as it pertained to accounts of assassinations, the Vietnam War, and Watergate became problematic, suspect, and finally degraded[ing]. Roth best explained the impetus behind *The Great American Novel* in 1973, when he wrote,

> It was not a matter of demythologizing baseball—there was nothing in that to get fired up about—but of discovering in baseball a means to dramatize the *struggle* between the benign national myth of itself that a great power prefers to perpetuate, and the relentlessly insidious, very nearly demonic reality (like the kind we had known in the sixties) that will not give an inch in behalf of the idealized mythology. ("On *The Great American Novel*" 89–90)

Roth sees the actual events and beliefs of the 1960s as a way "to take hold of baseball" "through a countermythology" (90), a seeming reversal of the reasons an author would choose to write of sport in his fiction. His statement perhaps accounts for the frustration of critics who have chided Roth for the inconsistent, overlong, and often pointlessly excessive satire of *The Great American Novel*. Marvellous at best and almost unreadable at worst, *The Great American*

Novel is an experiment in form: just how much fiction can Roth squeeze out of baseball, what he called, "the literature of his boyhood"? Roth's statement that only "in college" did he discover literature, something with "a comparable emotional atmosphere and as strong an aesthetic appeal" as baseball ("My Baseball Years" 35) echoes Malamud's remark about a baseball childhood and the subsequent influence of college. Both authors acknowledge an early passion and a later one: baseball and literature, the aesthetic apperception of both and the possibilities of baseball as form. One should not look primarily for an angry historical novel in *The Great American Novel* but rather for a formal experiment to stretch the limits of a popular aesthetic form. *The Great American Novel* is not a novel about "baseball as history" as much as it is a total absorption of the "demonic reality" of history into the aesthetic form—history as baseball.

Such an intent is quite different from writing "myth as baseball," as Malamud had done, because Roth begins with a distrust of "idealized mythology," of any affirmative, complacent, authoritative narrative such as the one in *The Great American Novel* by which organized baseball perpetuates itself. This distrust is countered by Roth's play, in which he has stated that comic inventiveness took charge, the comic logic of farce, burlesque, and slapstick, not the logic of satire or "integrated psychology," but instead "a destructive, or lawless, playfulness" ("On *The Great American Novel*" 76). This excess of the "play beyond" in Roth continues until he has exhausted the materials in each scene, rather than combined them. What separates Roth from any sort of utopianizing in play or any serious philosophical examination of boundaries and limits is his will to remain in the absurd, to let energy and inventiveness carry *The Great American Novel* without any attention to synthesis. The exile of the characters in *The Great American Novel* from baseball history is a convenient stance for Roth, who wants to dance outside the house of satire in a "satyric" form, as he calls it, one in which he will indulge in "the sheer pleasure of exploring the anarchic and the unsocialized" ("On *The Great American Novel*" 76).

Roth doggedly operates in the play mode, a vantage point from which he skewers individual sports heroism, collective sports heroism, and anti-heroism as well. By playing with baseball history, rules, and heroic figures, Roth conceived of a "counter-myth" at the center of which is the Patriot League, a third major league that mysteriously disappears after 1945, riddled with communist infiltration. Only a ninety-year-old Ishmael of a sportswriter, Word Smith, is alive to tell the tale. The Orwellian domination and re-writing of history by officialdom is complete. Word Smith cantankerously makes his pilgrimmage to Cooperstown each year to cast his Hall of Fame vote for Patriot League hero Luke Gofannon; Bowie Kuhn patiently disqualifies it. The "demonic reality" of the Patriot League insisted on by Word Smith is the nightmare face of Roth's history that counters official baseball history, the "benign national myth of itself" that America fosters. Word Smith's outrage at Cooperstown over the Patriot League's disappearance from history concludes when he cries, "why must you bury the truth about the history of this game —*of this country*? Have you no conscience? Can you just take the past and flush it away, like so much shit?" (Roth 18).

History, cries Word Smith, is indeed that realm of necessity, the place where the potential, desire, and potency of the individual sports hero runs through experience. Baseball is not mythologized by Roth but rather historicized and made to focus on the losers, the outcasts, the victims in politicized terms. As Roth writes in a chapter preface, "In this chapter, the fortunate reader who has never felt himself a stranger in his own land may pick up some idea of what it is like" (133). Roth presents the worst team in major league history, the Ruppert Mundys. If baseball is the game with the most sentiment about home, Roth creates the always-*homeless* Mundys of 1943, their ballpark appropriated by the War Department as a troop staging area where soldiers may spend their last night on American soil sleeping on a big league diamond. The Mundys are dispossessed, the fundamental metaphor allowing Roth to comment on baseball's deepest structure. He writes of greed and wandering franchises, the historical textualization of "exile" in the economic imperatives of the collective. Word Smith imagines the O'Malleys and their ilk finally moving baseball off the earth to new interplanetary markets. Word Smith addresses "Mr. and Mrs. Roaring Success! Henceforth all *your* games will be played away, too. Away! Away! Far far away!. . . . Or, as we say so succinctly in America to the unfit, the failed, the floundering and forgotten, HIT THE ROAD, YA BUMS!" (45).

Such exile is recreated on an individual scale among the players on the Mundys. The catcher has one leg, the rightfielder has one arm; the third baseman is fifty-two, the second baseman is fourteen; the French shortstop is a spy for the Japanese, the first baseman is recruited from prison. Roth bridges what he calls the "incredible credible" of actual baseball history when the major leagues scraped the bottom of the barrel for players during World War II—with his own "credible incredible" ("On *The Great American Novel*" 91) roster of outcasts from the province of Tall Tales and every sort of physical humor (Rodgers 11–15). Roth works richly in this vein. In his revisionist history of the spitball, Roth introduces the infamous "Spit Baal." Enraged at his pitch being outlawed, Spit Baal loads one up by a different method. He then hitches up his pants and calls down to the batter, "Here comes the pissball, shithead—get ready!" (108). To trample on American inspirational tales of victory over adversity through sport, Roth knows no limit: the catcher's wooden leg comes off when a batter's backswing drives it cleanly up the third base line; the ball sticks in the mouth of the one-armed right fielder when he tries to strip the glove from his one hand for a throw. He must submit to an inspection, and bare his torso before a press conference, to prove he has one arm, before a trade will go through. The daughter of his new team owner can only cry "Ucch," "unable to suppress a shiver of revulsion" (220). Roth pursues the logic of the grotesque until the official face of American sport, its sanitized moral and physical health, has been devastated, as has the humanist sentiment surrounding physical differences or deviance.

Roth extends physical deviance to social history in commenting on sport's perception of itself as an American melting pot, where barriers break down in models for the whole country to learn from. He conceives of a battle between radical and assimilationist baseball midgets. The radical midget is actually a misshapen dwarf who hates the perfectly-formed, fraternity boy midget. In a mini-drama of "otherness" and attempts to raise America's consciousness of his state, he asks, "Is it like 'everybody else' to go into a public urinal and stand on tiptoes at the trough, while 'everybody else' is pissing over your shoulder?" (199). O. K. Ockatur loathes Bob Yamm, "the kind of midget who went around pretending he was nothing but a smaller edition of everybody else" accompanied by his "spic-and-span kewpie doll of a wife" (198). Ockatur parades his deformity.

He is small and angry with an "over-sized head and bandy legs" (198) and not about to forget his differences. Once more the incredible-credible—Bill Veeck's stunt of putting Eddie Gaedel at the plate for the St. Louis Browns in 1951—is historicized into a parable of race relations, perhaps a commentary on Brooklyn Dodger teammates Jackie Robinson and Roy Campanella and their different approaches to racial prejudice. Roth plays "difference" and "otherness" repeatedly in *The Great American Novel,* making them problematic subjects of their own, the driving forces in social history to parallel the production of difference itself. To follow the "logic" of anarchy in this regard, Roth created the ultimate "other," Gil Gamesh, the greatest rookie pitcher in history, the only Babylonian kid on his block, indeed the only Babylonian kid anywhere. As Gamesh remembers his miserable childhood, "First for a few blocks the Irish kids threw rocks at me. Then the German kids threw rocks at me. Then the Eye-talian, then the colored, then them Mohawk kids . . . hell, even the Jew kids threw rocks at me, while they was runnin' away from the kids throwin' rocks at them" (254).

Roth takes on in *The Great American Novel* every authoritative discourse that speaks monologically from baseball's official center: owners such as Fairsmith, Commissioner Oakhart, Bob Yamm, umpire Mike "the Mouth," Roland Agni's father, Angela Trust—all who wish to deny dialogue and control history through rhetoric. Gamesh, Ockatur, Agni, and other Mundys speak politically and are consumed by baseball. They embody their reality and live it in physical and emotional pain, while baseball history is, as it were, written on their backs.

Overlong and slapdash in many spots, Roth's book is nonetheless a series of brilliant black-outs in the best vaudeville tradition: the Mundy roster sketches, the red-light district of moms, the Gamesh-Mike "the Mouth" Oedipal battle, the midgets' war, the Mundys' annual game with the Asylum team. One wonders if, in straining so hard to be knowing on both sides of America's myth of itself, Roth didn't freeze on the discovery and do violence to what he knew to be the hard-won truth of aesthetic wholeness. By an act of anti-mythological stubbornness, he refused to allow *The Great American Novel* to be even a contender for a corner of that title. Such would unfortunately appear to be the self-defeating requiem for a wonderful baseball book, one that perhaps will never be matched in comic inventiveness. Roth chose to re-create the aesthetic shambles of "Great American Novel" production, to mime the truism that our best novels are excessive hybrids. No amount of Roth's explaining the novel's anarchic purposes can disguise the fact that he imagined a marvelous old narrator who could have bridged decades of baseball and sportswriting history and its links to literature. However, Roth appears to lose interest in Word Smith who disappears for huge stretches in the novel. Probably Roth is only being faithful to the disappearance of Hawthorne after the custom-house sketch prologue in *The Scarlet Letter* or to Ishmael's long absences in *Moby Dick* or to Huck Finn's baffling relinquishment of sensibility back under the umbrella of "Tom Sawyerism," but nonetheless his Word Smith remains merely inconsistent.

Like Malamud, albeit with a very different intent, Roth is more interested in baseball aesthetics and their associations than in paying any homage to baseball's official conception of itself, as were Irwin Shaw and Harris. Roth is similar to Malamud as well in his mandarin approach to the raw material of baseball. Only where Malamud made baseball ponderously mythic, Roth willfully keeps baseball inventive and chaotic. He resists integrating his narrative or "coming home": no restoration is implied or achieved. Roth should be given his precise due. He wished to tease out baseball's differences and contradictions and play himself a hard game to, one suspects, recapture the delight that baseball itself had always provided him.

Memory, that tool of evocation of baseball's past, the swing in a diamond arc back toward origins, is everywhere evident in Word Smith's narrative. He wants to stay up forever since the Patriot League will not, cannot die if he remains at the plate. Word Smith's tale is of a prior outrage to which there is no recourse except in the telling. A counter-track of baseball history must be preserved, a reflexive world of novelistic creation that demands acknowledgement—a parallel world rather than a substitution. Roth shows us how baseball narrative, which possesses time, possesses history itself and speaks to every facet of our experience.

Coover: Baseball and Metahistory

IN THE *Universal Baseball Association,* Coover provided metacommentary on both myth and history through baseball. It is a treatise on ordering patterns of any kind, of what "learning from the past" means, of how history is created and by whom. Coover depicts myth, history, and ritual as colliding planes of experience, best expressed in his *The Public Burning* (see chapter 5). These planes are all part of the artist's storehouse of effects as well as deeply-felt responses artist's storehouse of effects as well as deeply felt responses by individuals as they attempt to explain and shape their experience. If Malamud worked consciously in mythic modes in *The Natural,* if Roth sought a logic of comic anarchy in *The Great American Novel,* Coover's *The Universal Baseball Association* was no less imbued with a specific aesthetic goal. He once commented, "I wrote the baseball book not for baseball buffs or even for theologians but for other writers" (McCaffery 110).

What Coover would tell other writers about baseball and history in *The Universal Baseball Association* begins with his commitment to the hermeneutic of restoration and return already alluded to in baseball's structure. Coover wrote he was strongly influenced by the tales of Cervantes and praised him thusly: "For your stories also exemplified the dual nature of all good narrative art: they struggled against the unconscious mythic residue in human life and sought to synthesize the unsynthesizable, sallied forth against adolescent thought-modes and exhausted art forms, and returned home with new complexities" (*Pricksongs and Descants* 77). Coover envisions the stories *themselves* as questors or knight-errants, battling myth in favor of synthesis in the return home. The fiction is the living form itself which attempts to make that journey. What Cervantes, a pre-baseball hermeneuticist, brought "home" was the novel itself, which Coover now sees moving back toward the comic, the eternal, the supernatural. Coover stated that to combat this mystification, to lead us back to clarification, maturity, and revelation (79), we must use the very tools of mystery and mystification to surmount their pull, even as Cervantes had plundered worn-out romance forms to create the novel. In *The Universal Baseball Association,* Coover will use myth, ritual, and history against themselves to move back to the real.

Roth called himself "satyric" in *The Great American Novel;* Coover in the same punning spirit has written of "the mystification of history produced by our irrational terror of reality. . . . We need to perform a kind of racial historectomy on all humankind" ("The Cat in the Hat for President" 21). *The Universal Baseball Association* is Coover's argument for both the immense power of history and its paralysis. His response is indeed surgical, the gutting of history's rich womb of security and explanation to expose its uncertainty and fictional status. Henry Waugh's great passion for creation and historicizing makes the Universal Baseball Association at all times a living, reflexive historical arena as well as an aesthetic construct, where Coover is committed to the "use of the fabulous to probe beyond the phenomenological, beyond appearances, beyond randomly perceived events, beyond mere history" (*Pricksongs and Descants* 78).

The search of Western man to find the sacred in profane history or to praise himself in a sacred dimension within his life is seen by Roger Caillois and Mircea Eliade to be part hubris, part inevitable process of the celebration of man's potential for influence in a secular world where he must move back and write his way into history. Man craves to see manifestations of himself in every significant action.[1] Henry Waugh has a particular slant on this craving. He had attended real baseball games but "found out the score cards were enough. I didn't need the games" (121). He renounces the actual ballpark, its rituals, ceremonies of communion (beer and hot dogs), and the fellowship of other believers, in favor of history, dead and perfect in the realm of his imagination. Yet once he has given life to his players, their existence and his role become more complicated and dangerous. The man who has become the "god" of his association has increasingly moved out of his own history in order to *make* history, which becomes not merely a numerical record, nor a textualization of time, nor even an institutional space, but a universe that demands rationale for being and philosophical coherence—a complete creation, a world. This "game" must have "players" whose lives become the living subject of the game's narrative.

Coover presents through Henry Waugh the Christian parable of a god acting in history: the deaths of Damon and Casey, his "sons," and the resulting confusion and growth of sects. Henry Waugh had begun by appreciating baseball's solid and secure regularity but realized its power as well: "No other activity in the world had so precise and comprehensive a history, so specific an ethic, and at the same time, strange as it seemed, so much ultimate mystery" (38). This "mystery" plunges Henry into metahistory at the expense of a "comprehensiveness." The deaths of Damon and Casey unmoor his rational structure. He begins to seek "a new ordering, the disclosure of pattern" because he "had discovered that perfection wasn't a thing, a closed moment, a static fact, but *process,* yes, and the process was transformation" (152). The heightened metaphysical yearning of Henry is evident as the Association becomes more complex and potentially disastrous.[2] Henry begins to move from reality toward a sacred ordering. He cries out, "What we want in this Association is participation—not in real time—but in *significant* time" (155). This urge to witness in revelation signifies the Association's move from reality into received myths about itself and is the cry of a ritualist. This is historical interpretation of the first order, what Coover's Uncle Sam hopes to generate by the execution of the Rosenbergs in *The Public Burning.* At the end of *The Universal Baseball Association*'s penultimate chapter, Henry has constructed a set of warring political philosophies within the Association. Yet his imagination is running down. His players seemingly spill out of his brain as out of a cornucopia, trampling his order in a great procession. The last words in the chapter, *"Here they come!"* (157) signifies the profusion of individual life and reality in the Association which will continue after Henry is no longer in control.

What Roth effects in the collective sense of exile as the Mundys are sent away ("Hit the road, ya bums!") is literal, physical, and tormenting. Coover's *"Here they come!"* also suggests exile, spiritual and cultural, in which the players in the Association, one hundred years later in Damonsday CLVII, live in the wake of an uncertain, symbol-haunted culture that is ridden with ritual forms and is encrusted in old creeds. The progression from history to myth and ritual is complete. What the players need is a renewal of generative spontaneity; what they do is sift through the past shards of their belief. One player cries out "Nobody understands Casey anymore! Nobody understands *history*" (168). To counter the agony, players use puns, verbal play, masks, and obscenity, all to avoid the continual pressure of turning their lives into parables. History seemingly has collapsed, God is a "nut," and myth and ritual are failing as substitutes before Coover moves to give the game back to the players with the ball "hard and white and alive in the sun" (174).

Paul Trench has studied all the UBA sects, "the Damonites, Caseyites, Legalists, Guildsmen, and Universalists," and "has discovered, in the end, his own estrangement from them all. If anything, he is simply a willing accomplice to all heresies, but ultimately a partisan of none" (172). Such a statement defines Coover's stance. Alive to all the fictional potential of the forms of myth, ritual, and history, alive to their rich embodiment in baseball, he finally is no partisan but an interpreter of their strengths and weaknesses, a *player* with them even as he knows he is played by them. Coover's meditation on the creation of history itself makes the use of history by other novelists working with baseball seem scant and underconceptualized. Coover knows that each novel is its own history, even as baseball has a history and creates its own, continually, through time.

Finally, Coover is very indebted to baseball's own Legend of the Fall. Because of Damon's death and Henry's resultant tampering, the UBA players themselves lapse into an exile in which they are cut off from their creator. They are permanently banished from themselves after the historical collapse of Henry's structure. They live on to attempt an approximation of Doctorow's lovely metaphor for the individual in history from *Ragtime:* "the immigrant, as in every moment of his life, arriving eternally on the shore of his self" (269). The "immigrant" depends on journey and memory, voyage and origin, having made the trip around the diamond, having found self along the way. Coover plays to avoid capture by myth or history. He knows that while baseball encapsulates all voyages and returns, it is still firmly represented in the present as the material for a living history. Baseball does not have to be transcended or renounced.

Exile and Exclusion: Blacks and Baseball History

THREE DIFFERENT exiles occur in baseball fiction. One exile is the Fall from Grace, in the sense of the Black Sox or any tragic embodiment of desire, from Roy Hobbs' sell-out to Henry Waugh's cheating after Damon's death. Another is Self-Exile, as in Herrin's *The*

Rio Loja Ringmaster, Neugeboren's *Sam's Legacy,* or Charyn's *The Seventh Babe.* Finally, there is "Exclusion," which is a prior act of violence toward an individual or group and is dramatized most strongly in baseball fiction through the representation of baseball's black players, their long banishment from "organized" baseball, and the resultant personal and historical roles lived by the players. Disenfranchisement and alternative history are the tales of black baseball in America for much of baseball's official history. Such mirroring and conflict is, of course, America's tarnished legacy to and stipulated condition for black Americans. Black characters do not "come home" in baseball fiction. Exiled by race, origins are not part of their play. They must survive and make do beyond baseball's official boundaries.

Roth commented on the genesis of his own Rupert Mundys that, well into the writing of *The Great American Novel,* he was intrigued by accounts of the Indianapolis Clowns, a black barnstorming team managed by a black midget who wore a gold earring and was a CPA in the off-season; the Clowns were as "homeless as my own team," said Roth (Siegel 184). Other less inclusive images of homelessness have punctuated baseball fiction. And of course, midgets are everywhere, beginning with James Thurber's Pearl du Monville in "You Could Look it Up" (1942) through Eddie Gaedel (life imitating art), Malamud's Otto Zipp, Roth's Yamm and Ockatur, and Sayles' Pogo Burns. Pogo is in flight from a menacing 6'10" black pimp. The Bimbos are a carnival of outcasts and yearning losers, an all-white team that refuses to clown before an all-black audience; it is beneath their dignity. Hemphill's *Long Gone* presents Joe Louis "Jose" Brown, a thirty-eight-year-old black catcher pretending to be a "Latino" rookie on a Class D team in the deep South in the 1950's. When the Ku Klux Klan comes after "Jose," his white teammates lay them out with baseball bats.

Harris wrote of Perry Simpson, a young black second baseman on the Mammoths. He was refused accommodations at the team's hotel in training camp, roomed with Henry Wiggen in *The Southpaw,* then later in *Bang the Drum Slowly* split off from Henry and the rest of the closely knit rookie group from *The Southpaw* to room with a black player. The club had changed the room arrangements, not the players themselves. Innocently, they drift apart, and Henry clashes with Perry when Henry tries to get the black players to lay off Bruce

Pearson (without telling them the truth of his illness). When Henry tells them that Bruce doesn't mean to exclude them, that he says "hello" to Negroes down in Georgia, Perry shoots back, "And they probably said pardon me for living, . . . Mr. Pearson, please allow me to kiss your wonderful white ass. Do not tell me what Georgia is like, Author, for I been there once too often and seen for myself" (*Bang the Drum Slowly* 185). Harris quietly weaves this confrontation into the larger theme of the Mammoths all pulling in opposite directions before learning of Bruce's fate. Yet Perry's distrust of Bruce as a white southerner and of Henry's motives is sad and realistically presented: "Leave him leave," Perry says of Henry, "he probably rather hang with his own anyway," while Henry writes of the black players, "They are good boys, never purposely nasty except when they get kicked around a good deal where a white fellow might not" (184–85). Both players make their points and Harris does not take sides.

Three very different novels present black players at the center of the narrative: Brashler's *Bingo Long*, Barry Beckham's *Runner Mack* (1972), and Percival L. Everett's *Suder* (1983). *Bingo Long* is a realistic fictional history set in the Negro baseball leagues of the 1930s and '40s. The leading characters, catcher Bingo Long and pitcher Leon Carter, are loosely modeled on black immortals Josh Gibson and Satchel Paige. The drama surrounds what happens to a black team when it breaks away from paternalistic black ownership and strikes out on its own. The novel is fundamentally about black players sticking together and taking care of each other, much as Harris' Mammoths united around Bruce Pearson. The novel concludes on a pregnant historic moment with the youngest player on the All-Stars ticketed for assignment to the white minor leagues. Leon's arm goes dead and Bingo at thirty-five muses on his timing; all he needed was ten years. The last lines describe Bingo on the endless road: "He leaned back and found a comfortable position to ride out the miles" (237). After Bingo's players had learned to take care of themselves, an elite more powerful and manipulative than the black ownership moves in to appropriate their future. Brashler rewrites the triumphant moment of black entry into the white professional leagues as bittersweet, a moment which signals the end of their hard-won freedom on the road. Economically, the collective moves to claim what it had ravaged spiritually and emotionally. To be welcomed into organized white baseball is to lose the solidarity born of exclusion.

Beckham's *Runner Mack* plays in an absurdist vein on that welcome and exclusion through its bewildered, eager young hero, who is constantly outwitted and degraded by society. *Runner Mack* is a heavily symbolic mixture of nightmare and satire and strongly derivative of Ellison's *Invisible Man*. Beckham imagines a young black character up from the South who hopes for a major league try-out in New York City but instead is subjected to manipulation by scouts, managers, strange corporations, and their henchmen. He finds himself in the army in Alaska and part of an eerie black rebellion led by "Runner Mack," a comic charismatic. The novel's overtly named hero, Henry Adams, has as his virgin a pliant beautiful girl suitably named Beatrice, and for his dynamo, Mack and the Mack truck that stalks him with its grinning front grille.

Baseball stardom is Henry's dream but he is doomed to humiliation. In his one try-out in a surreal domed stadium, he is made to look like a fool by machines that pitch to him and hit fly balls that defy gravity and geometry. Although down home he has hit .415 with 63 home runs, and though he believes, "Look, this is the American pastime, they've got to be fair with me" (99), they do not. As his supervisor in the factory says, "Henry, I don't know *what* we're doing. Or what it means. Or what I'm doing and if that means anything. I'm supervising. And I get paid for it" (108). As Henry says when Beatrice tries to keep him from joining the army, "How do you expect me to play ball for a team if they know I didn't want to help keep the country safe? I'm a man" (145). *Runner Mack* is Ellison out of Kafka and *The Natural*.

Suder has as its protagonist a black third baseman for the Seattle Mariners. It would be interesting, in fact it is necessary, to portray a central black figure in organized baseball in the present era, but *Suder* is not that book. Craig Suder's baseball life is hardly drawn on at all by Everett who is more interested in his hero's relation to jazz, to his crazy mother, and to sexual traumas in childhood than in synthesizing baseball into the account. One wonders why Everett chose baseball as Suder's occupation since he made so little aesthetic use of it.

Neugeboren and Charyn: Counterhistories

NEUGEBOREN'S SAM'S *Legacy* and Charyn's *The Seventh Babe* contain by far the most imaginative studies of blacks, exiles, and baseball history. The novels do not meet the subject head-on in chronicle or sentiment but rather construct a play space in which whiteness and blackness are both damnation and salvation. Both novels have imagined Negro League histories at their center that define their protagonists' dilemmas.

Sam's Legacy depicts the quest for maturity of Sam Berman. In his mid-thirties, an aimless small-time Brooklyn gambler and sports afficionado, Sam reaches a crisis of the spirit. He identifies with sports figures who had "heart," who had survived physical pain and injury (Monte Stratton, Lou Brissie, Herb Score, Waitkus, Gehrig), especially New York Knick forward Dave Stallworth who had come back to play after a heart attack, telling a reporter, " 'It was like somebody was sitting on my chest. . . .' Sam knew the feeling, he knew it well" (Neugeboren 4). Sam becomes involved with Flo, a woman who is wheelchair bound, and most fundamentally identifies himself with the "cripple" he feels himself to be. His passage in the novel is to come into acceptance of that part of himself in suffering. He must learn the terms of his "legacy" from his father, Ben, and from all men; the father-son bond in Jewish American fiction is never stronger than in this novel.

The main narrative of *Sam's Legacy* is earnest moral fiction, containing fine scenes of the decay of Brooklyn's white ethnic communities,[3] some taut gambling passages, and a sad sports reunion of boyhood friends in a Long Island suburb. Yet the novel comes alive in three long interpolated sections entitled "My Life and Death in the Negro American Baseball League, a slave narrative," told by Mason Tidewater, a mysterious old black man who lives in the Bermans' apartment basement and who had grown up with Sam's father, Ben. Tidewater turns out to be one of the greatest pitchers and hitters from Negro League history, yet a man consumed by a complex racial pride and fears that invalidated him for success or for love. His cautionary tale unfolds at junctures throughout the main narrative.

Mason Tidewater is sensitive and highly educated. His conundrum is his light skin that affords him the opportunity to pass for white in the major leagues. His life is consumed by the black-white conflict that possesses him. He begins his slave narrative:

> I consider the high point of my life to have been that moment on the fifteenth day of February, 1928, in the city of Havana, Cuba, when, after I had pitched and hit my team, the Brooklyn Royal Dodgers, to a 1 to 0 triumph over a team composed of players from the New York Yankees, George Herman "Babe" Ruth mocked me again for having chosen the life that was mine, calling me a "make-believe nigger," whereupon I slammed my fist into the pasty flesh of his dark face and struck him down; it was a blow I should have struck long before that day, and one which, filling me momentarily with joy, would lead on that same afternoon, to my death as a player in the Negro American Baseball League.
>
> I was known by another name then, and was often called, for my abilities (though never to my face), "the Black Babe"; if things had been otherwise, however, he might have been named for me, and he often admitted as much in the privacy of our friendship. He called me a fool on that day, though, for he knew what was common knowledge at the time—that if I had chosen to hide my origins (as, I should note, others did, including two—an outfielder and a second baseman—whose bronze busts reside in the Coopers-town, New York, Hall of Fame), I could easily have done so, and I could thereby, as he put it, have had it all. (69)

Here are the torments in Tidewater's life: his "choice" to play "black" is exacerbated and driven by a wild desire to dominate Babe Ruth whose own career was always dogged by the whispers about his origins and taunts of "nigger" from opposing dugouts. Punching the "pasty flesh" of Ruth's "dark face" is Tidewater's reaction to the insistent mirror double who is Ruth, a man to whom he is irresistibly drawn in his "black whiteness," even as Tidewater himself exists in a "white blackness."

Neugeboren's daring ploy is to imagine a homosexual relationship between Ruth and Tidewater that is an eerie and transformative account of a physical battle resembling Joe Christmas' tormented love for JoAnna Burden in *Light in August*. Tidewater exists as did Joe Christmas on that line between martyr and murderer, where rage is always ready to dictate when pride will take the individual over the line. Tidewater begins with the sort of racial pride that motivated Ellison's narrator in the Battle Royal in *Invisible Man*. He wants to be accepted by a white crowd for defeating white players. Yet when John McGraw urges him to play "white," Tidewater's contorted reasoning sees the impossibility: "If I had accepted, I would have proven to them [his black teammates] the very thing I longed to disprove—that I was one of them" (77). Tidewater is in double exile. In the face of the exclusion from white baseball, he chooses further self-exclusion.

Like Ruth, Tidewater becomes a pitcher-slugger who dominates the game. Unlike Ruth, he is a loveless figure, an enigma to teammates and fans. He bests Ruth time and again on the mound in barnstorming games in which he also booms long home runs. What begins on the field as Ruth needling him about their respective colors culminates in a hotel room: "And then, close to me, his lips on my cheek, he was a child again. 'My skin's darker than yours' he whispered" (308). The seduction follows. Tidewater comes to realize a welter of emotions about Ruth: "I proved myself his master on the playing field, I would away from the playing field, forever submit myself to him. . . . I brought him low only by making myself lower. . . . if anything, his willingness to meet me and to love me, even in his vulgar way, made him seem to me, given who he actually was, brave" (309). Tidewater, then, cannot reveal Ruth's and his affair but will seek all the more to defeat him utterly on the mound.

Neugeboren's Babe Ruth is a wonderful imagining, blunt, zestful, coarse, and lonely. He has no sense of home either, no way to be reconciled to his grim childhood, yet he has a sense of kinship to Tidewater: "They might've named me after you, if ya think about it. That's how come I feel for ya. You could've had it all, just like me" (311). Similarly, Ruth's appeal for Tidewater is precisely "the very mystery of his origins. . . . I wanted to go on forever being able to ask myself the simple question, did I love a white man or a black man?" (314). He reasons further, "I wanted—oh so dearly— to defeat him, not, that is, because he had what I wanted, but because he had what I hated myself for wanting" (317).

Tidewater is driven by his passions to wondrous feats. In 1925– 27, he wins 37, 41, and 45 games, while hitting 54, 58, and 64 home runs. Neugeboren describes games in fine detail and surrounds Ruth and Tidewater with the greatest of Yankees and players from the black leagues. Tidewater's nemesis is an ancient blacker-than-black teammate, Brick Johnson, who sees through Tidewater's proud presumptions and continually taunts him as "fair ass," hinting at his desire for Ruth. Johnson purposely lets a pop fly fall in front of him in right field in the ninth inning to break up a no-hitter Tidewater is pitching against a Yankee barnstorming team. When Johnson chides him as a "make-believe nigger," Tidewater chokes him to death in the clubhouse: "I could feel his blackness seeping into my fingers" (334). Tidewater flees the scene to begin a life of wandering, never to play baseball again. With the murder of Johnson, he concludes with the Fall through his desire in actuality to match baseball's exclusion of him and his exclusion of self.

Neugeboren constructs an original baseball frame for the thematics of Faulkner and Ellison and traumatically imagines our greatest mythical baseball hero in a psychological clash with our most devastating historical baseball reality. Tidewater's own racial history and that of America sets cruel limits and contortions on his desire and determines his career. Tidewater disappears but Sam Berman learns from him not to exclude self in prior prideful decision. The creativity finally passes to Sam who chooses to stay in Brooklyn with memories and responsibilities; his father's moral is "You must bet more than you can see." The novel ends with Sam Berman's imagined vignette, one on perfect pitch with baseball fiction's deepest rhythm: "A week or so after Tidewater had vanished, a group of elderly black men had appeared at the door to the rummage shop; [Flo] had invited them in and they had told her that, for some time, they had been looking for a man whom they believed had once been their teammate" (370).

Charyn's Babe Ragland in *The Seventh Babe* also embodies all the exiles in baseball history. As a boy in Texas, Rags had "learned baseball from the niggers on [his] father's ranch," and even there, freedom is stressed because "they didn't have the big leagues sitting on their backs, teaching them how to hit and field the ball" (138). As a brash young star for the Red Sox in the mid-1920s, Rags is banned from baseball on a trumped-up gambling charge. He then begins an odyssey as the only white player on the Cincinnati Colored Giants, a magic team of barnstormers who never come near Cincinnati but wander the country in a fleet of Buicks. Charyn imagines Rags making the Giants his life-long "home." The Giants are a collection of "crazy devils" with their own traveling witch doctor, a temptress, and wondrous athletes, including Pharoah Yarbull, an infielder and slugger without peer. Charyn's metaphors show a deep commitment to the mythology and history of the Negro leagues, the players' prowess and poignancy. Rags had his "birthright" stolen from him. He moves outside major league history, indeed outside *any* history: "Nigger baseball took Rags out of any specific order of time. Seasons didn't count" (289). Rags doesn't even know what year it is as Charyn pointedly invokes baseball's timelessness. Rags is heedless of the decades for "no amount of magic could thrust a calendar into the kid's head" (289). In the 1940s, his best rookie leaves the Giants for the white minors, the same symbolic scene with which Brashler concluded *Bingo Long*. Charyn's naturalistic yet surrealistic narration follows Rags to a 1949 brief stay with the St. Louis Browns but "he just didn't care about the major leagues" (321). Rags becomes "boss-man and magician" of the Giants and resigns from the Negro National League. Into his fifties and sixties, the Giants "were baseball dinosaurs, the last of the barnstorming teams. You couldn't find another crew like them" (327). Rags and his wife Iva live in one of the team's old Buicks.

Charyn's novel grows increasingly more fanciful as it becomes more improbable. The violent loneliness of the early chapters, the stark and musical images of homeless players on the road are continued but in a richer vein:

> But the kid had his sport. He ate ground balls. He went into the hole, his glove snapping like the meanest turtle in America. He was Ragland of the Colored Giants. If he had a dizzy spell, he would blink twice and then sock a triple over a barn or a chicken-coop. Iva had to rub his legs in a vinegar solution to burn away the charley horses. (327)
> Baseball was a disease in the magician's head. Incurable by now. He'd have played fungo in the grass if no other team would walk onto the field with his Giants. . . . They would come into town with soot on their faces from a long, long ride. Refugees from

nowhere. You would have thought fifty sheriffs had been chasing them. But no one was on their tail except that bossman-magician. *Play your game,* he said. (328)

Charyn intimates that Rags is the spirit of baseball itself, divested of leagues, teams, fans, going wherever there is to be a game, like some baseball Johnny Appleseed. The novel's last scene occurs in 1978 when Rags comes to Holyoke, Massachusetts, and spirits away his 1923 Boston Red Sox teammate, Garland James, from a rest home. Rags and the Giants feature the "kid [who] had to be seventy or seventy-two. His back wasn't curled over. He didn't have wattles on his neck. His fingers were hooked and powerful: the proper claws of any third baseman" (343). His pitcher is the grandson of his old teammate, Yam Murray. Garland James had left baseball fifty years before to teach Greek and coach baseball at a small New England college: "He wanted his center field without the rigamarole and politics of a major league club" (346). Now Rags, who has made baseball his home, comes to reclaim his old teammate and they go rattling off with the Giants.

The Seventh Babe ends, as does *Sam's Legacy,* with a baseball reconciliation, bridging decades and recalling teammates to life. Like Neugeboren, Charyn, too, has taken the suggestive pose of outlawry and exile and made it meaningful in individual historical terms. The history of black exclusion in baseball taps veins of psycho-drama (Neugeboren) and inventive mythologizing (Charyn) to provide two of the most satisfying endings in baseball fiction.

Expansion Draft: Baseball Fiction 1980–88

AFTER THE transitional novels of Neugeboren, Charyn, and others with their links to the flowering of baseball fiction in Harris, Malamud, Roth, and Coover, more than thirty baseball fiction novels have been published since 1980. This is an unprecedented sports fiction expansion which brings with it the problems, perhaps only metaphorical, of any sports expansion—a thinning of talent, some ragged games, retread veterans, callow rookies, careers open to talent, a few major surprises, and re-alignment of the competition.[4] All this expanded activity is more tentatively played out against and in the shadow of the influence of past heroes (novelists) and teams (their works).

The baseball fiction of Harris, Malamud, Roth, and Coover had been informed by the authors' sense of baseball's aesthetic properties and by baseball's resultant bonding with literature. Each of their novels had been very different in intention and style. The fact that baseball could serve so many varied authorial purposes—comic realism, myth, satire, self-reflexive fiction—suggests that baseball as a cultural form with referential and aesthetic properties is solidly historical as well as endlessly allusive.

The majority of baseball novels still take place in the mode of baseball as education. Here is where a series of mostly orderly transactions between the individual sports hero and the collective takes place, in which the protagonist "adjusts to" or "rebels against" this-or-that social or economic power that the team may represent.[5] Such traditional novels are extant in all periods up to the present and always comprise the majority of any fiction.

A very orderly passage is contained in John Hough, Jr.'s *The Conduct of the Game* (1986), which has an umpire as the improbable protagonist. Young Lee Malcolm works his way up to a major league assignment and along the way learns judgment and tolerance, the tools of his trade, as well as the human foibles and weaknesses that skew "conduct." He loses a bad old girlfriend, wins a loyal new one, confronts a black super star, and defends a gay umpire, Roy Van Arsdale, against prejudice and exposure. When Van Arsdale commits suicide, Lee Malcolm calls his own game on account of the hypocrisy of the baseball establishment and walks away from sports. A quiet maturation novel of personal baseball history is Don J. Snyder's *Veteran's Park* (1987) in which promising pitcher Brad Schaffer spends a minor league summer in Maine learning his craft and deepening his emotional range. All the verities of baseball's geography and history are present: small towns, farms, a good woman, children, staunch oldtimers. *Veteran's Park* is Kinsella without the hocus-pocus and a good generic example of current neo-realistic fictional expression. The best recent narrative of baseball education is Ron Shelton's film *Bull Durham* (1988), a sensual, knowing account of a Lardnerian bumpkin-pitcher, "Nuke" Laloosh (Tim Robbins), and

the proud veteran minor league catcher, Crash Davis (Kevin Cost-
ner), who teaches him the game. They in turn compete for and are
sustained by the captivating Baseball Annie [Savoy] (Susan Saran-
don), who loves them toward their respective triumphs ("Nuke's"
call to the major leagues, Crash's resignation to his own accomplishments and baseball future, perhaps with Annie). *Bull Durham* is
ahistorical with a benign view of organized baseball and is antithetical
to both myth and fantasy.

Malamud and Roth, so concerned with myth and baseball history,
wrote in a more recognizably modernist vein. Rich, nightmarish,
ironic, satiric—their baseball novels were formally interesting and
important, even if both authors appear to have carried their experi-
ments to excess. Referential to mythical, historical, and literary culture, they presented baseball in a web of associations that could not
help but legitimize the subject matter for serious fiction. In the
postmodern era, baseball novels partake deeply of the sense of baseball as education as well as extend the legacy of fantasy and myth
that Malamud and Roth provided. Two veteran literati step up to the
plate with wit and style. George Plimpton's *The Curious Case of Sidd
Finch* (1987) is about a New York Met rookie pitcher with a 160 mph
fastball who also is an Eastern mystic. Wilfred Sheed's *The Boys of
Winter* (1987) is a wicked comedy of manners about a group of very
competitive writers and artists whose summer softball team on Long
Island affords them all sorts of plots, both literary and otherwise.
Also, current authors on the baseball beat have Coover's baseball
treatise as ultimate (universal) guide and influence in the sense that he
stipulated the making of universes as a proper inquiry and subject
matter for fictions of baseball.

Be this as it may, with such expert players in the baseball fiction
hall of fame, current authors, instilled with the same diamond religion of restoration and search for origins, appear somewhat derivative and sentimental at this juncture. Steve Kluger's *Changing Pitches*
(1984) is a shallow tale of a veteran left-handed pitcher's infatuation
with his catcher that strives to be utterly contemporary. The novel's
resolution comes when the pitcher learns that the catcher is really in
love with a pro football quarterback. Henry Wiggen and Bruce
Pearson would blush—and then be bored. David Carkeet's *The
Greatest Slump of All Time* (1984) has solid baseball action and strives

for Coover's metaphysics but has too many interchangeably depressed characters who are articulate without a Damonsday to vivify them.

The baseball history of the Yankees and Dodgers in the 1940s and 1950s has provided the nostalgic material for three recent novels. Two novels, Morgenstern's *The Man Who Wanted to Play Centerfield for the Yankees* and David Ritz's *The Man Who Brought the Dodgers Back to Brooklyn* (1981) are fictional extensions of the current baseball "fantasy camps" where adult males live out their childhood baseball dreams. Morgenstern's Danny Neuman in early mid-life crisis chases his goal of playing centerfield for the Yankees to the dismay of his wife and others. When the current Yankees call him up from the low minors at the climax of an improbable promotional campaign, he hits a home run in his only at-bat and then abruptly and rather pompously walks right out of Yankee Stadium and baseball. The reader is not so fortunate in Ritz's novel in which a Brooklyn kid from the 1940s now a Los Angeles tycoon in the 1980s, buys the Dodgers and installs his boyhood pal as manager. They build an exact replica of Ebbets Field and move the team back to Brooklyn. A delightful idea (to this life-long Dodger fan), but Ritz's characters are wooden, his nostalgia unfocused and poorly evoked.

Robert Mayer's *The Grace of Shortstops* (1984) is, however, quite successful in entwining baseball history with the education of his fourth-grade protagonist, Pee Wee Brunig, a Bronx boy who idolizes the 1947 Dodgers and grows in different ways during the season. Mayer utilizes real baseball events—Jackie Robinson's first game, the first regularly televised baseball games, the heart-stopping Dodger-Yankee World Series of '47—to punctuate Pee Wee's growing consciousness of winning, losing, and adult weaknesses as well as adult responsibilities. Pee Wee's idol is Pee Wee Reese and the boy wants to learn "the way a shortstop becomes what he was" (85). Mayer's adults lead lives of compromise and complexity. Pee Wee's father, a rabbi, worries about his position and debates whether to become involved in running guns to the Hagannah in Palestine. At novel's end, Pee Wee has helped save a tiny neighborhood girl through considerable courage but, as the Dodgers lose the World Series, he must try to summon the "grace" to understand and forgive his mother, whom he has accidentally found out to have been deeply in love with his best friend's father. Such a knowledge of error and loss (the Dodgers', his own) weighs heavily on the young boy at the novel's open-ended conclusion. Where Morgenstern and Ritz use a baseball childhood as stagnant nostalgia, Mayer depicted baseball's seasonal history to be dynamic as it moved ahead with personal history. *The Grace of Shortstops* is about growth and feeling different toward baseball and self, playing toward the future rather than re-covering the past.[6]

Two of the most prominent recent baseball novels, *The Seventh Babe* and *Shoeless Joe,* suffer from what Jameson has discerned in postmodernism, "a new depthlessness," "a whole new culture of the image or simulacrum" ("Postmodernism, or The Cultural Logic of Late Capitalism" 58). As Malamud's descendant, Charyn uses language that is simultaneously ornate and gritty, while his characters, settings, and themes are simple and transcending (the definition, perhaps, of myth). As an heir of Harris, Kinsella's tale is sincere and educates with no complicated plot or thematic devices. Both novels are (like *Bull Durham*) reverent toward baseball itself: there is no higher ground or authority, no questioning of history, no shaking of fists at the cosmos, no formal subversion into fragments. Both novels are static and vivid at the same time. Babe Ragland is and will ever be the mad ancient boy at third base with claws for hands. Joe Jackson and his Black Sox mates will patrol Kinsella's farm diamond for as long as he can summon them in mind and spirit. Babe Ragland is both Wiggen and Hobbs but devoid of any interior life, an external copy of their passage and rebellion. Kinsella attempts to speak of what endures in baseball and ends with thin images of players as ghostly copies of historical figures, shades of shades, who fittingly take J. D. Salinger off with them into a sort of baseball twilight zone. Finally, Charyn has no affective tone at all while Kinsella is *all* affect.

Kinsella's second novel, *The Iowa Baseball Confederacy* (1986), strives toward even greater magic and fantastic effects than his *Shoeless Joe*. *The Iowa Baseball Confederacy* seems both extensively copied and overly magical. The Confederacy is a regional league that *might* have existed from 1902 to 1908 and is lodged initially only in the minds of father and son Matthew and Gideon Clarke who want to keep its memory alive. The IBC itself thus becomes a cross between Roth's Patriot League and Coover's UBA. In addition, there are magical events—young lovers at carnivals struck by lightning (Hobbs and Wonderboy, Harriet Bird), "back to the future" time travel, a fifteen-foot Indian named Drifting Away who is in touch with tribal ancestors who may or may not be in control of all temporality. A movable Black Angel stone monument from an Iowa City cemetery ends up playing right field. Leonardo Da Vinci arrives in a balloon to announce he invented baseball in 1506. There is even a biblical flood. Kinsella tries hard to unfold all events through his baseball frame. A desperate man blows himself up on a baseball field; an isolated old pitcher builds a fence exactly 60′6″ around himself; Matthew Clarke is killed by a line drive. Many characters are notable baseball aestheticians, including the cosmic Indian. There are "cracks in time"; opinions that "life is full of evil jokes" (95); powers that float "suspended in the silk and satin of the darkness" (103).

The center to the novel is a 2,648 inning game that begins on July 4, 1908 between the Chicago Cubs and the IBC All-Stars and that goes on too long in every sense. Kinsella is unsure of what he wants to do with this creation and we see little of the field action. In about the 1,000th inning, when Gideon Clarke says, "I want to see more of this special magic" (220), he may be the only one. Kinsella has run out of magic by this juncture. He is confident that baseball has wondrous associations for the reader, but his own conceptualizations are not tied to larger myth patterns or to any ideology in his baseball historicizing or to substantive issues in the creation of fiction. With the richness of the 1908 season at hand (cf. Greenberg's *The Celebrant,* for instance), Kinsella chooses to trick up a history of his own that pays remarkably little attention to the real ballplayers. Nor does Kinsella take a significant interest in creating fictional baseball players, preferring to control the narrative from the standpoint of a magic spectator-historian. It is no mistake, however, that two imagined baseball players are exceptions: Johnny Baron, a boy in the IBC in 1908 and an old man in 1978 in the novel's present, and Stan Rogalski, a 1970s career minor leaguer hurled back into sudden stardom in the IBC–Cubs marathon in 1908, are Kinsella's most affecting pair of baseball characters. Kinsella is at his best when he gives his fictional game over to *his* players, as in *Shoeless Joe* where Moonlight Graham, Kid Scissons, and Ray Kinsella's father are more interesting than the Black Sox shades and Kinsella's presumptions with "Jerry"

Salinger. All the sweetness and solemnity of Matthew and Gideon Clarke's (and Kinsella's) love of baseball cannot compensate for the randomness of the special effects and the absence of much coherence to the general baseball metaphysics in *The Iowa Baseball Confederacy*.

Tony Ardizzone's *Heart of the Order* (1986) is a baseball novel of education clothed in magic raiment but glib and preachy in and around its fantasizing. The unpleasantly self-possessed first-person narrator, Daniel Bacigalupo, is a third baseman of considerable promise who as a youngster kills a playmate with a line drive and from then on must deal with enormous guilt that determines his relations with family, peers, and girls. He imagines that the dead boy, Mickey Meenan, comes back to life inside him and becomes an alternate source of control. This ventriloquist act makes the reader a bit queasy (in this era of *The Exorcist* and *Alien*), though actually Mickey is a somewhat harmless cut-up. Ardizzone plays for reader sympathy but his hero is such an egotist that little in his passage appears moving or sincere. Danny's first major league at-bat results in a near re-creation of Mickey's death, Mickey perhaps travels to another body, a magical son is found in the bullrushes for Danny, Mickey's father becomes an improbable avenger, and Danny is almost killed. The last page redresses much of the overbearing narrator's line but Ardizzone has waited too long.

Baseball novels by women have become a flourishing subgenre in recent sports fiction. Not surprisingly, in light of the women's sport and play modes propounded in chapter 6, women's baseball fiction centers on the mode of cooperation, of interaction and support among teammates. Baseball appears to be the team sport most congenial to women athletes with its lack of aggressive physical contact and premium on attributes other than size and strength. Competition and heroic striving are present in the fiction but are integrated with the team's other potentials: nurture, family, growth.

The histories involved in this fiction are personal histories. Sylvia Tennenbaum's *Rachel, the Rabbi's Wife* (1978) depicts a heroine whose crises in understanding with husband and son repeatedly have reference to the baseball she avidly played in her youth and now follows as a fan. Rachel is more an informed spectator. Two novels, Paul Rothweiler's *The Sensuous Southpaw* (1976) and Barbara Gregorich's *She's on First* (1987), inevitably take the female participation in base-

377

ball to its other extreme: "the first woman to play in the major leagues." Rothweiler's novel is silly and fun. Gregorich writes very seriously of her heroine, Linda Sunshine, a talented shortstop who is shocked to learn that she is the daughter of her major league team owner and of a great female player from the All-American Women's League of the 1940s. Both novels isolate their heroines in competition with men against men and thus re-create the most excessive male reactions in sport. The "first woman to . . ." paradigm prevents the women from the affiliative team experience. One speculates Gregorich's real imaginative task would be to re-create the historical fact of the All-American League in all its relations, but that women's team sport history makes only a cameo appearance to help explain the blood lines for her pioneer who is still in thrall to Daddy—progenitor and "owner."

Softball is a thriving team sport for women and the sport of choice in Sara Vogan's *In Shelly's Leg* (1981) and Ellen Cooney's *All the Way Home* (1984). Vogan's team plays fast-pitch softball and Cooney's team plays slow-pitch. The choices say much about the novels' respective viewpoints. Vogan writes a more intense romantic narrative about a pitcher and catcher on a state championship team who are vying for the same man. The novel is set against a Montana backdrop of open vistas, sentiment, and personal nostalgia. Cooney's women are suburban housewives and mothers who have never played organized ball or competed for anything until they are brought together in a common effort where they slowly learn to exercise muscles and their capabilities. In both novels, the female players come to know each other through their sport and its lessons. Baseball as an education is invoked yet again in a new context.

Shelly's Leg is the name of the bar that sponsors the women's softball team. Vogan's heroines Margaret (pitcher) and Rita (catcher) are very different personalities. Margaret is a transplanted easterner; she is all pattern and definition, desiring stability and control after a failed first marriage and two children. Rita is more of a free spirit from a bad childhood on an Indian reservation; she has little plan to her instinctive affiliations, except to keep struggling. Woody, the object of their affections, is a classic western dreamer who wants to go on the road and try for a country and western singing career. Woody wants Margaret to go with him; she hesitates and Rita presents herself as an alternative. The softball season for the Shelly's Leg team proceeds along with this central drama.

Vogan does an excellent job of adapting baseball's field aesthetics to the lives and reactions of her central characters without ever forcing the comparisons. Margaret is the star pitcher: she always wants the ball and will never come out of the game. In effect, by her temperament and choices, she "pitches" Woody to Rita who "catches" him. Yet Vogan gives the women a complex relation to each other in regard to their feelings of cooperation (on the field) and competition (for Woody). Vogan's baseball voices are authentic. She writes a fine scene of Margaret and Rita alone on a ball field at dusk after another Shelly's Leg victory. Margaret's children are off playing in the distance. The pitcher and catcher have it out. Rita takes the initiative and walks with Margaret off the mound toward the plate:

> "Get down here," Rita said. She crouched behind the plate, her knees splayed as if waiting for the pitch. "Things look different from down here."
> Margaret knelt next to Rita, looking out at her children on the pitcher's mound and across the still field. From this angle the field looked more rolling, not as flat as Margaret had always assumed. She saw hollows accentuated by the dusk light, rises that looked as if they would lead off into the trees. (200)

Vogan has used the subjective perspectives formed by positions on the diamond to catch her characters in relation to each other. To Margaret, choices are flat and either-or; to Rita, from where "things look different," there are "hollows" and "rises," open-ended choices. Vogan does not take sides: both women argue their field of vision. Rita says, "It's being in the prime of life that's so hard for a woman. You don't know whether to lead or be led" (200). They begin to walk the diamond in the dark. To Margaret, "it seemed . . . that women never had anywhere to go and men surely and always did" (203). She resents Woody, and Rita as well, who tells her, "You're just starting to make a home here, in a town that *is* my home. We'll know each other long after Woody's made his first million or gone belly-up for the fiftieth time" (203–4). The familiar tension in baseball fiction of leaving home and return is invoked in a female context.

Their heated dialogue flares and subsides as they explain selves and each other. Finally Margaret "felt the pressure of Rita's hands holding her own" (207); they acknowledge they are both afraid, that they are both doing what they must. Nurture holds an equal place with competition.

Shelly had been the star-crossed lover of Sullivan, the romantic who had rescued her from a bad marriage after she lost a leg; they opened the bar together. Her spirit, her longings, fill the memory of Sullivan who manages the softball team and dispenses consolation and wisdom to Margaret, Rita, Woody, and the other "Shelly's Leg" citizens. For once in a sports novel, the absent spirit is *female,* not a dead son or schoolboy hero, but a mourned love, mate, and architect of the team. Shelly invented the community in "Shelly's Leg" and Vogan blesses her characters through her. The team loses the state championship game (to the Butter Butte Bandits) for the first time in six years and the women react with some regret and a certain gracious style, "their arms looped over each other's shoulders, their voices raised in what might have been Christmas carols" (244). Sullivan gives the benediction: "There ain't nothing to feel sorry about in softball. Tragedies don't traffic in games" (245). Woody after a final plea to Margaret will leave with Rita. The novel concludes with Sullivan reaching out to take Margaret's hand while they watch Woody and Rita in a slow dance and Sullivan extends Shelly's sympathy to all the living romantics.

Cooney's *All The Way Home* is less evocative and more solidly realistic about its heroines. It is really an anatomy of a team whose women of various ages and circumstances hardly have time for romantic flight, are indeed barely coping with children, spouses, and parents. Cooney has her dark touches, a battered wife and child, the trauma of a double parental death that follows a woman into adulthood and mothering of her own. Yet there are warmer moments as well: the pride of a husband in a wife's new sports interest and competence, a family's encouragement of a middle-aged mom's attempt to lose weight and acquire softball skills and confidence. The Spurs' team is coached by the intense Gussie Cabrini, a star athlete now home in Currys Crossing, Massachusetts, after failing to stick with a traveling women's softball team in the Southwest. She has been in a horrible motorcycle accident that has left her scarred and with an all-but-useless leg. Yet her power and authority, almost that of the male ritualist, inspires her team to take shape and each woman to do her best; they, in turn, bring Gussie back to life.

Nancy Willard's *Things Invisible To See* (1984) is a fine example of how to wed the lyrical to the prosaic in baseball fiction. Willard's strategy is from the outset to invoke God-play that is nonetheless absolutely historical in its import:

> In Paradise, on the banks of the River of Time, the Lord of the Universe is playing ball with His archangels. Hundreds of spheres rest like white stones on the bottom of the river, and hundreds rise like bubbles from the water and fly to His hand that alone brings things to pass and gives them their true colors. What a show! He tosses a white ball which breaks into a yellow ball which breaks into a red ball, and in the northeast corner of the Sahara Desert the sand shifts and buries eight camels. The two herdsmen escape, and in a small town in southern Michigan Wanda Harkissian goes into labor with twins. She will name them Ben and Willie, but it's Esau and Jacob all over again. (3)

Everything and everyone, not just baseball, is determined by the same cosmic play; no privileges are reserved for narrators such as those of Kinsella and Ardizzone. Baseball resides within Willard's magic power and is part of the novel's original vision. No rhetorical claims about the sport's special magic need be made. Ben and Willie cut deals with God and Death, Ben paralyzes a girl with a batted ball (a variant of the new favored plot device in recent baseball fiction), and the girl, Clare, receives instruction in *her* powers from a guardian "ancestress."

Woven in and around this magic is an engagingly American Gothic story of families on the homefront in Ann Arbor, Michigan during early World War II, the grounding from which Willard repeatedly returns to cosmic play (36, 147, 218, 263). Her subject is the battle between love and death. The cosmic choicemaking occurs when a decision of some grave import is made about a character who nonetheless must carry it forward in courage and love within his or her own history. Clare takes the form of a bird to be shot down for food by the sailors as Ben's raft drifts helplessly in the South Pacific (191);

later, she steals into Ben's hospital room in Ann Arbor to metaphorically light the lamps of his body anew (251).

The novel's gravest encounter is the final baseball match proposed
by Ben to Death (to stave off Ben's own); it is the most portentous
"big game" in baseball fiction since the one on Coover's Damonsday. Death sets the terms: Ben's boys' team from Ann Arbor, the
South Side Rovers, will play the "Dead Knights," Death's squad of
baseball immortals, for three innings. If the Rovers win, they will
survive the war; if not, Death takes them. If any of the Rovers now
scattered all over the world cannot play, they must be replaced by
their next of kin. Death and his client, Willie Harkissian, contrive a
bus crash that injures the Rovers. They are replaced by their mothers, who "look like they all work in a defense plant" (253), perhaps
Cooney's women from *All The Way Home* now entering the lists
with their sons' lives in the balance. This inexperienced "team" faces
Mathewson, Gehrig, and other great stars and ultimately wins.
Death moans, "Do you think Matty had to walk Mrs. Bacco? They
want the living to win. Even the umpire wants the living to win.
They remember how it was. All the pain, all the trouble—they'd
choose it again—they'd go extra innings into infinity for the chance
to be alive again" (261). Clare pitches heroically, her Ancestress
telling her to put "the stuff of being alive" (258) on the ball.

Willard lets the fantasy go on just long enough (3 innings and 10
pages versus Kinsella's 2,648 innings and 249 pages in *The Iowa
Baseball Confederacy*). She reunites Clare and Ben after the final ball
toss by the Lord of the Universe: "Clare starts running and Ben runs
after her as they round the bases, past the living and the dead,
heading at top speed for home" (263). Baseball's finest diamond
ryhthm is invoked yet again. Willard has charmingly enlisted baseball to play through her magic and mothers to play for their sons in
a history coextensive with time itself.

Recent baseball fiction carries forward all the thematics heretofore
mentioned. Stein's *Hoopla* has Kinsella's Black Sox but only as historical replicas with their historical "image" intact. Kinsella, Willard,
and Ardizzone believe in magic while Vogan, Cooney, Herrin, Hays,
Hough, Snyder, and Shelton write solidly of baseball as education,
in the wake of many baseball novelists and narratives. Jameson writes,
"We are condemned to seek History by way of our own pop images

and simulacra of that history, which itself remains forever out of reach" ("Postmodernism" 71). The mix of characters in some of the most recent baseball fiction suggests just such a re-cycling of baseball history and popular culture: *Hoopla* (Cobb, Buck Weaver, John L. Sullivan, Jackson); *The Seventh Babe* (Ruth, Landis, Dizzy Dean); *Sam's Legacy* (Ruth); *Suder* (pianist Bud Powell); *Shoeless Joe* (Black Sox, Salinger); *Things Invisible To See* (the "Dead Knights"); *The Celebrant* (Matthewson, McGraw, Hal Chase, Black Sox); *The Iowa Baseball Confederacy* (the 1908 Cubs, Frank Luther Mott); and *Ragtime* (McGraw, Charlie Faust). Such "copying" is not necessarily enervating if delivered in inventive form, with *Ragtime* the primary example of a postmodern treatise on replication and copying.[7] Nonetheless, baseball fiction at present needs a less complacent use of magic and history, a stiffening against the national romance with baseball, without losing its memory and pleasure. A cinematic triumph such as *Bull Durham,* bawdy, wise, and sentimental, while respectful of baseball's passages and rhythms, may signal a narrative return to comic realism, the most enduring baseball fictional mode as exemplified by Lardner and Harris.

Furthermore, some hard edges need to be beveled around the diamond. They are installed in the baseball frame of William Kennedy's *Ironweed* (1983), which squarely addresses the issues of fantasy and sentimentality in a dialogue with personal history. Kennedy creates this dialogue within the action of the novel itself in the responses of its protagonist, the blasted ex-Washington Senators third baseman, Francis Phelan. For heart-stopping grief, *Ironweed*'s fictional presentation of the father-son relation in baseball is unmatched. Francis Phelan had been a wondrous fielder with great hands, but in 1916, as he is diapering his infant son Gerald, he unaccountably drops the baby on the floor. The baby suffers a broken neck and dies. Francis flees his family in mortal devastation, condemning himself to a guilty wandering and vagrancy in which he cannot forgive himself. The novel opens in late 1938 with Francis back in Albany on Halloween night where ghosts are rising.

Kennedy balances Francis' reveries, his visions of his past and his victims, with his unsparing and violent presentation of self. Francis has killed two men as well as Gerald; the first a strike-breaking trolley car conductor downed "with a smooth round stone the weight of a baseball" (Kennedy 25) in 1901, making him a labor hero and precipitating his first flight from Albany and into organized baseball, which then necessitated his leaving every year. His second murder victim is a bum, "Rowdy Dick" Doolan, who challenges him on the road. After this incident, Francis runs again as he "reconstituted a condition that was as pleasurable to his being as it was natural: the running of bases after the crack of the bat, the running from accusation . . . the running from family, from bondage, from destitution of the spirit" (75).

Francis has colloquy with all his dead spirits in *Ironweed,* including a lovely early summoning of the dead Gerald who redeems Francis through prophesying Francis' "final acts of expiation": "Then when these final acts are complete, you will stop trying to die because of me" (19). Francis attempts stewardship of his own meager flock of friends, Albany's male and female vagrants. His love and road companion, Helen, is a strong, tormented character in her own right, as Kennedy accords complex dignity and valid pasts to his gutted people in the present.

For Francis Phelan, *his* shades are haunting, not summoned as in Kinsella or Ardizzone to magic up baseball art. Kennedy finally has it out with fantasy and the pull of the past when Francis, having returned to his home and to wife Annie, tentatively opens an old trunk of baseball memorabilia and imagines the people of his past: "The bleachers were all up, and men were filing silently into them" and "They kept coming: forty-three men, four boys, and two mutts" (176), when suddenly Kennedy shifts from the mode of "summoning" that had informed *Ironweed* since Gerald's stunning appearance. Francis closes his eyes "to retch the vision out of his head" (176–77). Then, as the light brightens, "with it grew Francis' hatred of all fantasy, all insubstantiality"; "I am sick of your melancholy histories, your sentimental pieties, your goddamned unchanging faces." He concludes, "You're all dead, and if you ain't, you oughta be." "So get your ass gone, " for "I'm the one is livin'. I'm the one who puts you on the map" (177).

Within Francis, Kennedy has fought the battle between the pull of the past, the summoning of shades, the grief-filled magic, and the need for the living man to continue out of his paralysis. Kennedy has the power to "put [Francis] on the map" and the power to draw the map. The "livin'" writer chooses as well, in this case a positive agency in Francis Phelan (what other baseball fantasists lack in their dreaminess), to embrace the patterns his own history makes beyond the fantasies and myths he constructs to keep himself imprisoned in the past. Francis Phelan's internal debate between fantasy and history in representation, his private agony and public torment, are everywhere related through the baseball frame both real and imagined. Such antagonists in debate define the two major modes in the creation of baseball fiction at present. A lyrical author, Kennedy nonetheless works in the service of some hard lines. Francis learns that he has more left than just his guilt. He lays to rest his friend Rudy and Helen, takes a few good bat swings at a gang that comes to break up a hobo encampment, then flees to his own home at last. He forages in the old trunk for his warm-up jacket, not for pictures of ghosts, and thinks perhaps of moving his bed into his grandson Danny's room; a hope of a future bond born of Gerald's memory is held out at last. Kennedy ends with "sure hands" himself, in the rhythms of coming home, an exile ended. As son Gerald had hoped in the graveyard, his father Francis has "stop[ped] trying to die," his "fugitive dance" (215) at least in abeyance.

Further reaction against the control of myth and fantasy in baseball fiction is David Small's *Almost Famous* (1982), a decidedly anti-sentimental novel in which minor league stand-out Ward Sullivan loses his career and lover in an automobile accident at age twenty-one. Possessed of a Roy Hobbsian urgency and natural talent, he, however, will not have a mythic rebirth. Instead, half-crippled at age thirty-three, he lives past baseball in his personal history with his pride and sense of order, attempting to shut out a re-connection to his family and an emotional life. He buries his father, becomes a father, breaks a young woman's heart, grudgingly learns to admire an artist brother, and deals unsparingly with a mad and inspired mother. Ward Sullivan painfully comes home, not through victory or revelation but through a slow imperfect education to his own failings. He's still learning at novel's end, one in which his extended family plays a pick-up game in the fields on family property in Maine. Ward yells to his brother, "Get back, kid! I'm going to hit this one a country mile," whereupon "the kid turned and bounded like a gazelle toward the dark trees at the edge of the clearing" (416).

Small's final image (similar to Vogan's diamond at dusk in *In Shelly's Leg*) is of Ward's exultation as well as of the inner diamond (clearing) glossed with the "dark trees," the space beyond where life is always unknown, to which we must "turn." Small provides a fitting encapsulation of baseball's geometry and outer possibility.

Finally, the drama of baseball is played out in the play between, within batter's boxes, baselines, between safe zones of the bases, between the pitcher's mound and home plate. On a journey around the diamond, one is allowed leads but must jump back to safety. The play between is *always* occurring; it is always the mechanism by which one may play back toward origins or play beyond the diamond. Thus baseball's time and space always depends on the play between of bat-ball, pitcher-batter, fielder-runner, ball-strike. Baseball's history encapsulates an origin, fabricates a narrative return, and then seals the journey toward it as an imperative within the rules. Baseball's passage is imbued with a hermeneutic of restoration and return within its very structure that accounts in no small part for its nostalgia and sentiment. Yet baseball is at one and the same moment radically open in temporal and spatial possibilities that hurl it beyond the inner diamond. Baseball is the only major American team sport to possess both these capabilities which are profoundly satisfying and endlessly suggestive in their patterns for players, spectators, and novelists.

13.

Fictions of Basketball

O F   T H E   three major American team sports, basketball has been the least favored by novelists; there are four times as many baseball novels and twice as many football novels. Basketball denies authors the traditional aids in fictionalizing American team sport. The game does not possess a mythology of weather. It is not played by "the boys of summer" and does not turn with the seasons. Nor is there anything analogous to fabled football games fought in mud or in Arctic cold. Basketball is not the pastoral game of small towns or the colorful fall spectacle of American universities. It is not a simulation of the traditional directed American work world as football is, nor an escape into ideal relations with that world as baseball is seen to be. As the youngest of the three popular American team sports, basketball has no deep school tradition and a shorter professional tradition than baseball or football.

Basketball is a difficult sport to write about for the sports reporter or the fiction writer. Basketball possesses too many adagio plays and too few real climaxes. Rather than building in a pattern of plays and strategy, it provides continual flow, frustrating to the writer who would pace the development of character and plot with competition, victories, and defeats. Basketball does not possess language in any form. If baseball is a sport interpreted by language (the umpire's calls of "strike," "ball," "safe," and "out") and football is a sport initiated by language (the quarterback's signals), basketball is a wordless ballet of shifting patterns, relentlessly consuming present time, as Updike sensed when he narrated the *Rabbit* trilogy in third person, present tense, a rare narration for extended fiction but one that catches the movement of the game. Rarer still is Barry Beckham's second person, present tense narration in *Double Dunk* (1980). Basketball allows only a few seconds to create plays that are run, used up, and then the action careens to the other end of the floor. Plays are completed in virtuoso movement that almost defies language to keep up with the pace.

Basketball like baseball has a circular symbolism but in a different vein. In basketball, players do not follow a [base]–line on solid ground but rather soar into the air to drop a circular ball through another circle. The act is not one of return or of a search for origins but rather of a transcendence in which the player becomes "at one" with the ball and rim, the goal becoming that of a touch that results in no touch with the rim, a clean descent of circle through circle, an aesthetic that places basketball at the furthest remove from football's collisions. Basketball's "touch" has little in common with "touch" posited by women writers in a sports frame. While the women "touch" in support and affiliation, basketball's "touch" enhances an individual escape to a personal realm without communication. Basketball's touch is an *object* touch rather than the touch of *subjects*.

In the fiction of the Ritual Sports Hero, particularly that of Hemingway, the hero searched for "the good place." Basketball's individual sports heroes search for "good space" where, if they internalize a sense of touch and the right moves, they may achieve freedom. Basketball fiction searches for this freedom for the individual through a playful creativity. The great contradiction of basketball as a team sport is that its novelists continually conceive of individual heroes who play to the music in their heads; the analogy to jazz with its improvisation within pattern has frequently been cited (Oriard, *A Dreaming of Heroes* 66–67; Novak 101).

Basketball players crave a clear space, an upward space where they can break through barriers of sense and reason. No guilt is evinced about love of basketball in the fiction, none of football fiction's "God help me, but I love it." Basketball is a religious communion for its devotees. Peace is achieved when a player feels, "I have my game," in the aforementioned "good space." At this point, by playing the game, he has "played beyond," breaking out of constraints, lost in improvised patterns, free at the peak of a jump shot, glorious in the power and artistry of a creative slam dunk.

Basketball fiction remains for the most part in the play-anti-heroism negations. It is a fiercely subject-centered fiction; indeed, of fifteen novels under discussion here, nine have first person narration. Yet basketball has specific historicization which recurs in two major areas: the point-shaving scandals of the early 1950s and 1960s and the current domination of the sport by black players. These two strains are linked by the fact that victims of the scandals are seen to be the ghetto blacks who fell prey first to the collective's enticements and then to its witch hunts. Thus basketball fiction sets up a firm tension between its transcendant aesthetics and its largely naturalistic historicization.

Basketball's Arena: The Playground

BASKETBALL FICTION'S central arena is the schoolyard or playground. The game there is not on a printed schedule or between fixed teams and is not a media spectacle in its pure form. The battles on the playground are most often learning experiences of skill and fortitude. Playground basketball is an education but its mystique is not that of the academy but rather of the neighborhood crucible in major American cities.

The playground game in the cities belongs to the players and the immediate community. The definition of playground-schoolyard is loose. Mack Davis in Neugeboren's *Big Man* (1966) has the proper definition: "I call it a schoolyard even though there's no school there, but any time you got some baskets with a wire fence around them, man, that's a schoolyard" (138). The playground is a free area where a democracy of talent reigns: to stay on the court, you must continue to win. The collective oppression that may have marginalized the players *in* this place, *at* this time, is turned into a virtue. Here beyond owners, coaches, leagues, and systems is where basketball is *played,* where emphasis is on both pride and creativity, where one scores points on both competitive nature and degree of difficulty. As David Wolf writes in *Foul* (1972), his nonfictional treatment of the odyssey of Connie Hawkins, "A kid could walk into a playground and find himself in pickup games with pros or All-Americans defending their reputations against the challenge of neighborhood heroes" (31). Thus for Wolf, the schoolyard match takes on the quality of the frontier challenge where the lone gun passes through the neighborhood in his high-tops. The myth of equality on the playground democratizes the oppression of the collective. Robert Lipsyte cynically opposes the myth of the playground when he writes, " 'the world's greatest player' has always just overdosed. Basketball almost saved him, but . . ." (Lipsyte 144). Countering both myth and scepticism is Beckham's vision of Harlem legend Earl Manigault, what he means to the playground and what the playground means to him: "You are renewed. You must show them something. They are here to see theatrics, something astonishing, some expression of a natural ability loosed spontaneously. . . . It all hangs together, because of it you feel like a catalyst. They have come to see you, have come to depend on you to give them some blessed relief, something to take their minds off the hell they may be living" (*Double Dunk* 29).

"Heaven is a playground," suggests Rick Telander in the title of his recent nonfiction basketball study. Updike's *Rabbit, Run* begins with boys playing ball in an alley. Al Young's *Ask Me Now* (1980), Robert Greenfield's *Haymon's Crowd* (1978), Bob Levin's *The Best Ride to New York* (1978), and Neugeboren's *Big Man* conclude on the playground. No basketball novel can totally ignore the power of this arena. Neugeboren's Mack Davis exclaims, "Oh man, I was king then. I mean, you make it big-time-high school, college, pro, I don't care where, it never compares with being king of your own school-yard" (*Big Man* 60). The competition there is almost always individual, the player practicing endlessly or taking on an opponent one-on-one in a more ballet-like version of boxing's confrontations. Players are described in alleys, in empty arenas, in littered playgrounds, in settings prosaic and drab. Yet the players' presence is where the game is. Levin's veteran Jake Baer describes the quintessential arena: "It was a great park. The trees were warped and stunted. The grass was gray. Smoke floated in the air like bats. . . . But there in the corner was the spread of macadam, the two stiff poles, the scuffling, struggling three-on-three game that I wanted" (*The Best Ride to New York* 66). Greenfield writes in *Haymon's Crowd,* "In summer, the school-yard is open and empty, a great desert of scorched and shimmering concrete," but "by the end of August, the breeze blowing through the schoolyard at night has lost its fire. The games are more fiercely contested, the [school] steps crowded" (39, 41). In Lawrence Shain-berg's *One on One* (1972), Elwood Baskin relates, "The court had metal backboards, no nets on the rims, no space at all between the court and the fence. . . . The players were seven Negroes, a Puerto Rican, two whites. . . . No laughter, no talk, no teamwork. Unlike college and professional players, they took the game down to its most essential problem: put the ball in the basket as quickly and as often as the other team allowed. *Playground basketball*" (61; emphasis Shainberg's).

Variations of the playground game abound. In *Inside Moves* (1978) by Todd Walton, an empty San Francisco arena is the site of a one-on-one battle between a small, lame white playground guard and a young, tall black NBA forward. Walter Kaylin's *The Power Forward* (1979) depicts a white pro star in a continuing psychic and emotional relationship with a black playground legend banned in a point-shaving scandal. Naked and exultant, the two play one-on-one at the white star's beachfront court where eventually dozens of NBLA players arrive to protest the banning of Muley Bishop and to play pick-up games in a camp atmosphere. Beckham's arena for Earl Manigault is always the schoolyard, the only place he can truly express himself. In *Ask Me Now,* Young's Durward Knight, an ex-pro guard, plays his only playground basketball on the novel's last page; his teammates are his son and his daughter's boyfriend. At odds with both of them throughout the novel, now he has learned to understand them and take pride in his son's talent in jazz. In the novel's last lines, "They sprinted through the gate onto the play-ground. . . . It felt so good to be saying what he meant and doing it at the same time. He couldn't wait to get his hands on the ball" (294).

The playground as arena houses many of basketball's disaffected and unaffiliated. David Shields' *Heroes* (1984) is narrated by a forty-year-old sportswriter and ex-college player, Al Biederman, who describes the playground hero come to the college town. Belvyn Menkus is perhaps the last white inner-city basketball genius, an instinctive master of the game with no academic or social skills. *Heroes* is a school sports tale that promises an expose', but the facts never quite cohere into an indictment. At novel's end, Menkus is neither star nor victim of the system but rather a frightened, injured player after a variant of playground duelling. Here Biederman and Menkus meet on the court when Biederman, who admires the kid greatly, bets Menkus he can score once before Menkus gets to ten baskets. Biederman watches in awe as Menkus soars over and around him. Almost hypnotized, he fails to move out of the way when Menkus makes his tenth basket with a thunderous stuff. The kid's knee is torn in an awkward landing. The playground challenge and moves have claimed Menkus, his future as a player is problematic.

Playground stars may be losers to the larger society, but through the action on court they come alive. Walton's *Inside Moves* extends this metaphor to encompass an urban society of broken men and women who need purpose and a sense of worth. They find it in San Francisco at Max's bar, owned by Max, a legless philosopher, and home to Jerry Maxwell, who tends bar, has a lame leg, and is afraid to dream of basketball stardom. The novel is narrated by Roary, a disabled Vietnam veteran, whose recovery and courage are the book's primary subjects. Yet, as in *Heroes,* the novel's sensibility is keyed to the wondrous basketball player. Jerry works two jobs but plays three hours every day in the schoolyard and serves as a bridge for Max's people to the world of great athletic achievement. Jerry and Roary bait Alvin Martin, an NBA forward with the Warriors, into a one-on-one contest in a deserted pavilion. Jerry wins, 32–28, in heroic fashion. Martin is outraged and frustrated, but Jerry says, trembling, "You know I beat you. That's all that matters' " and " 'Anytime you want a basketball lesson, come on down to Edison Park. I'm there most any lunchtime' " (Walton 26). Later, Martin helps them pay for an operation on Jerry's leg; at full strength, Jerry fights his way onto the Warriors as a scrappy guard and helps them win an NBA championship.

Walton almost pulls off a classic boys sport fiction fantasy ending within a contemporary adult novel by never descending into bathos or rhetoric. In his success, Jerry has his crisis of forgetting his roots among his friends at Max's and Roary must move past him. At the novel's conclusion, Jerry may be a star but Roary has grown into command of his life and future. As sour a novel as *Inside Moves* is sweet, Greenfield's *Haymon's Crowd* features Haymon Jacobs, an aloof, boorish seven-foot white journeyman who, by a series of implausible events, tip-stuffs a rebound to win an NBA title at the buzzer. *Haymon's Crowd* is full of half-characterized playground survivors, including Max Trapp, a gambler and fixer closely modeled on Jack Molinas, the mastermind of the late 1950s college basketball scandals and a fitting presiding spirit in a leaden, unpleasant book.

The great majority of schoolyard players do not crack the larger world of sports achievement; they are denied by fate, choice, or circumstance. Jake Baer in *The Best Ride to New York* has been working at the playground game for most of his life. A loner and court philosopher, he plays minor league basketball in Pennsylvania in his mid-thirties against largely black competition. His real job, however, is to set up young talent for contact with point shavers and gamblers. In this compromised role, he rationalizes the hard truths about competition in Tough Guy narration. Baer's assignment is to get close to a wondrous Philadelphia high school star, Sidney Nightingale. He thinks, "He had seventeen years on me, some inches, and his jumps made me look like I was falling down stairs. I figured that I had him . . . basketball might be his game, but it was how I made my living" (73). In a tense three-on-three schoolyard game, Baer pulls out all his tricks and gamesmanship against Sidney Nightingale to win by a few points. Sidney is ensnared, prompting Baer to think of him without sentiment: "There was always something you could not stand up to. I am sorry but you had to learn it sometime"(92). The playground test, then, is "schooling." Jake Baer—fatalist, minor hood, basketball gamesman—is reminiscent of Hemingway's boxer Jack Brennan in "Fifty Grand": he is "covered anywhere you can hit him." To authors, every sport has some degree of determinism, where the physical fact of vulnerability is displayed against a relationship of power. Basketball has this naturalistic side depicted in its legacy of fixes and scandals in the city game. Therefore playground basketball rivals boxing with the playground becoming an elemental arena for the one-on-one battle.

The schoolyard game is heavily ironic, because, in the case of most ghetto ballplayers, school has been only the place of dismal failure. Shields' Belvyn Menkus in *Heroes* is a dyslexic whose illiteracy has been covered up for years in school transcripts. Wolf describes Connie Hawkins with his "general" diploma from Brooklyn's Boys' High, signifying attendance and his seventh grade reading level. "In September of 1960 . . . [Connie] packed his sneakers and his comic books and went off to be Joe College" at the University of Iowa where at the end of the year he would be quickly mustered off campus when his loose involvement with the college scandals was uncovered in New York City. Hawkins said, "I didn't want to flunk out and have people laugh. I wanted to stay and play ball, so I'd be respected. But the readin' was killin' me" (92). Sadly, three decades later, the process of recruitment and retention of "student"-athletes is both more refined and more absurd, with financial scandals, drug tragedies, and even less pretense of educational standards. Neugeboren's point-shaver Mack Davis put the college basketball experience in perspective in the 1960s before the real big money: "All these guys always wanting to know why I did it, they give me a pain. I did it for the money, what they think? The college paid me, I did what they wanted; gamblers paid, I worked for them; bookies paid more than gamblers, I sign up with them. Shit, man, nobody give me an education cause they like my looks" (18).[1]

The playground may be the place where a reputation begins but it also functions as the place of bittersweet return. Mack Davis is back on the streets working in a car wash five years after his banishment from big time basketball. He drifts through his days until he is cajoled and taunted by his strong girl friend, Willa, to play for five dollars a night with a team sponsored by the car wash. In a game at the Jewish Community Center (a playground variant), he explodes against Nat Morgan, a fellow dumper from the scandals who is hanging around Willa and Mack's brother, Ronnie. Mack humiliates and punishes Morgan in the game. When asked by a small-time gambler to "play ball" and perhaps replace Morgan on the payroll, Mack knocks him out. In the novel's positive last scene, Mack is at the schoolyard. He plans to re-enroll in college and help Ronnie with his game. Beyond that, "nobody gonna get me back in that car wash. My hands, they clean enough" and "Oh yeah, man. We back in the big time. Nobody gonna beat me and Ronnie. We gonna take on all comers" (202–3).

Neugeboren and Young conclude their basketball novels with reconciliation of the black characters in the schoolyard. Beckham, too, in *Double Dunk* suggests that Earl Manigault's destiny is forever to be a presence to young black players in the schoolyard. Pointedly, Levin's Jake Baer in *The Best Ride to New York* concludes on a deserted, lighted court, doing his lonely shooting drill. In general, for the black basketball culture, the schoolyard is a community and a test; for the white player, a focused test on hostile turf. Both find their art and their competition there.

Basketball and the Black Experience

THE DOMINATION of American basketball by blacks in the last few decades has given birth to a unique situation. Basketball is the first major American sport to be redefined in its standards of play, its folk culture, its mores, and its language by a specific subculture with basketball's resultant dislocation in the white psyche and overemphasis in the black psyche. Not all of the implications of this shift are as yet evident in the fiction of black or white authors but the first returns are tabulated in recent basketball fiction. Not surprisingly, basketball fiction confronts this new dispensation in evasion and/or overcompensation through a symbolic intensity.

The novels by Young, Neugeboren, Beckham, Kaylin, plus Charles Rosen's *Have Jump Shot, Will Travel* (1975), all center on black experience in basketball. Of the five writers, Young and Beckham are black. Yet no easy categorizing may be done along these lines. Young's *Ask Me Now* has Durwood Knight as protagonist, a thirty-nine-year-old ex-NBA guard in San Francisco who is having trouble adjusting to being a full-time husband and father to his three teenage children. Like Percival Everett's baseball novel, *Suder, Ask Me Now* has a black athlete at its center but fails to capitalize symbolically on that fact. Like *Suder* as well, *Ask Me Now* has much feeling for jazz. Young Leon Knight is an aspiring saxophonist and Durwood, an ex-trumpeter, hopes to open a record shop. Woody Knight is a decent man but the novel is tired. The few basketball scenes are pro forma and without nuance. In a sense, Young is a prisoner of reader expectations. Black writers such as Everett and Young may be wary of pervasive conceptions in white America about "natural" black athletes, believing them to be mere corollaries to "natural" rhythm. Black writers may shy away from sport as subject matter as too stereotypical. Young feels compelled to de-emphasize any primacy for basketball. In an interview, Durwood Knight declares, "All I'm saying is you learn everything there is to know about life no matter what line of endeavor you take up" (287).

Yet all American authors today sense popular culture as the great common ground out of which to create new statements. Certainly Barry Beckham found ways to mix baseball, the American success myth, and the hallucinatory quality of black urban experience in *Runner Mack*. In the spirit of postmodern simulacra and the nonfiction novel, Beckham's *Double Dunk* is another interesting experiment because it fictionalizes the star-crossed career of Earl Manigault, the best-known black schoolyard great after Connie Hawkins. Manigaultt was brought to notoriety by Pete Axthelm who included a chapter on him in *The City Game* (1970). Entitled "The Fallen Idol: The Harlem Tragedy of Earl Manigault," the chapter was part of playground profiles set in juxtaposition to Axthelm's accounts of the 1969–70 New York Knickerbockers. Axthelm did more to set a historical specificity to the rough poetry and competition of city basketball than any other sportswriter.

Manigault's "tragedy" concerned his sweet, lost quality, a heroin addiction, resultant prison term, and lack of opportunity to prove his greatness beyond the high school level. Beckham writes documentary fashion, recounting Manigault's history through a second person, present tense narration that has the bounce and feel of the playground game, that provides the heart, music, and crowd language of the schoolyard. Beckham resists giving Manigault the consciousness of the urbanologist. When he does link and sustain basketball metaphors, it is through Manigault's dazzling skill that punctuates a schoolyard scene:

> What is there about the dunk shot that puts basketball on a different level? Why is the shot so special? Rising is one thing. Getting off the ground higher than anybody expects you to at six feet, one inch; leaving the sidewalk with its chalk marks and painted signs [*Robert loves Gina; Boys High full of punks; pussy is good*] and tiny pieces of glass from soda and beer bottles. Off that cement that even has blood stains and piss spots; the same cement or gravel or whatever kind of sidewalk they call it technically, the cement you have skinned your knees on as a child; off of it and away from it and into the air. Rising, flying, taking off from above all of this one the sidewalk, moving away from it at least temporarily. (126–27)

The passage is about "upward space" but the specifics detail the grim, earthbound society that remains the truth of the schoolyard and of the players in Harlem who would fly over it. Beckham's Manigault is a true folk hero in Harlem whose feats are embellished by the spectators: "What could be hipper than being around those who admire you while they make up stories about you?" (72). The other pole to his basketball wonder is the hopelessness of his failure at Winston Salem College that leads him to a dead end in Harlem and to addiction: "Brothers and sisters look out on the terribleness of the day, the scare of the night, the nothing of it all, the nothing of anything, especially they lives and see nothing. You know this. You know deep down inside you are as scared and confused as all the other brothers. *There ain't nothing to turn to.* Dig it: what is the other choice? Where you gonna go, watcha gonna be?" (159–60).

Beckham doesn't have the answers. Earl is last seen at age twenty-five, having failed a pro try-out with the ABA Utah Stars after his prison term. He turns back toward Harlem with the hopes of running the second year of his own schoolyard tournament and giving talks at high schools. As the greatest player never seen by the larger sports culture, he has a legendary quality. He belongs to the blasted black culture as a victim, not quite brave or smart enough to match his physical greatness with discipline. However, he is authentic, not fabricated by any spectacle or media (until Axthelm's and Beckham's retrospectives), not tainted by the scandals of the collective. Beckham establishes this fact; he does not trade on it in sentiment. He tells Earl's story *as* Earl's story, leaving the implications and neuroses to others.

Twenty-five years ago, Jeremy Larner in *Drive, He Said* (1964) wrote, "There are only two styles of basketball in America, and of the two the white boss grimly prevails over the Negro. The loose lost Negro style with its reckless beauty is the more joyful to watch or play, if you can, but it is the white boss style that wins" (Larner 110–11). Larner's statement still seems pertinent in the late 1980s, although basketball itself is almost completely black at its most skilled level as well as in its current mythography. Lipsyte wrote that as a consequence of these facts, "white males . . . were suddenly faced with the first major sport in which they felt racially outnumbered and culturally alienated" (168). One way for an author to deal with this pressure is evidenced by Shields' creation of Belvyn Menkus in *Heroes*. Menkus is a black character in every respect—language, socialization, style of play, background—but he is white. More believable are the attempts to show a white player in real conflict with basketball as it is defined at present.

Charles Rosen's *Have Jump Shot, Will Travel* was the first fictional assessment of the impact of basketball's black domination on the individual white player. Rosen's Bo Lassner, a moderately successful center at Hunter College, has been drafted by the Wellington Rifles, a minor league pro team that plucked "any large, ambulatory white body who lived within 150 miles of any team in the league" (*Have Jump Shot, Will Travel* 13). Bo says, "I made the Rifles' squad because I was the only white player who showed up" (14). As the last man off the bench, he is alternately ignored and taunted by his teammates: "I was positive that my every word was repeated at parties all over Harlem and Brownsville. I mean they were friendly, but they made it clear that I was nothing but a white trampoline" (20–21). Rosen makes clear Bo's alien status, his irrelevance to the restless beat of the schoolyard game in which "everybody spent the next two hours trying to score as many points as possible and totally avoid any body contact" (32).

The clash of what Bo needs from the game and the game he is forced to play is focused in his personal duel with huge, ex-Harlem Globetrotter Tarzan Cooper who physically wants to crush him. As Bo says to his team sage, "Foothead" Jones, "getting my bones broken for some stupid ritual is low on the list . . . I don't need the game to get me out of a ghetto, right? I want it to be beauty and precision and grace . . . like a magic concert in the Fillmore East. . . . It's creation and energy and even a kind of low-grade communion" (149). Bo is denied this game and concludes with the view of a true outsider at the schoolyard: "I just can't be a member of the club that's on the floor now. Either I'll wait for my next, or I just won't play" (151). Bo wants a transcendent harmony from basketball on his terms but the Wellington Rifles provide other lessons of schoolyard survival and one-on-one magic. The gap between the white and black basketball cultures appears too wide for Rosen.

Rosen's second basketball novel, *A Mile Above the Rim* (1976), is dull and programmatic in comparison. Here he attempts the anatomy of the New York Stars' pro franchise, the structure associated with football fiction's obsession with the collective organization. *A Mile Above the Rim* focuses on three figures: Silky Sims, a vain, black superstar-to-be; Wayne Smalley, his venal young mediocrity of a coach; and generic white guard Dave Brooks, so "fundamentally sound" as to make readers crave more slammin' and jammin'. Rosen doesn't have the space to develop many of the characters because he is committed to the anatomy form. Brooks quits the game after Silky Sims wins the NBA title for the Stars at the buzzer with a rebound stuff against Kareem Abdul-Jabbar. Like Bo Lassner, Brooks won't be a member of this team at this time. Silky and Wayne Smalley take turns plotting to undercut one another. Drugs, women, and money dominate the narrative between games. Rosen has one puckish moment: in the box score of a playoff game is the insertion of "Lassner ——DID NOT PLAY——" for Utah. Bo remains faithful to his role.

Kaylin's *The Power Forward* is a psychological novel about black-white pathology that happens to choose basketball as a frame. *The Power Forward* is one of the most intriguing and ultimately frustrating novels in contemporary sports fiction. Kaylin's plot is instantly compelling: a veteran white pro basketball star modeled on Bill Bradley is suddenly confronted with his black contemporary from Brooklyn high school days, the extremely powerful and volatile Isiah "Muley" Bishop, who had been banned from organized basketball at age nineteen for supposed involvement in point-shaving scandals. Muley Bishop has spent over a decade clowning with a barnstorming team, the Ebony Pharoahs, while the Bradley figure, "Peso Pete" Pendleton, has become a Rhodes Scholar and respected small forward on the New York Heroes' NBLA championship team whose veteran starting five bear the initials of the early 1970s New York Knick starters, Dan Dryden (Dave DeBusschere), Del Bowie (Dick Barnett), and so on. Pendleton, a good liberal who hopes to get into politics after pro ball, is a cautious, cerebral player who has difficulty responding to any situation with sensuality or physical force. His marriage is sexless, his wife insecure about her own femininity. Into their lives come the visceral Muley Bishop and his bewitching sister, Masai, who tantalizes both Pete Pendleton and his wife, Ruth, and later seduces Ruth. The Bishops hide a terrible secret: Masai was gang-raped by Muley's high school teammates. Muley's fury and subsequent impregnating of his own sister, the resultant botched abortion and her mutilated genitalia are their desperate truths. Muley had allowed his name to be banned to protect his sister from public acknowledgment of the events as well as to protect himself from her threats to use the information to punish him.

Pete Pendleton gradually learns the facts of Muley Bishop's case and goes on a hunger strike to win Muley's reinstatement. Muley is finally signed with great fanfare by the Heroes to play power forward. By halftime of his first game, he has twenty-seven points, but he is an erratic defender and frequent fouler, nervous and highstrung. In the last quarter, he disputes a referee's call, gets more and more furious, and finally snaps. When he is ejected from the game, he begins to circle the floor braying "Hee Haw!", his comic routine from the Ebony Pharoahs. Police and photographers descend upon him, his teammates are stunned. Pete Pendleton attempts to speak to him in the locker room where he is coiled against the back wall.

Masai rushes in, beseeches the doctors to let her administer a tran-
quilizer shot to her brother, then plunges the needle straight into
Muley's chest. He dies.

"Bill Bradley" a guilty, impotent man? His wife in a lesbian
relationship with "Connie Hawkins'" or "Earl Manigault's" sister?
Death and madness in the fourth quarter at Madison Square Garden?
What's going on here?

What we have is a heavily plotted, ambitious attempt to portray
white-black relations though basketball and a racial doubling of mirror images and insecurities. The black Bishops hide a maimed and
vicious sexual past; the white Pendletons have no sexual life at all.
Pete "plays" rapist with Ruth under their beachfront cottage but she
is not aroused or amused. Pete would seduce Masai, but she is not a
whole woman. His relations with Muley have always been those in
which Muley's superior strength and power forced Pete to change
his "game" and become a "skilled machine," whereas Muley is a
physical marvel.

All Pete's skills—intricate patterns, constant movement, soft, precise shooting—are learned skills, almost code language for white
basketball virtues. Perhaps one reason the Bradley-era New York
Knicks were so apotheosized as a team was that, despite three black
starters, they played "white" and succeeded. The Knicks won not so
much with "white boss" style as with a cerebration and precision
that lacked any classic loose schoolyard moves. Pete Pendleton is a
spokesman for the end of that style: "The game's changing. As we
start fading away, no attempt is being made to replace us with
players like ourselves. Our kind has had its day, the deft and brainy"
(118). Instead, the move is to "racehorse kids," a pejorative here in a
passage where race is never mentioned but is heavily present.

Kaylin goes to lengths to underscore the similarities and differences between Pete's and Muley's games. Pete explains to Ruth, "I
play that kind of game, slipping around, moving without the ball,
because I'm that kind of guy. I'm not a crasher. I'm not a one-on-
oner. I'm a fitter-inner" (20). Whereas Pete "figured [Muley] to
weigh no less than 240, a massive man with a neck like a python"
(47), Muley "jumped like a big killer cat sailing into a tree, attaining
remarkable heights and hanging there for inordinate lengths of time"
(220–21). In contrast, Masai repeatedly tells Pete, "you're such a

cautious little person" and "poor tiny little white guy" (142, 147). The Bishops are almost caricatures of disturbed personalities from whom the Pendletons frequently recoil. With Masai as a maimed black killer lesbian, Kaylin has run out of negatives. Pete sees Masai suddenly "for one frozen moment as a demented child" (144); Pete tells Ruth the Bishops are "devious people. They're way off-center. I don't know what it is with either of them" (275). And neither does Kaylin, one suspects. Having created a sexually and racially powerful situation within basketball's current historicization, he fails to make any of the characters really gain reader knowledge or sympathy. Muley is an obscene, lumbering boar of a man; Masai and Ruth are fey and brittle. Another black character, Orville Enders, the antagonist in the Bishop family drama, is a sort of *deus ex auctoris,* a bloodless black stand-in for Pete Pendleton whom Kaylin can't bring himself to place in direct relation to Muley's initial demise. Pete Pendleton is wooden, a first-person narrator who proclaims his own flatness.

The repeated violence within Kaylin's plot is always performed by blacks against blacks. There is an uncomfortable evasion of responsibility, an absolution of whites from any sins other than lack of spontaneous sexuality and, by extension, hang time and aggressive power. (Two exceptions are Dan Dryden's wife, an eager sex manual devotee, and Jerry Maslow, a master-fixer from basketball scandals, yet another fictional stand-in for the real life Jack Molinas.) The ultimate feeling from *The Power Forward* is that its black characters are ripped off by a serious author not really in sympathy with their being. Muley and Masai destroy each other in terrible love and explosive anger: that, too, is a way to de-humanize them. The Pendletons simply go home to Old Harbor, Connecticut.

The Power Forward portrays white alienation in basketball by making it an example of the deeper alienation and fear of white impotency and black sexual power. The Bishops are a tragic if melodramatic pair of siblings, the Pendletons as drab as Pete protests they are. Working within the relationship of a "Bill Bradley" and a nightmare version of a "Connie Hawkins," Kaylin has exposed the rawest of issues that basketball at present plays out in American culture. Masai hectors Pete Pendleton to aid Muley: "What's the matter with you, Pete? Don't you know with you and Muley it's a two-way street?" (212). In basketball, as in racial conflict. Kaylin gets the game plan right, even if his execution and politics leave something to be desired.

Rosen's *Have Jump Shot, Will Travel* retained the authority of the black basketball culture with Bo Lassner an alien within it. His status as a "white trampoline" was more humorous than the stiff Pete Pendleton whose "kind has had its day." Kaylin reserves the authoritative voice within basketball for white culture: it is the Bishops in *The Power Forward* who are the aliens. These two attempts by white authors to deal with white dislocation within the sport will undoubtedly be followed by others. For now, readers must choose between Rosen who has all the good lines and Kaylin who has the shocking scenes. In the last analysis, Beckham in *Double Dunk,* by staying within the legend of one black player and in the schoolyard itself, has produced the authentic fictional documentary of contemporary basketball culture and has left the white authors to work out their problematic relations to that culture.

"I Have My Game": The Pursuit of Upward Space

WHAT ALL players, black and white, search for in basketball fiction is to get "inside" their game. They wish to lose themselves in a pattern, or to become the pattern as in ritual sport, where one impulse is to "make me other" (see chapter 5). Jake Baer in *The Best Ride to New York* states, "In all those parks and schoolyards and under all those sets of rules I have always played my game. . . . I always looked for different games to test my game in" (Levin 68). For black players, the goal is "upward space" where one can soar. For white players, it is more a sense of the "good space." Lacking the aesthetic (not to mention the physical ability) of flight, their game will be to play as a solitary within a reverie. The play-anti-heroism negations are coolly traversed in bliss, waiting for the Satori that heralds, "I Have My Game."

For white ballplayers, the shot itself is the key to beginning this transcendence. Jake Baer comments, "Some people have religion to believe in. . . . My jumpshot is what I've held onto" (Levin 75); Bo Lassner feels, "You don't have to see the hoop, or follow through, or even know where you are. . . . Then you silently tremble with the Presence as you watch it descend in a perfect parabola" (Rosen, *Have Jump Shot, Will Travel* 145); Elwood Baskin believes, "there was almost no relationship between the person I was before the jump shot and the person I was after" (Shainberg 30). As white players launch the ball into the air, they identify with that floating ease. They achieve the "upward space" through release of the shot which becomes an extension of self in the air, a seamless motion of player, ball, and hoop that approaches unity. Jake Baer "swirled in the lights with the smoke" and "was everywhere, all places, simultaneously all things. . . . a whole, specific, encapsulated, removed, contained secure within himself" (Levin 142).

A more ritualized variant of the personal game and of "upward space" is found in Gerald Duff's *Indian Giver* (1983) in which an Indian, Sam Houston Leaping Deer, goes from a reservation in Texas to play ball for the University of Illinois. Duff contrives to equate basketball at its best with the mystical ceremonies of the Alabama Coushatta tribe: "The hoop waited in its roundness, solid and unmoving, while all around it things moved and slid and fell away. [Its] plane was fixed parallel to the earth, matching the balance the Nation's elders claimed Abba Mikko had given the world to start it" (86–87). Sam ritually possesses the "good space" that, predictably, he does not find at Illinois. James Welch in *The Death of Jim Loney* (1979) more simply and effectively portrays his Jim Loney as an ex-high school basketball player, an Indian drifting in a quiet melancholy of depression and visions. Loney kills his ex-teammate, Marvin Pretty Weasel, in a tragic hunting accident and walks back to the reservation to await the tribal police and his last rites.

The quest for the personal game and for "upward space" is at vast remove from the other strong sports metaphor that grows from the playground/schoolyard, that of pride in competition. The search for the game and space is in pure flight from competition, a "freedom from," a play *beyond*. Yet this play takes on no socially utopian vision, no heroic struggle against the collective or its beleaguered members. Although basketball is a team sport, its fictional heroes are almost never team players, their poetry and art inimical to any collective praxis. An exception would be Shields' ace playmaker Belvyn Menkus in *Heroes,* who learned team play ironically when he "used to come home howling because [the black kids] let him keep playing only if he passed them the ball" (69). The flight from group responsibilities in basketball fiction is almost pathological, from Updike's Rabbit Angstrom in 1960 to basketball's fictional heroes in the present.

Shainberg's *One on One* features the most neurotic of basketball's individual heroes. Elwood Baskin confesses at the outset, "The truth about me, from any logical point of view, is that I'm too fucked up to be an athlete, too good an athlete to be a regular big man, too big to be a regular man" (13). Baskin is 6'9" and 245 pounds and about to play in his first college game for NYU against Duke in Madison Square Garden. He is the most heralded big man in the East since Lew Alcindor. The novel relates the events of game day but also swoops in and out of Baskin's mind and past, alternating his narration with commentary by his witnesses—mother, father, girlfriend, student acolytes, his psychiatrist, and a mad sculptor. Baskin is in considerable psychic distress with the various claims made on him. Basketball's flow is his refuge: "It's like finding the central current in a river and letting it carry you downstream. . . . The only thing you have to do is let it happen" (66).[2] Baskin's final quest for upward space is expressed by the sculptor who wants to catch him at the peak of his jump off the floor. Baskin has fantasized that, in a moment of renunciation, he froze in the air in Madison Square Garden but could not let the ball go and stayed suspended there as his teammates tugged on his legs. Chud the sculptor then conceives of sculpting the entire floor, two teams in action poses. Baskin imagines a mock-courtroom trial for his own murder at which Chud confesses, "To DO him! Yes, of course, the word no longer meant what it had before, not merely to preserve a figure in its motion . . . but only to *contain* it, contain him, remove him from time and space, from my own time, my own space, from his time and space" (195).

The death-in-plaster hallucination of Chud and Baskin is an extension of the artist's desire to wrest the hero out of time, akin to Meyer's aesthetic in Coover's *Gloomy Gus*. Chud would capture Baskin as a performance artist in the impermanency of a permanant upward leap, what Morris expressed through Lawrence's daring half volleys in *The Huge Season*. Shainberg provides a most positive conclusion, similar to Coover's pitch-catch ritual at the end of *The*

Universal Baseball Association. Baskin, having mastered himself playing all the roles of evasion through aesthetics, as "one *commenting* on one," will begin his career as superstar: "The smile stayed with me as I walked toward the locker room, spread through my body while I dressed, and grew until it filled the Garden when I came out on the court" (206). The realistic novel that Shainberg did *not* write is about to begin. Baskin has his game.

To be in the game at an intense level is to become the game itself, as Jake Baer knows: "Suddenly, at some point, I don't know when . . . it had me someplace I had never been. I was still in the game and isolated from what was outside it; but I had gone one step farther —and was isolated in it" (Levin 141). An anonymity reigns here, akin to what Rabbit Angstrom achieves at the end of *Rabbit, Run,* a safe haven, a positive *ilinx,* a calm at the eye ("I") of the action.

White players are "in" the game at their best; black players are above it. To "stay up forever" in basketball means something very different than in baseball. In basketball, black players defy gravity and space rather than time. Transcendence will be active creation in the air through the body. White players invest the ball with their body's oneness. They soar in imaginative unity. Black players in basketball fiction actualize the dream: they float *with* the ball. They don't need to be sculpted in "upward space." They get there on their own. Mack Davis in *Big Man* exults in floating up to pick a dime off the top of the backboard: "I could of died right then. I die happy" (Neugeboren 61). Yet it is Beckham's Earl Manigault in *Double Dunk* who fully expresses the creative limits of "upward space" for the black basketball player.

Upward space for Earl Manigault is where you "do something spectacular"; "this is your dance, your expression of style and freedom" (29–30). This space is where he is masterful: "Most of all you stay in the air, hovering, floating, gliding, turning in circles. Nobody you've seen yet can get as high and stay as long as you have been able to" (72). His double dunk is creative basketball genius; he is the first player ever to think of it, much less achieve it, an insouciance of gravity-defying physical skill. Beckham, however, pointedly links the "high" of Earl's greatest plays to the depths of his subsequent heroin addiction when his basketball career is thwarted: "High is so nice. . . . You float. . . . You can't help but dunk the ball from way up here in the sky" (165). Stumbling through the Harlem streets as junkie, pusher, and petty thief, Earl tries at times to soar at the playground but he is thickened and slowed, a pitiful sight. Finally, he quits "cold turkey" in a detoxification cell in New York City's Tombs, with visions of his flying dunks to sustain him in his physical agony.

The catalyst that makes him at last move to salvage his life at age twenty-four is the story of Harlem schoolboy basketball star Kenny Bellinger, an addict at sixteen, dead after an attempted robbery when he desperately jumped fifteen feet across rooftops in a last effort to escape the police: "You can see his body hurtling through the air with the chimneys and antennas in the background. Hurtling and falling to the sidewalk" (203). The nightmare of Kenny Bellinger's death converts the "flying" of the great schoolyard player to "falling," the "downward space" into squalid death. This denial of flight, of free space, moves Earl to try and recapture space of his own. Beckham finds the way to use his strongest basketball metaphor to unite his hero's creativity and the tragedy of Kenny Bellinger in a wasted and hopeless environment. Beckham's *Double Dunk* reminds us that the magic of flying, slamming, and jamming is in response to the sorrow of deprivation, frustration, and loss. Whites may choose the inner game of transcendence in basketball fiction. Blacks see that game as necessity. For them to be earthbound here at this time, in this urban America, is to be in want.

Upward Space: Updike's Rabbit Trilogy

JOHN UPDIKE has worked out the most intricate basketball symbology of any American author. In *Rabbit, Run* (1960), he was the first American novelist to realize the aesthetics of the sport in fictional narrative. Indeed, no single work since *Rabbit, Run* has been as suggestive in this regard. Updike began with no models, with only the strong school sports tradition of the ex–schoolboy star. Thus his conceptions have almost a pre-basketball lore-and-legend caste. Furthermore, the basketball material is always at the behest of his search for a self-transcendence. Updike's fiction is created in response to his reading of Kierkegaard and Karl Barth rather than through interest in the basketball scandals or in schoolyard mythology. His basketball features set shots made by white high school players in the late 1940s. Yet everything that later authors would come to understand about flow, upward space, and the interior game may be found in Harry "Rabbit" Angstrom. Updike's second and third novels in the *Rabbit* trilogy, *Rabbit Redux* (1971) and *Rabbit is Rich* (1981), extend and continue the conception of upward space in the metaphors of "outer" and "downward" space, respectively. These novels together comprise a unique attempt by Updike to take a single American male through three decades (the 1950s, 1960s, 1970s) of his adult life, to integrate Harry "Rabbit" Angstrom's personal history with the larger American history of the era. Updike has checked in with Rabbit in each succeeding decade to see how things are going with him and, by extension, with America itself.

Updike has been a traditional realistic author with playful yearnings. He can write, "What we need is a greater respect for reality, its secrecy, its music. Too many people are studying maps and not enough are visiting places" (*Picked-Up Pieces* 503), while also writing, "I find I cannot imagine being a writer without wanting somehow to play, to make these patterns, to insert these secrets into my books" (499). He has commented that "art is part game, part grim erotic tussle with Things As They Are; the boxes must have holes where reality can look out and readers can look in" (208), while countering with the statement that "in each of my books there has been in my mind at least, a different experiment, an adventure" (494). His sense of play can be set against his commitment to a writing style that he defines as "pictorial, not only in its groping for visual precision but in the way the books are conceived as objects in space, with events and persons composed within them like shapes on a canvas" (35). Perhaps Updike's great ability to present realistic scenes in a multi-dimensional painter or photographer's conception has been the single most inhibiting factor in his reluctance to break a commitment to realism. Updike is contemporary American Fiction's finest creator of textures and his decision to work within fiction that he has lovingly described as "earthbound" does not prevent him from being deeply engaged with the aesthetics of space and its transcendence while he is committed to a *mimetic* mode.

Updike has long shown an intense interest in the games of American sport as well as in the game of novelistic play. His *New Yorker* essay, "Hub Fans Bid Kid Adieu," on the occasion of Ted Williams' last game for the Boston Red Sox in 1960, is one of the finest pieces of American sports journalism. He has written short lyric sketches on the glories of golf. As novelist, he constructed a self-reflexive playful frame for *Bech: A Book* (1970) and a sly narrative persona in *The Coup* (1978). He created a novel with its own mythic analogue in *The Centaur* (1963) and wrote of suburban games at the center of society in *Couples* (1968). In addition, he has reviewed a wide range of Continental and Third World fiction of experimental nature and has published review essays on fiction's master-players, Jorge Luis Borges and Nabokov.

This discussion will be limited to the *Rabbit* trilogy as it depicts Updike's spatialization of basketball and golf and the resultant implications for his work. *Rabbit, Run* explicitly comments on several familiar themes of American sports fiction. Rabbit Angstrom is an individual, isolated American hero very much in the tradition of American transcendental seekers: one, who as Ralph Waldo Emerson wrote in "The American Scholar," will "plant himself indomitably on his instincts, and there abide, the huge world will come round to him" (79). Rabbit is the "natural" who is seeking space in which to live and move. He is also a sports hero pursued by an entire society of witnesses to his heroism, including his family, mistress, minister, and ex-basketball coach, all of whom seek the riddle of his special inarticulate grace. Also, Rabbit represents yet another dead-end of the American School Sports Hero: a twenty-six-year-old ex-high school basketball scoring champion who now demonstrates a kitchen gadget in the window of a department store. Rabbit has been a star and now he is nothing at all. He retains his skills but has no game to perform in.

Updike uses basketball to underscore two essential patterns in *Rabbit, Run*. First, Rabbit's basketball "touch" is enlarged by Updike to become Rabbit's fundamental way to relate to his physical and moral environment. Rabbit "touches" everyone in the novel, either through their identification with his physical prowess or his spiritual rebellion or by actual sexual "touch" as with his wife, Janice, and his mistress, Ruth. Yet that "touch" is often as alienating and defeating with people as it is magical with objects.[3] Secondly, Updike has spun a web of nets and circles in the novel that begins most fundamentally with the basketball rim and net, but which then ranges far in its metamorphosis toward the achievement of unity in the sexual act and culminates in the ensnaring nets of a middle-class society that would enclose Rabbit. Finally, Rabbit is stumbling toward a perfect circle of knowledge and peace.

Initially, Rabbit's touch is what makes him special. He has been a star and now he is decidedly second-rate at almost everything in his life. The novel opens with Updike's version of a schoolyard game where "boys are playing basketball around a telephone pole with a basket bolted to it" (*Rabbit, Run* 7). As Rabbit plays with the kids, "he sinks shots one-handed, two-handed, underhanded, flat-footed, and out of the pivot, jump and set. Flat and soft the ball lifts. That his touch still lives in his hands elates him. He feels liberated from long gloom" (9).

Rabbit often experiences literally through his skin: "He now and then touches with his hand the rough bark of a tree . . . to give himself the small answer of a texture" (17); "At the same time he feels abnormally sensitive on the surface, as if his skin is thinking. The steering wheel is thin as a whip in his hands" (35). Touch, which would later become *the* religion in basketball fiction, here provides the mystical clarity: "When he was hot he could see the separate threads wound into the strings looping the hoop" (35). Touch also isolates him within his body: " 'all I know is what feels right' " (252), Rabbit can say, but he also states, "all I know is what's inside *me*. That's all I have' " (91). When Rabbit "has his game," touch internalizes all his experience, "he's safe inside his own skin" (105) in retreat where he is jiggling and lifting his hands "as though thoughts were basketballs" (107), the equation made explicit.

Along with Rabbit's sense of touch is Updike's pattern of circles and nets created to fuse Rabbit's perception of his sport, his sexual life, and his religious yearnings.[4]. The basketball rim and net are explicitly sexual in Updike's description: "The ball rocketing off the crotch of the rim" (7); "It drops into the circle of the rim, whipping the net with a ladylike whisper" (8); "There was you and sometimes the ball and then the hole, the high perfect hole with its pretty skirt of net" (35).

The net also becomes the web of responsibilities he falls into and then escapes from, exactly as a ball will be held up momentarily on its flight through the circle of the rim by the net before release into the hands of a waiting player. To achieve the circle, to score a goal, to be held momentarily in the net's thrall, and then to be off running again is the path of the ball; Updike equates Rabbit's passage with that of the ball itself. The nets close in on him in varying mutations. As he considers flight from Janice, his pregnant wife, "the problem knits in front of him and he feels sickened by the intricacy" (16). As he looks at a road map, "the names melt away and he sees the map whole, a net, all those red lines and blue lines and stars, a net he is somewhere caught in" (34). In exasperation, Rabbit rips the map and wads it into a ball, touch providing a comforting circle. As he flees south from Pennsylvania through Maryland, he thinks of the world of responsibilities he has left behind as "a net of telephone calls and hasty trips . . . an invisible net overlaying the steep streets" (37). After the death of his baby daughter, Rabbit is the only mourner genuinely moved at the grave site. He panics one final time at the net of family grief and accusation and runs blindly away into a dense forest. While running uphill toward the road and to light, the forest greets him with another net: "Such an unnatural darkness, clogged with spider-fine twigs that finger his face incessantly"(246). This "network" plagues Rabbit in his last reckless attempt toward "upward space."

The circle of the rim likewise mutates into crescents on bedroom wallpaper, the circular black ears of the head mouseketeer on the Mickey Mouse Club, a hem of a slip, the half-moons on Rabbit's fingernails, the seductive sun of the South, a stained glass church window, and, most centrally, Rabbit's heart, which is alluded to constantly throughout the novel (54, 65, 73, 135). In the novel's final scene, the images of nets and circles come together in a crescendo. The image of a cold circle with nets and a hole in the middle of the net signifies the "hardness of heart" which is part of the novel's inscription. Yet a blank heart is signified as well, a void or zero at the core of Rabbit's being. Within the heart is a net but within the net is a circle. Within that circle, one can posit a net as well in an infinite regress of circles and nets, nets and circles. In Rabbit's life, sexual intercourse creates the nets of children and marital responsibilities which lead to renewed desire outside these nets and thus to sex and new nets (the pregnancy of his mistress, Ruth). The circle and net imagery is relentless and constant. No contemporary American author other than Updike has come close to developing the elemental basketball symbols of circle and net in their sexual and spatial configurations and in their adaptation to describe the social space of a restrictive community.

Rabbit constantly seeks the space that all good shooters need, the opening to get off the shot. His evasive pattern as a cornered Rabbit resembles nothing so much as a basketball player running his patterns, shaking himself loose for space, using other bodies to set picks and screens, and fouling most egregiously when he must. Rabbit goes one-on-one not only with Janice and Ruth in a sexual sense, but also with male figures—ex-teammate Ronnie Harrison, coach Tothero, and Reverend Eccles. In most basketball fiction, such space as Rabbit seeks is primarily the freedom to move beyond constraint. Freedom as an unexamined goal is the conceptual limit of most basketball fiction. Yet for Updike, *upward* space has specific theological associations. As Rabbit stands with Ruth atop Mt. Judge, Updike writes, "His day had been bothered by God. . . . It seems plain, standing here, that if there is this floor there is a ceiling, that the true space in which we live is upward space" (96).

At the novel's conclusion, Rabbit runs for the last time down one street of row houses after another, seeking refuge within himself. He thinks, "Goodness lies inside, there is nothing outside, those things he was trying to balance have no weight. He feels his inside as very real suddenly, a pure blank space in the middle of a dense net" (254). As in an earlier dream, Rabbit's heart is a labyrinth of self-pity and sympathy. He hides in this heart which is a final, canceled subjective circle. Finally, Updike returns to one last basketball image to describe Rabbit's escape:

> It's like when they heard you were great and put two men on you and no matter which way you turned you bumped into one of them and the only thing to do was to pass. So you passed and the ball belonged to the others and your hands were empty and the men on you looked foolish because in effect there was nobody there. (255)

Society in the arena has hemmed him in, but Rabbit renounces the net of defenders by passing off. The novel's last net encircles the "pure blank space." If he cannot achieve the circle, he will leave the center of the game. He has no responsibility, he is no one; the player without the ball is invisible. Rabbit has disappeared into the inwardly spiraling circle, the controlling symbol of the novel. A representative basketball image has claimed him, and a most familiar one in basketball fiction: renunciation of the society in isolated selfhood "inside" the game.

In this realistic novel, Updike is moving his existential hero toward a structural fate. Rabbit is immersed in the very sporting symbols that have given him creative life: touch and the circles and nets. Like Gary Harkness in *End Zone* and J. Henry Waugh in *The Universal Baseball Association,* Rabbit disappears into the primary sports images of the narrative. Gary Harkness slips into what appears to be a coma, the burden of consciousness and language in nuclear war and football having become too great. J. Henry Waugh is a creative suicide, having lost his son and control of his baseball history, which reels on without him. Rabbit, too, tentatively disappears. Updike's last line ends, "he runs. Ah: runs. Runs" (255) as Rabbit first grasps the imperative of physical running, then the exhilaration of being free, and finally the promise of a larger search, though all of this final intimation comes out of a "sweet panic," instinct rather than free will. Rabbit is a stubborn, blind survivor guided by the only reality he knows: the touch and feel of the game in pursuit of the circle that promises intimation of upward space.

Basketball is only incidental to the structure of Updike's sequels, *Rabbit Redux* and *Rabbit is Rich.* Yet insofar as Harry Angstrom is still the subject of the novels, he retains the legacy of his past and its intimacies felt most strongly through sport. At the outset of *Rabbit Redux,* where Rabbit is now thirty-six instead of twenty-six, he muses about basketball: "The game different now, everything the jump shot, big looping hungry blacks lifting and floating there a second while a pink palm as long as your forearm launched the ball" (*Rabbit Redux* 18). Rabbit feels cut off from his sport as he does from most primary experience in the novel. Yet blacks and "lifting," "floating," and "launching" are central to the novel's imagery. The "upward space" of *Rabbit Redux* is that of outer space itself, constantly invoked through Updike's controlling imagery of the Apollo 11 trip to the moon. The novel is bathed in a cool, pale light, both that of the moon and the television screen. The colors are starkly white-blond, as in the hair and skin of Jill, the runaway teenager Rabbit takes in after Janice walks out on him, and black as in Skeeter, the young black activist who also comes to live with Rabbit by a series of events and who attempts Rabbit's political education.

Rabbit Redux is a despairing book. Rabbit thrashes in the bewildering culture of the late 1960s, an American patriot without a rationale; he is a large, white, soft, pale, washed-out man who does not play, who in fact has lost sexual desire as well as existential yearning. In *Rabbit Redux,* upward space is reserved for the bland, technological astronauts. Apollo 11 lifts off, "the swift diminishment into a retreating speck, a jiggling star" (7), repeating the language of Rabbit's memorable golf shot in *Rabbit, Run,* but now there is no exultation and no freedom. Watching the moon launch on television, "the men dark along the bar murmur among themselves. They have not been lifted. They are left here" (7). There is no religious leap for the believer, no transcendent ball floating toward basket or cup on the green.

Thus Rabbit's spiritlessness in *Rabbit Redux* negates the natural, instinctual patterns of *Rabbit, Run.* Updike might have invented Skeeter as a representative of the black basketball culture and have Rabbit engage him on that plane but Updike was seemingly not interested in such a structure. Skeeter only makes a few disparaging remarks about Rabbit's earthbound set shot: "Shit, boy, a one-armed dwarf could have blocked it" (272); they have a desultory scrimmage. Skeeter is a slender, nervous figure and no athlete. He represents the violent world of the television screen, of racial disturbance and Vietnam come home to Rabbit. Skeeter is the dramatic presence in the household, turning Jill on to drugs, giving manic history lectures from a revolutionary perspective. Skeeter casts Jill and Rabbit in a master-slave ritual where Rabbit plays a black man helplessly watching a black girl (played by Jill) be ravished by a white man (Skeeter). In this masque, Updike has done well what Kaylin strove for in the diminution of Pete Pendleton by Masai and Muley Bishop in *The Power Forward.* Rabbit is rendered impotent and immobile as he mimes black sexuality and rage. Skeeter is often moving and profound as he lectures; just as often, he is shrill and pathetic. An unstable redeemer and seeker after truth, Skeeter has replaced Rabbit in that role from *Rabbit, Run. Skeeter* runs in *Rabbit Redux.* Rabbit is left behind to clean up the mess of Jill's death by fire, his son's devastation, his ruined house. At novel's end, he and wife Janice have tentatively reconciled. He goes to meet her in his old high school athletic jacket: "Zipped, it binds across his chest and belly, but he begins that way" (392).

Rabbit is not pursuing any game nor projecting into an upward space in *Rabbit Redux*. That imagery is canceled for him while the floating he does is in melancholy sex with the haunted Jill before the television's glow. Rabbit is not connected or coordinated with his body or instincts. Jill is a lost daughter, the drowned baby Becky from *Rabbit, Run,* whom he is doomed to lose again and again, partly through his own guilt.

Updike does give Jill a lovely speech in which she espouses an amended Schillerian view of *man* as *play* as the mediation: "Man is a mechanism for turning things into spirit and spirit into things" (159). Too often, men imprint on the creation in negative ways, but for Updike, the artist leaves his imprint in whatever medium in a positive vein. In summation, Jill believes, "anything that is good is in ecstasy. The world is what God made and it doesn't stink of money, it's never tired, too much or too little, it's always exactly full. The second after an earthquake, the stones are calm. Everywhere is *play*" (159). A world "always exactly full" is indeed an ecstatic *mimesis* for Updike, who sees God's aesthetic as impeccable. Man is the mediating force of play in his actions while God plays in the natural world. Skeeter and Jill are the ministerial voices in *Rabbit Redux,* exiled and doomed, while Rabbit listens and learns, but cannot play in any freedom.

Updike here appears to be adopting a view of play closely akin to that of Gadamer in *Truth and Method* when Gadamer wrote, "Nature, inasmuch as it is without purpose or intention, as it is without exertion, a constantly self-renewing Play, can appear as a model for art" (94). Gadamer's strongest view of play is that of the game itself, an object–play that is between interpreters or dialogicians and is what we as players are caught *in*. Jill's vision of a "world always exactly full" is Updike's most intense phrasing of his commitment to realism, to earthbound glories in a union of art and nature. Such commitment is the dialectical opposite to his perception of "upward space" as a positive quest through basketball in *Rabbit, Run*. The play of the world in a Gadamerian sense lives in tension with the aesthetics of transcendence described in Rabbit's golf shot in *Rabbit, Run*. Thus Updike can at once imagine a creative, solitary, playful subject, as in *Rabbit, Run,* as well as imagine a *mimetic,* objective, play-ful world in *Rabbit Redux*. It remained for Updike to yoke his two visions of sport and play to some fuller synthesis of the individual and the collective in *Rabbit is Rich*.

In *Rabbit is Rich,* "upward space" has become "downward space." Rabbit broods more about the dead and begins to confront his own death. Basketball has been erased from his instinctive responses. Rather, it is golf once again that dominates the spatial conception of sport. *Rabbit is Rich* finds Harry Angstrom a "success" at last, a stolid, middle-aged married man who has taken over his dead father-in-law's Toyota dealership. His intimations are new: "The great thing about the dead, they make space" (5). However, that space now is defined with reference to the earth. For Rabbit, things are "a soft wedge shot away" (13); golf gives him the "bliss that used to come thinking of women" (50)—it is the game of his middle years. Rabbit now "wants less. Freedom, that he always thought was outward motion, turns out to be this inner dwindling" (97). Updike stipulates Rabbit's expiration of sense, of desire, as a liberation, though such relaxation may be just a more poetic version of middle-class security.

Rabbit seeks no transcendence: "He doesn't want to think about the invisible anyway, every time in his life he's made a move toward it somebody has gotten killed" (162). Golf provides a "downward space" worthy of Whitman in *Leaves of Grass:* "The fairway springy beneath his feet blankets the dead" (177). Hit *down,* he tells himself where "Dead Skeeter roams below, cackling" (178–79). To look up is "dizzying and terrible" (181). At night, he masturbates by thrusting upward in bed against the (winding) sheet (191) in Updike's brilliant yoking of "upward space" and mortality. As a boy, Rabbit had felt God "spread in the dark above his bed." Then, at puberty, "He entered into the blood and muscle and nerve as an odd command and now he had withdrawn . . . but for a calling card left in the pit of the stomach, a bit of lead true as a plumb bob pulling Harry down toward all those leaden dead in the hollow earth below" (231).

Harry "Rabbit" Angstrom has come back down through desire and his pursuit of upward space to the true knowledge of how and where "the world is always exactly full," to where we all ultimately model the certainty of death. Updike had intimated this curve and downward return at the climax of that first extraordinary golf shot in *Rabbit, Run* two decades before where Rabbit's ball "with a kind of visible sob takes a last bite of space before vanishing in falling" (*Rabbit, Run* 113). By the conclusion of *Rabbit is Rich*, Rabbit's triumphant "That's *it!*", so spontaneously expressed to Eccles in *Rabbit, Run* after the golf shot, has been matured in sadness and contains much more than natural athletic skill but is encompassed by nature, which is pronounced in its full passage. "*It*" has been both magic and *mimetic* in expressing transcendence and mortality.

Updike stretches the aesthetic potential of sports such as basketball and golf but always in the service of more fully portraying both an American hero and his societal relations. As Updike deepens Rabbit's perception of his own passage from novel to novel, he allows the reader a similar interpretive delight that comes from seeing familiar sporting enthusiasms depicted in growing complexity. Here are sport and play in fiction at their best.

Conclusion

BASKETBALL FICTION is still largely a potential sports fiction genre. With the exception of Updike, basketball fiction does not have its Malamud, Roth, Coover, or DeLillo, nor does it have its *Bang the Drum Slowly* or *Semi-Tough*. Basketball is present tense, flow, wordless, and transcendent. It does not lend itself easily to fiction which is evocative of past and future, serial, linguistic, and realistic. Yet the present position of basketball in American culture suggests future fictional riches. For white players, basketball is a mystical experience, for black players, a cultural event. A consequence of white withdrawal from basketball is their impulse to take the game with them, to privatize it in possession: "I have my game." A consequence of black domination within basketball is the tendency toward stereotypical figures within the sports spectacle, public characters objectified without private dimension: the schoolyard game.

Basketball's economic and social myths need to be explored in this present context. How will white alienation and black over-identification be conceptualized by white and black authors? What will be the ironies inherent in such fiction? Some white pioneer re-integrating a future NBA? Black players renouncing basketball as racially demeaning? What aesthetic will be demanded as white and black authors play between residual and dominant practice in the battle for upward space and cultural definition?

Conclusion

SUCH A SEMANTICS as I have proposed in the introduction and used throughout this book inevitably passes for a variant of a Hegelian universal history project, one that would contain a built-in drama of an individual journeying from initial questioning through diverse experiences to estrangements and conflicts, crises and spiritual deaths, to a final recovery in self-knowledge. Such a structure is almost inevitable when animating any fictional text with characters. Sports narratives appear particularly suggestive for fiction. Sports themselves provide dramas through their own rules, field dynamics, versions of plot, and inherent thematics. Not all sports fiction begins with play or returns to it; novels cut into the potentially cyclical structure at various junctures. Some authors illuminate a corner of the sport-and-play configuration, such as commodity reification (Gent) or anti-heroism (Exley) or female play in response to the dominant (Levin). Some authors and their characters literally wallow or bellow in anger in such corners. An author such as Kesey, more obsessed with freedom, plays his characters toward transcendence. Coover, a Promethean at the heart of his talent, wants to display the full panoply of his characters' relations through sport and play and drives the metaphors of the imagination and the social configurations of sport as far as they can go.

In sports fiction, characters cannot simply rest in a play space or an anti-heroism, but must move out again into time, space, and history where the imperative of such struggle is itself competition. To know "what is me" and "what is not me" is always an alteration in cycles: not a final retreat into play or art but a coming out again as well, a process wherein a character intimates that "the true is the whole." Such a journey recalls the "approach to the sacred" that my earlier volume characterized Hemingway and Faulkner taking through sport; repetitive, symbolic, formal, patterned, ceremonial; in short, play formalized in ritual.[1] Such play is often a strategy to counter the oppression of the "whole" through substitution and deferrals, a control of creative time, whereas sport is often a journey through real time managed in the game, a search for the possibility of control through the larger pattern that has immediate social and cultural relevance.

The dominant structure in sports fiction is the *collective sports heroism* that has as its contrary the residual *individual sports heroism,* as well as its implied opposite, the personal revolutionary critique of *anti-heroism,* an emergent practice, a potential alternative that would dismantle the dominant structure. *Play* fuels this revolt in re-presenting rather than in posing agonistic roles. Yet American sports fiction also models our Gadamerian sense that we are caught in the game, sometimes joyfully, sometimes angrily, but at play in a world that is also playing us in its totality. Sports fiction portrays a world of rules and competition as well as a world of internal and external reward. Sports fiction portrays a world of both positive and negative individualism and community.

The form of contemporary sports fiction has been quite traditional for the most part. Although the time period spanned in this study has covered a shift from high modernism to various post-modernisms, the fiction of sport and play has not been very experimental. In what remains the best attempt to classify the various games of recent fiction, Robert Detweiler in 1976 suggested that "contemporary American sports fiction is the most conventional of all ludic fiction" (52). His statement is valid, perhaps most fundamentally because of the relentlessly empirical quality of sports narratives' unfolding, its mimetic necessities, its preordained narrative structures. It could be argued that while the sports fiction most dialectically engaged with a powerful play spirit has provided sports fiction's finest achievements (Malamud, Roth, DeLillo, Kesey, Coover), the majority of sports fiction has been perhaps less interested in foregrounding play than the general run of contemporary fiction has as a whole.

Within this general estimate, the different narratives examined here under the categories of the individual sports hero, the collective sports hero, and the anti-hero exhibit some general structural qualities and preoccupations. The sports fiction of chapters 1–4 is quite naturalistic and realistic in presentation, depicting archaic and residual sporting practices in a contemporary world that has lost its relation to nature and to a primal or primary arena. The narration of ritual sports fiction in particular is individualized and inquisitive of heroic conduct. It along with the sports fiction of chapters 7–8 is concerned with what Brian McHale has called epistemological modernist preoccupations, some of which are "How can I interpret this world of which I am a part?" "What am I in it?" "How does the object of knowledge change from knower to knower?" (9). School sport and witness fiction is the most subject-oriented sports fiction, producing novels of sensibility, frame narration, and personal testament from Knowles through Exley to Ford. More intimately, the play responses to the competitive dominant of the heroes and heroines of Kesey, Coover, Towne, and Levin (chapters 5–6) bracket the threats to individual freedom and survival with powerful mimetic performance.[2]

The team sport chapters (9–13), chronicling the collective sports hero focus more specifically on large game structures and therefore more on object-play, the athlete or player in the social and historical world and the resultant tension there. Such fiction would appear to afford the opportunity to ask the more ontological, postmodernist questions, such as "What is a world?" "Which world is this?" "What happens when different kinds of worlds are placed in confrontation?" (McHale 10). Yet only baseball fiction has actually done this to any appreciable extent. Football fiction (chapter 9), like its naturalistic counterpart, boxing fiction (chapter 4), has stayed between the lines/ropes empirically, wondering "how to live in it," not questioning its premises for the most part, except in the novels of Coover, Whitehead, and DeLillo (chapter 10), where the very principles of collision and world-scrutiny get a metaphysical vantage point on the realistic poetics of the football fiction described in chapter 9. Basketball fiction (chapter 13) is primarily narrated in first person and is subject-centered. Basketball is the team sport most individualized in an epistemological quest, its narratives still very much in the modernist preoccupation of "What am I in this world?"

Baseball fiction (chapters 11–12) appears to take its cue from baseball itself to provide something for every spectator-reader in the past several decades. Timeless baseball with its inner geometry and outward space invites world-modeling and counter-history as Coover, Roth, Neugeboren, Charyn, Kinsella, and Willard have made clear. Baseball is the sports subject of postmodernist fictional choice well into the contemporary era. Yet baseball fiction is capacious enough to include high modernist myth-questing (Malamud and descendants) and a firm legacy of realistic coming-of-age narrative (Harris and descendants) as well.

Finally, legacies *are* authorial as well as generic. For example, in the authorial genealogy of the sports fiction subject, Fitzgerald's true heir is Updike, who in his interest in school sport has continued in a vein of romantic nostalgia to write of the tensions between the gifted sensual player and his culture. Hemingway bequeathed different things to different authors in the contemporary fiction of sport and play. Mailer intuits Hemingway's paranoia, defenses, and dominant maleness. Gent and other football and boxing authors tell us how to "take it" in the body's defeat, while DeLillo knows the terror of minimal language zones, of "what is left out" and of the silent screams we come to hear there. Lardner's comic realism is the satiric legacy to Harris and Jenkins, the wide commonality of a much-loved American voice and sub-ject matter. This comedy's darker counterpart is the tragi-comedy of Kesey and Coover, sports fiction's master-players, whose bit-ter mirth reigns over universe-making that dazzles and moves us. Such play is Faulknerian and partakes of both the comic mythog-raphy of *The Hamlet* and the sacred ontogeny of *Go Down, Moses*.

The author's reign as player is both literal and temporal with occasional acknowledgement of self and reader in play. When Faulkner drew his map of Yoknapatawpha County in 1936 for *Absalom, Absalom!*, he signed it, "William Faulkner, Sole Owner & Proprietor," most likely Coover's inspiration for the full title of *The Universal Baseball Association*, which adds *Henry J. Waugh, Prop*. Such calling of attention to the author's domain is matched in Faulkner by acknowledgement of the reader's partnership in the game of the novel. When Shreve McCannon and Quentin Compson fashion one of the narratives of the Sutpen tragedy in Chapter 8 of *Absalom, Absalom!*, they compete in their Harvard rooms as they embellish the story. At one juncture, Shreve ur-gently and simply asks, "Let me play a while now" (280). Shreve's statement underscores the shared nature of producing the reality of any text that lies between the author and reader. Such self-consciousness of that inter-play is a cornerstone of postmodern fictional experiment and of an entire reader-response school of contemporary literary criticism. A remaining question in the analysis of sports fiction would be to inquire if there is anything unique about the poetics of both creating and reading the play and sport fiction text. Such an inquiry will only be sketched here.

Sport represented in a novel is clearly a mixture of conventional and inventional elements. Novelists may use sport as a formal element to discuss crises of heroism and spectating in society or as a way to speak of society's economic and social relations. A sport's given structures and symbols may intrigue an author's aesthetic sense of time and space as well as enhance the terms of the dialectic of sport and novelistic play. All fiction about sport is an individual authorial representation of a cultural representation. Any narrative portraying sport is already initially reflexive, con-taining a textual copy of the sport in all its structures and formal elements, directed back to its likeness with the sport providing a dramatic center of recognition for the reader. The performance of the sport in sports fiction expands to fill much of the narrative space in the simplest of such texts which function as little more than the transmission of sports reality. In the more complex fictional usage of sport, symbolic and formal properties of the sport expand markedly, less to fill the novel's action than to map the structure of the novel's world and perhaps shape its linguistic structure as well. The clearest examples are Coover's *The Universal Baseball Association,* DeLillo's *End Zone,* and Updike's *Rabbit, Run.*

Ultimately an author's formal aim in any narrative is to allow readers to recognize through the text a world that the author represents in mimetic gesturing while also challenging the reader with a re-imagined subjective model of that world.[3] The reader must stay in the reader's game to perceive the game in/of the arena/novel. For example, Faulkner in "The Bear" invokes the "ancient and immitigable rules" (192) of the hunt that must be followed in ritual, even as he radically alters rules in his fiction *about* the hunt which breaks up traditions of chronology, plotting, and dramatic tension. Likewise, Faulkner telescopes the total curve of the sport-author-text-reader relation in the opening of "The Bear." The men of Jefferson, Mississippi, gather each fall in the hunt to participate in "the yearly pageant rite of the old bear's furious immortality" (194), which Faulkner calls "the best game of all, the best of all breathing," ritual sport made actual. The legends surrounding the animal and hunt are "the best of all talking" (191), the sports fiction narrative itself, the oral history re-imagined as text. Finally, the tale of the hunt is "forever the best of all listening" (192), the good talk around the campfire that becomes the reader's active participation with sport and narrative.

Thus the game of the novel is produced somewhere between the "talking" of the novel and the "listening" of the reader, between the author's text and the reader's experience, the processes that sport, play, and their narrative transformations show in such an intense light. The player or spectator always has images in front of him. Readers must imagine their context and relationships as well. The reader finally integrates his familiarity with the rules of the sport with the author's complication of all rules to, in

Coover's phrase, "return home with new complexities" (*Pricksongs and Descants* 77), a succinct description of not only the rhythm of Coover's own sports fiction, but of the dialogics of fiction itself. Sports fiction is *not* a genre, unique in itself, as much as sport *in* fiction is a structure, a symbolic universe, a referential activity in society, a competitive paradigm, a heroic conferral, a shaping against mortality. Sport in a novel becomes an inner environment in which one may grasp its relation to other worlds of experience, beginning with its effect on our bodies and moving toward realms of the spirit.

Play is what the Western liberal democratic system would begin with in monadic, individualistic freedom from libertarians through existentialists. This conception of play is anathema to a Marxist hermeneutic descended from Hegelian misgivings that would describe freedom as achieved only at the utopian moment of a collective partial liberation from necessity. This fundamental ideological debate between freedom as origin and freedom as goal is a wider contextual and historical version of the split identified by Derrida in "Structure, Sign, and Play" between the play toward origins and the play beyond sure substitution. Marxists score the capitalist collective model and its fragile idealism about individual liberties and believe the whole individual-collective dialectic itself to be defective and deluding. Play comes under strong attack from Marxists as apolitical, private, and "humanizing" unless, as Marcuse and Jameson point out, it can be enlisted in the service of some larger liberation.[4] At the same time, play has always been under attack by generations of Western capitalist writers who criticize play for being not serious enough in the realm of acquisition, production, and consumption. Play in the fascinating American dispensation of Puritan-capitalist dogma is not serious enough before both daily works and Final Things. Current American sports fiction models Western heroic individualism, while the individual's play models that individualism's rest points and origins. Sports heroes suspiciously eye the collective and its insistence on production and consumption while the collective returns the suspicious glance at the insurgency of the heroes' play.

What are the summary statements we can make about the relations of play and sport? For the most part, play challenges collective structures from an individual's point of control. Yet as Sutton-Smith has observed, "There have been ever so many more comments about play as a dimension of the experience of the individual learning how to survive as a social organism, and far fewer from the perspective of the group maintaining the social organisms of which we're all a part" ("Overview: Play as Flow" 277). Sport helps to redress that imbalance. Part of the dynamism of sport is that it not only carries play into the center of simulated winning and losing but that the tally sheet of a sports contest is a control against life's randomness. As Sutton-Smith writes, "Winning and losing, which are relatively unmanageable outside of play, in games become operating principles for a continuing series of cooperative engagements" ("Epilogue: Play as Performance" 309). Within what Sutton-Smith calls a *ludic dialectic,* sport may contain both competition and cooperation, both striving and interaction. If we place our harsh realities in play frames, we also place our playfulness and cooperation under the physical and social stress of competition and games. The human spirit has need of and partakes of both.

Play may put competition under momentary arrest; likewise competition may enlist play to drive for high stakes. In the dialectic of sport and play, each grants the other the "freedom" to come under its influence for a time. However, "freedom" must be a continually re-examined concept. Lentricchia has identified freedom as the individualistic, romantic touchstone of much contemporary critical thought from the New Critics to some exponents of post-structuralism (Lentricchia 169). I concur with Lentricchia that such freedom is in part a legacy of Schiller's play theorizing to the various current aesthetic, linguistic, and social criticisms. Freedom embodies what Lentricchia calls "aesthetic humanism," "the most visible philosophy of poetics down through Frye" (20). Such freedom is strongly countered by "a deterministic vision" that is "derived from historical or natural order" (21) that suggests realities more strongly in the life world than in aesthetic or linguistic construction. Between these two visions, between the idealism of an individual freedom and the determinisms of social and historical experience, are where play and sport have their interaction.[5]

The dialectical swing of play and sport together are what comprise the form that intrigues contemporary American authors, from Mailer's obsessions to Kesey's multiple roles to Coover's universe-making. Such a dialectic emerges as the form and voice of women in play and sports narratives as well. Play denies the power of history and culture. Play is radical in its attempts to seize momentary control of time, space, and narrative. However, it is conservative in its flight from the pain of that time and space. These "twin interpretations" are always present in the same moment of play—both appropriation of reality and a substitution of reality—and function as the dramatic tension in the fiction of sport and play.

Likewise, sport in all its manifestations of cooperation, competition, performance, ritual, and spectacle is both a re-creation of the culture's social and economic realities, as well as a turning from them, a substitution of and denial of the "real," the historical. Victories and defeats may be celebrated and mourned without actual, historical consequences and may yield physical, emotional, and aesthetic satisfaction for both participant and spectator. Finally, sport and the spirit of play are authorial, hence human choices, constraints chosen in response to constraint. They allow both the competition and the dance, the agonistic and the imaginative, the miming for and potentially in all of us in our pitiless passage through what is.

Notes

INTRODUCTION

1. On Schiller's aesthetics as inspiration for romantic poetry, see M. H. Abrams, *Natural Supernaturalism,* pp. 212–17.

2. See Jacques Ehrmann, "Homo Ludens Revisited," in his *Game, Play, Literature,* pp. 35–36. Ehrmann cites the linguist Emil Benveniste on his vision of the once unitary image of the sacred that has broken into two halves of play—play in action and play in words.

3. In "The Origin of the Work of Art" (1950), an essay Heidegger refined for decades, art stands between *physis* and *logos,* between earth and world. Truth happens *within* the work of art.

4. The Heideggerian surmise that the "essence of Being is play itself" (Axelos 20), that the world is *Spielraum* (Steiner, *Heidegger 149,* was enlarged

rhetorically by hermeneuticists and phenomenologists who were eager to speak of play as fundamentally centered and powerful.

5. Marcuse's chapter 9, "The Aesthetic Dimension," in *Eros and Civilization* champions the aesthetic as the impulse that will reconcile pleasure and morality by liberating man "from inhuman existential conditions." He concludes, "the play impulse is the vehicle of this liberation. The impulse does not aim at playing 'with' something; rather it is the play of life itself . . . and thus the manisfestation of freedom itself" (187).

6. Jameson in *Marxism and Form* does not cite Marcuse's pre-Jamesonian recuperation of Schiller in *Eros and Civilization.*

7. Jameson quotes Paul Ricouer from *Freud and Philosophy* (1970): "At one pole, hermeneutics is understood as the mainfestation and restoration of a meaning addressed to me in the manner of a message, a proclamation, or as is sometimes said, a kerygma; according to the other pole, it is understood as a demystification, as a reduction of illusion." Jameson, *The Political Unconscious,* p. 284.

8. Marxist critics of literature such as Terry Eagleton and neo-Marxist critics of sport and culture such as Max Horkheimer and T. W. Adorno see play and "the game" as a sanctioned siphoning off of revolutionary energy in the present. Horkheimer and Adorno are wary of the sports subject and of society's fascination with it. They conceive of sport as a deformed mirror-image of an already defective competitive capitalism.

9. For critiques of Greimas' structure, see Jonathan Culler, *Structuralist Poetics,* pp. 92–95, 224–28; Jameson, *The Prison House of Language,* pp. 163–68; *The Political Unconscious,* pp. 46–49, 121–27, 166–68, 254–57; Foreword to Greimas, *On Meaning: Selected Writings in Semiotic Theory,* vi–xxii; Robert Scholes, *Structuralism in Literature,* pp. 102–11.

10. Greimas' semiotic square is an adaptation of the logical concepts of the contrary and the contradictory and is a cornerstone of his major contribution to structural semantics. In my adaptation, Collective Sports Heroism is a *contrary* to Individual Sports Heroism. It has a positive value of its own, yet is antithetical to Individual Sports Heroism, while Anti-Heroism is the *contradiction* of Individual Sports Heroism. The first generated term, in this case the Individual Sports Heroism, will always include its antithesis; thus the one arbitrary critical decision is the choice of the first term's content. The creation of the fourth term (Play) allows for the negation of the Collective Sports Heroism which is already antithetical to Individual Heroism. The fourth term becomes the negation of the negation, the "not-not Individual Heroism," giving the double negative a positive valence that may be expressed by Play. Play is latent in the public assignments of sports heroism in the individual and collective spheres and coexistent in subversive spirit

with the negation inherent in Anti-Heroism. Thus the top two terms in antithetical relation (Individual Sports Heroism–Collective Sports Heroism) comprise the public world of sports heroism, while the bottom two terms (Play–Anti-Heroism) are potentially in revolt.

11. All fixed terms in the semiotic square may function to mediate in a series of three terms. Play "plays between," but so do Individual Sports Heroism, Collective Sports Heroism, and Anti-Heroism "play between," staving off and controlling oppositions (for better or worse) for characters in the fiction of sport and play.

12. For the rest of this book, the four terms on the semiotic square will be not be capitalized, except in specific representations in diagram form.

13. To Marxist critics, such a figure has retreated into the insufficiency of the monad as a marginalized individual. To existentialists, such a figure is poised to undertake a spiritual journey. Play's usefulness most often depends on the meta-rhetoric of the critic.

14. Hobbs' feat thus combines the play categories of Johan Huizinga, *Homo Ludens* (1950) and Roger Caillois, *Men, Play, and Games* (1961).

15. Rabbit would come into a relation to the golf club of what Heidegger called *Zuhandenheit,* a "readiness to hand" (Steiner 89), that would reveal to object-use spanning the things (golf club), nature (the golf course), and the world (Eccles' society, Rabbit's responsibilities there). Updike's philosophical grounding has most often been associated with his theological interest in Soren Kierkegaard and Karl Barth as well as Pascal, all of whom had a demonstrable influence on the young Heidegger.

16. That touch is a renewed phallic mastery. Women in sport and play fictional narratives have their own conception of touch as a liberation from males such as Rabbit Angstrom. See chapter 6.

I . THE DECLINE OF THE RITUAL SPORTS HERO

1. See Messenger, *Sport and the Spirit of Play in American Fiction: Hawthorne to Faulkner.* (Hereafter referred to as "Messenger, Book I"). Chapters 1–2 and 10–12 contain extended discussions of the Ritual Sports Hero in American fiction before the contemporary period.

2. Charles Gaines' *Stay Hungry* (1972), a novel about body-builders, highlighted the body itself as subject, which, without doing *anything* had become a work of art. To strike a "pose," is to make a "clean line," to refrain from movement or engagement and become the total embodiment of self. However, *Stay Hungry* does end in violent, sacrificial ritual.

3. Girard points out that an incorrect sacrificial victim unlocks more murders (Girard 49).

4. Anthropologist Victor Turner's classification of *liminal* and *liminoid* genres is useful in identifying ritual sports frames. Liminal genres are tribal genres while a liminoid genre is more fragmentary and pluralistic in the nature of a spectacle, carnival, or major sporting event such as the bullfight or boxing. Liminal genres are sequestered (private) and public: the former corresponds to the initiation rites of an adept, presided over by mentors who humble or level the initiate. The latter is public ceremony, perhaps a seasonal hunt or group activity with biological or socio-structural implications (Turner 43–47).

5. McGuane's *Ninety-Two in the Shade* (1973) contains similar violent dynamics of ritual testing and gamesmanship played by central figures Thomas Skelton and Nichol Dance, the Quinn and Stanton of the novel, respectively. The locale of *Ninety-Two* is Key West where, its competitors ply the Hemingwayesque trade of fishing boat guides.

6. In another mode, consider Richard Brautigan's "Trout Fishing in America Shorty," a "legless, screaming, middle-aged wino" who roams San Francisco "in a magnificent chrome-plated wheelchair." Brautigan, *Trout Fishing in America,* p. 45. Brautigan meets Shorty for the last time ten miles outside Ketchum, Idaho, just after Hemingway's death there.

7. Mailer's vision of "technology fill[ing] the pause" after Hemingway's death is a replacing of the engine of the body, in fact rendering the body inert and passive in a technological violation. The bodies of the Apollo 11 astronauts are wired, strapped, confined, and made impotent. To be individual heroes, they must murder their vital, active, masculine selves. Technology "does to" the men what as subject the Ritual Sports Hero had done to others in his compulsive encounters. Beyond the essential image of Promethean athletes bound, Mailer strove to affix the appropriate sports image to everyone connected with the mission of Apollo 11. Mailer's sports images establish the leadership roles in sport—headmaster, coach, quarterback, shortstop—and serve to contrast such physically healthy adept men with their roles as mere accessories to the space capsule (*Moon* 17, 25, 28, 31, 355).

8. This key statement was first identified by Richard Poirier, *The Performing Self,* p. 103, as a key to Mailer's vision of self, but Poirier does not carry the image through to other Mailer texts.

9. To engage the world is to set yourself at a fierce pitch of competition, to choose your terror and confront it again and again in ritual. Mailer best captured these imperatives in a ritual sports image when he wrote of Joe DiMaggio's "art" which demanded the "consistent courage" to "face into

thousands of fast balls any one of which could kill or cripple him" ("Married to Marilyn" 12). Tom Wolfe in *The Right Stuff* seconded this image with his tight-lipped band of heroic test pilots whose standard of performance stipulated "that a man should have the ability to go up in a hurtling piece of machinery and put his hide on the line and then have the moxie, the reflexes, the experience, the coolness, to pull it back in the last yawning moment— and then go up again *the next day,* and the next day and every next day" (Wolfe 18–19).

10. In *An American Dream,* Mailer also became surely the first writer to inscribe three wives (Jeanne Campbell, Beverly Bentley, Carol Stevens) in one character (Cherry Melanie). See Peter Manso, *Mailer: His Life and Times,* p. 399.

2. MAILER: THE BODY AS ARENA

1. Croft's cry almost directly reverses Ike McCaslin's trajectory in *Go Down, Moses,* for Ike comes to hate everything that *is* himself.

2. Andrew Gordon in *An American Dreamer* (1980) proposed a theory of anality to explain Mailer's aggression and compulsive private myth-making. The outlines of Gordon's argument are convincing, but he has limited discussion to Mailer's fiction and *The Armies of the Night* and does not go beyond the Mailer of 1968. While he gains psychoanalytic case histories in the persons of Mailer's central characters, he fails to confront adequately the richness of Mailer's nonfiction, the seedbed of all his novelistic themes.

3. See Raymond Williams, *Marxism and Literature.* Chapter 8, "Dominant, Residual, and Emergent," discusses the various cultural practices that make up any hegemonic reality.

4. Michael Cimino's film *The Deer Hunter* (1978) carries these configurations to Vietnam itself, extending the "killer brothers," Mike (Robert DeNiro) and Nick (Christopher Walken), into a terrifying Russian roulette game staged by their Viet Cong captors. Mike's Natty Bumppo-like Ritual Sports Hero's code of always using one bullet when deer-hunting in Pennsylvania is perverted by necessity. Mike persuades the soldiers to let them play with three bullets. Heroically, Mike and Nick turn their guns on the Viet Cong and escape. However, Nick has been severely traumatized. Seeking the grace of last rites in a repetition-compulsion, he now haunts Saigon as "the American," playing Russian roulette for money in the collective's "sport." He ultimately takes his own life before a horrified Mike. Cimino's tragedy is complete and hermetic. The killer-brothers have been destroyed, Nick literally, Mike as adept Ritual Sports Hero in a devastated competitive rite.

3. MAILER: BOXING AND THE ART OF HIS NARRATIVE

1. How this dramatization will be a record of Mailer's own war is suggested by Mailer's bizarre anecdote of Harry Greb, one of the toughest American fighters of the 1920s, who would visit a brothel before a bout, have two prostitutes in the same bed and "so absorb[ed] into his system all the small, nasty, concentrated evils which had accumulated from carloads of men." Mailer, *Cannibals and Christians,* p. 217. Greb's act is homoerotic by proxy with the prostitute as surrogate providing him with a raider's feast of poisons from the male.

2. On Mailer's and wife Beverley Bentley's relations with Miles Davis, see Manso, *Mailer: His Life and Times,* pp. 373, 401.

3. Mailer re-creates this psychic battle through sexual struggle in the days-long combat between the gods Horus and Set in *Ancient Evenings.*

4. Santiago still lives for Mailer. Tim Madden in *Tough Guys Don't Dance* (New York: Random House, 1984) comments on his aged father, Dougy, "he squinted at me like an old fisherman" (178), after Dougy has buried at sea the severed heads of two women (with appropriate skill).

5. Mailer traces the curve of this truth in a disquisition on a roster of heroes and their "war of form" in *Moon:* "The real heroism, he thought, was to understand, and because one understood, be even more full of fear at the enormity of what one understood, yet at that moment continue to be ready for the feat one had decided it was essential to perform. So Julien Sorel had been brave when he kissed Madame de Renal and Jimmy Dean had been brave in *Rebel Without a Cause,* and Namath when he mocked the Baltimore Colts knowing the only visions he would arouse in his enemy were visions of murder. So had Cassius Clay been brave—to dare to be rude to Liston—and Floyd Patterson brave to come back to boxing after terrible humiliation, and Hemingway conceivably brave to continue to write in short sentences after being exposed to the lividities of the literary world" (101).

6. Mailer's continuing sense of competition with Hemingway surfaces again in the circuitous wish that Hemingway had not been allowed to publish one of his most acclaimed works.

4. FICTIONS OF BOXING

1. See Messenger, Book I, pp. 255–56, 351.

2. For details of Schulberg's appearances and his own rationale, see Victor S. Navasky, *Naming Names,* pp. 286, 306, 310–11.

3. Schulberg's "novelization," *Waterfront* (1955), was much harsher with Terry Malloy's death merely part of a negative ending with no inspirational climax.

4. Eakins' only real rival in boxing art was George Bellows whose "Stag at Sharkey's" (1909), "Between the Ropes" (1923), and "Dempsey Through the Ropes" (1924) established him as the painter of boxing's Predator-Prey opposition.

5. The primordial California hero and his mate-woman were an increasingly familiar London pair in *Burning Daylight* (1910), *The Valley of the Moon* (1913), and *The Little Lady of the Big House* (1915).

6. John Wayne starred as Pat Glendon in a 1936 film version of *The Abysmal Brute* with Jean Rogers (Flash Gordon's Dale Arden) as his mate.

7. Only the tabloid adventures of Mike Tyson, an intriguing mix of Youth and Predator both in and out of the ring, have broken Rocky's hold on the public imagination (as of August 1989).

5. PLAY, SACRIFICE, PERFORMANCE: KESEY AND COOVER

1. For a critical view of Play's apolitical limitations, see Terry Eagleton, *Walter Benjamin; or, Towards a Revolutionary Criticism*, pp. 148–50.

2. An introductory survey of criticism on *Cuckoo's Nest* is found in Stephen L. Tanner, *Ken Kesey*, pp. 44–50.

3. This series was conceived after reading J. H. Duthie, "Athletics: The Ritual of a Technological Society?," in Schwartzman, ed., *Play and Culture*, pp. 91–97.

4. *Acid Test* and *The Right Stuff* tell similar stories. Any freedom to play and create in the books is available only to adherents of the true religion, the Pranksters or the Brotherhood of the Right Stuff. Both narratives portray ritualists seeking control. However, Wolfe has no awe before anything, secular or sacred; all is cultural process. For example, in *Moon*, Mailer is terrified of the astronauts having been violated as males by chemicals and technology and inscribes them in his sexual anxiety narrative. Wolfe jokes about them as "lab rabbits" with "a wire up the kazoo" (*The Right Stuff* 63), the blow being one to their pride as pilots, not overtly to their genitals. Wolfe never really allows in his subjects nor appears to question in himself his dependence on or the potential of an independence from a social order that is monolithic and determining in all his works.

5. On Coover and performance, see Thomas LeClair, "Robert Coover, *The Public Burning*, and the Art of Excess."

6. In his novel *The Bonfire of the Vanities* (1987), Wolfe finally joins the

novelists' team in writing the sort of urban narrative of society that he had consistently called for from American novelists of the contemporary period.

6. WOMEN IN SPORTS NARRATIVE: THE STRATEGIES OF MIMICRY

1. Jacques Derrida, "Deconstruction in America: An Interview with Jacques Derrida," p. 32.

2. What Nabokov will not do is give Lolita herself a language or any desiring imagination. She is the most extreme example of fictional representation solely through the male gaze.

3. There is enormous physical and/or sexual violence done to and by women in *The World According to Garp,* including Jenny Fields, Roberta Muldoon, Ellen James, Helen Garp, and Pooh Percy.

4. Marge Piercy's *The High Cost of Living* (1978) seriously attempts to portray that lesbian community as well as a variety of straight and gay gender roles. Piercy's heroine, Leslie, is a Black Belt in karate, but Piercy has little interest in sport beyond karate as a metaphor. Leslie is moral, guilty, disciplined, and uneasy in all her public and private relations. She must learn what she can go after and in which sphere: "Funny, you could study self-defense but not self-opening" (287). See also John Sayles' film *Lianna* (1983).

5. Baseball fiction by and about women is discussed in Chapter 12.

6. Sarge and Ilana's responses fit perfectly what Julia Kristeva has called the "symbolic" and the "emiotic," respectively, imperfect forms of paternal and maternal language that continually interact. The male symbolic is logical, abstract, phallocentric; the female emiotic is pre-verbal, maternal, and linked to body contact. See Linda Williams, "'Something Else Besides a Mother': *Stella Dallas* and the Maternal Melodrama," p. 11.

7. Irigaray both calls for the "goddess mother" role and warns against its logic as playing the man's game. Stanton, "Difference on Trial," p. 162.

8. See Williams, "*Personal Best:* Women in Love," pp. 1, 11–12.

9. Isolated instances of male professional athletes coming forward to proclaim their homosexuality include the NFL's Dave Kopay and Jerry Smith, and baseball's Glenn Burke.

10. Rita Mae Brown's *Sudden Death* (1983) is a breezy roman à clef about the women's pro tennis tour and a fictionalizing of Brown's one-time relationship with Navratilova. Brown does not respect athletes, nor does she acknowledge the complexities of sexual and athletic response in men and women. She repeats cliches of aggressive male-like female competitors and

their suffering female lovers: "Harriet never thought of Carmen [tennis champion] as a woman. She rarely acted like one. She wasn't responsive or nurturing. All her energy was fixed on a goal outside herself" (158).

11. Levin introduces the reader to a new issue in an era of changing sexual relations when Kaz concludes about Raina that "physical sameness did not lead to lack of mystery" (*Snow* 403).

7. THE DECLINE OF THE SCHOOL SPORTS HERO

1. See Messenger, Book I, chaps. 6–9, on the School Sports Hero in American Fiction before the contemporary period.

2. Two exceptions were Joel Sayre's *Rackety Rax* (1932) and George Weller's *Not to Eat, Not For Love* (1933).

3. See Messenger, Book I, pp. 218–24.

4. Wolfe met Fitzgerald in Paris in June 1930 at the Ritz Bar and reported him "entirely surrounded by Princeton boys, all nineteen years old, all drunk and all half-raw" (Andrew Turnbull, *Scott Fitzgerald*, p. 196). Wolfe may also have had in mind one Augustine William Folger, a star athlete at the University of North Carolina in 1916–17 (Robert J. Higgs, *Laurel & Thorn*, p. 187).

5. Walker Percy's Lancelot Lamar in *Lancelot* (1977), a far more complex and ironic Arthurian, nonetheless had his day of football glory when he returned a punt the ultimate 110 yards for a touchdown against Alabama.

6. A model for Frank Prescott may be Oliver Alden in George Santayana's *The Last Puritan* (1936).

7. For a detailed account of athletes in modern American drama, see Higgs, *Laurel & Thorn*, pp. 55–60, 82–87.

8. Jason Miller's *That Championship Season* (1964) centers on an absent School Sports hero, Martin, the high school basketball star who does not attend the team's reunion with its powerful and dying coach. Martin cannot redeem their lives with his "time," even as his absence passes judgment on their inhumanities and compromises.

9. In Edward Albee's *Who's Afraid of Virginia Woolf* (1963), the schoolboy hero takes on his strangest recombinant form. Rather than an actual sports hero or object of desire, he is the wholly imaginary son-figure played by his parents for and against each other until he is destroyed by them in a ritual sacrifice. The tenuous nature of the conception is nowhere more powerfully expressed than in the competition between George and Martha initially to supress, then to embellish, and finally to kill their dangerous "little all-American something-or-other," their "little bugger," their "blonde-eyed,

blue-haired son" (Albee 70, 72, 196). The son becomes the sacrificial victim to deflect murder from the surrogate victims, George and Martha, who had been killing themselves and each other. Now they must find what, if anything, lies beyond their play. Albee leaves the question unanswered.

10. Knowles' early school sports story, "A Turn With the Sun," climaxes on a Forsterian plot disruption when Lawrence, the schoolboy outcast, abruptly drowns. The tone is similar to Forster's famous "Gerald died that afternoon" that opens chapter 5 of *The Longest Journey.*

11. Knowles' *Peace Breaks Out* (1981) is a novel of post–World War II Devon with similar plot mechanisms and language to *A Separate Peace:* a contradictory death of a schoolboy, a rhetorical search for "truth," an inert narration. What *Peace Breaks Out* lacks is a vital school sports frame and a Phineas.

12. Morris has written about the fatal allure of the past for American authors in *The Territory Ahead* (1957).

13. For another version of the tennis natural, see Barry Hannah, "Return to Return," in his *Airships* (1978). The story was incorporated into Hannah's novel *The Tennis Handsome* (1983).

14. On Tilden's dominant and strange career in men's tennis, see Frank Deford, *Big Bill Tilden* (1976).

15. In *Lolita,* the highest moment of Lolita's grace and beauty come for Humbert when she is playing tennis. Like Morris in *The Huge Season,* Nabokov strove to fix images of tennis motion as suspended emblems of art. Lolita at tennis gives Humbert the spatial-temporal music ("a bar or two of white-lined time") to match his lyricism to the physical occasion without self-conscious reference to his guilt or to Lolita's imprisonment. Tennis gives Humbert the space for aesthetic play where his descriptio cannot be captured by his desire nor by his perverted spirit. Yet even here, most appropriately, Humbert's double, Clare Quilty, stealthily intrudes. Humbert reappears after his rapturous tennis description to find his "double" playing doubles with Lolita. On the motif of tennis in *Lolita,* see Alfred Appel, Jr., *Nabokov's Dark Cinema,* pp. 116–18.

8. ANTI-HEROISM: THE WITNESS AT THE CENTER

1. *The Catcher in the Rye* has other citations relevant to sports fiction tradition. Holden enjoyed *The Great Gatsby* , especially "Old Gatsby. Old sport. That killed me" (128), while Holden's plunge into New York City is not unlike Fitzgerald's more benign conception of his prep school hero Basil Duke Lee confronting the big city in the 1920s. Next to his brother, D. B.,

Holden's favorite author is Ring Lardner; surely Salinger is saluting Lardner's ear for colloquial language as would Mark Harris in *The Southpaw.* Also, like many Lardnerian narrators, Holden is stubbornly moral while hating pretension and verbal sham, and he responds deeply to the sad Lardner short story he relates. Salinger's citations of Fitzgerald and Lardner are both charming and apt.

2. Suggested by Alan Wilde's arguments of depths and surfaces in modern and postmodern fiction. Wilde, *Horizons of Assent,* pp. 3, 41–44.

3. Frank Conroy's autobiography/novel *Stop-Time* (1967) is as studiedly elegant and cool as *A Fan's Notes* is grotesque and garrulous but similarly concentrates through play and game on the control of time. See especially chapter 8, "A Yo-Yo Going Down, a Mad Squirrel Coming Up."

4. "He knew that when he kissed this girl, and forever wed his unutterable visions to her perishable breath, his mind would never romp again like the mind of God. So he waited, listening for a moment longer to the tuning fork that had been struck upon a star. Then he kissed her. At his lips' touch she blossomed for him like a flower and the incarnation was complete." Fitzgerald, *The Great Gatsby,* p. 112.

5. Exceptions would include James Thurber's earnest but thick football players such as Bolenciewcz in "University Days" (1933) and the cheerfully obtuse Joe Ferguson in Thurber's and Elliott Nugent's *The Male Animal* (1940).

6. Wilde calls "suspensiveness" the most inclusive of postmodern effects, one that "embrace[s] chaos at all conceivable levels." Wilde, *Horizons of Assent,* p. 135.

9. FICTIONS OF FOOTBALL: BETWEEN THE LINES

1. See Messenger, Book I, chapters 3–5, for an analysis of the Popular Sports Hero in American Fiction through Ring Lardner.

2. McMurtry wrote, "Most of my smalltown contemporaries spent their high-school years trying desperately to be good athletes." Charles D. Peavy, *Larry McMurtry,* p. 102.

3. See Messenger, Book I, pp. 186, 196, 266.

4. The world of Texas football hardly contains the full range of literary production in and about Texas. See A.C. Greene, "The Texas Literati: Whose Home is this Range, Anyhow?"

5. Maule also wrote fiction. His *Footsteps* (1964) was about college football. He also wrote a children's series about the Los Angeles Rams in *Championship Quarterback* (1963) and *The Receiver* (1968).

6. Jenkins' college football reports were collected in *Saturday's Heroes* (1970).

7. This pattern is mentioned by Michael Oriard, *Dreaming of Heroes*, p. 132; Neil David Berman, *Playful Fictions and Fictional Players*, pp. 39–41.

8. DeLillo in *Libra* (1988) has written the definitive fictional imagining of the life of Lee Harvey Oswald and surrounding plots.

9. From 1966 to 1970, the Dallas Cowboys went 52–16–2 and won five straight NFC Eastern Conference titles. However, in each post-season, they were defeated in what passed for a pigskin morality play.

10. FICTIONS OF FOOTBALL: WHY WE ARE PLAYING

1. In his 1987 revision of *Gus*, Coover has left the football material untouched. He concentrated on the deepening the historical context of the 1930s, specifically the Spanish Civil War and labor strife, as well as Meyer's Jewish consciousness.

2. See David L. VanDerWerken, "From Tackle to Teacher: James Whitehead's *Joiner*."

3. See Messenger, Book I, chapter 6, "The Incarnation of the College Athletic Hero," pp. 131–54.

4. A primer on the experimental fiction of the last two decades might include Robert Alter, *Partial Magic*; Scholes, *The Fabulators; Structuralism in Literature; Structural Fabulation*; Ihab Hassan, *The Dismemberment of Orpheus: Toward a Post-Modern Literature; Paracriticisms: Seven Speculations of the Times*; Susan Sontag, "The Aesthetics of Silence"; George Steiner, *Language and Silence*; Alan Thiher, *Words in Reflection*; and Wilde, *Horizons of Assent*.

5. On DeLillo's use of Wittgenstein, see Gary Storoff, "The Failure of Games in Don DeLillo's *End Zone*," pp. 240–41.

6. James McManus' *Chin Music* (1985) confronts nuclear war directly (see chapter 11). McManus, however, uses baseball in its rhythms of family and "coming home" to counter the apocalypse, whereas for DeLillo, football patterns the apocalypse.

11. FICTIONS OF BASEBALL: BASEBALL AND PASSAGES

1. Charles Victor Faust was the most famous baseball mascot of the early part of the century. John McGraw actually pitched him in two meaningless games in the 1911 season. Reportedly, the Cincinnati Reds took exaggerated

swings against him and allowed him to walk, steal two bases, and score a run.

2. On the question of a unique Jewish voice in modern and contemporary American fiction and the contradictory pull of assimilation, see Allen Guttmann, *The Jewish Writer in America* (1971) and Irving Malin, ed., *Contemporary Jewish American Literature: Critical Essays* (1973).

3. Harris' two other Wiggen books, *A Ticket for a Seamstitch* (1956) and *It Looked Like For Ever* (1979) are quite scant and an ill-advised comeback, respectively.

12. FICTIONS OF BASEBALL: BASEBALL HISTORICIZED

1. See Caillois, *Man, Play, and Games* (1961); Mircea Eliade, *The Sacred and the Profane* (1959); *The Quest: History and Meaning in Religion* (1969).

2. Such a search informs the beleaguered McDuff in Coover's "Casey at the Bat" adaptation, "McDuff on the Mound."

3. Neugeboren has written two fine baseball short stories, "Ebbets Field" and "Corky's Brother," collected in *Corky's Brother*.

4. In contrast, from 1971 to 1978 in what might be called the discovery of football as fictional subject, there were about half as many football novels published (I cite fifteen in chapter 9) as there were baseball novels published from 1980 to 1988. Football fiction has slowed to a very few titles in the 1980s.

5. Mixed genre baseball novels have begun to appear. In detective and crime fiction, we have Robert B. Parker, *Mortal Stakes* (1975); James Magnuson, *The Rundown* (1977); Gary Pomeranz, *Out At Home* (1985); and R. D. Rosen, *Strike Three, You're Dead* (1985). The thriller is represented by Charles Brady, *Seven Games in October* (1979); and Daniel Keith Cohler, *Gamemaker* (1980).

6. *The Grace of Shortstops* is similar to Gerald Green's *To Brooklyn With Love* (1967) in its evocation of Brooklyn, neighborhood baseball, and father-son tensions.

7. Jameson cites *Ragtime* as "the most peculiar and stunning monument to the aesthetic situation engendered by the disappearance of the historical referent." ("Postmodernism, or The Cultural Logic of Late Capitalism").

13. FICTIONS OF BASKETBALL

1. See also Neugeboren's story "Something is Rotten in the Borough of Brooklyn," in *Corky's Brother*. A novel on the college basketball scandals

and their aftermath is Leo Rutman's *Five Good Boys*. For historical accounts, see Charles Rosen, *Scandals of '51: How the Gamblers Almost Killed College Basketball*, and Stanley Cohen, *The Game They Played*.

2. For extended commentary on *One on One*, see Berman, *Playful Fiction and Fictional Players*, pp. 72–86.

3. Piet Hanema, the "builder" and sexual athlete in *Couples*, recapitulates the same dynamic success and failure through "touch."

4. The pattern of circles and nets in *Rabbit, Run* was initially identified by John C. Stubbs, "The Search for Perfection in *Rabbit, Run*."

CONCLUSION

1. See Messenger, Book I, chapter 12, "Sport Approaches the Sacred."

2. The best example of such a progression toward freedom in American Literature would be *Huckleberry Finn* in which Huck plays to survive while he learns self-determination and the self-consciousness to decide actively to work for Jim's freedom.

3. This book has centered on the hermeneutics and criticism of sport and play in contemporary American fiction. The poetics of the study have yet to be attempted. Key questions to be asked would be: 1. Can we describe how the bound motifs of a sport are integrated into the free motifs of a fictional plot that de-familiarizes the known sport? 2. How does sports competence (playing, spectating) interact with literary competence (writing, reading)?

4. In these terms, a collective revolutionary use of play and illusion appear to be beyond American sports fiction's conceptual points at present. Herman Melville's "Benito Cereno" (1854) remains the most suggestive revolutionary text in American play in fiction.

5. These visions refer as well to the differences in modernist and post-modernist representation, the foregrounding of individual or structural questions. Critics take to the battlements along these same lines in the debate between post-structuralism and a more social and politically based criticism (Foucault, Jameson, Habermas).

Bibliography

PRIMARY WORKS CITED

Albee, Edward. *Who's Afraid of Virginia Woolf.* New York: Atheneum, 1963.
Algren, Nelson. *Never Come Morning.* New York: Harper & Row, 1942.
Angell, Roger. *The Summer Game.* New York: Viking, 1972.
Ardizzone, Tony. *Heart of the Order.* New York: Henry Holt and Co., 1986.
Asinof, Eliot. *Eight Men Out.* New York: Ace, 1963.
—— *Man on Spikes.* New York: McGraw-Hill, 1955.
Auchincloss, Louis. *The Rector of Justin.* Boston: Houghton-Mifflin, 1964.
Barthelme, Donald. "Brain Damage." In his *City Life,* pp. 141–56. New York: Bantam, 1970.
Beckham, Barry. *Double Dunk.* Los Angeles: Holloway House, 1980.
—— *Runner Mack.* New York: Popular Library, 1972.
Bellow, Saul. *Dangling Man* [1944]. New York: Meridian, 1960.

Berry, Elliot. *Four Quarters Make a Season*. New York: Curtis Brown, 1973.

Bogdanovich, Peter. *The Last Picture Show*. Film, 1971.

Brady, Charles. *Seven Games in October*. Boston: Little, Brown, 1979.

Brashler, William. *The Bingo Long Travelling All-Stars and Motor Kings* [1973]. New York: Signet, 1975.

Brautigan, Richard. *Trout Fishing in America*. New York: Dell, 1970.

Broun, Heywood. *The Sun Field*. New York: Putnam, 1923.

Brown, Rita Mae. *Sudden Death*. New York: Bantam, 1983.

Carkeet, David. *The Greatest Slump of All Time*. New York: Harper & Row, 1984.

Cartwright, Gary. *The Hundred Yard War*. New York: Dell, 1968.

Charyn, Jerome. *The Seventh Babe*. New York: Arbor House, 1979.

Cimino, Michael. *The Deer Hunter*. Film, 1978.

Cohler, David Keith. *Gamemaker*. New York: Doubleday, 1980.

Cooney, Ellen. *All the Way Home*. New York: G. P. Putnam's Sons, 1984.

Cooper, James Fenimore. *The Pioneers*. New York: Signet, 1964.

Coover, Robert. "McDuff on the Mound." *Iowa Review* (Fall 1971), 2(4): 111–20.

—— *Pricksongs and Descants*. New York: Plume, 1969.

—— *The Public Burning*. New York: Viking, 1977.

—— *The Universal Baseball Association, J. Henry Waugh, Prop*. New York: Signet, 1968.

—— *Whatever Happened to Gloomy Gus of the Chicago Bears? American Review* 22 (Bantam, 1975), 34–110; printed in hardback novel form with additions, New York: Simon & Schuster, 1987.

Crane, Stephen. *The Red Badge of Courage* [1894]. New York: W. W. Norton, 1962.

Cronley, Jay. *Fall Guy*. New York: Signet, 1978.

Crews, Harry. *A Feast of Snakes*. New York: Ballantine Books, 1976.

Daley, Robert. *Only a Game*. New York: Signet, 1967.

Dawson, Fielding. *A Great Day for a Ball Game*. Indianapolis: Bobbs-Merrill, 1973.

Deal, Babs H. *The Grail* [1952]. New York: McKay, 1963.

Deford, Frank. *Big Bill Tilden*. New York: Simon and Schuster, 1976.

—— *Cut 'n Run*. New York: Viking, 1973.

—— *Everybody's All-American*. New York: Viking, 1981.

—— "Letter From the Publisher." *Sports Illustrated*, October 30, 1972, p. 5.

DeLillo, Don. *End Zone* [1972]. New York: Pocket Books, 1973.

—— "An Interview with Don DeLillo." *Contemporary Literature* (Winter 1982), 3 (1):19–37.

—— *Ratner's Star*. New York: Knopf, 1976.

Dickey, James. *Deliverance*. New York: Dell, 1970.

—— "For the Death of Vince Lombardi." *Esquire,* September 1971, p. 142.

Doctorow, E. L. *Ragtime*. New York: Random House, 1975.

Duff, Gerald. *Indian Giver*. Bloomington: Indiana UP, 1983.

Einstein, Charles. *The Only Game in Town*. New York: Dell, 1955.

Ellison, Ralph. *Invisible Man*. New York: Signet, 1952.

Emerson, Ralph Waldo. "The American Scholar." *Selections from Ralph Waldo Emerson,* pp. 63–80. Boston: Riverside, 1957.

—— *Representative Men* [1850]. Boston: Houghton Mifflin, 1884.

Everett, Percival L. *Suder*. New York: Viking, 1983.

Exley, Frederick. *A Fan's Notes*. New York: Harper & Row, 1968.

—— *Pages from a Cold Island*. New York: Random House, 1975.

Farrell, James. *My Baseball Diary*. New York: A. S. Barnes, 1957.

—— *Young Lonigan*. New York: Vanguard Press, 1932.

Faulkner, William. *Absalom, Absalom!* New York: Random House, 1936.

—— *As I Lay Dying* [1930]. New York: Vintage, 1957.

—— "The Bear." In his *Go Down, Moses,* pp. 191–334. New York: Modern Library, 1942.

—— *The Hamlet*. New York: Random House, 1940.

—— *Light in August* [1932]. New York: Modern Library, 1950.

—— "The Old People." In his *Go Down Moses,* pp. 163–190.

—— *The Unvanquished*. New York: Knopf, 1938.

Faust, Irwin. *The Steagle* [1966]. New York: Avon, 1971.

Fitzgerald, F. Scott. "The Bowl." *Saturday Evening Post,* January 21, 1928.

—— *The Great Gatsby*. New York: Scribner's, 1925.

—— *Tender is the Night*. New York: Scribner's, 1934.

—— *This Side of Paradise*. New York: Scribner's, 1920.

Ford, Ford Maddox. *The Good Soldier* [1915]. New York: Vintage, 1955.

Ford, Richard. *The Sportswriter*. New York: Vintage, 1986.

Forster, E. M. *The Longest Journey* [1907]. New York: Knopf, 1922.

Foster, Alan S. *Goodbye Bobby Thomson! Goodbye John Wayne!* New York: Simon & Schuster, 1973.

Frank, Morry. *Every Young Man's Dream*. Chicago: Silverback Books, 1984.

Gaines, Charles. *Stay Hungry*. New York: Doubleday, 1972.

Gardner, Leonard. *Fat City*. New York: Dell, 1969.

Gent, Peter. *The Franchise*. New York: Villard, 1983.

—— *North Dallas Forty*. New York: Signet, 1973.

—— *Texas Celebrity Turkey Trot*. New York: William Morrow, 1978.

Gerson, Noel. *The Sunday Heroes*. New York: William Morrow, 1972.

Green, Gerald. *To Brooklyn With Love*. New York: Trident Press, 1967.

Greenberg, Eric Rolfe. *The Celebrant* [1983]. New York: Penguin, 1986.

Greenfield, Robert. *Haymon's Crowd*. New York: Summit Books, 1978.

Gregorich, Barbara. *She's on First*. New York: Contemporary Books, 1987.

Guy, David. *Football Dreams*. New York: Seaview Books, 1980.

Hamill, Pete. *Flesh and Blood*. New York: Bantam, 1977.

Hannah, Barry. "Return to Return." In his *Airships*, pp. 67–96. New York: Delta, 1978.

—— *The Tennis Handsome*. New York: Knopf, 1983.

Harris, Mark. *Bang the Drum Slowly* [1956]. New York: Dell, 1973.

—— *It Looked Like For Ever*. New York: McGraw-Hill, 1979.

—— *The Southpaw*. Indianapolis: Bobbs-Merrill, 1953.

—— *Ticket for a Seamstitch*. New York: Knopf, 1957.

Hawthorne, Nathaniel. *The Scarlet Letter*. Boston: Houghton Mifflin, 1960.

Hays, Donald. *The Dixie Association*. New York: Simon & Schuster, 1984.

Heinz, W. C. *The Professional*. New York: Harper & Row, 1958.

Hemingway, Ernest. "The Battler." In his *In Our Time*, pp. 63–80. New York: Scribner's, 1930.

—— "Big Two-Hearted River" (parts 1 and 2). In his *In Our Time*, pp. 175–212.

—— *Death in the Afternoon*. New York: Scribner's, 1932.

—— "The Doctor and the Doctor's Wife." In his *In Our Time*, pp. 23–32.

—— *A Farewell to Arms*. New York: Scribner's 1929.

—— "Fifty Grand." In his *Snows of Kilimanjaro and Other Stories*, pp. 95–120. New York: Scribner's, 1936.

—— "Indian Camp." In his *In Our Time*, pp. 13–22.

—— *The Old Man and the Sea*. New York: Scribner's, 1952.

—— *The Sun Also Rises*. New York: Scribner's, 1926.

—— *To Have and Have Not*. New York: Scribner's, 1937.

—— *The Torrents of Spring* [1926]. Middlesex: Penguin, 1966.

Hemphill, Paul. *Long Gone*. New York: Viking, 1979.

Herrin, Lamar. *The Rio Loja Ringmaster*. New York: Viking, 1977.

Hough, John, Jr. *The Conduct of the Game*. New York: Harcourt Brace Jovanovich, 1986.

Honig, Donald. *The Last Great Season*. New York: Simon and Schuster, 1979.

Hughes, Thomas. *Tom Brown at Oxford*. New York: F. M. Lupton, 1862.

—— *Tom Brown's Schooldays*. New York: Belford, Clarke, 1884.

Irving, John. *The Hotel New Hampshire*. New York: E. P. Dutton, 1981.

—— *The 158 Lb. Marriage*. New York: Pocket Books, 1974.

—— *Setting Free the Bears*. New York: Ballantine, 1970.

—— *The World According to Garp*. New York: Pocket Books, 1978.

Jenkins, Dan. *Life Its Ownself*. New York: Simon & Schuster, 1984.

—— *Semi-Tough* [1972]. New York: Signet, 1973.

—— "The Making of *Semi-Tough*." *Sports Illustrated*, November 7, 1977, pp. 78–90.

—— "There's No Show Biz Like Nobis." *Sports Illustrated*, October 18, 1965, pp. 40–42, 47–50, 55.

—— "When Frogs Were Princes." *Sports Illustrated*, August 31, 1981, pp. 77–90.

Johnson, Owen. *Stover at Yale* [1911]. New York: Collier Books, 1968.

Jones, James. *From Here to Eternity*. New York: Scribner's, 1951.

Kahn, Roger. *The Boys of Summer*. New York: Harper & Row, 1972.

—— *A Season in the Sun*. New York: Harper & Row, 1977.

—— *The Seventh Game*. New York: New American Library, 1982.

Kaylin, Walter. *The Power Forward*. New York: Atheneum, 1979.

Kazan, Elia. *On the Waterfront*. Film, 1954.

Kennedy, Lucy. *The Sunlit Field*. New York: Crown, 1950.

Kennedy, William. *Ironweed* [1983]. New York: Penguin, 1984.

Kesey, Ken. *One Flew Over the Cuckoo's Nest* [1962]. New York: Penguin, 1976.

—— *Sometimes A Great Notion* [1964]. New York: Bantam, 1965.

—— "Blows to the Spirit" (interview). *Esquire*, June 1986, pp. 266–75.

Kinsella, W. P. *The Iowa Baseball Confederacy*. New York: Ballantine, 1986.

—— *Shoeless Joe*. Boston: Houghton Mifflin, 1982.

—— *The Thrill of the Grass*. New York: Penguin, 1984.

Kluger, Steve. *Changing Pitches*. New York: St. Martin's, 1984.

Knowles, John. *Peace Breaks Out*. New York: Holt, Rinehart & Winston, 1981.

—— *A Separate Peace* [1960]. New York: Bantam, 1966.

—— "A Turn With the Sun." In his *Phineas*, pp. 3–30. New York: Random House, 1968.

Koperwas, Sam. *Westchester Bull*. New York: Simon and Schuster, 1976.

Kramer, Jerry. *Instant Replay*. New York: World, 1968.

Lampell, Millard. *The Hero*. New York: J. Messner, 1949.

Lardner, Ring. "Alibi Ike." In his *The Ring Lardner Reader*, pp. 477–94. New York: Scribner's, 1963.

—— "Champion." In his *The Ring Lardner Reader*, pp. 239–57.

—— "Horseshoes." In his *Haircut and Other Stories*, pp. 9–21. New York: Scribner's, 1954.

—— "My Roomy." In his *The Ring Lardner Reader*, pp. 495–514.

—— *You Know Me, Al* [1916]. New York: Scribner's, 1960.

Larner, Jeremy. *Drive, He Said*. New York: Delta, 1964.

Levin, Bob. *The Best Ride to New York*. New York: Harper & Row, 1978.

Levin, Jenifer. *Snow*. New York: Poseidon, 1983.

—— *Water Dancer*. New York: Poseidon, 1982.

London, Jack. *The Abysmal Brute*. New York: Century, 1913.

—— "The Battle of the Century." In Shepard, Irving R., ed, *Jack London's Tales of Adventure*, pp. 140–41. Garden City, N.Y.: Hanover House, 1956.

—— *The Game*. New York: McKinley, Stone & Mackenzie, 1905.

—— "The Madness of John Harned." *Everybody's Magazine*, November 1910, pp. 657–66.

—— "The Mexican." *Saturday Evening Post*, August 19, 1911, pp. 27–30, 184, 186, 188.

—— "A Piece of Steak." *Saturday Evening Post*, November 20, 1909, pp. 6–8, 36–38.

Lorenz, Tom. *Guys Like Us*. New York: Viking, 1980.

Lowry, Robert. *The Violent Wedding*. Westport, Conn.: Greenwood, 1953.

Magnuson, James. *The Rundown*. New York: Dial, 1977.

McGuane, Thomas. *Ninety-Two in the Shade*. New York: Bantam, 1973.

—— *The Sporting Club* [1969]. Middlesex, England: Penguin, 1978.

McManus, James. *Chin Music*. New York, Crown, 1985.

McMurtry, Larry. *The Last Picture Show*. New York: Dell, 1966.

Mailer, Norman. *Advertisements for Myself*. New York: Signet, 1959.

—— *An American Dream*. New York: Dell, 1964.

—— *Ancient Evenings*. Boston: Little, Brown, 1983.

—— *The Armies of the Night*. New York: Signet, 1968.

—— *Barbary Shore*. New York: New American Library, 1951.

—— *Cannibals and Christians*. New York: Dell, 1966.

—— *The Deer Park*. New York: G. P. Putnam's Sons, 1955.

—— *The Executioner's Song*. Boston: Little, Brown, 1979.

—— "Existential Aesthetics." In his *Pontifications*, pp. 68–79. Boston: Little, Brown, 1982.

—— The Fight. Boston: Little, Brown, 1975.

—— "King of the Hill." In his *Existential Errands*. Boston; Little, Brown, 1972.

—— "Married to Marilyn." *New York Review of Books*, August 9, 1973, pp. 11–14.

—— "The Metaphysics of the Belly." In his *The Presidential Papers of Norman Mailer*, pp. 277–302. New York: Bantam, 1964.

—— *The Naked and the Dead*. New York: Signet, 1948.

—— *Of a Fire on the Moon*. New York: Signet, 1971.

—— "On Waste." In his *The Presidential Papers of Norman Mailer*, pp. 269–302.